SOLDIERS OF
DESTRUCTION

SOLDIERS OF DESTRUCTION

The SS Death's Head Division,
1933–1945

CHARLES W. SYDNOR, JR.

PRINCETON UNIVERSITY PRESS
PRINCETON, NEW JERSEY

Published by Princeton University Press, Princeton, New Jersey
In the United Kingdom: Princeton University Press
Guildford, Surrey

Library of Congress Cataloging in Publication Data
will be found on the last printed page of this book

Publication of this book has been aided by a grant from
the Paul Mellon Fund of Princeton University Press

Printed in the United States of America
by Princeton University Press, Princeton, New Jersey

To Linda

CONTENTS

LIST OF ILLUSTRATIONS

ix

LIST OF ABBREVIATIONS

BAKO	Bundesarchiv, Koblenz
BAMA	Bundesarchiv-Militärarchiv, Freiburg im Breisgau
HSSPF	Höhere SS- und Polizei Führer (higher SS and police leader)
IFZ	Institut für Zeitgeschichte
KZ	Konzentrationslager (concentration camp)
LSSAH	Leibstandarte SS Adolf Hitler
NA	National Archives of the United States
OKH	Oberkommando des Heeres (High Command of the German Army)
OKW	Oberkommando der Wehrmacht (High Command of the German Armed Forces)
RFSS	Reichsführer SS (Himmler's official title as Reich leader of the SS)
RuSHA	Rasse- und Siedlungshauptamt (Race and Resettlement Office)
SD	Sicherheitsdienst (Security Service of the SS)
SSFHA	SS Führungshauptamt (SS Operational Office)
SSTK	SS Totenkopfdivision (SS Death's Head Division)
SSTV	SS Totenkopfverbände (SS Death's Head units)
SSVT	SS Verfügungstruppe (SS Special Service troops)
SS WVHA	SS Wirtschafts- und Verwaltungshauptamt (Main SS Economic and Administrative Office)
USDC	United States Document Center, West Berlin

ACKNOWLEDGMENTS

THE preparation of this study would not have been possible without the assistance of a small army of very kind individuals. Much of the credit for its completion belongs to Professor Charles F. Delzell, who directed my graduate studies at Vanderbilt University. Professor Albert S. Hanser also provided encouragement and assistance. The opportunity for archival research in the Federal Republic of Germany was made possible by a generous grant from the Deutscher Akademischer Austauschdienst. Subsequent research and the completion of the work were underwritten by grants from the Longwood Foundation of Longwood College and the National Endowment for the Humanities. I am deeply grateful to these organizations for their part in making this book possible.

My archival labors in Europe were eased considerably by a number of helpful people. In the Bundesarchiv at Koblenz, Frau Elisabeth Kinder on two occasions placed at my disposal her unrivaled knowledge of the materials in the Himmler files and the papers of the ministries and agencies of the Third Reich. The staff of the Bundesarchiv-Militärarchiv at Freiburg im Breisgau made my nine-month stay there a stimulating pleasure. To Dr. Friedrich-Christian Stahl, the director, and to Herrn Ziggel, Moser, and Binger I should like to express my thanks for their advice and assistance. To Frau Erna Danzl, the staff, and community of scholars at the Institut für Zeitgeschichte in Munich I am also indebted for their interest in this study—appreciation I owe in equal measure to Mr. Richard Bauer, Herr Werner Pix, and the personnel of the Berlin Document Center.

The completion of the European phase of the research was made possible by the cooperation of a number of people on the staffs of the Library of Albert-Ludwigs Universität in Freiburg, the Wiener Library and Leo Black Institute of Contemporary History in London, and through the help of Professor Dr. Czeslaw Pilichowski, director of the Central Commission for the Study of Hitlerite Crimes in Poland, in Warsaw.

In the United States, I was aided in locating and obtaining a

wide variety of materials by Mr. Robert Wolfe of the National
Archives, and by many individuals in the Joint University Library
in Nashville, Tennessee, the New York Public Library, the Ohio
State University Library, and the Dabney S. Lancaster Library of
Longwood College.

Much of any literary and substantive merit this work may have
can be attributed to the critical efforts of four scholars: Professors
Richard J. Bazillion, Allan R. Millett, George H. Stein, and
Harold J. Gordon, Jr. Each read the entire manuscript at various
times, and all—especially Professor Gordon—offered incisive
and invaluable criticisms and suggestions. Any errors or omis-
sions that have persisted into the text in spite of their efforts, however, are solely my own responsibility. For enduring my numerous idiosyncrasies, and for sparing no effort in the editorial and
technical completion of the manuscript, I am indebted to Miss R.
Miriam Brokaw, to my editor Mr. Robert E. Brown, and to the
splendid staff of Princeton University Press.

I would also like to express my appreciation to the Presses Universitaires de France, and to the editors of *Revue d'histoire de la
deuxième guerre mondiale* and *Central European History* for
kindly permitting me to reprint earlier versions of material now in
chapters eight and nine.

Finally, I would like to acknowledge the personal influences
that, in the beginning and in the end, were indispensable to the
successful completion of this study. From my grandparents, who
taught me as a boy to love life and to revere learning, I first
learned the basic beliefs that have shaped my whole intellectual
development. They were extraordinary people, in whom the ability to love was exceeded only by the capacity for wisdom. Their
example was decisive, their influence definitive, and their memory is indelibly etched in my character. To my undergraduate
major professor, George Stevenson, a gifted teacher of immense
learning and deep commitment to the principles of humanist education, I owe the original inspiration for my own academic career.
And to my wife Linda, I am above all indebted for having shared
so encouragingly and tolerated so unselfishly the omnipresence of
this project for the last eight years.

Rice, Virginia   CHARLES W. SYDNOR, JR.
November 10, 1976

INTRODUCTION

THE thirty years that have passed since Adolf Hitler's squalid suicide in the ruins of Berlin have seen the growth of a vast literature in a variety of languages devoted to nearly every aspect of the history of Nazi Germany. Stimulated partly by the declassification and microfilming of the voluminous captured German documents,[1] a growing number of historians during the last decade have concentrated upon the Schutzstaffel, or the SS, in attempts to analyze and describe the ideological and institutional foundations of the Third Reich. Founded in 1925, the SS originally was an adjunct of the Sturmabteilung, or SA, the Nazi party's Brown Shirt Army, and initially received a variety of routine political and security assignments. After Hitler's appointment as chancellor in 1933, the SS under the direction of Heinrich Himmler assumed a growing number of official administrative, police, and military functions.[2] By the outbreak of the Second World War, the SS had

[1] The best available compilation of captured German documents is the American Historical Association, Committee for the Study of War Documents, *Guides to the German Records Microfilmed at Alexandria, Virginia* (Washington, D. C., 1958—). The bulk of the German documents already declassified, microfilmed, and listed in the above *Guides* are available through the National Archives. The originals of the documents have been returned to West Germany and deposited in the Federal Archives system.

[2] To date, the most complete surveys of books and periodicals devoted to the SS and published prior to 1965 are two articles by Karl O. Paetel, "The Black Order: A Survey of the Literature on the SS," *Wiener Library Bulletin*, 12, Nos. 3-4 (1959), 34-35; and "Die SS: Ein Beitrag zur Soziologie des Nationalsozialismus," *Vierteljahrshefte für Zeitgeschichte*, 2 (January 1954), 1-33. Additional bibliographical information on the SS may be found in Hans Buchheim, "Die SS in der Verfassung des Dritten Reiches," *Vierteljahrshefte für Zeitgeschichte*, 3 (April 1955), 127-57; and in Robert Koehl, "The Character of the Nazi SS," *The Journal of Modern History*, 34 (September 1962), 275-83. In the absence of major published bibliographical essays on the SS since 1965, the bibliographies of several important SS-related studies are especially valuable as guides to the more recent literature on the subject. These include, Heinz Höhne, *Der Orden unter dem Totenkopf: Die Geschichte der SS* (Gütersloh, 1967). English ed., *The Order of the Death's Head: The Story of Hitler's SS* (New York, 1971); Josef Ackermann, *Heinrich Himmler als Ideologue* (Göttingen, 1970); Shlomo Aronson, *Reinhard Heydrich und die Frühgeschichte von Gestapo und SD* (Stuttgart, 1971); and, most importantly, Michael H. Kater, *Das "Ahnenerbe" der SS, 1935-1945: Ein Beitrag zur Kulturpolitik des Dritten Reiches* (Stuttgart, 1974). Kater's book, a

grown into one of the largest and most powerful institutions in the Third Reich, and had become the dynamic core of the National Socialist state.[3]

The coming of the war in 1939 also witnessed the full emergence of the Waffen SS, or armed SS. These militarized SS formations had existed prior to 1939, and with the outbreak of war were organized and equipped as regular army units and eventually fought alongside the German Army on all fronts in the European theater of the war. Hitler and Himmler originally intended the Waffen SS to be an elite, racially pure Nazi force—a thoroughly trained and indoctrinated cadre of armed men fanatically loyal to the führer and to National Socialist Germany. During the first years of the war, as German armies swept from victory to victory, Hitler limited the size of the Waffen SS with a view to using it as the core of a future Nazi party army that would protect the postwar Reich and German-dominated Europe from foreign and domestic dangers. As the war lengthened and turned against him, Hitler authorized a vast expansion of the Waffen SS in an attempt to capitalize upon its superb fighting qualities and thereby avert the defeat that finally engulfed Germany in 1945. When the war ended, the Waffen SS was a huge, multinational army of over 900,000 men, many of them conscripts from German-occupied countries, and a political and military institution that the war apparently had transformed completely from its original form.[4]

---

massive, invaluable study of Himmler's SS office for ancestral and racial research, contains the most exhaustive current bibliography of books and articles devoted to the subject of the SS.

[3] This is the dominant theme in Helmut Krausnick et al., *Anatomie des SS Staates*, 2 vols. (Olten and Freiburg im Breisgau, 1965). English ed., *Anatomy of the SS State* (New York, 1968). This brilliant and powerful work, a collaborative effort by four of West Germany's most talented historians, remains the most authoritative analysis of the SS that has appeared in any language.

[4] At present, the best book in any language devoted to the Waffen SS is the American scholar George H. Stein's *The Waffen SS: Hitler's Elite Guard at War, 1939-1945* (Ithaca, N. Y., 1966). Two important and more recent studies are, Robert A. Gelwick, "Personnel Policies and Procedures of the Waffen SS," Diss. Nebraska 1971; and James J. Weingartner, *Hitler's Guard: The Story of the Leibstandarte SS Adolf Hitler, 1933-1945* (Carbondale, Ill., 1974). In West Germany, the Munin Verlag in Osnabrück has published a number of Waffen SS unit histories and documentary studies. To date, the most significant are: Dr. K. G. Klietmann, *Die Waffen SS: Eine Dokumentation* (Osnabrück, 1965); Otto

This book represents an effort to document specifically one particular part of the history of the Waffen SS. The focus of the study is threefold. First it examines comprehensively the origins, evolution, and wartime political and military role of a single armed SS formation, the SS Totenkopfdivision (SS Death's Head Division), one of the original and throughout the war one of the very best Waffen SS divisions. Secondly, this work relates the history of the SS Totenkopfdivision to the ideological and institutional development of the SS—especially to the multi-purpose political, military, and criminal functions of the SS as a principal center of power in Nazi Germany. Finally, this study addresses what in the opinion of this writer are three major problems in perceiving the history of the SS. These problems involve the questions of how and for what purposes the Waffen SS served the collection of institutions that constituted the SS; the extent to which Himmler, as Reichsführer SS, exercised effective control over the armed SS; and the degree to which the Waffen SS was involved in criminal acts attributed to the Schutzstaffel.[5]

In his *Discourse on Method* (1637), René Descartes concluded that the problems of nature and of mind could be solved scientifically if men would " 'divide each problem into as many parts as possible; that each part being more easily conceived, the whole may be more intelligible.' "[6] Confronted as the present generation

---

Weidinger, *Division Das Reich, 1934-1941*, 2 vols. (Osnabrück, 1967-69); Friedrich Husemann, *Die guten Glaubens waren: Der Weg der SS Polizei-Division, 1939-1942* (Osnabrück, 1971); Wilhelm Tieke, *Tragödie um die Treue: Kampf und Untergang des III. (Germ.) SS Panzer-korps* (Osnabrück, 1970); and Peter Strassner, *Europäische Freiwillige: Die Geschichte der 5. SS-Panzer Division "Wiking"* (Osnabrück, 1969).

[5] The problem of understanding the institutional complexity of the SS, and the role and functions of the Waffen SS within it, has been compounded by the efforts of the postwar apologists for the Waffen SS to portray it as an army of anti-Communist idealists who belonged to an organization separate, independent, and distinct from the SS. The apologists have further claimed, and have secured wide public credence for the thesis, that the men who served in the Waffen SS as frontline soldiers were in no way involved in or responsible for crimes committed by other SS agencies during the Second World War. A condensed version of these problems as they relate to the history of the Waffen SS may be found in Charles W. Sydnor, Jr., "The History of the SS *Totenkopfdivision* and the Postwar Mythology of the *Waffen SS*," *Central European History*, 6 (December 1973), 339-62.

[6] The quote from Descartes, as well as the conceptual and methodological inspiration for the structure of this study, came from William S. Allen, *The Nazi Sei-*

still is by the absence of an analysis of the National Socialist phenomenon that is both intelligible and whole, the undiminished weight of Descartes' words provide more than sufficient inspiration and justification for an entire book devoted to the history of a single SS division. To the extent that any institutional and personal example can make any part of the history of the SS and Nazism "more intelligible," the unique perspective afforded by the experience of the Totenkopfdivision can. The prewar origins of the SS Death's Head Division, the characteristics and beliefs of the men who organized and built it, and the purposes for which it was used, make it ideal as a model with which to enlarge—however modestly—upon our present knowledge of the organizational complexity of the SS, the destructive nature of National Socialism, and the unparalleled ordeal of the Second World War.

---

zure of Power: The Experience of a Single German Town, 1930-1935 (Chicago, 1965), one of the few truly classic works in the massive historical literature of the Third Reich.

SOLDIERS OF
DESTRUCTION

CHAPTER ONE

The Prewar Background: The Development of the Concentration Camp System and the SS Totenkopfverbände

THE Waffen SS Totenkopfdivision emerged from two significant interrelated forces in the structure of Adolf Hitler's Third Reich. These forces were individual and personal on the one hand, and institutional and ideological on the other. Individually, the SS Totenkopfdivision in a real sense was the personal creation of Theodor Eicke. A major figure in the SS, Eicke was the architect, builder, and director of the prewar German concentration camp system, and the founder and commander of the SS Totenkopfdivision until his death in Russia in 1943. Ideologically, the SS Totenkopfdivision was the institutional outgrowth of the sinister SS Death's Head Units (SS Totenkopfverbände), the militarized SS formations Eicke recruited, organized, and trained to guard and administer the concentration camps of the Reich.[1]

From its activation in October 1939 until its dissolution in May 1945 the SS Totenkopfdivision retained a distinct and individual identity, ethos, and character that stamped it indelibly with the imprint of Theodor Eicke's personality and marked it unmistakably as the product of its prewar origins. Since the interrelationships of these factors antecedent to the creation of the SS Totenkopfdivision are so vital to a clear and comprehensive perception of the division's wartime role and significance, they are the natural and necessary point of departure for this study.

The pattern of Theodor Eicke's life before his entry into the Nazi party and the SS was similar to that of many prominent figures in Hitler's movement. Born on October 17, 1892, in the

---

[1] George H. Stein, *The Waffen SS: Hitler's Elite Guard at War, 1939-1945* (Ithaca, N. Y., 1966), pp. 27-34, for a general description of the background and organization of the first Waffen SS divisions in 1939.

then German province of Alsace, Eicke was the eleventh child in a family originally from the town of Gittelda in the Harz Mountains of Germany. His father, Heinrich Eicke, was the railroad stationmaster in the Alsatian village of Hampont.[2] Theodor Eicke attended both the Volkschule and the Realschule in Hampont, but was a poor student and left school without finishing in 1909. As a youth of seventeen, Eicke enlisted in the Twenty-third Infantry Regiment at Landau in the Rhineland-Palatinate and embarked on an undistinguished service career as a clerk and paymaster. During the First World War, Eicke served successively as a paymaster with the Third and Twenty-second Bavarian Infantry Regiments—earning in the process the Iron Cross, Second Class. After the armistice and the German revolutions, Eicke resigned from the army in 1919 with the rank of career assistant paymaster and found himself thrown into the chaotic cauldron of postwar Germany.[3]

Without prospects for a new career and filled with hatred for the new government of the Weimar Republic, Eicke and his wife[4] settled in Ilmenau in Thuringia, near her family. When his meager savings evaporated and his father-in-law refused to extend financial support, Eicke in desperation secured employment as a paid police informer in Ilmenau. He remained an informer until July 1920, when he was dismissed by the police for engaging in political agitation against the Republic.

Eicke found police work so agreeable that he tried repeatedly during the following eighteen months to make it his new career. From Ilmenau Eicke moved successively to Cottbus, Weimar, Sorau-Niederausitz, and finally to Ludwigshafen am Rhein in his frustrated odyssey for status and security as a professional policeman. In each location, Eicke succeeded in gaining em-

[2] United States Document Center, West Berlin, SS Personalakte Eicke, Lebenslauf (hereafter cited as USDC, SS Personalakte Eicke, Lebenslauf). See also Helmuth Krausnick et al., *Anatomie des SS Staates*, 2 vols. (Freiburg im Breisgau, 1965), II, p. 56 (hereafter, Krausnick, *Anatomie*); and Shlomo Aronson, *Reinhard Heydrich und die Frühgeschichte von Gestapo und SD* (Stuttgart, 1971), p. 105.

[3] USDC, SS Personalakte Eicke, Lebenslauf; Aronson, p. 105.

[4] Eicke married Bertha Schwebel on December 26, 1914. They had two children—a daughter, Irma, born April 5, 1916, and a son, Hermann, born May 4, 1920 (USDC, SS Personalakte Eicke, Lebenslauf).

ployment, but in each instance he held it only briefly before being dismissed either for expressing his fierce hatred of the Republic or for participating in antigovernment demonstrations.[5]

Finally, in January 1923, his luck changed and he secured employment, first as a salesman and then as a security officer in the I. G. Farben plant in Ludwigshafen. From 1923 until his entry into full-time service with the SS in 1932, Eicke remained employed by I. G. Farben as a security officer.[6]

Eicke spent the years from 1923 to 1928 settled in Ludwigshafen, but remained unreconciled to Germany's defeat and to his own postwar civilian existence. The intensity of his hatred for the Weimar Republic eventually attracted him to the Nazi party, which by 1928 had become aggressive and successful in recruiting in the Rhineland-Palatinate. On December 1, 1928, Theodor Eicke, having found a group that shared his political views and offered him membership in a paramilitary formation, joined the Nazi party, with Party Card No. 114-901. At the same time, he entered the ranks of the party's storm troops (the Sturmabteilung, or SA).[7]

Eicke remained in the Ludwigshafen SA until August 20, 1930, when he transferred to the smaller and better-disciplined SS (Schutzstaffel), a separate group within the SA used to protect party speakers and to maintain order at party political rallies. Opportunities for influence in the smaller SS seemed to Eicke much greater—an assumption amply confirmed by the meteoric rise that within four years carried him to one of the most important positions in the SS.[8]

On November 27, 1930, Heinrich Himmler, Hitler's loyal Reichsführer SS, appointed Eicke to the rank of SS Sturmführer (second lieutenant) and gave him command of Sturm (platoon) No. 148 at Ludwigshafen am Rhein. Eicke's energetic recruiting and organizing abilities were so obvious and successful that within three months Himmler promoted him to SS Sturm-

[5] Aronson, p. 105; Krausnick, *Anatomie*, II, pp. 56-57.
[6] USDC, SS Personalakte Eicke, Lebenslauf; Krausnick, *Anatomie*, II, p. 57; Aronson, p. 105.
[7] USDC, SS Personalakte Eicke, Lebenslauf; see also *Dienstaltersliste der Schutzstaffel der NSDAP: Stand vom 1 Juli 1935* (Berlin, 1935), pp. 2-3.
[8] USDC, SS Personalakte Eicke, Lebenslauf.

bannführer (major) and ordered Eicke to create a second SS Sturmbann (battalion) for the projected Tenth SS Standarte (Regiment) of the Rhineland-Palatinate. By the summer of 1931 Eicke had filled the ranks of the new SS Sturmbann. His success and single-minded zeal earned for him Himmler's admiring recognition, and on November 15, 1931, the Reichsführer SS promoted Eicke to SS Standartenführer (colonel) and gave him command of the Tenth SS Standarte.[9]

By this time the combination of the depression and his SS activities cost Eicke his job with I. G. Farben. Free to devote his time and energy to his SS command and to party activities, Eicke embarked on a new career in political violence. On March 6, 1932, Eicke was jailed for illegal possession of high explosives and for conspiring to carry out a series of bombings and political assassinations in Bavaria.[10] He remained in custody until July 7, 1932, when a Bavarian court sentenced him to two years in prison. The sympathetic Bavarian minister of justice, Franz Gürtner (later Hitler's minister of justice) quickly intervened and granted Eicke a temporary parole to "regain his health" before beginning his prison sentence. Upon his release on July 16, 1932, Eicke returned directly to Ludwigshafen and resumed his political activities.[11]

The police quickly noted his reappearance and forced Eicke into hiding with party friends in Landau. These circumstances clearly embarrassed Himmler, who ordered Eicke via courier to come secretly to Munich for important instructions. Himmler had decided to remove Eicke to some location where he would do no harm and would be out of the reach of the authorities. Consequently, when Eicke arrived in Munich Himmler sent him immediately to Italy. On September 18, 1932, complete with disguise and false papers, Eicke traveled through Austria to Malcesine in northern Italy. As a sop, the Reichsführer SS promoted

[9] Ibid.

[10] USDC, SS Personalakte Eicke, telegram dated March 6, 1932 from the Ludwigshafen Schutzpolizei (security police) to the SS regional office in Munich; and Aronson, pp. 105, 282.

[11] USDC, SS Personalakte Eicke, Lebenslauf; Krausnick, *Anatomie*, II, pp. 55-58; Aronson, pp. 105, 282.

him to SS Oberführer[12] and gave him command of the fugitive SS camp which Mussolini's government had organized at Malcesine on Lake Garda to house similar exiles.[13]

While he was in Italy, Eicke's command of the Tenth SS Standarte was threatened by the swaggering Gauleiter of the Palatinate, Josef Bürckel. Bürckel and Eicke had begun a fierce quarrel in 1931, when the Gauleiter (district leader) attempted to coordinate all the SA and SS units in the Palatinate under his own control. Eicke's successful resistance killed the plan but not Bürckel's ambitions. With Eicke conveniently in Italy, Bürckel tried to strip the SS Oberführer of his power in the Palatinate by having him expelled from the party. Word of Bürckel's machinations reached Eicke in Italy, and in a series of letters written to his comrades in Ludwigshafen during the winter of 1932-1933 he swore that upon returning to Germany he would use the "old methods" to prevent Bürckel from imposing "Jesuit politics" on the Nazi revolution.[14]

Hitler's appointment as chancellor of the Weimar Republic on January 30, 1933 liberated Eicke from exile. Franz Gürtner thoughtfully provided amnesty for his 1932 Bavarian conviction, and on March 10, 1933 Eicke returned to Ludwigshafen—after promising Himmler that he would not renew the old quarrel with Bürckel. Once in Ludwigshafen, however, Eicke forgot his prom-

---

[12] The rank of SS Oberführer had no equivalent in either the German Wehrmacht or the U.S. Army. It was a special SS rank between Standartenführer (colonel) and Brigadeführer (brigadier general). USDC, SS Personalakte Eicke, Dienstlaufbahn; and Stein, p. 295.

[13] USDC, SS Personalakte Eicke, Lebenslauf; Krausnick, *Anatomie*, ii, pp. 57-58; Aronson, pp. 105, 282.

[14] USDC, SS Personalakte Eicke, letter from Eicke to "Mein treuer Kamerad Philip" dated January 30, 1933. See also Aronson, p. 282. By the "old methods" Eicke meant specifically using leftover bombs to blow up "that swine" Bürckel. Eicke's exile also provided him with new opportunities to embarrass Himmler. He and his SS fugitives caused a sensation on October 28, 1932, by participating in full uniform in the Bolzano parade commemorating the tenth anniversary of Mussolini's march on Rome. The incident received wide coverge in both the Austrian and Italian press, and angered many Nazi sympathizers in the Tyrol. See USDC, SS Personalakte Eicke, "NSDAP Landesleitung für Österreich an den Führer, die Oberste SA Führung, und die Reichsführung der SS," dated November 4, 1932. The incident is also described in detail in Aronson, p. 282.

ise. With his loyal SS followers he celebrated his return by staging an armed putsch against Bürckel. Eicke and the mutineers stormed the Ludwigshafen Gau headquarters and locked Bürckel in a janitor's closet before the forces loyal to the Gauleiter managed to call in the local Schutzpolizei, who arrested the mutineers and forced Eicke to release Bürckel.[15]

The humiliated Gauleiter exacted full revenge upon his cantankerous enemy. He had Eicke arrested, judged "mentally ill and a danger to the community," and deposited for psychiatric observation in the Nervenklinik in Würzburg. An infuriated Himmler also removed Eicke's name from the service list of the SS on April 3, 1933, and consented to Eicke's indefinite confinement in the Würzburg clinic.[16] While in the clinic, Eicke managed to make friends with his psychiatrist, Dr. Werner Heyde, who later wrote to Himmler that Eicke appeared perfectly normal, always behaved quietly, and had given no one at the clinic the impression that he was either disturbed or a chronic troublemaker.[17]

Heyde's evaluation and Eicke's constant pleas to the Reichsführer SS finally persuaded Himmler to have Eicke released and reinstated into the ranks of the SS. On June 26, 1933, Eicke left the Würzburg clinic with his old rank of SS Oberführer, and with direct orders from Himmler, chief of the Bavarian political police, to assume a new post. The Reichsführer SS had

---

[15] USDC, SS Personalakte Eicke, "Bericht über die Vorgänge in Ludwigshafen am Rhein," dated March 20, 1933; and Aronson, pp. 105, 282-283. For an illuminating discussion of a similar struggle between the SS and the Nazi party at the local level, see Herbert S. Levine, "Local Authority and the SS State: The Conflict over Population Policy in Danzig-West Prussia, 1939-1945," *Central European History*, 2 (December 1969), 331-55.

[16] USDC, SS Personalakte Eicke, Lebenslauf; Aronson, pp. 282-283; Krausnick, *Anatomie*, II, pp. 57-58; and Heinz Höhne, *Der Orden unter dem Totenkopf: Die Geschichte der SS* (Gütersloh, 1967), p.189.

[17] USDC, SS Personalakte Eicke, letter from Heyde to Himmler of April 22, 1933; Aronson, p. 283. Dr. Heyde, who was not a party member but was a sympathizer in 1933, was later introduced to Himmler by Eicke, joined the party and the SS, and directed Hitler's euthanasia program during the war. For details see H. G. Adler, *Der verwaltete Mensch: Studien zur Deportation der Juden aus Deutschland* (Tübingen, 1974), pp. 236-37. The appearance of Adler's exhaustive and overpowering work represents a significant milestone in the historiography of the holocaust and in the advancement of our knowledge of the Third Reich.

selected Eicke to become commandant of one of the first Nazi concentration camps for political prisoners at Dachau.[18]

Himmler had established the Dachau camp on March 20, 1933, three days before and in anticipation of the passage of the Enabling Act in the Reichstag. This legislation gave Hitler the sweeping legal powers he needed to incarcerate the political enemies of the Nazi party. Like many of the other early "wild" concentration camps, Dachau initially was staffed by local SA and SS men who practiced indiscriminate brutality upon the helpless prisoners in their custody.[19]

Himmler's first SS commandant at Dachau, SS Sturmbannführer Hilmar Wäckerle, attempted to regulate the mistreatment of prisoners with stringent punishment regulations— rules that classified as crimes "violent insubordination" and "incitement to disobedience" and made them punishable by death. Hanging was imposed by a tribunal of camp SS officers, over which the camp commandant presided. In the determination of all sentences the commandant's vote was decisive, a procedure that invested him with absolute life-and-death power over every prisoner in the camp.[20]

Wäckerle's tenure as Dachau commandant ended in June 1933 when Himmler dismissed him to dampen the scandal that arose over the murder of several prisoners in the camp—murders which

[18] USDC, SS Personalakte Eicke, Dienstlaufbahn, and letters from Eicke to Himmler of March 29, April 13, and May 16, 1933.

[19] Aronson, p. 283; Höhne, p. 189; and Krausnick, *Anatomie*, II, pp. 57-58.

[20] Aronson, pp. 105-106; and Krausnick, *Anatomie*, II, p. 45. Much of the following discussion of the development of the concentration camp system is based on the excellent chapter by Martin Broszat, "Nationalsozialistische Konzentrationslager," in Krausnick, *Anatomie*, II, pp. 9-149. In addition, basic studies of the concentration camp system and the mistreatment of prisoners used in the preparation of this chapter include: Olga Wormser-Migot, *Le Système Concentrationnaire Nazi, 1933-1945* (Paris, 1968), esp. pp. 31-137; Joseph Billig, *Les camps de concentration dans L'Économie du Reich Hitlérien* (Paris, 1973); Günter Kimmel's authoritative chapter "Zum Beispiel: Tötungsverbrechen in nationalsozialistischen Konzentrationslagern," in Adalbert Rückerl, ed., *NS-Prozesse: Nach 25 Jahren Strafverfolgung, Möglichkeiten- Grenzen- Ergebnisse* (Karlsruhe, 1971), pp.107-29; H. G. Adler, "Selbstverwaltung und Widerstand in den Konzentrationslagern der SS," *Vierteljahrshefte für Zeitgeschichte*, 8 (July 1960), 221-36; and the valuable collaborative work on the institutional development of the major camps edited by Martin Broszat, *Studien zur Geschichte der*

subsequently resulted in charges against Wäckerle by the Bavarian criminal prosecutor's office.[21]

The direct result, then, of the publicity stemming from the Dachau murders was Eicke's appointment as the new commandant. At Dachau, Eicke began immediately to reorganize Wäckerle's rough outlines for administering the camp and to refine the regulations for oppressing the prisoners. The results were Eicke's own system of terror and organized brutality—hideous procedures that subsequently became standard practice in all the German concentration camps.

Eicke's first task at Dachau involved reshuffling the camp guard personnel. As commandant, Eicke was responsible directly to Sepp Dietrich, then commander of SS Oberabschnitt Süd (Southern Regional Administrative District) with headquarters in Munich. Dietrich controlled the selection of Eicke's replacements for the Dachau guard units, a situation Eicke claimed created serious problems in the camp. In letters to Himmler, Eicke charged that Dietrich sent him corrupt and undesirable asocials, whom Dietrich simply dumped into the camp command. This, Eicke complained, resulted initially in serious disciplinary problems and cases of theft—difficulties Eicke solved by transferring or dismissing some sixty of the SS men sent him. Eicke also complained of initial matériel shortages, and later wrote Himmler that at first there were no boots and socks for his men, few cartridges and rifles, no machine guns, and only dilapidated and unsanitary sleeping quarters for the SS guards.[22]

Konzentrationslager, Schriftenreihe der Vierteljahrshefte für Zeitgeschichte, No. 21 (Stuttgart, 1970). Finally, Eugen Kogon, *The Theory and Practice of Hell: The German Concentration Camps and the System behind Them,* trans. Heinz Norden (New York, 1958) is a classic eyewitness account by a prisoner who suffered horribly in the camps.

[21] Aronson, p. 105. The charges against Wäckerle stemmed from the murder of a prisoner named Sebastian Nefzer. See *Trials of the Major War Criminals before the International Military Tribunal,* (Nuremberg, 1947-49), vol. 26, Doc. No. PA-645. (Hereafter cited as *TMWC* with volume, document, and/or page numbers.)

[22] Aronson, pp. 105-106; Krausnick, *Anatomie,* II, pp. 64-65; and a letter from Eicke to Himmler dated August 10, 1936, in the Bundesarchiv, Koblenz, NS-19/neu-1925. (Hereafter cited as BAKO with document collection, individual identification and/or page numbers.)

Shortly after assuming command at Dachau, Eicke began urging Himmler to make the Dachau command independent of Dietrich's SS Oberabschnitt by subordinating the camp directly to the office of the Reichsführer SS.[23] As Eicke made a success of his tenure at Dachau, this desire to bypass Dietrich and increase his own power and independence grew into a restless craving for further power and influence that led him to guard jealously his own prerogatives and to look upon his important SS colleagues with suspicion, hostility, and hatred.

While commandant at Dachau, Eicke developed two basic camp policies that were to have enduring significance in the history of the Third Reich. The first was his unwritten code of conduct for the SS guards, and the second consisted of new, elaborate disciplinary and punishment regulations for use against camp prisoners. These latter regulations eventually established the "legal" basis for handling prisoners in all the German concentration camps; while the basic concepts in the code of conduct for the SS guards were refined, expanded, and implemented with horrific efficiency in the camps within the Reich, and in the wartime extermination centers in the German-occupied east.[24]

The code of conduct for the SS guards was based upon Eicke's demand for blind and absolute obedience to all orders from SS superior officers, and upon his insistence that each prisoner be treated with fanatical hatred as an enemy of the State. By drilling his SS guards constantly to hate the prisoner, and simultaneously by buttressing this hatred with the legality of orders (which enabled the guards to mete out the harshest punishments to prisoners), Eicke invented what subsequently became the standard SS formula for mistreating all concentration camp inmates.[25]

---

[23] BAKO, NS-19/neu-1925, letter from Eicke to Himmler of August 10, 1936.

[24] Aronson, pp. 168-69. See also Raul Hilberg, *The Destruction of the European Jews* (Chicago, 1960), pp. 555-56, 577-86; and Karl-Dietrich Bracher, *The German Dictatorship: The Origins, Structure and Effects of National Socialism* (New York, 1970), pp. 359-61.

[25] Aronson, pp. 168-69; Rudolf Höss, *Kommandant in Auschwitz*, vol. 5, *Quellen und Darstellungen zur Zeitgeschichte* (Stuttgart, 1958), pp. 53-67; and the testimony of Oswald Pohl, later Eicke's nominal superior as head of the prewar SS Administrative Office (SS Verwaltungsamt), in *Trials of War Criminals Before the Nuremberg Military Tribunals under Control Council Law No. 10* (Washington, D. C., 1950), vol. 5, case No. 4 *U.S.* v. *Oswald Pohl*, p. 437. (Hereafter cited as

Eicke's new regulations for the "Maintenance of Discipline and Order" (zur Aufrechterhaltung der Zucht und Ordnung) were issued on October 1, 1933. These regulations defined a number of crimes for which a prisoner could be punished, prescribed the penalties, and gave the SS guards extensive freedom to deal harshly with the "enemy behind the wire." To an extent, Eicke's regulations were patterned after Wäckerle's, especially in delegating to the camp commander full and absolute power to determine the punishment for prisoners convicted of infractions. Eicke's originality lay in his definition of the serious offenses that were punishable by death. These included political agitation, the spreading of propaganda, any acts of sabotage or mutiny, attempted escape or aid in an escape, attacking a sentry or guard tower; and a long list of less-serious infractions.[26]

In addition, Eicke devised a graded system (eight, fourteen, twenty-one, and forty-two days) of close confinement with a warm meal only every fourth day; he subjected prisoners to long periods of solitary confinement with only bread and water. To supplement these measures with physical abuse of the prisoners, Eicke introduced corporal punishment (Prügelstrafe) into the regulations. Eicke's corporal punishment usually consisted of twenty-five lashes with a whip, carried out at his specific order in the presence of the assembled SS guards, all the prisoners, and the camp commandant. Eicke rotated the responsibility for these

---

TWC/Green Series, with volume, document, and/or page numbers.) Eicke once remarked, in Höss's presence, that "any sympathy for enemies was unworthy of an SS man; that there was no place in the ranks of the SS for weaklings, and that such persons would do well to retire to a cloister quickly. He [Eicke] had use only for tough men who would obey unquestionably every order" (Höss, *Kommandant*, p. 56). For an illuminating and perceptive analysis of Eicke's influence on Rudolf Höss, later the notorious commandant of Auschwitz, see Joseph Tenenbaum, "Auschwitz in Retrospect: The Self-Portrait of Rudolf Höss, Commandant of Auschwitz," *Jewish Social Studies*, 15 (July-October 1953), 203-36.

[26] Erminhild Neusüss-Hunkel, *Die SS*, Schriftenreihe des Instituts für wissenschaftliche Politik in Marburg/Lahn (Hannover, 1956), p. 53; Aronson, pp. 168-69; Krausnick, *Anatomie*, II, pp. 58-59. Copies of the regulations may be found in *TMWC*, vol. 26, pp. 291-97; and in Jeremy Noakes and Geoffrey Pridham, eds., *Documents on Nazism, 1918-1945* (New York, 1974), pp. 284-86. In 1933-1934 the members of the Dachau guard were men from the Allgemeine SS (General SS), who were paid the same wages as regular office employees of the Allgemeine SS, and who received weapons training in the camps (Neusüss-Hunkel, p. 53).

whippings among the SS officers, noncommissioned officers (NCOs), and SS guards in the camp. This made the punishment more impersonal and hardened the SS camp personnel into laying-on the whip routinely and without flinching.[27] Other forms of punishment included suspension of mail privileges, especially heavy or dirty forms of manual labor, tying prisoners to stakes or trees for varying periods, and special exercises—usually performed with accompanying kicks and blows from the SS guards.[28]

Eicke also sought to instill among the guards a particular hatred for the Jewish prisoners. Being himself violently anti-Semitic, Eicke considered the Jews the most dangerous of all the enemies of National Socialism. He frequently delivered anti-Semitic lectures to the guards, and displayed regularly copies of Julius Streicher's notorious racist newspaper, *Der Stürmer*, on bulletin boards in the SS barracks and canteen. To foment anti-Semitic violence among the prisoners he posted copies of *Der Stürmer* all over the protective-custody camp as well.

Of all the punishments Eicke devised at Dachau, the most psychologically devastating was reserved for the Jewish inmates. Whenever an atrocity report about the concentration camps appeared in a foreign newspaper, Eicke ordered all the Jewish prisoners locked in their barracks. The windows were then nailed shut, and the Jews had to lie in the sealed barracks for one to three months—leaving their beds only at mealtime and for roll-call. Eicke insisted that all atrocity stories were circulated by emigrating German Jews, and that the Jews in the concentration camps should suffer collective punishment as a result.[29]

[27] Krausnick, *Anatomie*, II, pp. 58-59; and the discussion of the administration of the whippings and infliction of other bestial forms of punishment in, Kogon, pp. 108-15. The procedures for administering the whippings later were altered so that the lashings were conducted by SS NCOs and guards. A chilling description of one such whipping is in Höss, *Kommandant*, pp. 54-55.

[28] *TMWC*, vol. 26, pp. 291-97. Punishment regulations identical to those at Dachau, were drawn up August 1, 1934 by Eicke for the concentration camp at Esterwegen. See *SS im Einsatz: Eine Dokumentation über die Verbrechen der SS*, Herausgegeben vom Komitee der Antifaschistischen Widerstandskämpfer in der DDR (East Berlin, 1960), pp. 156-57. Comprehensive discussions of physical abuse of prisoners in camps may also be found in H. G. Adler, "Selbstverwaltung und Widerstand," pp. 221-63; in the chapter by Günter Kimmel in Rückerl, ed., *NS-Prozesse*, pp. 107-29; and throughout the memoirs of Eugen Kogon.

[29] Rudolf Hoess, *Commandant of Auschwitz* (New York, 1961), pp. 119-23.

To strengthen his own power as commandant and to make the camp run efficiently, Eicke also supervised the dividing of the camp administration into different departments. He secured a camp doctor to head a medical department, and appointed an administrative officer to run the camp pay office and purchase all supplies. Another office was established to keep the personal property surrendered by each prisoner upon entering the camp, and Eicke himself organized a camp repair and maintenance bureau to be responsible for maintaining the camp's physical plant, procuring supplies, and making uniforms for the prisoners.[30]

Eicke divided the inmates in the camp into "blocks" of 250 prisoners each. The commander of a "block" was an SS guard, usually an SS Scharführer (technical sergeant). He in turn was responsible to a Rapportführer (coordinating leader), who normally held the rank of SS Hauptscharführer (master sergeant). The Rapportführer's superior was designated detention camp officer (Schutzhaftlagerführer), and always held commissioned rank (SS Führer) in the SS. With the subsequent enlargement of Dachau, Eicke appointed additional Schutzhaftlager commanders to handle the increasing numbers of prisoners, and to rotate duty every twenty-four hours.[31]

Eicke's success in organizing Dachau into a model detention center for political enemies of the Nazi regime made a deep impression upon Himmler. On January 30, 1934, the Reichsführer SS promoted Eicke to SS Brigadeführer (brigadier general) and began to listen seriously to Eicke's complaints that subordination

---

This is the English edition of Höss's autobiography. This edition contains much valuable information that is omitted from the earlier German version—in the form of appendices in which Höss presents character sketches of the main figures who ran the concentration camp system. One of the lengthiest of these is devoted to Eicke. All subsequent references to Höss's autobiography in this chapter are taken from the English edition.

[30] Krausnick, *Anatomie*, II, pp. 66-67.

[31] Ibid. By 1935 Dachau had ten blocks of 250 prisoners each, with eight of the ten blocks consisting of political prisoners, and the other two a mixture of Jews, gypsies, asocials, and homosexuals. Eicke also initiated the practice at Dachau, later used in all the camps, of marking each prisoner according to category with a colored triangular patch of cloth sewn onto the uniform.

14

to SS Oberabschnitt Süd was hampering even greater progress at Dachau.[32]

Himmler apparently was motivated not only by Eicke's success but also by a desire to retain a firm grip on his own position by setting his subordinates in competition with each other. Eicke clearly was a talented, rising, and potentially important figure in the SS, and if he were given an independent command subordinate to Himmler, he could serve as a check against the Reichsführer's cunning and ambitious protégé, Reinhard Heydrich.[33]

By the time Himmler moved to Berlin to take command of the Prussian Gestapo in April 1934, he had decided to centralize all the SS-run concentration camps into one system by creating a specific SS office to organize and administer the camps. Because of his success at Dachau, Eicke appeared the natural choice to direct this new and vital organization. In May 1934 Himmler and Eicke discussed the prospects, and the Reichsführer SS told the elated Eicke he would have the responsibility for this reorganizing.

As a further sign of his confidence in Eicke, Himmler appointed him Führer im Stab (officer on the staff) of the Reichsführer SS on June 20, 1934. This appointment invested Eicke with the prestige of direct subordination to Himmler, and more importantly separated the Dachau command from SS Oberabschnitt Süd.[34] Eicke thus had reached a second and crucial stage in his SS career. In less than a year after his release from the psychiatric ward, he again possessed Himmler's personal confidence, commanded a significant institution in Hitler's terror apparatus, and stood within reach of vastly enlarged power in the SS as the muggy heat of June 1934 brought the dispute between Hitler and Ernst Röhm's SA to a climax.

[32] *Dienstaltersliste*, 1935, pp. 2-3.

[33] Aronson, pp. 111-12, 283. In January 1934 Heydrich was emerging as a major figure in both the SS and the police. He was chief of the SS Security Service (Sicherheitsdienst, or SD), and succeeded Himmler as chief of the Bavarian political police.

[34] Krausnick, *Anatomie*, ii, pp. 57-58, 64-65; Aronson, pp. 111-12, 283. Eicke later assured Himmler that conditions began to improve as soon as the Dachau command had been made independent and placed under the direct authority of the Reichsführer SS. BAKO, NS-19/neu-1925, Eicke's letter to Himmler of August 10, 1936.

The events leading to Hitler's purge of the SA leadership in the infamous "Night of the Long Knives" have often been described.[35] Until recently, little was known about the conspicuous and important role Theodor Eicke played in the SA purge. On direct orders from Hitler, Eicke murdered Röhm on the evening of July 1, 1934.[36]

Eicke's part in the purge began when he and men picked from the Dachau guard assisted Sepp Dietrich and two companies of the Leibstandarte SS Adolf Hitler (Hitler's personal SS bodyguard) in rounding up the important SA leaders during the night of June 30 and depositing them in the Stadelheim prison in Munich, where the executions were to take place. Sometime during the early afternoon of July 1, Hitler gave the order to liquidate Röhm. As a principal director of the purge, Himmler received the necessary instructions. The Reichsführer SS telephoned Eicke at the Munich offices of SS Oberabschnitt Süd in the Amalienstrasse, told him Hitler's decision, and ordered Röhm shot. The one qualification, at Hitler's insistence, was that Eicke first give Röhm the chance to commit suicide.[37]

Accompanied by his adjutant, SS Sturmbannführer Michael Lippert, and by SS Gruppenführer Heinrich Schmauser, the liaison officer between the SS and the army for the purge, Eicke set out by auto for the Stadelheim prison. When the three arrived and were taken to the prison director, Robert Koch, Eicke explained why they had come. Koch tried to stall, claiming that he could not deliver Röhm without the necessary instructions and papers. When Eicke began to shout and threaten, Koch telephoned the Nazi minister of justice, Hans Frank, and asked for orders. During the

[35] See especially Joachim C. Fest, *Hitler*, trans. Richard and Clara Winston (New York, 1974), pp. 456-67; Alan Bullock, *Hitler: A Study in Tyranny*, 2nd ed. (New York, 1964), pp. 284-311; Gerald Reitlinger, *The SS: Alibi of a Nation, 1922-1945* (London, 1957), pp. 58-60; and Hermann Mau, "Die Zweite Revolution, 30. Juni 1934," *Vierteljahrshefte für Zeitgeschichte*, 1 (April 1953), 119-37.

[36] Aronson, p. 193; and Höhne, pp. 90-125, esp. pp. 120-21.

[37] Höhne, p. 120; and Fest, p. 467. Both accounts of Eicke's role in the Röhm purge are based on testimony given during the 1956 trail of Sepp Dietrich and Michael Lippert for the murder of Röhm. *Anklageschrift gegen Josef Dietrich und Michael Lippert*, Landgericht München, 4. Juli 1956 (Munich, 1957), 1, pp. 2-4, 35.

conversation Eicke grabbed the receiver from Koch and screamed into the mouthpiece that Frank had no business interfering in the Röhm affair, as he (Eicke) was acting on direct orders from the führer. This satisfied Frank, who ordered Koch not to intervene further. Eicke, Lippert, and Schmauser then proceeded to the cell where Röhm was confined.

Entering the cell, Eicke announced loudly, "You have forfeited your life! The Führer gives you a last chance to avoid the consequences!" He then placed an extra pistol on the table and told Röhm he had ten minutes to end everything. Eicke, Lippert, and Schmauser withdrew and waited in the corridor for fifteen minutes. No sound came from Röhm's cell. Finally Eicke glanced at his watch and both he and Lippert drew their pistols.

Pushing the cell door open, Eicke shouted: "Chief of Staff, make yourself ready!" He and Lippert then fired at the same time, and Röhm collapsed to the floor. One of the two SS men then crossed the cell and shot Röhm point-blank through the heart.[38]

For Eicke, the Röhm purge was a significant career turningpoint. He had been entrusted personally with the task of killing Röhm—an indication of the confidence that Himmler and subsequently Hitler could place in him. In addition, the purge resulted in immediate tangible rewards for the concentration camp specialist. Four days after Röhm's murder, Eicke was officially appointed to the new SS office, inspector of concentration camps and leader of SS guard formations (Inspekteur der Konzentrationslager und Führer der SS Wachverbände). On July 11, 1934, in recognition of his service at Dachau and his performance during the Röhm crisis, Himmler promoted Eicke to SS Gruppenführer—the second-highest commissioned rank in the SS.[39]

Eicke began immediately the important task of organizing Germany's dispersed and locally administered concentration camps into one SS-controlled system. The initial steps involved gathering a staff, developing plans for the construction of the camps, and recruiting, training, and equipping more SS guard units.

[38] Höhne, p. 121; Aronson, p. 193; Fest, p. 467.
[39] *Dienstaltersliste, 1935*, pp. 2-3; Krausnick, *Anatomie*, II, pp. 57-58; Aronson, pp. 220-21.

17

Moving as quickly as possible, Eicke relinquished his Dachau command to SS Oberführer Heinrich Deubel, and moved to Berlin in October 1934 to establish quarters for his new inspectorate at No. 129 Friedrichstrasse.[40]

As inspector of concentration camps, Eicke had complete responsibility for formulating all policy matters concerning the administration of the camps. Each camp commander was his direct subordinate and received orders from his office on all internal administrative affairs for the particular camp. Eicke's inspectorate, in turn, was subordinated formally to the SS Hauptamt (SS main office), commanded in 1934 by SS Gruppenführer August Heissmeyer. In fact, however, Eicke was Himmler's immediate subordinate, and during his five-year tenure as inspector of concentration camps answered only to the Reichsführer SS. In the course of these years Eicke's own staff grew to forty-three, and he moved the inspectorate offices to the Sachsenhausen camp at Oranienburg north of Berlin, where the command of the inspectorate remained until the collapse of the Third Reich in 1945.[41]

Early in 1935, Eicke moved to bring all the widely scattered local camps, which had been established on a temporary basis after the Nazis seized power, under full SS control. He began by closing down most of the local camps and collecting all the prisoners into several large, permanent concentration camps. By March 1935 Eicke's inspectorate controlled seven large concentration camps with 9,000 prisoners in all. These camps included Dachau, Esterwegen, Lichtenburg, Sachsenburg in Saxony, Columbia-Haus in Berlin, Oranienburg near Berlin, and the Fehlsbüttel camp near Hamburg.[42]

With the first stage of his reorganization complete, Eicke pro-

---

[40] Krausnick, *Anatomie*, II, p. 73; Aronson, pp. 220-21.

[41] Krausnick, *Anatomie*, II, p. 73; Aronson, pp. 220-21. See also Enno Georg, *Die wirtschaftlichen Unternehmungen der SS*, Schriftenreihe der Vierteljahrshefte für Zeitgeschichte, No. 7 (Stuttgart, 1963), pp. 38-39. Among Eicke's closest associates in the prewar inspectorate was his deputy, Richard Glücks. Hand-picked by Eicke from the Allgemeine SS in 1936, Glücks remained with the inspectorate for his entire SS career, succeeding Eicke as inspector of concentration camps in October 1939 when the latter was transferred to the Waffen SS as commander of the SS Totenkopfdivision. See also Hoess (English, ed.), pp. 232-35.

[42] Krausnick, *Anatomie*, II, pp. 71-72; Neusüss-Hunkel, pp. 53-54; and Aronson, pp. 223-24.

ceeded to reduce further the number of concentration camps, while directing the construction of newer and larger camp installations. The original Oranienburg camp and Fehlsbüttel were closed during the first months of 1936. The Esterwegen camp and Columbia-Haus were closed in August 1936, and the prisoners from both were collected in the new Sachsenhausen facility near Oranienburg. The process was repeated when in July 1937 the Sachsenburg camp was terminated and its prisoners transferred to the sprawling new detention center Eicke had ordered built near Weimar. This huge complex opened officially in August 1937 as the Buchenwald concentration camp.[43]

By August 1937, Eicke had established a permanent concentration camp system based on four enormous camps within the borders of the Reich: Dachau, Sachsenhausen, Buchenwald, and a new camp at Lichtenburg, which was completed in the summer of 1937 and used exclusively for women prisoners. After the Anschluss in March 1938, Eicke engaged in building a new concentration camp in the incorporated Ostmark to hold the throngs of Austrian political prisoners collected by Gestapo dragnets. By July 1938 construction was completed and the new Mauthausen camp opened near Linz.

The internal structure of the individual concentration camps Eicke based on the "Dachau model" he had created. This involved both the established Dachau method of mistreating the prisoners and the Dachau example for the division of authority and responsibility in the management of the camp. The Dachau disciplinary and punishment regulations were drafted for each of the camps and remained in effect as the basis for handling prisoners until 1945. In all the camps, the death penalty was imposed for the same offenses Eicke had included in the Dachau regulations, and corporal punishment with the whip was inflicted in the manner prescribed by Eicke at Dachau. In addition, the use of forced labor, solitary confinement, and the other generally established forms of abuse became standard throughout the camp system.[44]

[43] Krausnick, *Anatomie*, II, pp. 75-76; Billig, pp. 14-19.

[44] Krausnick, *Anatomie*, II, pp. 76-77, 63-66; and a full copy of the orders drafted by Eicke on June 2, 1934 for the administration of the Lichtenburg concentration camp in, USDC, SS Personalakte Eicke.

The infliction of these cruelties on such a large scale soon caused Eicke trouble. With so many deaths in the camps from beatings and other physical tortures, and with so many dead prisoners reported as "shot while trying to escape," civilian prosecutors in the ministry of justice began to investigate events in the concentration camps. As a result, Eicke in April 1935 ordered his SS guards not to enforce strictly the harsh penalties in the punishment code, but to continue using them as threats against the prisoners. The Gestapo took advantage of Eicke's embarrassment and in October 1935 made what appeared to be a substantial incursion into his authority. With Himmler's approval, guidelines were promulgated requiring all concentration camp commanders to assist the Gestapo in investigating abnormal deaths of camp inmates. This forced Eicke to restrict all corporal punishment in the camps, with the result that the number of murders, though not the general tenor of the brutality, declined somewhat.[45]

During the winter of 1935-1936 Eicke also organized the administrative structure for each of the new camps. Drawing upon his experience at Dachau, he divided the administration of each camp into five sections. The first included the office of camp commandant, his adjutant, and the postal censoring bureau. The second was the political section, headed by a member of the Gestapo or the Kripo (criminal police), with an identification office to keep records on all the prisoners. The third section in the new organization was the detention camp itself. This section consisted of the SS NCOs who dealt with the prisoners, the Rapport- and Blockführer, and the guards detailed to command the prisoner work gangs. The fourth section was made up of the individual camp administrative offices. These consisted of the chief camp

---

[45] Krausnick, *Anatomie*, II, pp. 63-64; and Aronson, pp. 225, 236-38. The Gestapo did not, of course, intervene in camp policy in order to improve the plight of the prisoners. Gestapo interference came as a result of Heydrich's desire to discredit Eicke and gain a measure of control over the camps. Aronson, pp. 236-38, makes an extremely important point in concluding that the traditional Reich authorities from the first were powerless to stop Eicke's judicial murders in the camps, a fact that Gürtner, as minister of justice, and Wilhelm Frick, as minister of the interior, both had conceded by the spring of 1938. See Helmut Heiber, ed., *Reichsführer!* . . . *Briefe an und von Himmler* (Stuttgart, 1968), pp. 53-54, for a letter from Himmler to Gürtner of May 15, 1938 concerning the shooting of prisoners in the camps.

administrative officer and his staff, an office for handling the prisoners' personal property, and the camp engineer's office. The fifth section designated was the medical office, headed by the camp doctor.[46]

While organizing the new camp system, Eicke also decided to extend to all the camps the economic enterprises he had begun at Dachau. These activities originally involved construction work by the prisoners, but subsequently were expanded in Dachau to include a table and shoemaking shop, a locksmith's shop, an electric work, a saddlery, and a bakery. Initiated on Eicke's orders, these first economic activities in the camps were carried on as forced labor until they became too successful and aroused Himmler's interest. As a result, the Reichsführer SS in 1938 subordinated the economic activities in the camps to the SS Verwaltungsamt (SS Administrative Office), directed by SS Gruppenführer Oswald Pohl. Himmler thus removed from Eicke's hands control of the enterprises and the power to regulate their production.[47]

Himmler's efforts to restrict Eicke's empire-building, by giving Pohl authority over activities within the concentration camps, may be taken partly as an example of the Reichsführer's "divide and rule" policy with his subordinates, and partly as a further sign of the respect Himmler had for the restless former Dachau commander. Another indication of Eicke's major stature in the SS was the continuing feud he had with Reinhard Heydrich. Heydrich was the most cynical, ruthless, and feared of the important SS figures; in the jungle of constant and shifting struggles among Himmler's subordinates, confronting Heydrich required considerable skill and courage.

The hostility between the two dated from Eicke's appointment as commandant of Dachau. Then, as chief of the Bavarian politi-

[46] Krausnick, *Anatomie*, II, pp. 67-68.

[47] BAKO, NS-19/neu-1925, Eicke to Himmler, August 10, 1936. More extensive discussions of the initial economic and forced labor activities developed by Eicke in Dachau, and their significance as the model subsequently used for the huge slave labor enterprises of the wartime camp system, may be found in Georg, pp. 12-14, 36-37; Billig, pp. 138-39, 161, 185, 192; Kogon, pp. 91-93; and in the testimony of Oswald Pohl during his postwar trial, *TWC/Green Series*, vol. 5, case 4, p. 559.

cal police, Heydrich had attempted to take control of Dachau. Eicke's selection as commandant blocked this move, and earned for Eicke Heydrich's vehement and lasting hatred. Eicke, for his part, was just as ambitious, if not as subtle and cunning, as Heydrich, and regarded the hawk-nosed former naval officer as an immature and insolent upstart.[48]

Frustrated in his initial attempt to seize control of Dachau, Heydrich tried to undermine Eicke's authority as inspector of concentration camps, and to ruin his career through interference and the circulation of damaging rumors. His efforts, however, were partly offset by Eicke's constant and direct access to Himmler.[49]

The best example of this is the angry letter to Himmler that the Heydrich intrigues prompted Eicke to write on August 10, 1936. Reliable reports, Eicke wrote, indicated that Dr. Werner Best, Heydrich's deputy in the SD, had been circulating rumors that the SS guard formations would be removed from Eicke's control in the autumn of 1936 since the concentration camps were run by a group of swine, and since the time had come for all the camps to be controlled by the Gestapo.[50] Heydrich's attempts to sequester Eicke's camp empire never would have succeeded. Despite any reservations he had about Eicke, Himmler was not about to permit his zealous protégé to gain control of Germany's concentration camps. Eicke, with his own solid power base and proven, slavish loyalty to the Reichsführer SS, shrewdly and stubbornly matched Heydrich move for move.[51]

By 1937 Eicke had a formidable reputation among his SS col-

[48] Höhne, pp. 188-89; Aronson, pp. 111-12, 227; and Pohl's testimony in *TWC/Green Series*, vol. 5, case 4, pp. 439-41.

[49] Krausnick, *Anatomie*, I, p. 199; Höhne, pp. 190-91; Aronson, p. 227; and Pohl's testimony in *TWC/Green Series*, vol. 5, case 4, pp. 440-41. As chief of the security police and the SD, Heydrich had complete control over the incarceration and release of political prisoners in all camps in the Reich after June 17, 1936. Eicke and his camp commandants had no authority to decide who could be put into or taken out of the concentration camps (Krausnick, *Anatomie*, II, p. 75).

[50] BAKO, NS-19/neu-1925, Eicke to Himmler, August 10, 1936; and Krausnick, *Anatomie*, I, pp. 198. Höhne, p. 191; and Aronson, p. 112, feel that Eicke was a key factor in Himmler's "divide and rule" practice, and consequently served the Reichsführer SS as an important check against the ever-dangerous Heydrich.

[51] Aronson, pp. 112; 227; and Pohl testimony, *TWC/Green Series*, vol. 5, case 4, pp. 439-40.

leagues as a tough and vicious figure. Ever-suspicious, quarrel-some, cruel, humorless, and afflicted with a cancerous ambition, Eicke was a genuinely fanatic Nazi who had embraced the movement's political and racial liturgy with the zeal of the late convert, advancing rapidly and unshakeably into the power structure of the Third Reich. Moreover, Eicke had demonstrated that he possessed in abundance the basic qualities needed to get to the top in the SS—uncompromising ruthlessness in the service of obedience, a marked talent for organization, and a gift for inspiring and leading men.

These facets of Eicke's personality, in particular his unremitting hatred for everything and everyone non-Nazi, influenced definitively the development, the structure, and the uniquely inhumane ethos of the concentration camps. Eicke was convinced that the camps were the most effective instrument available for destroying the enemies of National Socialism. He regarded all prisoners as subhuman adversaries of the State, marked for immediate destruction if they offered the slightest resistance. Eicke eventually succeeded in nurturing this same attitude among many SS guards in the camps. The prisoners were treated harshly and impersonally, and to maintain discipline and avoid embarrassing inquiries, Eicke tolerated no independent brutality or individual acts of sadism by the guards.[52]

Like many of the concentration camp commanders he trained, Eicke basically was pitiless and cruelly insensitive to human suffering, and regarded qualities such as mercy and charity as useless, outmoded absurdities that could not be tolerated in the SS. His unique contribution to the consolidation of Hitler's dictatorship was to provide the regime with a network of extra-legal prisons, beyond the control of traditional law and authority, in which the "enemies of the State" were broken and destroyed by the organized, impersonal, and systematic brutalities he invented.[53]

In the spring of 1936, with the administrative structure of the

[52] Hoess, appendix 8, pp. 223-31; and USDC, SS Personalakte Eicke, commandant's order No. 1/34 of June 2, 1934 for Lichtenburg. See also BAKO, NS-3/448, Befehlsblatt des Führers der SSTV und KZ, dated February 16, 1937. This is one in a series of circular orders from Eicke to all his commandants. A similar evaluation of Eicke's beliefs and personality may be found in Tenenbaum, "Auschwitz in Retrospect," esp. pp. 209-11.
[53] Aronson, pp. 168-69, 236-38.

camp system nearly established, Eicke's interests shifted to the problems involved in expanding, equipping, and training the camp system's SS guard units, the SS Death's Head units (SS Totenkopfverbände).[54] As in the centralization of the camps, Eicke's organization and expansion of the SS Totenkopfverbände (SSTV) began with his experience at Dachau. The original guard units at Dachau consisted generally of sadists and bullies left over from the Nazi party's political struggle. Eicke weeded these men out soon after he became commandant, and replaced them with reliable, disciplined SS officers, NCOs, and enlisted men. As he expanded the camp system, Eicke's Dachau SS cadre, especially his most trusted subordinates, served as the nucleus of the additional SS guard units for the new concentration camps.[55]

In December 1934 the Dachau guard unit (Wachtruppe Oberbayern der Allgemeinen SS), and the guard units at the other camps were renamed with regional designations. By March 1935 Eicke had divided the SS Totenkopfverbände into six battalions, each assigned to one of the six concentration camps then in existence, and each named for its region. SS Oberbayern guarded the Dachau camp, while SS Ostfriesland was assigned to Esterwegen, and SS Sturmbann Elbe was quartered at Lichtenburg. SS Sachsen watched over the Sachsenburg camp, SS Brandenburg split its guard duty between the Oranienburg camp and Columbia-Haus in Berlin, and SS Hansa had responsibility for the Fehlsbüttel camp near Hamburg.[56]

At the Reichsparteitag in Nuremberg in September 1935 Hitler recognized publicly the SSTV as party formations in the service of the Reich, and subsequently ordered that the Reich government assume the costs for their maintenance—a directive that paved the way for the expansion of the Totenkopfverbände. At Eicke's re-

[54] Hoess, p. 226; and Pohl testimony, *TWC/Green Series*, vol. 5, case 4, p. 441.

[55] Hoess, appendix 8, p. 225; and Krausnick, *Anatomie*, II, p. 72. It was Eicke's idea to use the Totenkopf (Death's Head) on the right collar tab as a distinctive insignia for the SS guard units in the camps. All the insignia worn by the prewar SS were hand-made by craftsmen in the concentration camp tailor shops (Kogon, p. 93).

[56] Krausnick, *Anatomie*, II, p. 72, and I, p. 195. See also Hans Buchheim, *SS und Polizei im Nationalsozialistischen Staat* (Duisdorf bei Bonn, 1964), pp. 168-69.

quest, Himmler in March 1936 authorized an increase in the size of the SSTV from 1,800 to 3,500 men.[57] The SS Hauptamt directed the expansion by requesting each SS Oberabschnitt to handle the recruiting for the SSTV. The commander of each SS Oberarschnitt was requested to supply a list of eighty volunteers by March 25, 1936. These volunteer candidates were to be from seventeen to twenty-two years old, at least five feet ten inches tall, in perfect health, and of "racially pure stock." On March 29, 1936 Himmler designated the concentration camp guard units officially as SS Totenkopfverbände.[58]

In the initial stage of the expansion, SSTV volunteers were slightly older than Himmler wished, averaging between twenty-five and thirty years of age. Many SS officers who joined the SSTV were veterans of the First World War who had drifted through the SA and the Allgemeine SS before settling in Eicke's units. After April 1936, the majority of volunteers—both officers and men—was somewhat younger. The change seems to have been due principally to the new opportunities the SSTV offered. Many young men were attracted by the prestige of the black uniform, the prospect of quick promotion, or simply by the nature of the duty involved. The period of enlistment in the Totenkopfverbände initially was four years, but was changed in 1938 to twelve years.[59]

Oswald Pohl's SS Verwaltungsamt, a branch within the SS

---

[57] BAKO, NS-19/neu-1925, Eicke to Himmler, August 10, 1936. The Reich assumed the maintenance costs for the SSTV effective April 1, 1936. Until that date, Eicke had to secure funds by negotiating with the governments of the individual German states in which concentration camps were located (testimony of defendant August Frank in the Pohl trial, *TWC/Green Series*, vol. 5, case 4, p. 448).

[58] Krausnick, *Anatomie*, I, p. 195, and II, p. 74; BAKO, NS-7/426, circular letter from August Heissmeyer, chief of the SS Hauptamt, to all SS Oberabschnitten, March 16, 1936. On September 13, 1936, the SSTV were given the place of honor among the SS units parading before Hitler at the Nuremberg party rally, an event described in some detail in the German press (See *Die Frankfurter Zeitung*, 17 Sept. 1936).

[59] Krausnick, *Anatomie*, II, pp. 54-55; and BAKO, NS-19/neu-1652, Hitler's secret decree of August 17, 1938. Until shortly before the war, the major problem Eicke encountered in recruiting was the fact that service in the Totenkopfverbände did not count toward the compulsory military obligation all young German males had to fulfill. This fact was not altered until May 1939, when Hitler ordered that service in the SSTV count toward the military requirement. (See below, fn. 85).

Hauptamt, was responsible for maintaining and supplying the SSTV, and for negotiating with the Reich Finance Ministry the annual government allotment for the units. From April 1, 1936, the appropriations for the maintenance of the SSTV and the concentration camps were carried on the annual budget of the Reich Ministry of the Interior.[60]

In matters relating to the management and military training of the enlarged SSTV, Eicke appeared to be a formal subordinate of the SS Hauptamt. In fact, however, he enjoyed a wide and increasing freedom. An obvious indication of this was his own energetic effort to infuse into his Death's Head members a political fanaticism, elitism, and camaraderie that would give them a sense of their own uniqueness within the SS.

Eicke's belief in SSTV elitism grew from his concept of what the concentration camps were for. Since the camps were, in Eicke's view, the main repositories for the most dangerous political enemies of the State, and since the führer had given the SSTV—a racially select group of men—sole responsibility for guarding and running the camps, then the SSTV constituted an elite within the elite structure of the SS. Eicke repeated this theme constantly in orders, circulars, and memoranda in an unending attempt to convince his men that they served in the most important and finest formation in the SS.[61] Eicke's efforts produced one effect he desired by removing, in the minds of his men, the stigma of the SSTV as jailers or prison guards. Simultaneously, as the then and subsequent behavior of the SSTV suggests, he created an atmosphere conducive to indoctrination in political fanaticism.

In an administrative circular to the SSTV in February 1937, Eicke announced sharply that he wanted no outdated and useless military formalities practiced in the Totenkopfverbände. In his SSTV units, Eicke declared, it was absolutely necessary for a feeling of real comradeship to exist between a company commander and a sergeant. Likewise, in a March 1937 circular, Eicke

[60] Krausnick, *Anatomie*, II, p. 74; BAKO, NS-19/neu-1925, Eicke to Himmler, August 10, 1936.

[61] See especially USDC, SS Personalakte Eicke, orders drafted by Eicke for Lichtenburg on June 2, 1934; BAKO, NS-19/1958, circular order from Eicke to all SSTV battalion commanders, May 5, 1936; and BAKO, NS-3/448, long circular letter from Eicke to all concentration camp commandants, February 23, 1937.

wrote that the Totenkopfverbände were an integral, unique part of the SS. The SSTV, he insisted, possessed unsurpassed camaraderie, loyalty, and toughness, and belonged neither to the army, the police, nor the SS Verfügungstruppe—the fully armed SS troops that remained at Hitler's disposal for any internal emergency. Finally, Eicke declared that he would transfer to the Allgemeine SS any member of the SSTV who lacked the necessary spirit of camaraderie and who performed his duties routinely and unenthusiastically. Eicke based the whole of SSTV training on these concepts—elitism, toughness, and comradeship; and simultaneously imposed a ruthless discipline upon the SSTV, meting out harsh and often brutal punishments for the slightest infractions of SS rules.[62]

Members spent three weeks every month in training, followed by one week of guard duty within the concentration camp. The training, both political and military, was designed to instill in the SSTV soldier an attitude, outlook, or state of mind, while participation in camp guard duty was meant to give him exposure to the prisoners and conditions in the concentration camps. This experience, Eicke felt, would confirm the lessons learned by the SS man during his training, and would strengthen his belief that the prisoners were inferior but implacable enemies of the German nation against whom the SS had to wage an unending struggle.[63]

Eicke structured most of the SSTV soldier's three-week training program around political indoctrination. In the spring of 1937 he also appointed a chief education officer to the staff of the con-

---

[62] Krausnick, *Anatomie*, I, pp. 290-91, 294; BAKO, NS-3/448, administrative circulars distributed by Eicke on February 23 and March 2, 1937. Eicke also tried to convince his men that the other SS and police agencies were inferior to the SSTV. He referred repeatedly to members of such organizations as the Allgemeine SS and the Ordnungspolizei, then in the process of amalgamation into the SS, as "fat, complacent, petty officials," and instituted the policy of transferring men from the SSTV to these agencies as punishment for violations of the rules or for failure to measure up to the standards of the SSTV (BAKO, NS-3/448, administrative circular for February 23, 1937; and USDC, SS Personalakte Eicke, orders of June 2, 1934 for the Lichtenburg concentration camp). Krausnick, *Anatomy* (English ed.), p. 598, refers to the chronology of the incorporation of the Ordnungspolizei into the SS, beginning in 1937.

[63] BAKO, NS-3/448, circular order from Eicke to all camp commandants, March 2, 1937; Neusüss-Hunkel, pp. 55-56; and Krausnick, *Anatomie*, I, pp. 276-79.

centration camp inspectorate and placed an education officer in each battalion of the SSTV to conduct daily political training. SSTV members attended several lectures weekly, and were told repeatedly that the goal of their training was to shape them into political soldiers of the führer.[64]

Political training was divided into three broad areas. The first dealt with the history of the Nazi party, and included an examination of the party program. The second involved the history and racial beliefs of the SS—with special emphasis upon the SSTV. The third and most important part required a careful analysis of the enemies of National Socialism. In order of importance these were: (1) the Jews; (2) freemasonry; (3) bolshevism; and (4) the churches.[65]

Eicke placed ultimate emphasis upon the development of camaraderie and esprit de corps. Since, in Eicke's mind, the final purpose of the SSTV was to serve as an SS cadre upon which the führer could rely absolutely, the proper SS spirit had to imbue the men. This was necessary, Eicke maintained, because a high measure of esprit de corps was the one intangible asset that could make a unit invincible.[66]

Eicke held such theories in earnest, and believed that through their implementation he could make the SSTV into a fanatical and totally reliable super-elite—the finest single force within the SS. To achieve this objective, Eicke initiated some novel procedures and policies. He ordered unmarried officers in the SSTV to eat some of their meals in the enlisted men's mess; he himself spent

[64] USDC, SS Personalakte Eicke, orders for Lichtenburg of June 2, 1934; and BAKO, NS-3/448, Eicke's circular orders to his camp commandants, February 16 and March 2, 1937.

[65] BAKO, NS-3/448, circular order of March 2, 1937. For an interesting contrast to the kind of ideological training given to the prewar SSTV, see James J. Weingartner, *Hitler's Guard: The Story of the Leibstandarte SS Adolf Hitler, 1933-1945* (Carbondale, Ill., 1974), pp. 20-29. As did Sepp Dietrich in the Leibstandarte, Eicke initially used SS Leithefte (indoctrination journals), but found them too bland and relied later on his own more violent and coarse views to instill the proper attitudes in the SSTV soldiers. Within the prewar SSTV, as in the case of the Leibstandarte, it is impossible to judge the extent to which Eicke's programs were effective, although the subsequent behavior of the SSTV and the SS Totenkopfdivision bespeak considerable success.

[66] BAKO, NS-3/448, circular order of March 9, 1937.

28

long hours sitting and drinking with young SS recruits in the enlisted men's canteen.[67]

Another of Eicke's innovations was his vehement antireligious campaign. Since he aimed to create among his men a hatred for the churches as enemies of National Socialism, all members of the SSTV were pressured intensely to renounce their church affiliation. By late 1936, Eicke's efforts resulted in official renunciations of Christianity by a substantial majority of the men in the SSTV. These renunciations periodically resulted in serious and permanent breaches between Eicke's young recruits and their parents. Eicke responded by opening his own home to men in the SSTV who had been renounced by their parents and who wished to spend their leave at home with a family. In addition, he declared it the duty of every member of the SSTV to befriend comrades suffering such treatment at the hands of their parents.[68]

Eicke also visited all the camps regularly and developed the habit of talking alone with enlisted men, away from their immediate superiors. Moreover, in February 1937 he installed locked suggestion boxes, to which he alone possessed keys, in all the concentration camps. All officers and men in the SSTV thus had direct access to Eicke, a channel through which information and complaints could reach their commander.[69]

To complement these innovations Eicke constantly dismissed or transferred those he felt did not conform. He was always alert for disobedient or incompetent officers, and when any man in the SSTV incurred Eicke's displeasure, transfer to the Allgemeine

[67] Ibid., circular order of February 16, 1937; and Hoess, p. 224.

[68] BAKO, NS-19/neu-1925, Eicke to Himmler, August 10, 1936; and BAKO, NS-3/448, circular from Eicke to all camp commandants, dated March 2, 1937. Eicke's genuine hatred of Christianity was fittingly summarized in a 1940 circular he composed that subsequently became an SS motto in Auschwitz: "Prayerbooks are things for women and for those who wear panties. We hate the stink of incense; it destroys the German soul as the Jews do the race. We believe in God, but not in his son, for that would be idolatrous and paganistic. We believe in our Führer and in the greatness of our Fatherland. For these and nothing else we will fight. If we must therefore die, then not with 'Mary, pray for us.' We will depart as freely as we have lived. Our last breath: Adolf Hitler!" Quoted in Josef Ackermann, *Heinrich Himmler als Ideologue* (Göttingen, 1970), p. 93, (my translation).

[69] BAKO, NS-3/448, Eicke's circular order of February 16, 1937; and Hoess, p. 226.

29

SS, the police, or to a disagreeable post within the concentration camp system usually resulted.[70] To his SS officers he preached incessantly the need for rooting from the ranks the weak, the disobedient, the unreliable, and the lazy. The frequent announcements of such dismissals, transfers, and punishments in the weekly circulars of Eicke's inspectorate attest to the disciplinary thoroughness he exacted.[71]

By late 1937 Eicke's energy and drive clearly had transformed the SSTV into a crack paramilitary party formation. The concentration camp guards developed in Eicke's mold: ruthless, fanatical, pitiless creatures who obeyed every order with reflex instinctiveness, and who, like Eicke, became inured to the cruelties they practiced and indifferent to the sufferings they inflicted. Moreover, Eicke developed a close personal contact and rapport with his men unusual even in the SS, inspiring a near worshipful devotion from SS soldiers who both feared and revered him. By 1938 the success Eicke had achieved with the SS Totenkopfverbände was significant enough to elicit effusive praise from a highly impressed Himmler.[72]

During the last year before the Second World War, Eicke conducted a second and more extensive reorganization and expansion

[70] Hoess, pp. 228-29, claims that Eicke was a poor judge of character, and that he was lenient with those SS officers he liked. Hoess also maintains that many of the SSTV officers whom Eicke punished, demoted, or transferred during the prewar years subsequently ended up on the camp staff at Auschwitz.

[71] BAKO, NS-19/1958, Eicke's circular to the camp commandants, May 5, 1936; and ibid., NS-3/448, circulars of February 9, 16, and 23, and for March 2, 1937. Eicke was especially severe with SSTV officers who misused prisoners' labor for their own personal gain and with those guards who engaged in unauthorized acts of wanton brutality.

[72] The nature of Eicke's relations with the men in his command were described to this author independently by three veterans of the SS Totenkopfdivision (two of whom had served with Eicke in the prewar SSTV) in interviews held in Koblenz, West Germany on June 19-20, 1972 (hereafter cited as Koblenz interviews). For Himmler's comments on Eicke's success with the camp system and the SSTV, see USDC, SS Personalakte Eicke, letter from Himmler to Eicke, November 3, 1937; and the laudatory remarks made by the Reichsführer SS in the course of a speech delivered to a gathering of SS Gruppenführers on November 8, 1938, in BAKO, NS-19/H. R.-5, Gruppenführerbesprechung am 8. 11. 1938 im Führerheim der SS Standarte Deutschland. This lengthy and important speech recently appeared in the expertly compiled volume by Bradley F. Smith and Agnes Peterson, eds., *Heinrich Himmler Geheimreden, 1933 bis 1945* (Berlin, 1974), pp. 25-49 (text of the speech), and pp. 279-84 (notes and comments).

of the SS Death's Head units. By September 1937 the centralization of the camps had progressed far enough to allow Eicke to enlarge the five SSTV battalions then existing into three SS Totenkopfstandarten (Death's Head regiments). These, designated by name and number, were posted to the three enlarged concentration camps that were the nucleus of the system. SS Totenkopfstandarte I "Oberbayern" remained at Dachau, while SS Totenkopfstandarte II "Brandenburg" took over the Sachsenhausen camp at Oranienburg. SS Totenkopfstandarte III "Thuringen" received responsibility for guarding and running the huge Buchenwald camp at Weimar. The Anschluss enabled Eicke to add yet another regiment to the SSTV when SS Totenkopfstandarte IV "Ostmark" was organized in September 1938 to guard the Mauthausen camp near Linz.[73]

The final phase in the prewar expansion of the SSTV resulted directly from Hitler's growing belligerency in the conduct of foreign affairs. At this juncture, moreover, Himmler, having recognized fully the extent of Eicke's success in creating a powerful new force within the SS, began to exert greater direct authority in matters concerning the SSTV. In short, by 1938 Eicke had reached the limit of his authority and power within the SS. Although he retained command of the camps and the new SSTV units created after 1938, all policy matters concerning the Totenkopfverbände—when, where, how, and for what purposes they would be used—became an affair of state, conducted exclusively at the highest level between Hitler and Himmler.[74]

As Hitler's plans for the destruction of Czechoslovakia matured in the summer of 1938, Himmler initiated a lobbying campaign to expand the SSTV and the other armed SS formations. The Reichsführer SS saw in Germany's aggressive foreign policy, and in the threat of war it generated, a perfect opportunity to argue that an enlarged armed SS would add an extra measure of internal security for the Reich during crises. Himmler found the führer in a most receptive mood. With his personal control over the armed forces firmly established, Hitler could devote serious thought to

[73] Krausnick, *Anatomie*, I, p. 195; and II, p. 77.
[74] BAKO, NS-19/H. R.-5, one of the major points in Himmler's speech, November 8, 1938.

31

questions concerning his armed SS formations.[75] During the summer of 1938 he agreed to define legally their status and to specify the purposes for which they could be used. In so doing, Hitler provided Himmler the means for a sizable enlargement of Eicke's Totenkopfverbände.

Hitler enacted the decision in a secret decree of August 17, 1938. This decree stipulated that for special domestic tasks of a political nature, or for use by the German army in the event of mobilization, the SS Verfügungstruppe, the SS Junkerschulen (officer cadet schools), the SS Totenkopfverbände, and the reserve units of the SSTV were to be armed, trained, and organized as military units. In peacetime these armed formations would be commanded by Himmler, who would have sole responsibility for training them into a state of combat readiness.[76] Service in the SS Verfügungstruppe, Hitler ordered, was to count toward the compulsory military obligation, though membership in the SSTV was not. In the event of war, the decree specified that units of the SSTV could be transferred to the SS Verfügungstruppe as replacements.

Hitler also decreed that as party formations the SSTV belonged neither to the Wehrmacht nor to the police. Instead, he defined them as a standing armed force of the SS, available for any special tasks of a political nature that he might determine. Hitler ordered that the SSTV be subject to all ideological and political criteria laid down by him for the party.[77]

The decree also divided the SSTV into four regiments of three battalions each, with each battalion alloted three infantry companies and one machine gun company. Hitler further stipulated that Eicke's units be fully motorized with enough staff cars and trucks to transport all the men, their weapons, and equipment. Finally, Hitler reserved for himself—after consultation with

[75] Hitler acquired personal control over the German armed forces as a result of the Blomberg-Fritsch crisis of January 1938. The standard work on this significant episode is Harold C. Deutsch, *Hitler and His Generals: The Hidden Crisis, January-June 1938* (Minneapolis, Minn., 1974).

[76] Stein, p. 20; Krausnick, *Anatomie*, I, p. 208; and Neusüss-Hunkel, pp. 61-63. One of the ten photocopies made of the original führer decree of August 17, 1938, may be found in BAKO, NS-19/neu-1652.

[77] BAKO, NS-19/neu-1652, führer decree of August 17, 1938.

Himmler—the power to make any changes in the strength and organization of the Totenkopfverbände.[78]

The führer's view of the SSTV role in the event of mobilization was not clearly specified in the decree. Himmler immediately recognized this loophole and used it to enlarge the SSTV. The führer decree enumerated only the peacetime functions of the Totenkopfverbände as a "standing armed force of the SS" for use in "clearing up special tasks of a police nature"—specifically, guarding and running the concentration camps. In the event of mobilization, the decree directed, the original Totenkopfverbände would be replaced as concentration camp guards by members of the Allgemeine SS more than forty-five years old. The motorized SSTV, strengthened by a call-up of their reserve units, would then become a special and independent police force under Himmler's direct command.[79]

Using the provisions of the decree, and Hitler's mobilization of the armed SS for deployment in the Sudetenland during the Czech crisis, Himmler conducted a "police strengthening" (Polizeiverstärkung) in an emergency order (Notdienstverordnung) of October 15, 1938. This call-up activated members of the Allgemeine SS designated as reservists in the Totenkopfverbände for three months of duty in the concentration camps.[80]

The Polizeiverstärkung proved merely Himmler's first step in going beyond the provisions in Hitler's decree. The Reichsführer SS was determined to strengthen further the SSTV by dipping into the convenient manpower pool of the party and its various organizations. Accordingly, in early February 1939 Himmler ordered that men in the SS Verfügungstruppe whose enlistment was about to expire be given the chance to join the SSTV as NCO candi-

[78] Ibid. The decree also provided the SSTV with a medical company, a transport staff, and a communications platoon.

[79] Stein, pp. 23-24; and BAKO, NS-19/neu-1652, führer decree of August 17, 1938; and Neusüss-Hunkel, 62-63.

[80] Krausnick, *Anatomie*, I, pp. 209-11; Stein, pp. 19-20, 24-25; and Neusüss-Hunkel, pp. 62-63. A copy of the decree confirming the call-up, signed by Interior Minister Wilhelm Frick on February 12, 1939, may be found in BAKO, NS-7/426. Hitler placed four battalions from the Totenkopfverbände under army command during the mobilization. Two battalions from SSTV "Oberbayern" moved across the border even before the invasion to assist Konrad Henlein's Nazi Free Corps in preparing for the occupation (Stein, pp. 24-25).

dates; Eicke added the promise to promote to NCO within three months those from the Verfügungstruppe who proved qualified.[81]

Equally important was the agreement Himmler secured with Rudolf Hess, later confirmed by Hitler, by which the party circulated proclamations encouraging men in the SA to volunteer for service in the Totenkopfverbände. All SA men who joined the SSTV were promised retention of their SA insignia on the SS uniform and immediate return to their old SA units as soon as they were released from the SSTV.[82]

Figures compiled by Eicke sometime during the spring of 1939 indicate that Himmler's recruiting effort for the SSTV within the party and the SA was quite successful. According to Eicke's tabulation, the strength of the SSTV in mid-1939 stood at 22,033 men, of whom 755 were officers, 5,005 were NCOs, and 16,273 were SS enlisted men. The same summary indicates that the SSTV possessed weapons including pistols and gas masks for every man, 19,643 carbines, 325 heavy and 486 light machine guns, and 1,458 machine pistols. In less than a year, Eicke's formations had tripled in size and gained substantial quantities of weapons and equipment.[83]

This vast inundation strained Eicke's organizational and administrative abilities to the limit. In the remaining months of peace, he worked feverishly to train, equip, and organize the additional recruits into new Totenkopf regiments. Moreover, as international tension increased, Hitler recognized as permanent the expansion of the SSTV effected during the Czech crisis. In a new decree dealing with the armed SS, dated May 18, 1939, the führer fixed the permanent minimum size of Eicke's Totenkopfverbände at 14,000 men, and authorized Himmler to increase the SSTV to a strength of 25,000 men in the event of another mobilization. To protect Eicke's men from the manpower demands of the

[81] BAKO, SS Erlasssammlung, circular order from the SS Hauptamt to all units of the SS Verfügungstruppe, dated February 6, 1939.

[82] Ibid., NS-7/426, memorandum from Hess's office dated November 29, 1938, titled "Beorderungen von Angehörigen der Partei . . . für die Polizeiverstärkung," and a circular order from the SA command staff on the same subject, dated November 24, 1938.

[83] Ibid., NS-3/138, undated memorandum signed by Eicke and titled "Gliederung und Stärkenachweisung der Polizeiverstärkung, SS Totenkopfverbände."

Wehrmacht, Hitler finally decreed that service in the SSTV count for the military obligation of all SS officers and men who had joined the Death's Head units on or before September 20, 1938. Finally, the new decree defined the role of the SSTV in the event of war: the Totenkopfverbände would serve as combat replacements for units of the SS Verfügungstruppe.[84]

The conditions envisaged in Hitler's decree of May 18, 1939 materialized quickly. As the German dictator pushed Europe and the world toward conflagration, Himmler on August 30, 1939 issued an emergency call-up of all SSTV reservists. The Dachau, Buchenwald, Sachsenhausen, and Mauthausen concentration camps became assembly points for the new Death's Head regiments, which were outfitted, armed, and held ready in the camp complexes as police reserves. On September 7, 1939, with the war a week old, the overall strength of the Death's Head units was just under 24,000 men.[85]

As German armies smashed across Poland's frontiers on the morning of September 1, 1939, the three original Totenkopfstandarten Eicke had created—"Oberbayern," "Brandenburg," and "Thuringen"—prepared to leave their respective barracks compounds in the Dachau, Sachsenhausen, and Buchenwald camps for a secret assignment in the new war zone. Hitler had ordered the three Totenkopf Regiments deployed in the army rear areas in Poland, and had delegated to them full authority to conduct "police and security" measures behind the German lines.[86] The

[84] Institut für Zeitgeschichte, Munich, Nuremberg War Crimes Trials Document Collection, Doc. No. NG-5792, a copy of the führer decree of May 18, 1939. (Materials from the Institut für Zeitgeschichte hereafter cited as IFZ, with individual collection and document identification).

[85] BAKO, SS Erlasssammlung, SSTV strength-summary titled "Einberufung der Verstärkung der SS Totenkopfstandarten," dated August 30, 1939; and ibid., NS-7/426, circular order from the SS Hauptamt of September 8, 1939 outlining the tasks of the newly activated Totenkopf regiments.

[86] In a speech to the assembled officers of the SSTV at Oranienburg on September 1, 1939, Eicke alluded to the coming campaign of terror and mass murder the Death's Head units had been ordered to conduct in Poland. The severe laws of war, he declared, compelled every man in the SSTV to execute the harshest orders without hesitation. In protecting Hitler's State, the SS would have to incarcerate or annihilate every enemy of National Socialism, an endeavor that would challenge even the absolute and inflexible severity the SSTV had learned in the concentration camps. Hoess, pp. 73-74, 77-79, recalled the speech and its significance in his autobiography. A powerful and convincing argument of the thesis that Hitler

cover of these broad powers, the unique qualities the SSTV brought to this task, and the unprecedented ruthlessness of Hitler's aims in Poland combined to make Eicke's Death's Head units the advance apostles of a new and terrible creed of war.[87]

specifically ordered the SSTV and other SS units to murder Polish civilians is Helmut Krausnick, "Hitler und die Morde in Polen: Ein Beitrag zum Konflikt zwischen Heer und SS um die Verwaltung der besetzten Gebiete," *Vierteljahrshefte für Zeitgeschichte*, 11 (April 1963), 196-209.

[87] In a speech to his service chiefs at Berchtesgaden on August 22, 1939, Hitler revealed with shocking clarity the fate he was preparing for the Polish people, and referred specifically to the ruthless measures he intended to use to insure the destruction of the Polish nation. There are several unofficial versions of Hitler's August 22 address, each different with respect to specific details. The extensive notes of uncertain authorship found in the captured OKW files were reproduced as Nuremberg documents 798-PS and 1014-PS, and are in *TMWC*, vol. 26, pp. 338-44, and 523-24. A corroborating eyewitness version, based on shorthand notes made during the speech, is that of Colonel General Franz Halder, *Kriegstagebuch*, 3 vols. (Stuttgart, 1962), vol. 1, pp. 22-26. An English translation of the Halder account is in *Documents on German Foreign Policy, 1918-1945*, Series D, vol. 7 (Washington, D. C., 1956), pp. 557-59. The best scholarly analysis of the different versions of the August 22 speech, and a persuasive argument for the authenticity of Hitler's stated intention to liquidate the Polish national leadership and intelligentsia, is Winfried Baumgart, "Zur Ansprache Hitlers vor den Führern der Wehrmacht am 22. August 1939, Eine Quellenkritische Untersuchung," *Vierteljahrshefte für Zeitgeschichte*, 16 (April 1968), 120-49; and Baumgart's response to the critical remarks of Admiral Hermann Boehm, an eyewitness to the speech, in "Miszelle: Zur Ansprache Hitlers vor den Führern der Wehrmacht am 22. August 1939," *Vierteljahrshefte für Zeitgeschichte*, 16 (July 1971), 294-304.

CHAPTER TWO

The Polish Campaign and the
Creation of the SS Totenkopfdivision

THE initial phase of the war was crucial in transforming the Totenkopfverbände into the Totenkopfdivision. In the harsh crucible
of Poland, the grim heritage of the concentration camps was violently transformed into an ethos of war that became and remained
a key element in the Waffen SS character of Eicke's Totenkopf
formations. The SSTV made no tactical contribution to the German victory in Poland. Their military capabilities were employed
instead in terrorizing the civilian population through acts that included hunting down straggling Polish soldiers, confiscating agricultural produce and livestock, and torturing and murdering
large numbers of Polish political leaders, aristocrats, businessmen, priests, intellectuals, and Jews.[1]

To accomplish rapidly and thoroughly Hitler's goal of annihilat-
ing all actual and potential sources of Polish leadership and resistance, Himmler on September 7 deployed Eicke's three Totenkopf
regiments, "Oberbayern," "Brandenburg," and "Thuringen," in
Upper Silesia as independent SS Einsatzgruppen (action groups)
under Eicke's overall command. Totenkopfstandarten "Oberbayern" and "Thuringen" were sent into the rear of the operational zone of the German Tenth Army, and during the campaign
operated between Upper Silesia and the Vistula River just south of
Warsaw. SS "Brandenburg" followed the Eighth Army of Colonel General Johannes Blaskowitz into Poland, roaming over

[1] Höhne, pp. 270-81; Krausnick, "Hitler und die Morde in Polen," esp. pp.
203-9; and Martin Broszat, *Nationalsozialistische Polenpolitik, 1939-1945*
(Stuttgart, 1961), pp. 22-58 for a general discussion of Hitler's aims and the behavior of the SS in Poland in the autumn of 1939. See also Stein, *The Waffen SS*,
pp. 27-29; and Weingartner, *Hitler's Guard*, pp. 32-37 for a description of the
undistinguished combat role of the Leibstandarte SS Adolf Hitler and the units of
the SS Verfügungstruppe in Poland.

37

large areas of Poznan and the entire west-central portion of the country overrun by the Eighth Army.[2]

Eicke did not accompany the SSTV into the field, but directed their activities throughout September from Hitler's special headquarters train (Führersonderzug) with the official title of higher SS and police leader (Höhere SS und Polizei Führer, or HSSPF) for the regions of Poland conquered by the Eighth and Tenth Armies. This title empowered Eicke, as the direct representative of the Reichsführer SS, with sweeping authority to deal with the Polish population, and made him accountable to Himmler alone for any measures he took in "pacifying" the conquered areas. Accordingly, until they were withdrawn from Poland in early October to be reorganized into the cadre of the SS Totenkopfdivision, the three Death's Head regiments and the units of the security police and SD under Eicke's control acted as the supreme police authority of the Reich in the provinces of Poznan, Lodz, and Warsaw as they were released from direct army control.[3]

The nature and extent of the acts committed by the SSTV may

[2] BAKO, R58/825, Meldungen des Chefs der Sicherheitspolizei und des SD, "*Betrifft*, Amtschefbesprechung am 12. September 1939," dated September 13, 1939. A copy of the minutes of this same high-level meeting concerning the deployment of SS units in Poland may also be found in IFZ, microfilm collection, MA-433, frames 8509-8511. Units of the security police and the SD were organized into five separate Einsatzgruppen, and operated in conjunction with Eicke's SSTV. With the exception of SD Einsatzgruppe III behind the Eighth Army, which was placed under Eicke's direct command, the other SD Einsatzgruppen active in Poland remained under the control of Heydrich as chief of the security police and the SD (Höhne, pp. 273-74).

[3] BAKO, loc. cit.; and BAKO, B-162/29, fol. 1, Einsatzgruppen in Polen, Einsatzgruppen der Sicherheitspolizei, Selbstschutz und andere Formationen in der Zeit vom 1. September 1939 bis Frühjahr 1940, 38-40, (Hereafter cited as BAKO, Einsatzgruppen in Polen, with page numbers). This is a typescript copy of the lengthy report on the activities of the SSTV and SD units in Poland prepared by the war crimes investigation division in the office of the attorney general of the Federal Republic of Germany (Zentrale Stelle der Landesjustizverwaltungen) in 1963. Before the war the HSSPF acted as Himmler's direct agents for coordinating, independently from the regular state and military authorities, all SS and police activities in the SS Oberabschnitten in the event of mobilization. In the wartime occupied east, the HSSPF exercised even greater power, executing orders as Himmler's immediate subordinates in command of all SS and police units garrisoned in the individual occupied territories. The best analysis of the institutional significance of the HSSPF within the structure of the SS is the important article by Hans Buchheim, "Die Höheren SS und Polizei Führer," *Vierteljahrshefte für Zeitgeschichte*, 11 (October 1963), 362-91.

be judged from the amply documented record of SS Totenkopfstandarte "Brandenburg," which moved into Poland on September 13 to begin "cleansing and security measures" (Säuberungs- und Sicherheits Massnahmen).[4] SS "Brandenburg" was commanded by Standartenführer Paul Nostitz, a trusted Eicke subordinate who carried out his orders thoroughly and fanatically. During the three weeks it remained on active duty in Poland, SS "Brandenburg" gave the villages and towns through which it passed a fitting introduction to the character of German rule.[5]

In his report summarizing the actions of SS "Brandenburg" in Poland, Nostitz described how his SSTV had conducted house searches, secured villages from "insurgents," and had arrested and shot large numbers of "suspicious elements, plunderers, insurgents, Jews, and Poles," many of whom were killed "while trying to escape." In the perverse clerical jargon of the SS, this report referred to the savage measures SS "Brandenburg" took against the inhabitants of the cities of Włocławek (Leslau) and Bydgoszcz (Bromberg).[6]

SS "Brandenburg" arrived in Włocławek, some seventy miles northwest of Warsaw on the Vistula, on September 22, and began a four-day "Jewish action" (Judenaktion) that involved plundering Jewish shops, dynamiting and burning the city's synagogues, and arresting and executing en masse many leading members of the local Jewish community.[7] In the midst of the Włocławek ac-

[4] BAKO, Einsatzgruppen in Polen, pp. 38-39.
[5] Ibid.; USDC, SS Personalakte Nostitz, summary report of SS "Brandenburg" activities in Poland entitled, "Tätigkeitsbericht während des Einsatzes vom 13. bis 26. 9. 1939," and dated Oranienburg, September 28, 1939; and a letter to the author from Dr. Cz. Pilichowski, director of the Central Commission for the Study of Hitlerite Crimes in Poland (Główna Komisja Badania Zbrodni Hitlerowskich w Polsce), dated Warsaw, April 22, 1970. (Hereafter cited as Pilichowski letter).
[6] USDC, SS Personalakte Nostitz, report of September 28, 1939. SS "Brandenburg" took a route of march through Poland that may be retraced by pinpointing the villages and towns of Ostrovo, Kalisch, Turek, Zuki, Krosniewice, Klodava, Przedecz, Włocławek, Dembrice, Bydgoszcz, Wirsitz, Zarnikau, and Chodziez, in the McGraw-Hill International Atlas (Gütersloh, 1963), plates 101, 104-5, and 113.
[7] BAKO, Einsatzgruppen in Polen, pp. 38-41, 51-52, 93-94, 161-62; Pilichowski letter; and a corroborating eyewitness account in, Jacob Apenszlak, ed., The Black Book of Polish Jewry: An Account of the Martyrdom of Polish Jewry under Nazi Occupation (New York, 1943), pp. 7, 10-12. The SS soldiers also tortured several Jews into signing confessions that they started the synagogue

tion, Nostitz received a visit from SS Gruppenführer Günther Pancke. During September 1939, Pancke served as Eicke's deputy in transmitting personally orders from Hitler's headquarters train to the individual SSTV and SD Einsatzgruppen operating under Eicke's authority in the field. The purpose of Pancke's trip to Włocławek was to deliver an urgent, top secret order from Eicke. Nostitz received instructions from Eicke to dispatch two battalions of SS "Brandenburg" to Bydgoszcz (Bromberg) to conduct an "intelligentsia action" there. As a result, on September 24 two Sturmbanne of SS "Brandenburg" traveled to Bydgoszcz and during the following two days hunted down, arrested, and shot approximately 800 Polish civilians from the provinces of Poznan and Pomerania whose names the security police and SD had recorded on special death lists of intellectuals and potential resistance leaders. While two of his battalions conducted the round-up and killing of civilians in Bydgoszcz, Nostitz remained in Włocławek to direct the other battalion of SS "Brandenburg" in the "Jewish action."[8]

In addition to these murders, there were large-scale atrocities committed in Poland by other Death's Head units subsequently

---

fires, giving Nostitz a cynical pretext to levy a fine of 100,000 zloty against the Jewish community of Włocławek for arson. The precise number of Jews killed in Włocławek by SS "Brandenburg" has never been determined. The most thorough description of SS "Brandenburg" activities in Włocławek is the report of the then commander of Army Rear Area 581, Lieutenant General Alfred Boehm-Tettelbach, whose outraged protest to Eighth Army of September 25 indicates only that Nostitz had ordered 800 Jews arrested and had declared to army officers present that he intended to have all the Jews shot. This document, with a heading "Kdt. rückw. A. Geb. 581, An A. O. K. 8, Włocławek, den 25. 9. 1939," is reproduced in full in BAKO, Einsatzgruppen in Polen, p. 161.

[8] USDC, SS Personalakte Nostitz, report of September 28, 1939; and BAKO, Einsatzgruppen in Polen, pp. 41, 93. During the period SS "Brandenburg" and units of the security police and SD operated behind the Eighth Army, Pancke served as the liaison between Eicke and the units in the field with the title of "Special Police Commander with the Eighth Army" (Sonderbefehlshaber der Polizei beim A. O. K. 8), Pilichowski letter of April 22, 1970.

Photographs of the mass shootings during the "intelligentsia action" in Bydgoszcz may be found in Stanisław Poznanski, *Struggle, Death, Memory* (Warsaw, 1963), n.p., identified by caption only. This volume, one of several pictorial documentaries published by the Polish Council for the Preservation of the Monuments of Struggle and Martyrdom, also contains assorted photographs of SS soldiers from Death's Head units, clearly identifiable by the skull-and-crossbones emblem on their right collar tabs, physically abusing Polish Jews.

incorporated into the SS Totenkopfdivision. On September 8, 1939, the battalion SS "Heimwehr Danzig" shot thirty-three Polish civilians in the village of Ksiazki (Hohenkirch) in the province of Pomerania.[9] SS Wachsturmbann Eimann, a reserve SSTV organized in Danzig in June 1939, operated after September 13 in the area between Karthaus and Neustadt in the former Polish Corridor and carried out an undetermined number of massacres, the principal victims of which were Polish Jews.[10] In south-central Poland, in the province of Kielce (the rear area of the German Tenth Army), similar atrocities involving the torture and execution of large numbers of Jews, political and religious leaders, and captured Polish soldiers occurred in Nisko, Rawa Mazowiecka, and Ciepielow. These mass shootings almost certainly were the work of the other two original SSTV, SS "Oberbayern" and SS "Thuringen." These two Death's Head regiments operated behind Reichenau's Tenth Army, were under Eicke's command, and received orders to conduct actions against Polish Jews and civilians similar to the measures taken by SS "Brandenburg."[11]

When the original three Death's Head regiments left Poland in

[9] Szymon Datner, "Crimes Committed by the Wehrmacht During the September Campaign and the Period of Military Government (1 September 1939—25 October 1939)," *Polish Western Affairs*, 3 (September 1962), 294-338, esp. 305. SS "Heimwehr Danzig" was organized as SS Totenkopfsturmbann "Götze" in Danzig in the spring of 1939, but was renamed SS "Heimwehr Danzig" just before the war. In October 1939, SS "Heimwehr Danzig" was incorporated into the SS Totenkopfdivision as the nucleus of the artillery regiment (Stein, p. 28; Dr. K. G. Klietmann, *Die Waffen SS: Eine Dokumentation* (Osnabrück, 1965), pp. 419-21; and IFZ, newspaper collection, *Das Schwarze Korps* (the official SS newspaper), issues for August 24, 31, and September 28, 1939, for articles on SS "Heimwehr Danzig").

[10] BAKO, Einsatzgruppen in Polen, p. 36. In January 1940, SS Wachsturmbann Eimann was disbanded and its men divided among the SSTV serving as replacement/training units for the SS Totenkopfdivision.

[11] Though circumstantial, the evidence points overwhelmingly to SS "Oberbayern" and SS "Thuringen" as the perpetrators of the atrocities at Nisko, Rawa Mazowiecka, and Ciepielow. These two SSTV were the only SS units operating in these areas during September, and they were the only SS formations behind the Tenth Army that had the size, firepower, and mobility to conduct large-scale killings at different points scattered over so broad an area. See especially Gerald Reitlinger, *The SS* (New York: Viking 1968), p. 126; *The Final Solution: The Attempt to Exterminate the Jews of Europe, 1939-1945* (London, 1953), p. 43; and the photographs of SS soldiers conducting executions in Rawa Mazowiecka and Ciepielow in September 1939 in, Poznanski, *Struggle, Death, Memory*, pictures identified individually by caption.

41

early October 1939, they were replaced by newer SSTV that had been organized in 1938. One of these replacement regiments, the Twelfth SS Totenkopfstandarte, moved into the province of Poznan upon the departure of SS "Brandenburg." In late October, one company from the Twelfth SS Totenkopfstandarte occupied the town of Owińsk and began the systematic liquidation of the patients in the large psychiatric hospital there. The mentally ill were hauled away from the hospital in truckloads of fifty and shot by SSTV soldiers in groups on the edge of a mass grave. In less than a month, one company of Totenkopf soldiers murdered over 1,000 innocent, helplessly ill men and women. The men who served with the Twelfth SS Totenkopfstandarte in Poland, including those responsible for the Owińsk killings, eventually were called into the SS Totenkopfdivision as combat replacements.[12]

The behavior of the SS Death's Head units during and after the Polish campaign provoked an attitude of shock, disgust, and uneasiness among responsible senior officers of the German army. In the process, the shrewder army commanders saw the real purpose behind the presence of the Totenkopfverbände in Poland. Typical of this army sentiment and suspicion was the report to the Eighth Army by General Boehm-Tettelbach in Włocławek protesting the actions taken by SS "Brandenburg."[13] The general's clear impression was that SS "Brandenburg" had been sent to Włocławek solely for the purpose of taking violent measures against the Jews. To support this assertion, he cited Nostitz's repeated refusal to perform normal security assignments, such as having SS "Brandenburg" comb the forests south of Włocławek. The SS officers and men preferred instead to remain in Włocławek to torment Jews and other Polish civilians. The general also described how Gruppenführer Pancke had said openly that the SSTV would not obey army orders, since the SS had special tasks to per-

---

[12] Pilichowski letter of April 22, 1970. By the autumn of 1941, nearly all the men from the prewar replacement SSTV had been called into combat service with the SS Totenkopfdivision, or with one of the other Waffen SS formations fighting in Russia. Charles W. Sydnor, Jr., "The History of the SS *Totenkopfdivision* and the Postwar Mythology of the *Waffen SS*," *Central European History*, 6 (December 1973), 339-62, esp. 347-49, for a discussion of the movement of replacements from the SSTV into the SS Totenkopfdivision.

[13] BAKO, Einsatzgruppen in Polen, pp. 161-62.

form that were outside the competence of the army. The events in Włoclawek, he concluded, demonstrated that the SSTV commander was following orders from some nonmilitary authority to terrorize the local Jews.[14]

The report on the atrocities committed by SS "Brandenburg" in Włoclawek undoubtedly reached Colonel General Blaskowitz, and helped transform that iron-spined officer into the army's most bitter critic of SS behavior in Poland. As commander of the Eighth Army during the campaign, and as chief of the occupation zone Upper East (Ober Ost) after October 23, Blaskowitz dealt directly with the SS Totenkopfverbände and was constantly aware of their movements and actions. The Colonel General found all the Death's Head units loathsome and was so horrified by their excesses against the Poles that he composed a long memorandum cataloguing the crimes committed by the SSTV in Poland and sent it as a protest to Colonel General Walther von Brauchitsch, then commander-in-chief of the German army. Blaskowitz's protests, however, had no effect. Brauchitsch was too weak-willed to press the issue with Hitler, and the end result—months later—was nothing more than a perfunctory meeting between Himmler and Brauchitsch in which the Reichsführer SS promised that any such future activities would be conducted in a fashion inoffensive to the sensibilities of the army.[15]

In addition to blunting the army's criticism of SSTV behavior in Poland, Himmler won another important victory when Hitler agreed, during the first week of October 1939, to the creation of

[14] Ibid. The Włoclawek report confirms the conclusions of Professor Helmut Krausnick, "Hitler und die Morde in Polen," pp. 207-9, that the SS atrocities in Poland which appeared to be part of an undirected, uncontrollable orgy of sadism were, in fact, a series of actions Hitler had ordered specifically against the Polish population.

[15] Stein, pp. 30-31; IFZ, Nuremberg document NO-3011, a photostatic copy of Blaskowitz's lengthy memorandum to Brauchitsch of February 15, 1940. Blaskowitz was especially chagrined by the brutal manner in which the SSTV carried out executions, and was equally disgusted by the frequent incidents of public drunkenness and looting by members of the SS Death's Head units—particularly men belonging to the Eleventh SS Totenkopfstandarte. This SSTV was responsible for security in the area between Warsaw and Radom, and most of the incidents referred to by Blaskowitz occurred in Radom. The best discussion of Blaskowitz's courageous crusade against the SSTV is Harold C. Deutsch, *The Conspiracy Against Hitler in the Twilight War* (Minneapolis, Minn., 1968), pp. 182-89.

1. Himmler (foreground) and Theodor Eicke (over Himmler's left shoulder) inspect SS Totenkopfverbände in Poland, September 1939.

three SS field divisions for the projected western campaign. These new SS formations, designated officially as Waffen SS, included the führer's own pet Leibstandarte SS Adolf Hitler, which was to be enlarged to a fully motorized infantry regiment, the SS Verfügungsdivision (to be built around three regiments of Verfügungstruppen), the new SS Totenkopfdivision, and the SS Polizeidivision, which was to be made up chiefly from conscripts from the Ordnungspolizei.[16]

Eicke duly received orders to assume command of the new Totenkopfdivision, and proceeded to Dachau in early October to prepare for the organization of the division. By October 12, he had created the skeletal framework of an administrative service for the SS Totenkopfdivision (SSTK), and had transferred the inmates at Dachau to other camps within the Reich. With the prisoners out of the way, Eicke and the SSTK administrative service, which consisted of a supply office, a bakery company, and a butchering company, began feverish preparations for feeding the huge influx of SS men expected by October 25. All food and supplies had to be purchased daily from farmers and merchants in the immediate vicinity of Dachau, and the kitchens of the concentration camp hastily enlarged to handle all the cooking. The army, which was bitterly opposed to the creation of a Waffen SS, refused Eicke any supplies or assistance and left the infant SSTK to forage for itself.[17]

The structure of SSTK, as a motorized infantry division, corresponded roughly to that of the army's newer motorized formations. Eicke's new SSTK consisted of a division staff and units that included three motorized infantry regiments (regular-army motorized divisions had two), an artillery regiment, a communications battalion, an engineer battalion, a tank-destroyer battalion

[16] Stein, pp. 29, 32; and BAKO, NS-7/426, "Einstellungsbedingungen für die Waffen SS," an undated memorandum drafted sometime during the autumn of 1939.

[17] Bundesarchiv-Militärarchiv, Freiburg im Breisgau, Splitterakten der 3. SS Panzer Division "Totenkopf," 1939-1945, III SS, 42/1, Verwaltungsdienste, Kriegstagebuch 1, pp. 1-2, 61. (Hereafter cited by document collection, series, volume, and page number as BAMA, III SS, 42/1, pp. 1-2, 61). This collection of war diaries, unit reports, correspondence, memoranda, maps, telegrams, and teleprinter messages is the most important single source for the study of the SS Totenkopfdivision.

(Panzer Jäger Abteilung), a reconnaissance battalion, supply, administrative, transport, pay and postal battalions, and a medical and hospital unit. The personnel for the new Totenkopfdivision came from several branches of the SS. The nucleus of the SSTK, its three infantry regiments, consisted of Eicke's original three concentration camp guard regiments, SS "Oberbayern," SS "Brandenburg," and SS "Thuringen." SS "Heimwehr Danzig" provided most of the men for the artillery regiment, while the other units of SSTK were staffed with new recruits and SS men drawn from the Verfügungstruppen, the Allgemeine SS, the Ordnungspolizei, and the new SSTV created by Eicke during the last months of peace. To provide Eicke's new division with additional muscle, Himmler designated from among the new SSTV a replacement/training battalion for each regiment and a replacement company for each battalion of the SSTK.[18]

Eicke devoted most of his time and energy during the first three weeks of October to gathering a reliable staff for the SSTK to advise and assist him in his new command. The SSTK staff was, with several modifications, organized along traditional lines.[19]

[18] BAKO, NS-19/neu-1668, "Ausbildungstand," a memorandum written by Eicke and dated April 9, 1940, describing the progress of training the SSTK from its creation in October 1939. See also, BAMA, III SS, 41/8, i, 4-7, listing the location and size of the SSTK replacement units; and Stein, p. 33; and Klietmann, pp. 107, 115-17. The infantry regiments of the SSTK were divided into three battalions of four companies each, plus two replacement companies for each regiment. The artillery regiment was divided into three battalions, with each battalion having three batteries and each battery four field pieces. The engineer battalion and the tank destroyer battalion both consisted of three companies, while the reconnaissance battalion was divided into two motorcycle companies and an armored car platoon. The communications battalion was split into two companies, one for handling telephone traffic and the other radio communications (Klietmann, pp. 115-17).

[19] Eicke adopted the German army's Roman numeral designations for the sections within the SSTK staff. See BAMA, III SS, 41/5, ii, Anlagenband zum KTB No. 5, pp. 216-17. The SSTK staff included an operations officer (Ia), a supply and transport officer (Ib), and a division intelligence officer (Ic). Eicke's staff also included a training officer (Ausbildungsoffizier), or (Id) as in regular-army divisions. The SSTK training officer, however, received a different title—Offizier zur besondere Verwendung—(officer for special assignment), and performed duties much different from those of his counterpart in the army. In addition, Eicke had adjutants to handle personnel matters for officers (IIa), enlisted men (IIb), and a judge advocate (III) to preside over the SSTK courts martial. Also attached to the

The men Eicke chose for the division staff represented a remarkable blend of administrative and military talents. For the most part, those appointed to key positions on the SSTK staff—those closest to and most trusted by Eicke—had served before 1939 either in a camp guard unit or on the staff of Eicke's inspectorate at Oranienburg.

The sole exception was the first operations officer (Ia) of the SSTK, and the man most responsible for whipping the division into fighting shape, SS Standartenführer Cassius Freiherr von Montigny. An ascetic, dour, and brilliant aristocrat, Montigny had earned the Iron Cross, First Class while serving in the U-boat arm of the German navy during the First World War. Physically, he resembled the classic stereotype of the cold-eyed, waspishly thin, insufferably arrogant professional German officer.

Montigny's pre-SS career had included as much political intrigue as it had military distinction. After retiring from the navy in 1919, Montigny had served briefly with one of the naval units of the Freikorps—the postwar military formations that fought against the Poles and were used by the Republic to suppress the Communist uprisings in 1919. In 1920 Montigny began a fifteen-year career as a police officer, serving until the autumn of 1935 in several different cities. With the coming of German rearmament and renewed conscription, he found the lure of the military irresistible and resigned his police commission to join Hitler's new Wehrmacht as commander successively of the Thirty-first and 102nd Infantry Regiments.[20]

After joining the army, Montigny gravitated to the pro-Nazi circle of officers then associated with General Walter von Reichenau and began to dabble in political intrigue. His political activity on behalf of the Nazi party among the men in his command resulted in sharp criticism from the war minister, Field

---

staff were an administrative officer (IVa), the division medical officer (IVb), a motor transport officer (V) responsible for all repairs and maintenance, and the staff munitions officer. The staff roster also listed officially the commander of the division's military police unit (Feldgendarmarie) and included both the SSTK postmaster and paymaster. Finally, to assist the operations officer, Eicke had a map officer, four officers to handle special missions, and two interpreters.

[20] USDC, SS Personalakte von Montigny, summary of the materials in Montigny's SS service records, especially his Lebenslauf and Dienstlaufbahn.

Marshall Werner von Blomberg, and on April 30, 1937, Montigny was forced to resign from the army. Incensed, Montigny sometime during the first months after his resignation composed and sent to Himmler—the army's archenemy—a memorandum criticizing the army and its leaders for being anti-Nazi, bureaucratic, lethargic, and generally unimaginative. What the officer corps needed, he wrote, was a thoroughly politicized cadre of new men to drive out the ruling "Schleicher clique" and infuse the army with the proper National Socialist spirit. Himmler was so impressed with the memorandum that he forwarded it to Hitler for perusal and approached Montigny on the subject of a career as an SS officer.[21]

On April 1, 1938, at Himmler's request, Montigny joined the SS with the rank of Obersturmbannführer (lieutenant colonel), and was assigned by the Reichsführer SS to the SS Junkerschule at Bad Tölz as an instructor in military tactics, where he remained until Himmler suggested him for the post of Eicke's operations officer in October 1939.[22]

Among Eicke's closest and most trusted immediate subordinates, one who had been associated with him the longest was the commander of SSTK Infantry Regiment Number 1, SS Standartenführer Max Simon. As a corporal in the First Life Cuirassier Regiment during World War I, Simon won the Iron Cross, First Class for gallantry under fire. Unable to accept Germany's defeat or to adjust to civilian life at the end of the war, he joined the Freikorps Life Cuirassier Regiment early in 1919 and the following year succeeded in joining the Reichswehr with the rank of sergeant. Simon remained a member of the Sixteenth Cavalry Regiment until his voluntary retirement from the army in September 1929.

After four unsuccessful years at different odd jobs, he enlisted in the Allgemeine SS on May 1, 1933. Shortly thereafter, Simon became acquainted with Eicke, who had him transferred to the new camp inspectorate and promoted to SS Hauptsturmführer in

---

[21] Ibid., copy of a telegram from Blomberg to Montigny, dated April 28, 1937; and an undated memorandum signed by Montigny and initialed with favorable marginal comments by Himmler with instructions for forwarding to Hitler.

[22] Ibid., Montigny's Lebenslauf and Dienstlaufbahn.

the summer of 1934. Simon quickly gained Eicke's complete confidence and found a place for himself in the burgeoning concentration camp network. He became commander of the SS guard unit at Sachsenburg on November 9, 1934, remaining there until September 15, 1935. Eicke then moved him to the "Oberbayern" Death's Head unit and subsequently, on May 1, 1937, secured Simon's promotion to the rank of SS Sturmbannführer and gave him command of the First Battalion of SS "Oberbayern." Two months later, on July 10, 1937, Eicke gave Simon command of the regiment itself—a post Simon held until both he and SSTV "Oberbayern" were transferred to the new SS Totenkopfdivision in October 1939.[23]

The commander of the Second Infantry Regiment of SSTK, SS Obersturmbannführer Heinz Bertling, did not enjoy Eicke's confidence or get along well with him. Himmler had assigned Bertling to SSTV "Thuringen" in February 1938 as an SS Sturmbannführer and battalion commander. Bertling immediately incurred Eicke's suspicion and displeasure, and at Eicke's request transferred to the SS Regiment "Deutschland" in May 1938. After several months with SS "Deutschland," Bertling received a staff assignment with the Leibstandarte SS Adolf Hitler and remained there until Himmler forced him upon Eicke as a regimental commander in October 1939.[24]

[23] Ibid., SS Personalakte Simon, summary of the materials in Simon's SS service records, especially his Lebenslauf and Dienstlaufbahn. Simon is a figure of major importance in the history of the SS Totenkopfdivision and the Waffen SS. During the Second World War he became one of the premier SS field commanders, rising to the rank of SS Gruppenführer and assuming command of SSTK after Eicke was killed in Russia in February 1943. In April 1944, Simon received command of the Sixteenth SS Panzergrenadierdivision Reichsführer SS, and the following October became commander of the Thirteenth SS Army Corps, where he remained until the end of the war.

[24] Ibid., SS Personalakte Bertling, summary of the materials in Bertling's SS service records. Bertling was also a decorated veteran, having won the Iron Cross, First Class while serving with the Seventy-fourth Hanoverian Infantry Regiment in World War I. He subsequently joined the famous Ehrhardt Second Marine Brigade, and fought against the Spartacists in Wilhelmshaven and participated in the Kapp Putsch. After leaving the Freikorps, he served as a police officer until joining the SS in 1931. From March 1935 until his assignment to SS "Thuringen" in February 1938, Bertling was an instructor in tactics at the SS Junkerschule in Braunschweig. Eicke tried in vain to prevent his posting to SSTK, complaining to the SS Hauptamt that he had known Bertling for many years and considered him

The man who held what was initially the second most important post among Eicke's immediate subordinates in SSTK, that of division supply and transport officer (Ib), was SS Standartenführer Erich Tschimpke. Tschimpke had won the Iron Cross, First Class during World War I as a first lieutenant in the 157th Infantry Regiment, and had drifted aimlessly after the war from job to job until joining the SS in 1932. As a staff officer with SS Oberabschnitt Südwest, Tschimpke displayed marked talent for handling problems of supply and logistics. He was spotted by the ever-alert Eicke in the autumn of 1937, and transferred to the inspectorate of concentration camps in January 1938—remaining at Oranienburg until Eicke had him placed on the staff of SSTK. Tschimpke's organizational talents were considerable, and to him belongs most of the credit for solving, in the face of the army's stingy and hostile attitude, the nearly insurmountable initial problems involved in supplying and feeding the new SSTK.[25]

The first administrative officer (Verwaltungsleiter) of the SSTK, SS Obersturmbannführer Anton Kaindl, was also a veteran of the prewar concentration camp system. His SS career, which began in 1935, had been confined, because of his bad health and poor eyesight, to administrative duties. As an efficient member of the staff of the SS Verwaltungsamt, Kaindl volunteered in 1936 for service with Eicke's SSTV and was transferred to the inspectorate headquarters at Oranienburg to serve as paymaster of the SS Death's Head units. In April 1937, Eicke promoted him to the position of chief administrative officer in the inspectorate, and subsequently assigned Kaindl to the staff of the SSTK with the same title.[26]

The surgeon of the new Totenkopfdivision, SS Standartenführer Karl Genzken, also came with Eicke directly from the in-

---

incompetent as a leader of men. Consequently, relations were strained between the two until Bertling obtained a transfer to the political section of the Foreign Office in August 1940. See also, Stein, pp. 189-90.

[25] USDC, SS Personalakte Tschimpke, summary of the materials in Tschimpke's SS service records, especially his Lebenslauf and Dienstlaufbahn.

[26] Ibid., SS Personalakte Kaindl, Lebenslauf and Dienstlaufbahn, and the efficiency reports on Kaindl written by Eicke on January 8, 1937, January 5, 1938, and April 19, 1939. Eicke considered Kaindl ideally fitted for work in the concentration camp system. After serving for two years with the SSTK, Kaindl returned to the camp system and served as commandant of Sachsenhausen, 1942-1945.

spectorate of concentration camps. Before the war, Genzken had been the chief medical officer on the inspectorate staff, and his transfer to the SSTK subsequently proved most timely. At Oranienburg, Genzken and another surgeon had conducted a number of successful experiments for sterilizing professional criminals. Word of these activities leaked out and came to the attention of officials in the Reich Ministry of Justice, who began making inquiries about the medical experiments in the camps. Himmler referred all questions to Eicke's successor at Oranienburg, Richard Glücks. Glücks was able to quash any inquiry by admitting that the experiments had taken place—claiming that they were justified in view of the dangerous nature of the criminals who had been sterilized—and by asserting that it would be impossible for anyone from the ministry of justice to question the SS doctors involved, since they both had been transferred to the Totenkopfdivision and were serving "at the front." With that, the matter was dropped and Genzken was spared any embarrassment.[27]

The most sinister-looking member of Eicke's SSTK staff was his training officer, SS Sturmbannführer Dr. Wilhelm Fuhrländer. A squat, ugly man with a porcine appearance and a face full of dueling scars, Fuhrländer had earned a doctorate in civil administration at the University of Bonn after World War I. He too had arrived in the Totenkopfdivision after a long association with Eicke in the concentration camp system. Joining the SS in April 1932, Fuhrländer held a succession of unimportant posts until August 1935. At that time, while serving as a racial expert with SS Oberabschnitt West, he met and became friends with Eicke. The latter requested his transfer to the camp inspectorate and

[27] IFZ, microfilm collection, reel MA-293, frames 2550872-873, 882-884, a letter of May 3, 1939 from Eicke to SS Gruppenführer Karl Wolff, the chief of Himmler's personal staff; and a letter from Richard Glücks to Karl Wolff of December 2, 1939. Though his name is not mentioned in either letter, the SSTK records reveal that only two surgeons—Genzken and the surgeon for the SSTK artillery regiment, SS Sturmbannführer Dr. Edwin Jung—were transferred directly from the inspectorate of concentration camps at Oranienburg to the Totenkopfdivision in early October 1939 (BAMA, III SS, 46/1, Divisions Arzt, KTB No. 3, pp. 6-7). Genzken left SSTK on March 31, 1940 for a promotion to the medical inspectorate of the Waffen SS, and eventually became the wartime chief of the entire Waffen SS medical service. See also Hilberg, *Destruction*, pp. 601, 706.

made Fuhrländer his educational officer, responsible for determining the racial fitness of new SS recruits and for conducting the ideological and racial schooling of the men in the SSTV. In this capacity, Fuhrländer was sent in October 1935 to the SS Rasse- und Siedlungshauptamt (Race and Resettlement Office, or RuSHA) for intensified training in Nazi racial theory. He was then posted briefly to the SS Junkerschule at Braunschweig to gain lecturing experience as an instructor before returning permanently to Eicke's staff at Oranienburg in January 1936.[28]

As one of Eicke's most intimate associates, Fuhrländer accompanied him into the SSTK in October 1939 to perform the same tasks in the division that he had in the prewar Death's Head units. Responsible for the ideological education (weltanschauliche Erziehung) of the men in the SSTK, Fuhrländer was required to report to the RuSHA and to follow their pedagogical guidelines. In matters concerning discipline and promotion, however, he remained a subordinate of the division commander. During the first months after the creation of the SSTK, Fuhrländer's ideological education program made little progress, as Eicke and his staff devoted almost every hour of training to making the division combat-ready for the expected western campaign.[29]

The careers of the men mentioned above—those with major roles in creating the Totenkopfdivision—represent a combination of military and political experience that, when carried into the Waffen SS and applied to the training of SS soldiers, helped produce reckless bravery and calculated brutality, hallmarks of SSTK

[28] USDC, SS Personalakte Fuhrländer, letter from Eicke to the SS Hauptamt, dated August 16, 1935, requesting Fuhrländer's transfer to the SSTV; and a summary of the other materials in Fuhrländer's SS service records, especially his Lebenslauf and Dienstlaufbahn.

[29] Ibid., copy of a circular signed by Himmler on November 2, 1939, confirming Fuhrländer's appointment and outlining his responsibilities. Himmler assigned a training officer to each of the original three Waffen SS divisions created in the autumn of 1939. These men concerned themselves almost exclusively with the political and racial indoctrination of SS soldiers. Responsibility for the military training of the men rested with the division's operations officer and the individual unit commanders. In addition to his duties as training officer of the SSTK, Fuhrländer screened for Himmler all marriage applications filed by members of the division, and administered in conjunction with the SS Versorgungsamt (benefits office) the payment of benefits to wounded men and to the families of SSTK soldiers killed in action (BAMA, III SS, 41/8, 1, pp. 36-38).

behavior during the war. Most of Eicke's staff had seen combat during World War I, and many had emerged from the war as highly decorated soldiers. Nearly all of them had succumbed to the lure of the postwar Freikorps, with their fanatical loyalty to individual officers, and freebooter, soldier-of-fortune spirit and camaraderie. Consequently, as the fragmentary evidence in their SS service records suggests, they became misfits in civilian life. Blacklisted by the labor unions, jobless and aimless, they were among the most politically explosive malcontents in the society of Weimar Germany. Most of them eventually sought refuge either in police work or in a return to military life through a career in the Reichswehr.

For all of them, the SS became a home and, with the sole exception of Montigny, work in the concentration camp system a specialty. In the SS Death's Head units, Eicke's rigid discipline and disposition of blind obedience provided them with the security they had not found in civilian life. At the same time, the miasma in the camps made them anesthetic to the infliction of cruelty as routine duty, and instilled in them a zealous hatred for Germany's foes. Except for Bertling and Montigny, all had been hand-picked and trained by Eicke, who brought them into the Totenkopfdivision solely to help him build the division into the kind of formation the prewar SS Totenkopfverbände had been.

During the first months after the creation of the SSTK, Eicke, his staff, and his unit commanders devoted all their energy and patience to the three most urgent problems facing the new division: the organization of its units and the combat and technical training of the troops; the procurement of weapons and equipment; and the creation of a sense of discipline and esprit de corps. The question of combat training was the most pressing issue, with the goal of achieving the highest level of proficiency in the shortest time.[30]

---

[30] BAMA, III SS, 41/8, 1, pp. 9-11. Himmler was lobbying with Hitler during these months to have the new SS divisions committed in the first attack waves of the western campaign. The target date for the invasion of France and the Low Countries was postponed repeatedly during November and December because of bad weather and the reservations of Halder and Brauchitsch. Hitler finally agreed to postpone the campaign until the spring of 1940. These postponements proved most fortunate for Eicke and the SSTK, as the division was in no condition during

By the third week of October, all the men designated for the new SSTK had arrived at Dachau. Eicke held his first full-dress inspection early on the morning of October 24, and announced a projected three-month training schedule he and Montigny had drawn up. The vigorous training program, which began that same day, consisted of continuous formal lectures, combat exercises, drills for familiarizing the men with all types of weapons, and extensive practice in the coordination of light- and heavy-weapons fire. The goal of the division's combat training program, Eicke declared, was to teach the SS soldier how to handle himself and his weapons in every possible battle situation.

Unit training exercises began at the squad and platoon level and, beginning in November, broadened each succeeding week into exercises on the next-largest unit level—to company, battalion, and finally regiment scale. The SSTK officers received instruction in such problems as issuing clear and precise orders, scouting and reconnaissance, proper utilization of training, and coordinated infantry and heavy-weapons fire. In addition, each SS officer was trained extensively in the problems of command at the next-highest unit level—platoon commanders received training in company command, and company commanders instruction in battalion command.[31]

During the two months the Totenkopfdivision remained at Dachau, training exercises for SS officers also included the handling of different types of weapons, tactics of camouflage, deployment and surprise attack, and the methods of breakthrough and pursuit. The small-unit exercises of the first weeks were broadened in December to mock assaults of company and battalion size carried out with artillery support. In late November, moreover, Eicke began taking the entire division into the coun-

---

the autumn and winter to be employed among the second- and third-line formations designated for such a campaign. For details concerning the planning of the western offensive, see the memoirs of Colonel General Heinz Guderian, *Panzer Leader* (New York, 1957), pp. 67-75; and those of the commander whose plan was subsequently adopted, Field Marshal Erich von Manstein, *Verlorene Siege* (Bonn, 1956), pp. 61-124; and the thorough discussion in Telford Taylor, *The March of Conquest: The German Victories in Western Europe, 1940* (New York, 1958), pp. 155-86.

[31] BAMA, III SS, 41/8, I, pp. 9-12.

tryside on practice marches to give his officers and men experience in assembling, moving, and dispersing large motorized formations.

For the more technical aspects of military training, the SSTK began to receive some help from the army. At the beginning of November, the army made arrangements to accept seventy men from the SSTK for a three-week course in radio and telephone training at the signal corps school at Halle.[32]

Despite the hurried nature of the training exercises and the initial shortages in equipment, which caused delays in the weapons training schedule, Eicke felt that the program was making progress and yielding results. His optimistic appraisal was seconded by the Reichsführer SS, who paid his first inspection visit to the SSTK on November 4, 1939. Himmler reviewed the men, looked over their equipment and watched a training exercise, conferred with Eicke, and left three hours after arriving—seemingly satisfied with what he had seen.[33]

Combat-readiness and full mobility, however, remained objectives out of Eicke's immediate reach. The slow pace at which the SSTK approached these goals during the winter of 1939-1940 was due more to the frightful shortages of weapons, equipment, and other supplies than to the enthusiastic but often clumsy SS approach to military training.

From October until mid-December 1939 the Totenkopfdivision was short of everything except zeal and determination. Even the process of feeding the division was an uncertain, day-to-day, emergency affair. The army persisted in its refusal to allocate any food for the SSTK, using the argument that since the SSTK was not yet under army operational command, it could not receive any of the vital foodstuffs appropriated by the Wehrmacht for the war effort.[34] Himmler and Eicke protested in vain. Not until the SSTK moved from Dachau at the beginning of December and was

[32] Ibid., pp. 11-15, 43-44.

[33] Ibid., pp. 21, 24-25, 29; and III SS, 44/2, pp. 26-27. In a special order of the day on Saturday, October 28, Eicke praised his men for their hard work, dedication, and spirit. He then lifted the ban he had placed on alcoholic beverages in the SSTK canteens, and declared Sunday, October 29, a holiday for the troops.

[34] Ibid., III SS, 42/1, Verwaltungsdienst, KTB No. 1, 3-4.

placed under army command did the Wehrmacht grudgingly give in and agree to help supply the division regularly.

During October and November, Eicke appealed repeatedly to the local grocers and businessmen in the Dachau area for help in acquiring food. The community apparently cooperated, as the SSTK succeeded in buying nearly all of the food it needed from local merchants. Food supplies that could not be purchased locally, Tschimpke found and bought in Munich.[35]

Overcoming the shortages in weapons and equipment required enormous ingenuity and perseverance; it taxed Eicke and his staff to the limit. The Wehrmacht, arguing that production in the armaments industry lagged behind the expanded demands of the three armed services, refused to give the SSTK any significant quantities of weapons and vehicles out of its own allotments. This forced Eicke to hunt on his own, scraping together what he needed wherever he could find it. By applying his relentless tenacity to the field of "requisitioning," Eicke managed eventually to find almost everything he needed for his new division and earned a reputation as the most original, resourceful—and successful—stealer of weapons, supplies, and equipment in the SS. From his desk in Dachau, he flooded the Reich with telephone calls to Himmler, the concentration camps, SS Oberabschnitten headquarters, the commanders of new SSTV, and army supply dumps, begging, demanding, threatening, cajoling, and somehow nearly always managing to locate and obtain what he wanted or needed.

Most of the equipment required initially by the SSTK, except for heavier weapons such as 105 mm artillery pieces and armored cars, which were received in small amounts from the army, Eicke succeeded in acquiring from sources within the SS. From the SS Kaserne at Buchenwald, for example, he procured four truckloads of clothing, and from the SS medical center in Berlin-Lichtenberg, five truckloads of medical supplies. In addition, during the first week of November Eicke's men raided the motor pool of the concentration camp inspectorate at Oranienburg, driving away with twenty-two Opel-Blitz trucks and nineteen motorcycles. Several days later, Eicke received Himmler's permission to take from the inspectorate radio equipment urgently needed by the

[35] Ibid.

SSTK signals battalion. During the same week, he also managed to squeeze several thousand rifles out of the reserve SSTV, several hundred thousand rounds of rifle and pistol ammunition from SS dumps in Oranienburg and Buchenwald, and two field howitzers from the Junkerschulen at Bad Tölz and Braunschweig.[36]

The above items represent, of course, only a fraction of the matériel needed by a fully motorized infantry division. They simply illustrate the manner by which Eicke got what he needed throughout the autumn and winter of 1939-1940. During these months, SSTK convoys shuttled daily in and out of Dachau, going to and coming from all parts of the Reich as Eicke worked ceaselessly dredging up the items he needed to make his division ready for the western campaign. His unrelenting zeal led to much resentment and hostility among those who suffered from his pilfering, and the friction caused by his larcenous ebullience resulted finally in a showdown with Himmler.

In late December, Eicke dispatched a convoy of thirty drivers to Oranienburg to obtain any additional trucks and vehicles that were not urgently needed by the inspectorate. Glücks, who evidently felt that his former boss was going too far, protested to Himmler. The Reichsführer agreed, refused to release any of the vehicles to the SSTK, and scolded Eicke for his high-handed tactics. Himmler then treated Eicke in kind by summarily transferring ten of the thirty SSTK drivers to the Eleventh SS Totenkopfstandarte in Warsaw. The remaining twenty men were put on a train and sent back to Eicke.[37]

---

[36] BAMA, III SS, 41/8, I, pp. 57, 157, 160, 165, 167, 218; and 44/2, 20. A good example of the frustrations caused by the equipment shortages can be seen in the experience of the SSTK bakery company, which was formed in mid-November. The only equipment the company received were 142 worn-out bicycles and ten World War I vintage, Czech-made, horsedrawn baking ovens. The ovens, which were wood burning and weighed two and one-half tons apiece, were practically useless. There were too few horses available to pull them, and they had to be loaded or unloaded from their wagon beds by the use of cranes—items even the persistent Eicke was unable to obtain (ibid., 42/1, KTB No. 1, p. 37).

[37] BAKO, NS-19/neu-1668, telegram from Glücks to Himmler; a copy of a letter from Himmler to Eicke; and a report written by SS Obersturmbannführer Walter Reder of Glücks' staff, all of which are dated December 30, 1939. In his letter to Eicke, Himmler stated categorically that the SSTK could have no more vehicles from SS motor pools, and that Eicke would have to get along with what he had until the army released more vehicles to the Waffen SS. Eicke in response pro-

In mid-November, Eicke's difficulties eased slightly when the Wehrmacht, largely as the result of Himmler's entreaties to Hitler, authorized the release of small quantities of heavy weapons and vehicles to the SSTK. By the end of the month, Eicke had enough motorcycles to equip fully the reconnaissance battalion, and had received sixteen 37 mm antitank guns (PAK) from the army depot in Kassel for the division's tank-destroyer battalion.[38] In addition, the SSTK received from army supply dumps and vehicle parks mortars, armored cars, motorcycle side cars, field kitchens, ten Czech-made trucks, and twelve field howitzers. The SSTK artillery regiment still had no 150 mm artillery pieces, with no immediate prospect of receiving any, and lacked sufficient medium halftracks to tow the 105 mm pieces it did have. By the beginning of December, moreover, the division still lacked the necessary trucks, halftracks, armored cars, and armored personnel carriers to make the three infantry regiments and the reconnaissance battalion fully motorized. Consequently, the constant postponements of the planned offensive in the west worked to the definite advantage of the Totenkopfdivision, which was far from operational readiness.[39]

The third major problem Eicke and his staff had to contend with before the western campaign was that of maintaining discipline and building esprit de corps in the SSTK. The difficulties Eicke encountered in this area came from two sources: the composition of the personnel in the division, and the temptations of being near Munich. Of the original complement of 15,000 men who made up the SSTK, about 7,000—less than half—had been members of the original three prewar Totenkopfverbände. The remainder of the men, drawn from the Ordnungspolizei, the Allgemeine SS, and the newer Death's Head units, were not as well disciplined as the men who had served under Eicke in SS "Oberbayern," SS "Brandenburg," and SS "Thuringen." Most of Eicke's initial discipline and morale problems in SSTK involved units within the division consisting of these less-experienced and less-disciplined men.

---

tested that he had only done his duty, and begged Himmler at least to send back the men transferred to Warsaw, since they were ten of the best drivers in the SSTK.

[38] BAMA, III SS, 44/2, p. 8; III SS, 41/8, I, pp. 215-18, 157.

[39] Ibid., pp. 62-63, 75-89; 41/8, I, pp. 215-18; and Stein, p. 50.

Eicke considered the proper esprit de corps even more important for the new SSTK than it had been for the prewar SSTV
since, as he imagined, the new division would play a much larger
and more direct role in the destruction of Nazi Germany's
enemies than had the prewar Death's Head formations. In a special order of the day on November 17, 1939, in which he announced that Hitler had confirmed officially his appointment as
commander of the SSTK, Eicke reiterated his conviction that the
strongest ingredient any SS unit could have was a superior esprit
de corps (Korpsgeist). He admitted that the SSTK still had far to
go in this respect, but affirmed his belief that the division would
develop the discipline and morale which would solve any problem, no matter how difficult, and would bind all the men in the
division together in the same fraternal spirit that had existed in the
SSTV. On both counts, Eicke's predictions proved premature.[40]

A week before issuing his first official pronouncement about
discipline and morale, he had had to warn his men about unauthorized absences from the Kaserne, and had sent Fuhrländer
around to all the units to lecture on the wartime military criminal
code and the offenses that were punishable by death. At the same
time, Eicke began a disciplinary policy that quickly became
standard wartime procedure in the SSTK. For disobeying orders
from a superior officer, an SS Untersturmführer (second lieutenant) in the supply section was confined for five days then transferred to the concentration camp inspectorate at Oranienburg for
reassignment to a concentration camp or to one of the reserve
SSTV in occupied Poland.[41]

During that same week, the temptations of Munich made themselves felt in Eicke's new division. The war diary of the SSTK
supply section indicates that several men from the division had
been frequenting the less wholesome Munich brothels. The result

[40] BAMA, III SS, 41/8, I, p. 45.

[41] Ibid., 44/2, p. 35; and 41/8, I, p. 179, Tagesbefehl No. 29, November 8,
1939. Eicke announced that he was making this particular case public so that any
future offenders might know what to expect as punishment. On the same day,
Eicke demanded that an unknown SSTK officer, who had been involved in a traffic
accident in Munich and had left an injured civilian in the Nymphenburg hospital
without reporting the accident to the police, turn himself in immediately. Two
days later this officer was transferred to duty in the concentration camp system
(ibid., 41/8, I, p. 176).

was the first appearance in the SSTK of social diseases that have menaced armies the world over. These first cases elicited a sharp warning from Eicke and brought on another round of lectures by Fuhrländer.[42]

By mid-November, the judicial procedures had been worked out for handling those in the SSTK guilty of committing crimes or charged with breaches of discipline. On November 13, Eicke announced that all violations of the wartime criminal code would be subject to the jurisdiction of a tribunal of the Totenkopfdivision. This SS court-martial would have sole competence to try and sentence all men in the division in accordance with the existing military laws. As division commander, Eicke was to be the convening authority (Gerichtsherr) with the right of final review in all cases.[43] Eicke also informed his men that the SSTK, as a formation subject to all SS and party racial regulations, was bound to comply with the standards established by the Reichsführer SS and the RuSHA for marriage applications. Consequently, any member of the SSTK who wished to marry had to send his own personal complete Ahnentafel (ancestral chart) and that of his prospective bride to Eicke, who, after examining the materials, passed them on through Fuhrländer to the RuSHA for final approval.[44]

Some of Eicke's officers made the mistake of not taking his many warnings seriously. On November 20, Eicke announced in an order of the day that he was relieving from duty SS Obersturmbannführer Werner, commander of the signals battalion, and transferring him to the inspectorate at Oranienburg for disobeying specific orders applying to the use of motor vehicles on convoy duty. To emphasize his seriousness, Eicke added that

[42] BAMA, III SS, 44/2, pp. 42-43.

[43] Ibid., 41/8, I, pp. 182-83. These courts-martial in the new SS field divisions and the reserve SSTV were created as the result of a decree of the Ministerial Council for the Defense of the Reich, dated October 17, 1939. This decree gave the SS field formations judicial independence from the army. Although still subject to the same laws as the army, the SS could try its own men for offenses that came under the military code, whereas before SS men had been tried by Wehrmacht tribunals. The demand by Himmler for judicial separation from the army came as the result of an atrocity committed during the Polish campaign, when two SS men shot fifty Jews and the army demanded a trial and stiff penalties (Stein, p. 30).

[44] BAMA, III SS, 41/8, I, p. 184.

in the future any officer who disobeyed specific orders would be relieved of command. He also prohibited any further three-day passes, citing as the reason poor troop performance and lack of spirit during training exercises.[45]

On the very day Eicke cancelled all leaves and issued his disciplinary warnings, the problems confronting him all boiled over in an embarrassing crisis. On the night of November 20-21, six enlisted men from the Fourteenth Company of the Second Infantry Regiment of SSTK stole an Opel-Blitz truck, left the Kaserne unnoticed, and proceeded into Munich for an evening's frivolity. While in the city, they made the rounds in a number of bars, becoming more inebriated as the evening wore on. Shortly before midnight, the six set out for Dachau. Leaving Munich, the driver lost control of the stolen truck and collided head-on with a streetcar in the Dachauerstrasse. The collision derailed the tram, badly damaged the Opel-Blitz, and knocked unconscious the SS driver. The commotion quickly drew a large crowd, and when the police arrived in considerable force they found the dazed and curious streetcar passengers peering into the back of the truck, where the other five SS men were snoring loudly and contentedly— oblivious to what had happened.[46]

Through considerable effort, Eicke managed to avoid any publicity, and the incident seems to have escaped Himmler's attention. The enraged Eicke, however, turned on the hapless six offenders with the full force of his passion for punishing those who disobeyed him. Determined to end his discipline problems by making an example of these SS men, he stripped them of all rank, expelled them from the SS, and had them committed to the Buchenwald concentration camp. This punishment was technically illegal, since Eicke had no authority, as an SS division commander, to incarcerate at will in concentration camps those in his command who violated the military criminal code. In sending the men to Buchenwald, however, Eicke acted in accordance with his own interpretation of his judicial authority as a division com-

[45] Ibid., pp. 194, 197.

[46] Ibid., pp. 55-56. The account of this incident is taken from a special order drafted by Eicke describing the events in detail. In this order, Eicke declared that anyone else who stole or even used a military vehicle for unauthorized purposes would face either the concentration camp or a firing squad.

mander. Even more important is the fact that he succeeded in placing the men in the camp for an indefinite period. His sentences went either unnoticed or unchallenged—even by the Gestapo. As a result, the incident established a practice Eicke used for the next several months—that of turning his troublemakers into concentration camp inmates.

The threat of incarceration in a concentration camp, made even more effective by their familiarity with the camps, hung like a poised blade over the heads of the men in the SSTK. The day after the tram-truck incident in Munich, a disgruntled SS private in the Fifth Company of the Third Infantry Regiment asked to transfer from the SSTK so he could resign from the SS, using as justification the perfectly legal argument that he had already fulfilled his compulsory military obligation in the army. Eicke's reaction was swift and severe. He expelled the young recruit from the SS, had him dressed in the uniform of a camp inmate, paraded before the entire assembled division, and then shipped off for indefinite incarceration in Buchenwald.[47] For the singleminded, fanatical Eicke, the concentration camp rapidly became a panacea for the division's disciplinary ills. His men, moreover, were trapped. If they demonstrated incompetence or displeased Eicke in the performance of their duties, they were, upon his whim, transferred back to the concentration camp inspectorate. If, on the other hand, they committed a crime as defined by the wartime military code, or if in dissatisfaction they requested a transfer from the SSTK or tried to resign from the SS, they faced the alternative of moving to the concentration camps as prisoners instead of guards.

The threat of the concentration camp, utilized by Eicke with great skill, had an immediate effect on the division. Any men in the SSTK still dissatisfied or unenthusiastic about serving under Eicke resigned themselves to their predicament. There were no further requests for transfers or attempts to resign from the SS, and the discipline problems subsided immediately in number and seriousness.[48] By the beginning of December, moreover, the

[47] Ibid.

[48] On November 23, 1939, Eicke published a special order outlining the crimes defined in the wartime criminal code and the punishments they carried. He warned that any member of the SSTK who violated the laws of war would, without regard to rank or person, be tried and punished by the court-martial. Eicke also warned

62

court-martial of the SSTK began sitting regularly, thus systematizing the administration of justice in the division and relieving Eicke of many headaches. On December 1, the tribunal of the SSTK announced the results of its first cases, handing down sentences totalling one and one-half years in prison to five young enlisted men convicted of petty theft. In confirming the sentences, Eicke directed that the convicted men serve their time in regular jails instead of a concentration camp, since he did not regard petty larceny as an offense that merited such incarceration.[49]

In the midst of these developments, Eicke received orders from the army to prepare for moving the SSTK to more suitable training quarters at Ludwigsburg, just north of Stuttgart. The Totenkopfdivision was to be placed in the second-line reserve formations that the Army High Command (OKH) was assembling for the imminent campaign in the west. Eicke and his staff thus spent the last ten days of November engaged in intensive preparations for the coming move. By November 26, enough vehicles had been found to move the administrative services and the first of the combat units, and on the twenty-eighth the equipment, vehicles, and artillery pieces too heavy for road transport were loaded on trains. Eicke and his staff left their quarters on December 2, and three days later the entire SSTK had moved into new quarters spread out among five different army Kasernes in the Ludwigsburg-Heilbronn area. The move, Eicke naively hoped, would bring final preparations for the campaign against France.[50]

---

that any man found guilty would be expelled automatically from the SS, a fact that would make him an outcast from the German community (Volksgemeinschaft) and thus prevent him from ever securing a good job or becoming an acceptable member of society (BAMA, III SS, 41/8, I, pp. 61-62). For a detailed examination of the extensive wartime relationships between the SS Totenkopfdivision and the concentration camp system, see below, chapter nine.

[49] BAMA, III SS, 41/8, I, pp. 60.
[50] Ibid., pp. 53-54, 70, 203-5, 211; III SS, 42/1, pp. 5-7; III SS, 44/2, p. 60.

CHAPTER THREE

Growing Pains: December 1939-May 1940

In the five months and ten days between its departure from Dachau and Hitler's attack against France and the Low Countries, the SS Totenkopfdivision underwent a major transformation. The untrained, ill-equipped, and partially disciplined SSTK of October developed during the winter into a fully motorized, well-equipped, and intensively trained elite formation. The major credit for this startling metamorphosis belonged to Eicke. With his gift for improvisation and talent for organization the former concentration camp czar utilized a number of factors to unusual advantage. The most important was time.

The long-range postponement of the attack in the west enabled the units of SSTK to undergo unusually thorough tactical and technical training. In addition, Eicke and his men benefitted from the increased interest that both Hitler and Himmler began showing in the new Waffen SS formations. Himmler's persistent lobbying at the chancellery resulted in greater—if still reluctant—cooperation from the army. This vital assistance soon included larger allotments of weapons and equipment and the admission of men from SSTK to army technical schools and specialized training courses. Finally, with sufficient time for the creation of an unusually harsh disciplinary code, Eicke managed to raise morale while weeding out numerous undesirables—including many hardened criminals.

By mid-December 1939, the entire Totenkopfdivision was settled into its new quarters in the Ludwigsburg-Heilbronn area. Eicke and the division staff located in Heilbronn, while the rest of the division's units were quartered in barracks in small villages to the east and north. The training exercises begun in Dachau and interrupted by the move had to be curtailed when severe winter weather set in. As a result, during December and January the major emphasis in training centered on physical conditioning and

64

on studies of the technical problems involved in moving and handling a motorized infantry division.

This enforced period of textbook concentration in mobile warfare also gave Eicke time to formulate his own rules for conducting military operations. Using existing army manuals as guidelines, Eicke and his staff devised regulations for deploying the units of the Totenkopfdivision for combat. These basic army rules were altered slightly so as to concentrate an even larger mass of infantry, heavy weapons, and fast reconnaissance vehicles in the forward attack waves of the division. This reflected Eicke's view—shared by many other SS commanders—that the army's gospel of offensive speed and surprise could be improved by concentrating all available mass and firepower in the forward units, and by reckless, zealous pursuit of the attack until the enemy surrendered or was annihilated. In the more complex and sophisticated theories of motorized operations, Eicke had neither learning nor the slightest interest. In his blunt and impatient mind the rules were fixed plainly enough: concentrate every available soldier, weapon, and vehicle in the front line, then smash away at the enemy with relentless fury until he crumbled. This uncomplicated formula represented the extent of Eicke's tactical knowledge of mobile warfare, and served as the basis upon which he directed the Totenkopfdivision in battle until his death in Russia.[1]

In mid-January 1940, SSTK first received invitations to send its men to a number of technical training courses in army schools throughout Germany. These included openings for ten noncommissioned officers (NCOs) in a three-month course in mortar gunnery, an unspecified number of NCOs for a three-month course in firefighting, and notification that the army would accept SS trainees in its weaponry school at Berlin-Treptow. In addition, officers from Eicke's artillery regiment were invited during the first week of February to attend a two-day series of lectures in Koblenz on directing artillery fire with spotter aircraft. Finally, the Wehrmacht also began training men from the division at the

[1] BAMA, III SS, 47/1, Nachrichtenabteilung, KTB No. 1, pp. 8-14, summary of weather reports for December and January; and ibid., 41/8, i, pp. 84-86, memorandum outlining the functions and order of march of all the vehicles in the Totenkopfdivision.

Ulm munitions depot in handling and storing ammunition, and allowed Eicke to send several of his officers to the army's gas warfare school at Celle.[2]

Despite the complications imposed by the weather and a lack of fuel, Eicke managed to conduct several large-scale exercises during January and February. The experience gained came at some cost, however, as the road conditions and poor training of the drivers caused a number of vehicular accidents—several of which resulted in serious injuries and considerable property damage.[3] Indeed, the progress of training generally during the winter seems to have been minimal at best. The records of the Totenkopfdivision are filled with entries for these months that reflect gloom and despair.

At the end of January, Eicke turned to Karl Wolff, his friend and the chief of Himmler's personal staff, and poured out all his frustrations. In a long litany of woe encompassing everything from bad weather to shady politics, Eicke railed against his situation. What most angered him, he confided to Wolff, was the condescending attitude and the impossible training demands of the Army High Command (OKH). He implored Wolff to explain to Himmler that if the SSTK vehicles were taken out again in the severe winter weather it would require at least three weeks to repair them—an impossibility itself since there were not enough spare parts. Considering the circumstances, Eicke fumed, he was simply not in any position to obey the unendurable orders and training schedules sent him by the army. Eicke concluded this long lamentation with the fatuous request that Himmler authorize the transfer of SSTK to Pirmasens in the Palatinate so the division could engage in valuable training by skirmishing with French border patrols and by shelling positions in the Maginot Line.[4]

---

[2] BAMA, III SS, 41/8, 1, pp. 88-89, 292; 44/2, Nachschubdienst, pp. 145, 157, 169-70, 173. In announcing these openings for trainees, Eicke warned that the men selected from SSTK to attend were obligated to make the best possible impression, that failure on their part would not be tolerated, and that any SS man who caused trouble while attending one of the courses could expect severe punishment upon his return to SSTK.

[3] BAMA, III SS, 44/2, pp. 136-38.

[4] BAKO, NS-19/neu-1668, letter from Eicke to Karl Wolff, dated January 23, 1940.

The general tone of despair in Eicke's letter was amplified even more a month later in a gloomy memorandum written by Montigny, Eicke's operations officer, as an evaluation of the progress made in training. The report implied that the division was far from ready for combat. Recent exercises, Montigny concluded, had revealed a number of weaknesses in the individual units. Regimental commanders had erred in massing too many vehicles along stretches of open road, thus presenting an inviting target for enemy aircraft; and the men had made far too much noise with their vehicles in the assembly areas. There were, he continued, too many vehicle breakdowns and far too few skilled mechanics to handle the repairs. Those vehicles that did remain in running order often were involved in huge traffic jams caused by confused commanders who used the wrong roads and entangled themselves with other units.

In addition, Montigny wrote, the division markedly lacked coordination of firepower, and was slowed considerably by the excessive time certain units took to change positions. Most serious of all was the report's conclusion that widespread poor leadership among the officers and a general lack of discipline among the men were the two main problems in the training program. Eicke was greatly disturbed by Montigny's report, and two days after receiving the memorandum announced plans for renewed intensive training even before the onset of good weather. Special emphasis was to be placed upon weapons training and upon developing leadership qualities among the officer corps.[5]

The problems involving combat training during the winter months left little time for concentrated political indoctrination. Evidently, the first chance Eicke had to schedule any such activity was in mid-January 1940. At that time, each unit in the Totenkopfdivision heard a series of lectures on the dangers of and defenses against enemy propaganda. A number of sessions were also held for instructing the men in how to write letters to their relatives without divulging vital information about the division or its location. Eicke also continued to exert all possible pressure on

[5] BAMA, III SS, 41/8, i, pp. 112-13, Montigny's memorandum of February 22, 1940; and ibid., pp. 319, 325, 331, 336, for the complete schedule of training exercises for the SSTK during the remainder of February and March 1940.

the men to renounce their church affiliation. Indeed, his stated goal was to have the SSTK free of any religious association except that of worshiping the führer and National Socialist Germany.[6]

The winter months of 1939-1940 were also a period of frustration and delay in Eicke's attempt to equip fully all the units of his division. In this respect, as in the case of the training program, time worked ultimately to his advantage. Most of the winter clothing urgently needed by SSTK, Eicke obtained from SS agencies. The clothing depot in the Dachau concentration camp supplied coats, shirts, camouflage jackets, and long underwear in regular installments during January and February, while the Hauptamt Haushalt und Bauten (Main Office for Budget and Buildings), an SS-run agency that regulated all labor and production in the concentration camps, began supplying SSTK with boots and trousers made by the prisoners in the camps. Despite these regular deliveries, the men in SSTK suffered some during the winter months as a result of Eicke's inability to procure enough socks. Many SS men were forced to make artificial foot wrappings or had to stuff newspaper into their boots to protect against the cold. The situation became so serious that Eicke finally issued elaborate instructions on methods of avoiding frostbite.[7]

For supplies of weapons, vehicles, fuel, and ammunition, Eicke remained dependent upon the army. Beginning in January, the Wehrmacht procurement office became extremely generous in providing communications equipment, light vehicles, tools, and items other than arms. The signals battalion, for example, re-

[6] Ibid., III SS, 44/2, p. 147; 41/8, 1, p. 346; 42/1, KTB No. 1, pp. 16-18. One interesting piece of political propaganda from this period is a completely unimaginative memorandum written by Eicke. The paper attempts first, by giving a grossly distorted version of the history of Alsace-Lorraine, to justify an attack in the west. Eicke then follows more orthodox propaganda by depicting Britain and France as decaying states run by corrupt Jews, and therefore incapable of winning the war (ibid., III SS, 41/8, 1, pp. 94-100).

[7] BAMA, III SS, 42/1, KTB No. 1, pp. 69-72; 44/2, pp. 125-33; and 41/8, 1, pp. 252-53, 286. The records of the Totenkopfdivision indicated that supplies of clothing and other articles produced by slave labor were received frequently throughout the war. After the invasion of Russia, SSTK also enjoyed the patronage of several of the higher SS and police leaders in the occupied east. They often supplied the division with looted materials and tribute taken from civilians and deposited in special SS warehouses.

ceived during January eight radio and telephone trucks, six armor-plated radio sets, ten cipher machines, six truckloads of telephone cable, portable radio sets and field telephones, and large quantities of spare tubes, batteries, wire, and tools. In addition, Eicke obtained from the army thirty ammunition trailers, sixty three-ton Opel-Blitz trucks, several thousand hand grenades, five truckloads of rifle ammunition, ten trench mortars, and limited quantities of shells for the tank-destroyer battalion's guns.[8]

Food procurement for the division ceased to be a problem after the move to Ludwigsburg, as the army undertook to supply SSTK regularly. Eicke's men appear, as a result, to have eaten as well as soldiers of the regular armed forces, suffering only from temporary shortages of meat during the winter. For the SS soldier, the typical daily menu of hearty German fare began with a breakfast of coffee (or a coffee substitute), 80 grams of jelly or marmalade on bread, and 100 grams of sausage. The big midday meal nearly always included 200 grams of meat (usually beef, veal, sausage, or liver), 400-500 grams of potatoes served with sauerkraut, beans or rice in varying quantities, and a wartime treat of 15 grams of fat. All of this the SS men washed down with tea, beer, or—on special occasions—wine. At the end of the day, a soldier in the Totenkopfdivision could expect a solid meal of coffee, a thick soup or goulash stew, and quite often a bonus ration consisting of a cup of fresh milk and 400 grams of potato salad.[9]

The fact that the men were so well fed during the winter of 1939-1940 was due mainly to Eicke, who when requesting food—or anything else from the army—always asked for much more than was needed so he could be sure of getting enough. Keeping his men well fed was one of Eicke's major concerns,

[8] Ibid., III SS, 41/8, I, pp. 262, 265, 279, 297, 303; 42/1, KTB No. 1, pp. 7-9; and 44/2, pp. 125-26, 153, 213. The army also graciously allowed SSTK to obtain its share of musical instruments from manufacturers with army contracts—including some seventy accordions and 729 harmonicas from the firm of Gustav Spranger in Klingenthal (ibid., 41/8, I, pp. 308-9).

[9] BAMA, III SS, 42/1, Verwaltungsdienst, KTB No. 1, pp. 39-41, menu for the Totenkopfdivision for the week of January 11-20, 1940. These meal schedules were followed regularly during periods in which SSTK remained settled in one location. While out on exercises during the winter months, the men had to carry along several-days' supplies of rations owing to the difficulties involved in lugging around the ponderous field kitchens.

since he reasoned that a full stomach would insure a high level of morale and help maintain the physical fitness of the troops. The measure of success Eicke achieved in the mess hall may be gauged from conclusions he himself drew after members of his staff examined the kitchen slop buckets. After an inspection of the division's mess facilities at the end of February, Eicke learned that a sample of garbage thrown out one evening had contained thirty-five untouched loaves of bread, numerous half-loaves, and a score of unopened bags of fresh potato salad. Reacting in an angry order of the day, he announced that such waste in wartime amounted to sabotage, that those responsible did not deserve to belong to the SS, and that in future strict measures would be enforced to prevent such criminal waste of precious food.[10]

No such embarrassing surpluses resulted from his efforts to obtain weapons. Throughout the winter, repeated requests to the Wehrmacht for heavy weapons (mortars, antitank guns, howitzers, and artillery pieces) were either rejected or ignored. These rebuffs led Eicke to turn in desperation to Himmler, and to expect the Reichsführer SS to cut through army red tape and hostility and provide the Totenkopfdivision with whatever it needed. Consequently, Eicke's relations with Himmler and with other offices and agencies of the SS became noticeably strained. This was owing as much to Eicke's tone and attitude as it was to the frequency with which he pestered Himmler. To the SSTK commander, the division was his own private empire, subject exclusively to his control. In running the division, Eicke tolerated no interference from any of his subordinates and did not hesitate to resist Himmler's attempts to intervene in matters concerning SSTK. In fact, after the beginning of the western campaign Eicke on occasion even disobeyed specific orders from the Reichsführer SS that he thought encroached upon his own authority as a division commander. On the other hand, he never hesitated to call

[10] Ibid., III SS, 41/8, 1, p. 330. Eicke's desire to provide his men with morale-boosting rations of wine also led to trouble. In early March, several trucks among a convoy returning from a trip to Ulm for wine were involved in a grinding chain-reaction series of collisions caused by icy road conditions (and perhaps some sampling of the cargo by SSTK drivers). The accident demolished two of the trucks and hospitalized five men with serious injuries (ibid., 42/1, KTB No. 1, pp. 12-13).

upon Himmler when he wanted something, and regularly became furious when any SS agency refused to yield immediately to his whimsical demands. Throughout the spring and summer of 1940, Eicke's demands upon Himmler became more incessant and unreasonable, while his acts of disobedience grew in number and flagrancy. By the autumn of 1940 Eicke was causing so much difficulty that several of his most powerful antagonists (with Himmler's approval) formed an alliance to bring him down to size.

One excellent example of the trouble Eicke caused Himmler during the winter of 1939-1940 was the dispute over creating a heavy-artillery battalion for the Totenkopfdivision. Late in January Eicke wrote again to Karl Wolff, relating excitedly his discovery that at the Skoda works in Pilsen there were many newly-made 150 mm heavy-artillery pieces and sufficient eight-ton halftracks to pull them. Having learned this, he continued, he would not rest until he got enough of the guns to form his own heavy-artillery battalion. Since he would need only three weeks to organize the battalion, the most important thing was to get the field pieces as quickly as possible. To this end, Eicke continued, there were two possibilities. The first involved the simple dispatch of a raiding party from SSTK to steal the guns from the Skoda works in the middle of the night. To Wolff's undoubted relief, Eicke readily admitted that this was impractical, since his own reputation for requisitioning would make it too easy for the army to guess who had stolen the guns and to recover them quickly.[11]

Turning to the second and more practical alternative, Eicke urged Wolff to put the question of a heavy-artillery battalion for SSTK directly to Himmler. This, Eicke claimed, was the only method that would produce results, since the chief of the SS Procurement Office, SS Oberführer Heinrich Gärtner, was unenthusiastic, and the commander-in-chief of the replacement army, General Friedrich Fromm, was determined under all circumstances to prevent the armed SS from creating its own heavy-

[11] BAKO, NS-19/neu-1668, letter from Eicke to Karl Wolff of January 27, 1940. The guns in question at Pilsen were intended originally for export, but had been frozen by the occupation of Czechoslovakia and the outbreak of the war. They subsequently became Wehrmacht property along with the Skoda works (Stein, p. 53).

artillery units. Eicke's nagging request was doubtless an unwelcome irritation to Himmler, who at that very moment was negotiating gingerly with the army for enough of the 150 mm guns at Skoda to make one heavy-artillery battalion for the Waffen SS.[12] The squabbling dragged on until late March, Eicke making two trips to Berlin to plead his case personally with Himmler. On March 26, Hitler sided with Himmler and the SS and authorized the formation of a heavy-artillery battalion for the armed SS. For Eicke, however, the victory proved hollow, as none of the twelve Skoda heavy pieces released by the Wehrmacht were earmarked for immediate delivery to the SSTK.

This decision sent the volatile SSTK commander into a towering rage. Still unwilling to concede defeat, Eicke dispatched a long and bitter letter to Himmler on March 29. In it, he claimed that his own "private intelligence sources" had confirmed that the army had 206 of the desired heavy-artillery pieces hidden away in depots at Magdeburg, Kunersdorf, and Pilsen. Furthermore, he snorted, since the führer himself had ordered SSTK to be committed among the first waves in the coming campaign, it was more entitled to the guns than were the reserve army units. Eicke concluded by stating flatly that had the Skoda decision not come directly and personally from the führer, he and his men would have carried out the proposed raid on the Pilsen works. A week later, the much-harrassed Wolff telephoned Eicke at Himmler's behest and attempted to smooth matters. Since the decision was final, he could offer only the advice of calm and patience and relay a warning from Himmler not to initiate a private quarrel with the Wehrmacht over the matter.[13]

[12] BAKO, NS-19/neu-1668, Eicke to Karl Wolff, January 27, 1940. In the same letter Eicke undiplomatically reminded Wolff that Himmler had promised a consignment of captured high-powered Polish rifles fitted with sniper scopes. These, Eicke intoned, were urgently needed by the SSTK, so "would the Reichsführer SS please see to the matter immediately." For an extensive discussion of Himmler's fight for heavy weapons during the winter of 1939-1940 and the controversy over the artillery pieces at the Skoda works, see Stein, pp. 50-55.

[13] BAKO, NS-19/neu-1668, Eicke to Himmler, March 29, 1940; and the transcript of a telephone call from Wolff to Eicke on April 4, 1940. For Eicke's comments to his own men, see BAMA, III SS, 41/8, 1, pp. 371-72. The agreement to give the Waffen SS a heavy artillery battalion was actually a compromise. The army gave in and relinquished twelve of the heavy guns with the understanding that Himmler would not get any more heavy pieces until the seventh and eighth waves of the army had been fully outfitted with artillery.

When the dispute over the heavy artillery was building to a climax, a long-smoldering jurisdictional quarrel begun by Eicke erupted into a row between the SS and the Nazi party. The point of dispute concerned the reserve Totenkopfstandarten and thus the reserve units of SSTK. The difficulty grew out of a practice Eicke had initiated during the call-up of reservists to the SSTV at the beginning of the war: drafting full-time employees and political leaders of the Nazi party into the Death's Head units. After Eicke became commander of the Totenkopfdivision, this practice was continued by Gottlob Berger, chief of the Waffen SS Recruiting Office (Ergänzungsamt der Waffen SS).

By the spring of 1940, career party officials who had been exempted from Wehrmacht service because of the nature of their work were still being conscripted into the reserve Totenkopfstandarten. As a result, many ended up in Death's Head units designated as replacement/training formations of the SSTK and were therefore liable for immediate transfer to active, front-line duty in the Totenkopfdivision. Eicke categorically refused to release any of the men in his replacement units who were party officials, ignoring with malicious glee the mounting protests of Kreis- and Gauleiters trying to rescue friends and cronies from military service. In February 1940, a group of local party officials finally appealed to the highest level and Rudolf Hess intervened. The whole question was settled by an agreement which permitted the Waffen SS to continue drafting party personnel but gave Gauleiters the power to veto the call-up of individual party officials.[14]

Within the division during these winter months, Eicke's discipline problems became as serious a source of trouble to him as his

[14] BAKO, NS-7/426, circular from the SS Hauptamt dated February 16, 1940 and headed "Einberufung von hauptberuflichen Politischen Leitern zu den bewaffneten Einheiten der SS." The records of the Totenkopfdivision and the materials in the Himmler files do not indicate whether any important party officials actually were called into the SSTK. At the time of the dispute, the replacement units of the Totenkopfdivision included three Death's Head battalions (garrisoned at Radolfzell, Lichtenburg, and Breslau), plus antitank, motorcycle, communications, engineer, artillery and medical companies scattered throughout the Reich and the occupied territories. The paper strength of these units was 4,945 men. Eicke, however, considered all the Totenkopf units, including the concentration camp inspectorate and its guard contingents, as quasi-replacements for the Totenkopfdivision. In the spring of 1940, all these reserve Death's Head formations had a combined total strength of nearly 25,000 men.

73

own nagging was to Himmler and Wolff. The task of keeping the SSTK men in line was complicated by several factors. The first of these was Eicke's unusually stiff and at times unreasonable disciplinary rules. Any breach of regulations, however slight, was usually punished in the harshest fashion. In addition, the records of the division courts-martial and the numerous complaints Eicke directed to Berger's recruiting office make clear that the ranks of the Totenkopfdivision were infested with many social misfits, convicted felons, and other potential criminal types.[15]

At the same time, the competition for manpower between the army and the SS was creating a shortage of replacements. This new development forced Eicke to keep many men he otherwise would have rejected, and even compelled him to alter his disciplinary procedures. The initial policy of transferring problem cases to the concentration camps was abandoned and replaced with a more practical form of punishment. Eicke created a penal section or Sonderkommando for the engineer battalion. The ranks of this unit, which was given unusually dirty or dangerous tasks to perform, were filled gradually with men sentenced to prison terms. After expelling them from the SS, Eicke simply commuted their sentences and assigned the men indefinitely to the Sonderkommando.[16]

In addition, Eicke began using among his own men the "sharp arrest" punishment he had developed for the prisoners in the prewar concentration camp system. He intended to discourage first-time offenders and prevent them from turning into persistent troublemakers. Eicke defined "sharp arrest" the same way he had in the camps, namely solitary confinement for up to thirty days with two pieces of bread and a liter of water as daily sustenance, with one warm meal every fourth day. As a result, many men received stiff first sentences ranging from several-days' to three-weeks' confinement for such things as smoking in the motor pool, returning a few hours late from leave, or getting drunk while off

[15] According to the division records, during January and February 1940 eleven men were given sentences totalling ten years and eight months in prison. Another nineteen men received collectively 153 days of "sharp arrest," or temporary solitary confinement. See BAMA, III SS, 41/8, I, pp. 275-335.

[16] Ibid., 44/2, p. 144; 41/8, I, pp. 278, 281, 291-94, 303.

duty. One SS soldier was sentenced to two weeks of solitary confinement for committing adultery with the wife of another SS man. The strict rules also left the men at the mercy of their unit commanders, who often recommended punishment or preferred charges for the slightest infractions.[17]

The harsh discipline and brutal punishments during the winter produced one of the few recorded instances of discontent within the ranks. In the middle of January, Eicke expelled an SS private serving with the artillery regiment for writing a letter to his former employer filled with complaints about life in the Totenkopfdivision. The young man claimed that conditions generally were terrible, that there were chronic shortages of winter clothing and heated quarters, and that a great many men in the division were disillusioned and dissatisfied. The letter, discovered by Eicke's censoring office, evidently was accurate in its description of life and conditions in SSTK. An obviously worried Eicke disclosed all the details of the letter in an order of the day, expressing his disgust and contempt for its writer. He concluded with the ominous warning that anyone found writing such letters in the future would be considered guilty of treason and dealt with accordingly.[18]

Many civilians and regular soldiers would have rendered a much harsher judgment than that of the disgruntled SS private. During this same winter a number of Eicke's officers and men became involved in damaging scrapes with civilians and Wehrmacht personnel. There is ample evidence that these incidents were frequent, often deliberately provoked by SSTK soldiers, and occasionally bloody. In fact, Eicke's own records leave the impression that during January 1940 drunken brawling and malicious destruc-

[17] BAMA, III SS, 44/2, pp. 149-50, 215-16; 41/8, 1, pp. 253, 261-62. Eicke announced that during wartime he would make no distinction between leave and active duty, so that any man who overstayed the time limit of his pass would be punished as though he had disobeyed orders in the face of the enemy. He set a penalty of one day of sharp arrest for every hour any SS man stayed away after his pass expired. This penalty extended to the twenty-third hour of lateness. After the twenty-fourth hour of absence without leave, Eicke considered the SS man automatically subject to court-martial and liable to punishment as defined in the military criminal code (ibid., 41/8, 1, pp. 247-48).

[18] Ibid., pp. 261-62.

tion of civilian property were the only forms of recreation his men enjoyed. The tendency to mischief was enhanced by the fact that the location of SSTK allowed the men easy access to Stuttgart, an important military rail and communications center which had become a bustling garrison city jammed with thousands of soldiers.

Among regular-army personnel and the local authorities, Eicke's men soon became well known. The district commander of the Wehrmacht field police in Stuttgart lodged an official complaint against SSTK at the end of December 1939, charging that for some weeks large gangs of Eicke's soldiers had been roaming the streets of Stuttgart at night, picking fights with regular soldiers, beating them up, and then stealing their sidearms. The only incident referred to specifically in the police report was about a corporal in the SSTK artillery regiment who allegedly got drunk in a bar and started a disturbance there that quickly developed into a melee involving a score of army and SS men. The SS corporal was arrested by army field policemen and put in a stockade. Eicke denied formally the allegations in the police report, but hastily expelled from the division and the SS the corporal charged with starting the brawl, and left him in army custody for punishment.[19]

Mere brawling, however, was beneath the dignity of Eicke's officers, who preferred the more gentlemanly diversion of shooting up the saloons and Gasthäuser of the city. The crowded bar at the Neckar Hotel was the scene of the wildest such episode. After an evening of strenuous imbibing, an Obersturmführer in the signals battalion became "blind drunk" (sinnlos besoffnen), drew his pistol, and began firing at the light fixtures and into the ceiling. This caused a general panic, and in the ensuing rush for the exits—a scene of great confusion—the clientele wrecked the premises. The SS paid for the damage and Eicke promptly placed the Neckar off-limits to the division. The officer who indulged in the shooting spree was quickly relieved of his command and sent to the inspectorate of concentration camps for reassignment.[20]

No sooner had Eicke curbed the social exuberance of his offi-

[19] BAMA, III SS, 44/2, p. 123.

[20] Ibid., III SS, 41/8, I, p. 272. Eicke also cashiered an Obersturmführer in the supply administration and packed him off to the camp inspectorate for speeding around Stuttgart in his service vehicle with several women (ibid., III SS, 41/8, I, p. 104).

cers and men than he was faced with another major problem that threatened to get him into serious trouble with Himmler. A number of angry merchants and tavern owners in the Dachau area had written letters to both Eicke and Himmler demanding payment of bills and accounts that men in SSTK had not settled before the division moved in early December. Eicke ordered each unit commander to see that the men paid their bills immediately and to impress upon them that such actions caused "irreparable harm to the image of the Totenkopfdivision." Even more serious were the complaints received in Berlin and at Eicke's office in Heilbronn about SSTK soldiers stealing army equipment and supplies while participating in Wehrmacht training courses. After a careful investigation, Eicke had three men from the SSTK field hospital court-martialed for stealing sheets, towels, and clothing while attending the army medical instruction school at Neustadt, and made profuse apologies to the school's commander. He then announced to the division that any more stealing from the army would be dealt with most ruthlessly, since such activity besmirched the image of SSTK in the eyes of its comrades in arms.[21]

In the last dreary, bitter-cold days of February 1940, Eicke reached the nadir of his problem-filled winter. OKH finally agreed to a specific assignment for the Totenkopfdivision for the coming western campaign. Instead of a place among the armored and motorized formations picked to spearhead the German offensive, Eicke learned with disappointment and bitterness that SSTK would be confined to a reserve role during the coming campaign. The Totenkopfdivision was assigned at the end of February to the Second Army, an untrained reserve force composed of three new infantry divisions and SSTK. The only role envisaged for the Second Army during the coming campaign was that of a standing reserve deployed in the area around Kassel in Westphalia. Protests by both Eicke and Himmler were to no avail. The chief of the army general staff, Colonel General Franz Halder, stood by the decision and refused to reconsider Eicke's assignment. As a result, SSTK received its marching orders at the end of February, and during the first week in March moved north from Heilbronn to

[21] BAMA, III SS, 41/8, 1, pp. 92, 104, 294, 310.

new quarters in the vicinity of Korbach, a little village fifteen miles west of Kassel.[22]

This disappointing assignment, however, soon brought about a change in the division's fortunes. SSTK was for the first time placed under the operational orders of OKH, and Eicke became the direct subordinate of a senior army commander, Colonel General Freiherr Maximilien von Weichs—the commander-designate of the Second Army. In the comparative quiet of the area around Kassel, Eicke would have additional time to whip his men into fighting shape. As a direct subordinate of Weichs, moreover, he could expect experienced guidance from the army in training his men, and perhaps a bit more cooperation in his efforts to obtain weapons and equipment.

By March 3, the Totenkopfdivision was once again settled in new quarters. With the coming of warmer weather, Eicke began intensive combat training exercises and renewed his efforts to acquire the needed quantities of weapons and equipment before the onset of the campaigning season. Himmler came on March 6 to inspect SSTK and its new quarters. While in Korbach, he ordered Eicke to tighten all security regulations and to crack down even more severely on problem cases in the division. The Reichsführer clearly wanted the Totenkopfdivision to make a better impression within the army than it had in the past. Following Himmler's visit, Eicke banned all visits to bars and restaurants. He ordered his men instead to drink together in their own canteens on free evenings, and instructed his unit commanders to bear down in enforcing the disciplinary regulations during the weeks ahead.[23]

---

[22] Stein, p. 57-58; Halder, *KTB*, I, p. 179; BAMA, III SS, 44/2, pp. 192-93; and BAMA, III SS, 42/1, KTB No. 1, pp. 13-16.

[23] BAMA, III SS, 41/8, I, p. 357; 44/2, p. 201. Himmler evidently scheduled his visit for March 6 after learning from Eicke that Colonel General Weichs planned to inspect the Totenkopfdivision on March 7. The anxious Reichsführer SS hurried to Korbach in order to satisfy himself that Weichs would receive a favorable impression when he arrived. Weichs, however, changed his plans at the last minute and did not visit SSTK until nearly a month later.

Eicke later expanded the ban on drinking in bars to include dancing in public places. Dancing was a form of recreation Eicke loathed especially, and an activity he described to his men as a "degrading Jewish diversion" (ibid., III SS, 44/2, pp. 229, 245).

The stepped-up tempo of the training and the harsh disciplinary procedures introduced during the winter began to produce results. Between March 1 and the opening of the western campaign, only twelve men were brought before the division court-martial. Facing charges that ranged from petty theft to direct disobedience of orders, these twelve received prison sentences totalling thirteen years and five months. The decline in the number of men court-martialed was accompanied by a marked increase in the severity of the sentences inflicted. Six of the twelve men convicted—those receiving the lightest sentences—were transferred to the Sonder-kommando of the engineer battalion, while the remaining six were turned over to the criminal police for incarceration.[24]

One of the cases heard by the SSTK tribunal involved a young SS sergeant (SS Unterscharführer) charged with revealing state secrets in letters written to several women. The sergeant had described the exact route of march taken by SSTK from Heilbronn to Kassel, and had made uncomplimentary observations about life in the division and the officers in his unit. He had then compounded matters by attempting to send the letters through the public mail rather than the division post office. Tried at Eicke's insistence for breach of security and insubordination, the sergeant was sentenced to a year in a concentration camp and expelled from the SS.[25]

Eicke seemed more irritated by the thought that his men were making negative comments about the division and its officers than he was worried about any dangerous breaches of security. He warned his men that he considered it unsoldierly to write home about individual problems and anxieties, thus creating a "false impression on the home front of the spirit and state of the troops." In another of his threatening proclamations, he warned that in the

[24] Ibid., III SS, 41/8, I, pp. 332, 342, 382, 385-86.

[25] Ibid., pp. 123-24. This particular case caused an important change that subsequently affected every man in the Totenkopfdivision. As of April 1, 1940, Eicke ordered the complete double censorship of all outgoing mail. No man in the SSTK could send a letter without first having it scrutinized by his company commander, who had to approve and stamp it before the SSTK field post office would accept it for mailing. In addition, SSTK intelligence officers continued the usual censoring procedures—with the dual purpose of monitoring the diligence of the unit commanders and double-checking for security leaks.

future any man caught making critical comments about SSTK would be liable for immediate court-martial.[26]

The demoralizing effect that this removal of privacy had on the men in SSTK was alleviated in some measure by the arrival of warm, spring weather and by the increase in daily activities. The last two months before the attack in the west were marked by frantic efforts to acquire needed matériel and to complete the planned training programs.

The Wehrmacht even grew generous in March and April, and, as regular-army units acquired all they needed, released leftover stocks of war matériel to the SSTK and other formations of the Waffen SS. By mid-March, all the Czech-manufactured equipment, including the ancient field kitchens, had been collected by Tschimpke and turned over to the army in exchange for German-made weapons and vehicles. In addition, Eicke received from the Wehrmacht forty heavy diesel- and gasoline-carrying tank trucks to keep the division fueled while on the move, and found another twelve Opel-Blitz trucks to use as troop transports. The Wehrmacht also agreed to give SSTK additional consignments of machine pistols, mortars, grenades, and rifle and machine-gun ammunition. By the beginning of April, moreover, the shortages in boots, socks, and other articles of clothing had been alleviated, and Eicke had procured 3,000 camouflage jackets from the SS clothing depot at Dachau.[27] By the end of the month, Eicke had obtained virtually all the weapons and equipment needed by a fully motorized infantry division. When viewed against the background of the army's formidable and stingy hostility, and the quarreling and hopeless confusion among the myriad

---

[26] Ibid., pp. 123-25. Eicke used the occasion of his discourse on letter writing to expound at length on the subject of "racial self-consciousness in the SS." Maintaining that those in SSTK who complained were "racially flawed" individuals, Eicke declared that without high standards of racial selectivity the armed SS would experience a disastrous erosion from within that would make it useless in the coming struggle (ibid., pp. 121-22).

[27] BAMA, III SS, 44/2, pp. 195-96, 203-4; 41/8, 1, pp. 346-47, 349, 352-53. Keeping the Totenkopfdivision supplied with camouflage jackets was an obsession with Eicke. His concern was due primarily to incidents that had involved the SS Totenkopfverbände during the Polish campaign. Evidently, snipers among straggling bands of Polish soldiers and partisan groups had easily recognized SS officers by their jaunty insignia, singled them out as prime targets, and killed several.

SS supply and administrative agencies, this was no small accomplishment.

Even more impressive, especially to the persistent skeptics and professional SS-baiters in the army, was the progress made during March and April in combat training. Eicke and his staff drove themselves and the entire division at a relentless pace in an attempt to master the combat fundamentals of mobile warfare. With Montigny's February memorandum as a beginning, every effort was made to overcome the numerous deficiencies the operations officer had spotted. Eicke tackled the problem of improving leadership quality in the SSTK by selecting larger numbers of older and more-seasoned NCOs to send to the SS Junkerschulen, and by making an effort to know his individual officers.[28]

As the warmer weather improved road conditions, units of the Totenkopfdivision began practicing daily the techniques of assembly, coordinated movement, and deployment for action. Drills were intensified in marksmanship, coordination of heavy and light infantry weapons fire, and in the tactics of assault in battalion strength—emphasizing the use of high explosives to reduce fortified positions. In addition, Eicke's staff developed a new schedule of training exercises in hand-to-hand combat, street fighting, night fighting, and the techniques of crossing rivers and moving through heavily wooded areas. During the remainder of March, these grueling exercises continued seven days a week from dawn to dusk. By the beginning of April, the progress that had been made surprised everybody—particularly the headquarters staff of the Second Army.[29]

[28] BAMA, III SS, 41/8, I, pp. 331, 346. Eicke also sought to indoctrinate his men more thoroughly in his own brand of antireligious harshness. Fuhrländer stepped up the pressure on the men to renounce their church membership, and the new SSTK Intelligence Officer (Ic), SS Hauptsturmführer Alfred Franke-Gricksch (sent to Eicke by the Sicherheitsdienst), began lecturing the troops regularly on political subjects. An earnest, efficient, and intelligent young SS officer, Franke-Gricksch considered himself a Heydrich protégé; thus, in his indoctrination programs for the soldiers in the SSTK, he disdained the crude fanaticism characteristic of Eicke's approach to political questions. See especially the long memorandum he wrote and sent to Himmler on the subject of ideological training in the Waffen SS, in BAKO, NS-34/15, Alfred Franke-Gricksch, Ic der SS T.-Div., "Denkschrift über die weltanschauliche Führung in der SS," dated February 10, 1941.

[29] BAKO, NS-19/neu-1668, "Ausbildungstand," dated April 9, 1940. This is a

On April 2, 1940, Colonel General Weichs and his staff made a day-long inspection of the Totenkopfdivision. The visit proved highly significant in view of what transpired, and marked an important turning point in Eicke's struggle to win for his division the respect of professional soldiers in the German army. Colonel General Weichs had not previously seen the Totenkopfdivision and knew very little about it. He did, however, know a great deal about Eicke's sordid career as the architect of the concentration camp system. As an aristocrat, a devout Catholic, and a senior member of the German officer corps, he had a very low opinion of the SS. Upon his arrival in Korbach, it was clear that he expected to be confronted by an undisciplined mob of street brawlers. His behavior toward Eicke bordered on open hostility as the latter made his welcoming remarks and began to explain the organization and composition of SSTK. Weichs, however, was surprised that the Totenkopfdivision was fully motorized and possessed an abundance of the latest types of military vehicles. As Eicke led the general and his staff from one exercise to another and through a series of inspections of the men and their quarters, Weichs's attitude changed markedly. At one point midway through the morning, he even asked Eicke to convey his best wishes to the Reichsführer SS the next time they met.

The tour was interrupted at noon for luncheon at the nearby estate of Josiah Erbprinz zu Waldeck und Pyrmont, the higher SS and police leader (HSSPF) of Fulda-Werra and one of Himmler's most respectable cronies. The choice of this luncheon site was a shrewd move by Eicke, as Weichs loosened up even more in the company of the garrulous Erbprinz zu Waldeck—one of the premier showpiece aristocrats in the SS. Following lunch, Eicke's guests attended several lectures in tactics and then witnessed a full-scale assault with live ammunition by SSTK Infantry Regiment No. 1 (SSTK/I. R. 1) against a dummy system of pillboxes and fortified trenches. Beginning with artillery fire directed by spotter aircraft and then attacking behind a thick smokescreen, the assault troops used mortar barrages, grenades, concentrated machine gun fire, and precisely placed satchel charges of high explo-

lengthy memorandum prepared by Montigny for the Ia of the Second Army. It outlines the training program and assesses the condition of the Totenkopfdivision at the beginning of April 1940.

sives to reduce the entire set of concrete and barbed wire fortifications to a smoking shambles. Weichs and his staff were impressed.

Eicke then whisked his dazzled guests to another exercise ground, where the SSTK engineer battalion performed by systematically and expertly destroying an entire minefield that had been planted by another unit the night before as part of the exercise. Weichs showed enthusiasm and friendliness after watching the engineers in action, and complimented personally the officers who had directed the exercise. At this point, with perfect timing, Eicke announced to the general and his entourage that the Totenkopfdivision was in the process of organizing a heavy-artillery section. Would the general, Eicke wondered, be able to help in "clearing up a few difficulties that had arisen about getting the necessary number of heavy guns?" Weichs quickly promised to help Eicke in every way he could, declaring that he would send people from his staff to Korbach within the week to see what was needed. Upon leaving that evening, Weichs told Eicke he had been highly gratified with everything he had seen, that he was proud to have the Totenkopfdivision in his command, and that he wished to return again "very soon" for another visit.[30]

The conversion of Weichs was authentic, as he subsequently made good his promises to Eicke. The chief of engineers in the Second Army arrived several days after the visit to discuss the equipment and vehicle shortages, and Weichs' staff began checking almost daily with Eicke on a number of matters concerning the training and equipping of the Totenkopfdivision.

Colonel General Weichs and his staff returned on April 26 to witness what amounted to Eicke's dress rehearsal for the coming western campaign. According to Eicke's jubilant report to Himmler, what the colonel general observed brought him near ecstasy. Weichs spent most of the day watching assault exercises carried out by the infantry and artillery regiments. For the morning exercise, an assault was mounted in battalion strength against camouflaged fortifications. To impress Weichs, Eicke deliberately

---

[30] Ibid., a lengthy report of April 4, 1940 from Eicke to Himmler, describing in detail Weichs' visit. See also the special laudatory order drafted by Eicke and read to the assembled troops on the morning of April 3, in BAMA, III SS, 41/8, I, pp. 131-32; and the account of Weichs' visit in Stein, pp. 57-59.

chose for the exercise a dense wooded area crossed by deep ravines and numerous thickets. When the assault began, Weichs became engrossed in what was happening but was unable to follow the advance because the assault groups were so successfully camouflaged. Finally, he insisted on moving into the middle of the advance to observe more closely.

After lunch, the general and his staff witnessed another assault by a different battalion. For this exercise, Eicke had had a special observation tower constructed behind the attack objective so Weichs could see the assault coming head-on. Once again neither the general nor any members of his staff could fault the conduct of the exercise. Following the mock assault the general told Eicke he was most pleased by the superb physical condition of the SS troops, who showed no signs of fatigue after a strenuous three-hour exercise. Weichs also remarked upon the reckless ferocity with which the SS men demolished their objective, and complimented Eicke especially on the "passion and spirit" of the men, which he found "astonishing." At the end of the day, Weichs accepted Eicke's invitation to tea and remained chatting amiably for nearly two hours before departing.[31]

The general's enthusiasm for the Totenkopfdivision produced visible results in Eicke's final efforts to obtain the arms and equipment he wanted. By the middle of April, all supply shortages had been overcome and just before the end of the month SSTK received the first battery of four 150 mm pieces for the heavy artillery section. In the meantime, Colonel General Weichs also helped arrange the enrollment of picked men from the SSTK artillery regiment in a special gunnery course at Arolson, and secured permission from the high command for Eicke to send five officers and two NCOs to a month-long class at the army artillery school at Jüterbog.[32]

[31] BAKO, NS-19/neu-1668, report by Eicke to Himmler dated April 29, 1940; BAMA, III SS, 41/1, KTB No. 2, pp. 10-12. During his second visit, Weichs told Eicke that he wanted to return on May 6 to see firing drills with the 150 mm guns of the heavy artillery section. These heavy pieces had arrived after Weichs' first visit, but were not ready for firing on April 26. The general's proposed third visit, however, was canceled as a result of the alert prior to the attack in the west on May 10.

[32] BAMA, III SS, 41/1, KTB No. 2, pp. 8-12; 44/2, p. 240.

The last hectic weeks before Hitler's attack in the west filled Eicke and his men with excitement and anticipation. On April 19 all extended leaves were cancelled and those men at home were ordered to return immediately. Tight security measures were put in force, and Eicke ordered his men, under pain of court-martial for treason, to say nothing to any civilian about activities within the division. During the last week of April, just before Weichs' second visit, Eicke took all the combat units of SSTK out during the night for a fifty-mile practice march.

On May 1, the unit combat exercises ended and the last shipments of uniforms, helmets, and camouflage jackets arrived from Dachau. Three days later, all units in SSTK were assembled individually for a thorough political briefing by Fuhrländer and Franke-Gricksch. On this occasion, Eicke and Fuhrländer also made a last effort to get the few remaining hold-outs in the division to renounce their church membership.[33]

On the evening of May 9, 1940, Second Army signaled Eicke to have the Totenkopfdivision on full alert by dawn the next morning and ready to move on short notice. Several hours later, as the German army moved into final positions along the Dutch and Belgian borders, Eicke received instructions to send a truck column to Kassel to pick up the sixty tons of field rations allotted SSTK for the first phase of the campaign. Eicke called his staff together and issued the necessary orders. Then, shortly after dawn on May 10, as German tanks crashed through the Dutch and Belgian border defenses, OKH put the Second Army on full alert. In accordance with his mobilization orders, Eicke authorized the distribution of field rations sufficient for a ten-day march, notified his unit commanders to be ready to assemble with the entire division within twelve hours, and expectantly awaited orders to move toward the front.[34]

At that time, Eicke and his staff had no idea where or in what manner the Totenkopfdivision might be employed, or indeed even

[33] Ibid., 44/2, pp. 234-35; 41/1, KTB No. 2, pp. 16-20, 76. In his address to the troops on May 4, Eicke announced that there were only four men left in SSTK—all Catholics—who had not formally renounced Christianity and their church affiliation.

[34] Ibid., 42/1, KTB No. 1, pp. 19-20, 76-77.

if it would be used in the vast campaign about to unfold. Eicke's orders stated nothing more specific than to prepare to move upon receipt of march instructions from the army group to which he would be assigned. As he sat nervously and waited, frequently telephoning Second Army headquarters in Bonn, Eicke must have reflected bitterly on the insignificant role he and his men had been given. The grueling training program of the spring, whose results had surprised and pleased even the professionally skeptical Weichs, appeared a wasted effort. The hours diligently spent in locating, acquiring, and stockpiling guns, ammunition, vehicles, and other war matériel, seemed to have gained Eicke nothing. As the first days of the campaign passed without any further word from Second Army or OKH, Eicke began fearing that SSTK would be used only as an occupation force, moving to the west into the combat zone after all the decisive battles had been fought.[35]

Much of Eicke's bitterness was justified. At a time when only seven of the 157 divisions in the German army were motorized, and both the SS Verfügungsdivision and the Leibstandarte Adolf Hitler were committed with the first waves, the decision to hold the Totenkopfdivision in reserve appears to have been based solely upon the army's dislike of the former concentration camp guards and its contempt for Eicke as a "police general."[36] The slight was one that Eicke deeply resented and never forgot.

Fortunately for Eicke's nerves and the division's morale, the breathtaking successes achieved by Hitler's armored formations during the first stage of the offensive prevented the Totenkopfdivision from being left behind during the decisive phase of the battle of France. The lightning advances in the opening days of the campaign and the constantly expanding area of operations dictated the quick call-up of additional mobile strength. Less than a week after the campaign began, the Totenkopfdivision was out of OKH reserve and on its way to combat.

[35] Ibid., pp. 12-24, 74-80.
[36] BAMA, III SS, 42/1, KTB No. 2, pp. 36-37; Jacobsen, *Fall Gelb*, p. 259; and the comments in Halder's *KTB*, I, p. 179, that the Totenkopfdivision presented a nice appearance but was not ready to be trusted with front-line duty. SSTK was certainly as fully mobile as any of the army's other motorized divisions. Eicke had over 3,500 vehicles in the division on the eve of the French campaign.

CHAPTER FOUR

The SS Totenkopfdivision and the
Battle of France

THE German plan of campaign in the west envisaged an assault on a scale then unknown in the history of warfare. The finest armored, motorized, and infantry divisions in the world, protected from above by a vast armada of nearly 2,000 Luftwaffe fighters and bombers, assembled along the German frontier to deliver a series of lightning blows designed to paralyze the enemy in blitzkrieg fashion.

The ninety-three divisions that moved into their jumping-off positions after receipt of the code-word "Danzig" from Hitler's HQ on the evening of May 9, 1940, were arrayed in three great army groups that stretched the entire length of Germany's Rhine boundary from Holland to Switzerland. In the north Army Group B, commanded by Colonel General Fedor von Bock, disposed of twenty-nine divisions and stood poised to slam into Holland and northern Belgium. In the center Army Group A, led by Colonel General Gerd von Rundstedt, was to be the Schwerpunkt (point of main effort) of the western offensive, delivering the crucial armored blows through southern Belgium and northeastern France. This massive force consisted of forty-five divisions, including the bulk of the German armor, and was to be led by three powerful, echeloned and densely packed panzer corps containing nearly 2,000 tanks. Assigned as a back-up force exclusively for Army Group A was the entire OKH reserve of forty-five divisions, including the Second Army and the SSTK. Army Group C, the weakest of the three German forces, formed the southern end of the German front facing Alsace and Lorraine. Army Group C was commanded by Colonel General Wilhelm Ritter von Leeb, and with its modest force of nineteen infantry divisions was to stand on the defensive opposite the Maginot Line once the German attack began.[1]

[1] The text of the German plan "Fall Gelb" (Case Yellow) may be found in

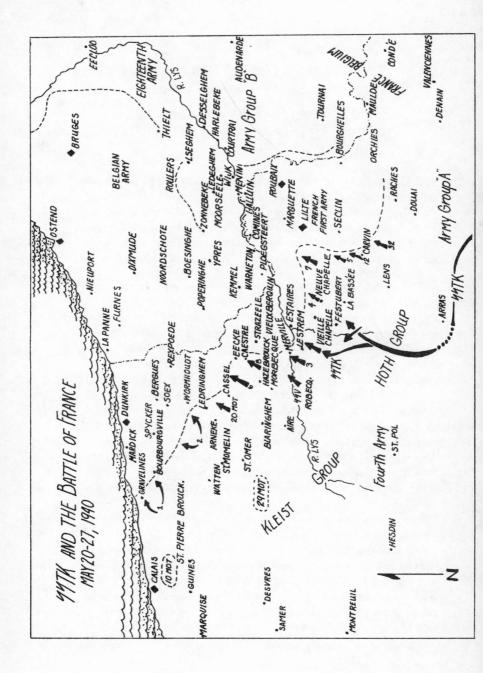

OKW AND THE BATTLE OF FRANCE
MAY 20-27, 1940

At dawn on May 10, 1940, "Fall Gelb" (Case Yellow) began. As specified in the plan, the initial German attacks were delivered by Army Group B in Holland and northern Belgium. The sudden and violent German invasion of Holland, combining savage attacks upon the Dutch frontier with simultaneous and daring airborne assaults upon the Hague and Rotterdam 100 miles to the rear, created a brilliantly calculated diversion that made the Allies believe Bock's thrust was the main German attack. In addition, "Plan D" as formulated by the Allied commander in chief, French General Maurice Gamelin, called for the immediate commitment to Belgium of the entire Allied left wing in response to the German invasion. Consequently, by design and by accident the Allies blundered fatally—as the German plan had foreseen—by moving their armies into Belgium to meet the feint they expected was the brunt of the German offensive. Once the Allies had committed themselves, the German trap began to close. To the south, the bulk of the formations in Army Group A, led by Lieutenant General Heinz Guderian's powerful Nineteenth Panzer Corps, moved quickly into southern Belgium and Luxembourg, shearing through the supposedly impassable Ardennes Forest into the flank and rear of the Allied armies to the north.

Encountering only light resistance, Rundstedt's tanks made straight for the weakly held French positions at Sedan on the Meuse River. This sector of the front was thinly defended because the French expected the Ardennes, with its thickly wooded hills and narrow, winding roads, to serve as a shield against any large-scale German operations. As a result, the weak French units on the Meuse were taken by surprise and crumpled like wet cardboard under the massive weight of Guderian's tanks. By May 13, the Germans had crossed the Meuse in force and overrun the remaining French positions. Guderian spent the following day enlarging the bridgeheads on the west bank of the Meuse, and then on May

---

Walther Hubatsch, ed., *Hitlers Weisungen für die Kriegführung, 1939-1945* (Frankfurt am Main, 1962), pp. 46-50; and in English translation in H. R. Trevor-Roper, ed., *Blitzkrieg to Defeat: Hitler's War Directives, 1939-45* (New York, 1964), pp. 25-27. Helmuth Greiner, *Die Oberste Wehrmachtführung, 1939-1943* (Wiesbaden, 1951), pp. 55-110; and B. H. Liddell Hart, *Strategy*, 2nd ed. rev. (New York, 1967), pp. 222-31, both have thorough and reliable discussions of the evolution of German plans for the attack.

15 began the breakout that carried his armored formations fully into the rear of the British and French forces in the north. In the four days that followed, Guderian's tanks crossed the rolling plains of Artois and Picardy, reached the English Channel, and entombed the Allied armies in Belgium.[2]

For Eicke and his men, held in reserve far to the rear with the Second Army, the first three days of the campaign were a time of unbearable tension. The state of alert continued, and each passing hour brought more detailed news of the awesome initial successes achieved by the Wehrmacht's armored and motorized formations. By the late afternoon of May 12, with Guderian's tank columns in possession of Sedan and the north bank of the Meuse, the progress of Rundstedt's advance compelled OKH to make the first change in the Totenkopfdivision's status. Eicke received orders to move westward immediately to a new reserve staging area on the Belgian frontier. At 8 P.M. on May 12, the SSTK assembled and moved out of the Korbach area. Driving through the night in col-

---

[2] The literature on the battle of France is extensive. Works of special value used in this study include: Lionel F. Ellis, *The War in France and Flanders, 1939-1940* (London, 1953); B. H. Liddell Hart, *History of the Second World War*, 2 vols. (New York, 1972), vol. 1; and the previously cited book by Telford Taylor, *The March of Conquest*. In addition, Alistair Horne, *To Lose a Battle, France 1940* (Boston, 1969), is useful but must be read with caution, as the description of the German side of the campaign is frequently shoddy and erroneous. From the Allied side, Major General Sir Edward Spears, *Assignment to Catastrophe*, vol. 1, *Prelude to Dunkirk, July 1939—May 1940*, and vol. 2, *The Fall of France, June 1940* (New York, 1954-55), is a remarkable first hand account of the chaos, stupefaction, and paralysis that the German invasion produced in France. General Spears served as Prime Minister Winston Churchill's liaison with French Premier Paul Reynaud during the battle of France. Also important are Jacques Benoist-Mechin, *Sixty Days that Shook the West: The Fall of France in 1940* (New York, 1963); Guy Chapman, *Why France Fell: The Defeat of the French Army in 1940* (New York, 1968); Theodor Draper, *The Six Weeks War: France, May 10-June 25, 1940* (New York, 1954); and Sir Arthur Bryant, *The Turn of the Tide: A History of the War Years Based on the Diaries of Field Marshal Lord Alanbrooke, Chief of the Imperial General Staff* (New York, 1957), as they view the campaign from the perspective of a French defeat rather than a German victory. From the German side, the previously cited memoirs of General Guderian, *Panzer Leader*, are extremely valuable; as is Hans-Adolf Jacobsen's chapter on the battle of France as it culminated at Dunkirk, in Hans-Adolf Jacobsen and Jürgen Rohwer, eds., *Decisive Battles of World War II: The German View*, trans. Edward Fitzgerald (New York, 1965). The account in Alan Bullock, *Hitler: A Study in Tyranny*, 2nd ed. rev. (New York, 1964), pp. 507-93, is interesting; while Stein, pp. 60-92, is indispensable for an appreciation of the role of the Waffen SS in the battle of France.

umns that stretched for nearly twenty miles, the Totenkopfdivision passed through Cologne in the early morning darkness and then swung northwest toward the villages of Neukirchen and Wipperfürth on the Belgian border.[3]

Once in his new quarters, Eicke was forced to spend another frustrating four days waiting for final march orders. During that time, he sought to relieve the tension among his men with last-minute training exercises, pep talks, and baths and haircuts for all who wanted them. At 9:15 P.M. on May 14, as the spearheads of Army Group A prepared to break out of the Meuse bridgeheads, the operations section of OKH alerted Eicke to stand by for marching orders from Army Group A. Another forty-eight-hour delay ensued while the army group's tanks achieved their spectacular breakthrough between Sedan and Dinant. Once onto the open plain of northern France, the German armored divisions fanned out and began a headlong dash for the English Channel. The sheer size of the breakthrough and the surprising speed of the advances on May 15 and 16 startled even the senior German commanders, and dictated the call-up of reserves to fill in the gaps and protect the flanks of the rapidly widening armored salient.

Accordingly, the SS Totenkopfdivision was ordered out of OKH reserve and into action by Army Group A on May 17. Eicke was instructed to move west across the southern tip of Holland and through Belgium to link up with General Hermann Hoth's Fifteenth Panzer Corps (Fifth and Seventh Panzer Divisions), which was moving into France as the northern half of Rundstedt's armored wedge. The Totenkopfdivision was to be flung directly into action to add depth and muscle to Hoth's fast-moving corps.[4]

During the night of May 17-18, the entire Totenkopfdivision assembled into marching columns and, with Eicke leading in his command car, moved out in the darkness just before dawn. From Neukirchen, the division motored west to Roermund in Holland,

---

[3] BAMA, III SS, 42/1, KTB No. 1, pp. 19-20; 44/2, p. 252; 41/1, KTB No. 2, pp. 13-14. The SS Totenkopfdivision departed from Korbach for the front with a combat strength of 668 officers, 2,825 NCOs, and 17,818 troops. The SSTK thus began the western campaign with greater strength than the German army's armored and infantry divisions (Klietmann, p. 499; and BAMA, III SS, 41/1, KTB No. 2, pp. 36-37).

[4] BAMA, III SS, 41/1, KTB No. 2, pp. 13-14; Stein, p. 67; and Taylor, p. 229.

and there turned south on the highway leading into Belgium at Maastricht. Continuing southwest, SSTK detoured around Liège on the south and pushed through Huy toward Dinant. On their march through Holland and Belgium, Eicke's columns encountered no enemy resistance, as Bock's army group by May 18 had pushed the British and French back much further to the west.

The journey was not without difficulty, however, for Eicke and his men soon discovered that they were moving through the rear of the operational area of Army Group B and directly across the path of its axis of advance. This situation resulted in several mammoth traffic jams. Eicke's columns became entangled at road junctions with reserve units of Army Group B attempting to move northwest toward the front. The traffic tie-ups slowed progress considerably and enraged Eicke, who alighted from his command car several times at snarled intersections to bluster and threaten in an attempt to clear the roads for his vehicles. There were several ugly scenes along the route as Eicke and army commanders engaged in shouting contests over the right of way while truckloads of SS infantry traded insults with weary soldiers marching toward the front. Not until 5 P.M. on May 19 did the truck columns of the supply and administrative services, bringing up the rear of SSTK, clear the last of the traffic jams and arrive in Dinant.[5]

In the meantime, Eicke had received orders for SSTK's first combat assignment and had moved into northern France with the forward elements of the division. At 4 A.M. on May 19, while pausing to rest near the French border, he was alerted to prepare for enemy counterattacks in regimental strength from the north. This communiqué was followed a short time later by orders from Fifteenth Panzer Corps to move into France and proceed as quickly as possible to the village of Le Cateau. SSTK was to rescue one of the army's crack divisions, the Seventh Panzer, commanded by then Major General Erwin Rommel, which had been

[5] BAMA, III SS, 44/1, KTB No. 1, pp. 56-57; 41/1, KTB No. 2, pp. 14-15; 42/1, KTB No. 1, p. 20. On the morning of May 18, Eicke's men had their first glimpse of what lay ahead. The roads through Belgium were flanked by bombed-out homes and littered with wrecked and burning vehicles and the graves of German and Belgian soldiers. Very few of the traffic tie-ups seem to have resulted from vehicle breakdowns. The SSTK maintenance companies, moreover, proved surprisingly efficient in repairing quickly the disabled vehicles.

halted between Le Cateau and Cambrai and pinned down by a savage French counterattack.[6]

Detailing the Totenkopfdivision's First Infantry Regiment (SSTK/I. R. 1) and antitank, engineer, and artillery companies for the task, Eicke ordered an attack across the Sambre River toward both Le Cateau and Cambrai to relieve the pressure on Rommel. In their first contact with the enemy, a day-long engagement, Eicke's men methodically cleared French Moroccan troops from several small villages in vicious house-to-house, hand-to-hand fighting. After dislodging the Moroccans, the SS soldiers had to repulse a series of tank attacks. By mid-morning on May 20, Eicke's men had cleared the enemy from the area east and north of Cambrai, freeing the Fifteenth Panzer Corps to resume its advance that same afternoon. During this first engagement, units of the Totenkopfdivision captured 1,600 French prisoners, including two colonels and four majors, and hauled in a large cache of weapons and supplies. The savage nature of the fighting between the SS men and the Moroccans may be gauged from the respective casualty figures for the day. SSTK lost 16 dead and 53 wounded, while claiming 200 Moroccan soldiers killed and only 100 taken prisoner.[7]

With the full resumption of the advance by the German armor, Army Group A transferred SSTK to General Rudolf Schmidt's Thirty-ninth Corps on May 20, and inserted it into the slot between the Eighth Panzer Division on the south and the Seventh Panzer Division on the north. Eicke was ordered to keep pace between the two divisions moving west into the open country south of Arras. With German forces streaming almost unhindered toward the channel, OKH's objective was to plug the gaps along the line to prevent the escape of British and French units from Belgium and northern France into the area south of the Somme River.

[6] Ibid., 42/1, KTB No. 1, pp. 76-77; 41/1, KTB No. 2, pp. 15-16. The daily movements of the Totenkopfdivision during the French campaign were outlined in a published photo album, *Damals, Erinnerungen an Grosse Tage der SS Totenkopf-Division im französischen Feldzug* (Stuttgart, 1940), a copy of which is included among the division's war diaries and catalogued as BAMA, III SS, 48/1. The traffic jams in Belgium were serious enough to stop Eicke's rations from reaching the front, forcing him to draw food until May 21 from the Seventh Panzer Division and from captured enemy stores.

[7] BAMA, III SS, 41/1, KTB No. 2, pp. 16-21; Stein, pp. 67-68.

By early afternoon on May 20, Eicke had brushed aside the weak resistance offered by French rearguards, forced his way across the Canal du Nord at the village of Inchy-en-Artois, southwest of Cambrai, and begun advancing west toward Arras. In the meantime, Rommel's Seventh Panzer Division on Eicke's right had run into stiff resistance from British units digging in to the east of Arras. At about 4:30 that afternoon, SSTK reached the village of Mercatel, due south of Arras, where Eicke halted temporarily to await further orders. An hour later, instructions arrived for Eicke to swing the division northwest, assume a blocking position for the night, and prepare to encircle Arras the following day.

South of SSTK, on Eicke's left, the Eighth Panzer Division sped by in the early afternoon heading due west, and by nightfall on May 20 reached the town of Hesdin, only fifteen miles from the channel coast. Further to the south, the Second Panzer Division of Guderian's Nineteenth Panzer Corps, after an unopposed dash of fifty miles, reached the channel coast and seized the town of Abbeville at the mouth of the Somme River. The jaws of the gigantic armored trap had opened around the Allied armies in Belgium and northern France, and caught them between the rapidly converging steel teeth formed by the army groups of Bock and Rundstedt.[8]

The unexpected successes achieved so quickly by the German armor on May 20 caused a momentary fit of nervous paralysis at Hitler's HQ. While the führer argued with Brauchitsch and Halder over whether to commit the armored and motorized units of Rundstedt in a concerted drive north to reduce the surrounded Allied armies, the Totenkopfdivision, Rommel's Seventh Panzer Division, and their neighboring units sat through the night of May 20-21 without definite orders for action on the twenty-first. At midday on May 21, Hitler finally agreed on a full-scale attack northward by Rundstedt's armor and motorized infantry to de-

---

[8] BAMA, III SS, 41/1, KTB No. 2, pp. 21-22. See especially Ellis, pp. 79-80; and Horne, pp. 484-88 for details of the dispute between Hitler and the high command. Guderian's arrival at Abbeville made the führer extremely nervous and led him to accuse his generals of irresponsible recklessness. Hitler feared that the German divisions strung out between Luxembourg and the channel would be chopped up by Allied counterattacks from the north.

stroy the Allied divisions trapped between Bock and Rundstedt. Accordingly, Eicke received orders shortly before 2 P.M. to mass in force, cross the Scarpe River, and advance due north to the highway running west out of Arras.[9]

The eagerness and dispatch with which Eicke obeyed these orders probably saved the Totenkopfdivision from suffering a major setback. While SSTK deployed into attack columns, and engineers and assault groups from SSTK/I. R. 3 forced the Scarpe, the British armor counterattacked around Arras to the south and ran headlong into SSTK and the Seventh Panzer Division. The attack was part of an ill-fated Allied plan to smash open a corridor through the German lines with simultaneous assaults from the north and south. Owing to a series of misunderstandings between the French and British general staffs, the assault materialized only from the north. The attacking force consisted of units from the British Fifth and Thirtieth Divisions, and collided with SSTK and the Seventh Panzer Division shortly after 2:30 P.M. on May 21.

The confusing battle of tanks, armored cars, and infantry that followed was a sobering experience for the men in the Totenkopfdivision. Luckily for Eicke, the brunt of the attack in his sector by chance crashed squarely into the tank-destroyer battalion, which deployed quickly and began blazing away at the wildly careening British tanks. The antitank gunners immediately discovered that their 37 mm cannon were useless against the thirty-ton British "Matildas," which inflicted heavy losses especially upon the Third Company of the tank-destroyer battalion. After watching helplessly while their shells bounced off the enemy tanks, a number of the gun crews were blasted to pieces at close range or crushed beneath the treads of the relentless Matildas. Several companies of the tank-destroyer battalion abandoned their guns and retreated a short distance to regroup. Then, aided by soldiers from SSTK/I. R. 3 armed with mortars and heavy machine guns, the antitank gunners went after the British again, recklessly attacking the tanks singly and in pairs with hand grenades. This tactic also failed, resulting in even heavier casualties. After nearly an hour of desperate resistance, Eicke succeeded in stalling the tank

[9] BAMA, III SS, 41/1, KTB No. 2, p. 22; Horne, p. 490.

attack by firing over open sights on the British with his artillery. The timely arrival of Stukas finally drove off the remaining British tanks.[10]

This armored assault, the stiffest contact SSTK had then had with the enemy, cost Eicke 39 dead, 66 wounded, and 2 missing. In addition, evidence suggests that there was panic among some units during the first half-hour of the attack. This was particularly noticeable in one of the SSTK supply columns, whose men abandoned their vehicles and fled pell-mell as a group of British tanks approached. In general, however, the Totenkopfdivision appears to have performed commendably on May 21. And if there was momentary panic in SSTK, it was nowhere near as serious as the chaos that prevailed in Rommel's Seventh Panzer Division, which absorbed the impact of the center and left of the British attack. According to Rommel's own version of the events, the condition of his troops for a time was critical, verging on hysteria. Rommel even feared that the panic might turn into a rout, and sped from unit to unit in his command car restoring calm, regrouping his men, and directing counterattacks until the crisis passed.[11]

[10] BAMA, III SS, 41/1, KTB No. 2, pp. 21-23; 44/1, KTB No. 1, p. 17; and BAKO, NS-19/neu-1668, "Panzerangriff bei Mercatel am 21. 5. 40." This is a detailed account of the repulse of the British tank attack, written by SS Hauptsturmführer Hartkampf, the commander of the Fourteenth Company of the SSTK tank-destroyer battalion. The battalion claimed twenty-two British tanks knocked out in the fighting on May 21. For additional details concerning the local Allied counterthrust on May 21, see Ellis, pp. 83, 91, 94-95; Stein, pp. 68-69; Horne, pp. 501-4; Taylor, pp. 234-37; and Chapman, pp. 184-87. Most of the SS men seriously wounded on May 21 were hit in the lungs and stomach when running upright at the British tanks, thus exposing themselves fully to the tank gunners and the following British infantry. See especially, BAMA, III SS, 46/1, Divisions Arzt, KTB No. 4, pp. 13-14.

[11] BAMA, III SS, 41/1, KTB No. 2, pp. 30-31; Taylor, pp. 236-37; and B. H. Liddell Hart, ed., *The Rommel Papers* (London, 1953), pp. 29-43. The substantial role played by the Totenkopfdivision in repulsing the tank attack of May 21 has consciously or unconsciously been ignored by the military historians and memoirists who have written on the subject. General Guderian notes smugly (and incorrectly) in his memoirs (p. 92) that SSTK had not been in combat before May 21 and had shown "signs of panic" during the British attack. Horne (p. 504) accepts this judgment without censure, while vaguely stating earlier (p. 501) that the right-hand column of British tanks—the group who collided with SSTK—was stalled by stiff resistance and had to fall back on the village of Warlus after suffering heavy casualties. The tendency has been to accept Rommel's own version of the events at Arras on May 21, and to give the Seventh Panzer Division complete credit for halting the British attack.

The Allied counterthrust at Arras stunned the Germans temporarily and forced Eicke to halt his northward advance until the morning of the twenty-second. While his men enjoyed a well-earned rest on the night of May 21-22, Eicke received fresh orders from OKH. The Totenkopfdivision was transferred during the night to General Erich Hoepner's Sixteenth Panzer Corps, which also contained the SS Verfügungsdivision and the Third and Fourth Panzer Divisions. This powerful mechanized force was assigned the task of spearheading the drive by Rundstedt's armor to crush the constricting Allied pocket in the north. As a result of the nervousness caused by the unexpected tank attack at Arras, Hoepner ordered Eicke to advance northward with caution, and then only after carefully reconnoitering the area in his path. Inching forward slowly behind the reconnaissance battalion screen, SSTK encountered only isolated resistance on May 22. At his own HQ in Aubigny, however, Eicke had a few nervous moments as his soldiers beat off an attack by British light tanks in the early afternoon.[12]

The light contact on May 22 restored the Germans' self-confidence; for the following day Hoepner planned a full-scale attack across the line of the La Bassée Canal to prevent the retreating British from digging in along this natural defense line. Eicke was assigned the limited objective of advancing to the town of Bethune, lying astride the canal, and of probing along the waterway for a suitable crossing point. Reaching the outskirts of Bethune late in the afternoon, Eicke ordered an immediate crossing of the canal in battalion strength, without the precaution of reconnoitering the opposite bank. When his men had worked their way into town, they discovered the British were dug in strongly. Finding themselves caught by surprise in the open, the SS men withdrew across the canal in haste under heavy fire. In the meantime, Eicke had moved his artillery and antitank batteries into position along the canal and had brought up engineers to prepare bridges for a large-scale crossing. Faced by stiff British resistance, however, he changed his mind and ordered a reconnaissance in force along the south bank of the canal to find a weak spot where crossings might be made. This was all Eicke had orig-

[12] BAMA, III SS, 41/1, KTB No. 2, pp. 24-25.

inally been authorized by Hoepner to undertake. His deliberate disobedience of orders in attempting a precipitate crossing of the canal had resulted only in wasted casualties.[13]

While Eicke's men searched frantically for suitable crossing points, the British units bypassed to the southeast around Arras, withdrew northward, and began shuttling reinforcements into position along the northern bank opposite the Totenkopfdivision. Units of the British Second, Forty-fourth, and Forty-eighth Divisions arrived continuously throughout the night and dug in. Early on the morning of May 24, the Fourteenth Company of the Third Battalion/SSTK I. R. 1, accompanied by a Flak (antiaircraft) battery and using a pontoon bridge daringly constructed by engineers, managed to cross the canal and establish a bridgehead. With the bravado of a reckless amateur, Eicke—pistol in hand—led the attack. Once across, his group was pinned down temporarily by concentrated rifle and machine-gun fire. Ignoring the fusillade, Eicke radioed for three more companies to come across and began directing the fire of field pieces that had been lugged to the opposite bank. After about an hour, when the SS troops had a firm hold on the north bank, Eicke ordered the bridgehead expanded and signaled his units on the south side to prepare for a crossing.[14]

At this very moment, urgent orders from Sixteenth Panzer Corps were relayed to him by his HQ on the south bank. SSTK was to break off its attack, retire to the south bank, and prepare defensive positions for an expected enemy tank attack. This order to change to the defensive grew from a controversial decision made at Hitler's HQ on May 24 to halt the armored formations of Army Group A along the canal line so they could rest and refit for the second stage of the campaign. This was to be an attack south across the Somme along a broad front to roll up and destroy the

[13] Ibid., pp. 25-27.

[14] Ibid., pp. 27-28; Horne, pp. 526-29; and Ellis, pp. 131-32, for details of the British withdrawal to the canal line. The British had decided on the evening of May 23 to pull out of the constricting pocket between Lille and Arras and to form a new defensive line along the La Bassée Canal. This possibility had been foreseen by both Rundstedt and Hoepner, who had hoped to beat the British to the canal. Owing to the cautious movement of May 22, however, SSTK and the other divisions in Hoepner's corps arrived too late to prevent the British from establishing a formidable defensive system.

French armies that had not been trapped in the huge northern pocket.

For this major second offensive, Hitler argued, the armored and motorized units under Rundstedt's command would need rest and preparation. In the wrangling at Hitler's HQ on the twenty-fourth, the conclusion emerged that Bock's army group, despite its lack of armor, was capable of finishing off the Allied armies in northern France. The final decision, in which Rundstedt concurred with Hitler, called for Bock to push the enemy forces back against the stationary armored divisions along the canal line as the two German army groups converged.[15]

The halt order infuriated Eicke, especially because of the losses his engineers and infantrymen had taken in bridging the canal. The carnage that resulted as he tried to pull his men back across the canal was even worse. The British noted quickly the changed activity in the bridgehead and, sensing a withdrawal, began directing murderous fire onto Eicke's positions. This accurate cannonade, joined by British artillery to the north of Bethune, soon became so intense that an orderly, gradual withdrawal was impossible. Abandoning their rubber boats and heavy gear, the SS men simply raced for the canal, jumped in and swam across, then scrambled for cover on the south bank. Casualties were frightful. When the British finally ceased firing after an hour, SSTK had suffered losses of 42 killed, 121 wounded and 5 missing.[16]

Once safely back on the south side of the canal, Eicke encountered Hoepner, whose professional antipathy to the SS and doubts about SSTK's reliability had brought him to Bethune where he might examine the action at close range. Though no verbatim account of their conversation exists, a bitter exchange between the two men seems to have ensued. Eicke apparently challenged the halt and withdrawal order, sputtering at Hoepner that losses made no difference when one held a position and did not retreat in the face of the enemy. The angered Hoepner replied by reprimanding

---

[15] Ellis, pp. 131-32; Horne, pp. 533-35; and Taylor, pp. 255-62, for a full discussion of the reasons for the halt order on May 24 and an analysis of subsequent controversy surrounding it. See also the thoughtful article by Hans Meier-Welcker, "Der Entschluss zum Anhalten der deutschen Panzertruppen in Flandern 1940," *Vierteljahrshefte für Zeitgeschichte,* 2 (July 1954), 274-90.

[16] BAMA, III SS, 41/1, KTB No. 2, pp. 28-31.

2. Totenkopf soldiers give the Nazi salute over the grave of a fallen comrade, France, May 1940.

Eicke sharply in front of his own staff, accused him of caring nothing for the lives of his men, and allegedly even called the former concentration camp commander a "butcher" to his face.[17] Following the exchange, Hoepner and his aides departed, leaving Eicke to fume and the Totenkopfdivision to entrench in defensive positions along the south bank of the canal.

Eicke's irritation at his dressing-down and the anger and frustration his men felt over having to withdraw to defensive positions were not salved any by the events of the next two days. While SSTK sat immobile in drenching rain on May 25 and 26, the British strengthened their canal defenses and harrassed Eicke's forward units constantly with mortar and artillery fire. The British High Command had been astonished by this unexpected German halt and took full advantage of the situation by placing additional forces along the canal line. These British troops were to act as the main blocking force covering the general withdrawal of the Allied forces trying to escape through the pocket to the channel coast.

All day long on May 25 the British lobbed mortar and artillery fire on SSTK with deadly accuracy. Mounting casualties and the growing number of his vehicles set ablaze prompted Eicke, on his own initiative, to authorize small assault groups for canal crossings. These selected SS men were to reconnoiter the British positions on the opposite bank and silence as many mortar batteries as they could. The experience of one assault group reveals much about the manner in which Eicke had taught his men to wage war, and the methods they were beginning to employ in handling enemy prisoners.

The combat group, led by an Obersturmführer Harrer, crossed the canal safely and began moving along a road. Suddenly, the SS men spotted a British motorcycle courier speeding toward them. One of the SS soldiers quickly raised his Mauser and knocked the cyclist off his machine with a shot. The whole group then ap-

---

[17] Reitlinger, *The SS*, p. 148; and Gerhard Ritter, *Carl Goerdeler und die deutsche Widerstandsbewegung* (Stuttgart, 1954), p. 532. Professor Ritter, in attesting to Hoepner's moral courage while a member of the German resistance movement, recounts this incident as it was told to him by a Dr. Bothe-Berlin—one of Hoepner's aides who was present on May 24 when the exchange with Eicke occurred. Eicke's behavior reinforced Hoepner's already low opinion of the armed SS, and turned him into one of Eicke's most persistent and troublesome critics.

proached and found the British soldier lying in a ditch, his shoulder wounded. After pulling the man to his feet, the SS soldiers unsuccessfully tried to converse with him. Obersturmführer Harrer finally asked the wounded man in halting English if he spoke French. When the British soldier did not reply, Harrer calmly drew his pistol and shot the man through the head at point-blank range. The SS soldiers threw the body and the motorcycle into a drainage ditch out of sight from the road and continued on in the direction they had been moving.[18]

Later that afternoon these same men were ambushed as they walked unaware into a British roadblock. Several were taken prisoner, while Obersturmführer Harrer, though wounded, managed to get away. The German prisoners were transferred immediately to a compound near the channel coast. The account of their treatment at the hands of the British is most interesting in light of the incident mentioned above, and especially considering the behavior of the Totenkopfdivision during the next several days of bitter fighting.

At the rear-area compound, the SS prisoners were interrogated by a German-speaking captain. They were then given clean clothes, a warm meal, and cigarettes. During the last days of the fighting in northern France, these men were shuttled around behind the front. According to their own version of the captivity, they were not mistreated by the British. At one point, British soldiers even saved the prisoners from a French mob that tried to lynch them after the Luftwaffe had destroyed a small village and killed several civilians. Thereafter, they were dressed in British greatcoats and helmets so as not to attract the attention of the French population. The SS men finally escaped when the British soldiers guarding them simply walked away in the confusion to join the last units being evacuated from Dunkirk.[19]

[18] BAMA, III SS, 41/4, Anlagenband zum KTB Nos. 1-4, pp. 75-79. This is a copy of the transcript of the subsequent interrogation by SSTK intelligence officers of the men sent across the canal on May 25.

[19] Ibid., III SS 41/4, Anlagenband zum KTB, Nos. 1-4, pp. 75-79, 81-83. The three SSTK men captured on May 25, SS privates Hubert Schopfhauser, Konrad Radl, and Hugo Gieck, were picked up by units of the German army after being abandoned by their captors. All three men, listed originally as missing in action, managed to make their way quickly back to SSTK. All were interrogated closely about their experiences as prisoners of the British.

In the meantime, those at Hitler's HQ realized that the British were digging in along the canal line for a major defensive stand. As a result, late in the afternoon of May 26 OKH ordered a full resumption of the advance by all the German armored and motorized divisions strung out on the arc extending from the channel coast to Lille. Eicke received detailed orders from Sixteenth Panzer Corps at 4:30 P.M. on May 26. He was instructed to cross the canal again and establish a bridgehead between the villages of Locon and Le Cornet Malo. Once firmly in the bridgehead, Eicke was to launch an attack to the north on the morning of May 27. SSTK/I. R. 3, commanded by Standartenführer Friedmann Götze, began the crossing at 8:30 P.M., after Eicke's heavy-artillery battalion softened up the British positions. By midnight, Götze had secured a bridgehead on the north bank. On the left, SSTK/I. R. 2, commanded by Standartenführer Heinz Bertling, also began moving across the canal under cover of darkness. Bertling's regiment, however, ran into much stiffer resistance and was still struggling to consolidate its hold on the north bank at dawn on May 27. While the lead companies of infantry worked to establish bridgeheads, Eicke's engineers labored feverishly to complete the pontoon bridges before dawn.[20]

Shortly after dawn on May 27, Eicke received additional orders from Hoepner. He was to attack in force across the canal line, seize Bethune, then advance to the northeast and occupy the area between the villages of Estaires and Neuve Chapelle. Unfortunately for Eicke, Sixteenth Panzer Corps grossly underestimated the strength of the British forces along the canal in front of the Totenkopfdivision. As a result, Eicke's men were surprised by the unusually stubborn resistance they encountered. As the day wore on, the fighting along their front developed into the most savage and bitter of the French campaign. Maddened by the desperate struggle, units of the Totenkopfdivision committed wanton

---

[20] Ibid., III SS, 42/2, Divisions Tagesbefehle, Nos. 28-127, p. 137. The canal crossing in Eicke's sector was made especially difficult by the canal bypass north of Bethune. The canal, as originally constructed, looped to the south through Bethune. A bypass later had been dug to skirt the town on the north. Consequently, to advance due north as ordered, SSTK had to cross two canal lines instead of one. The British realized the value of this double barrier, and entrenched heavily on the north bank of the canal loop and the canal bypass. See Stein, p. 76.

brutalities on May 27, one of the blackest days in the division's history.

The SSTK assault began precisely at 8:00 A.M. on May 27. Using the assault tactics that had so impressed Weichs, Eicke's soldiers swarmed across the canal on the expertly constructed pontoon bridges while the artillery regiment unleashed a vicious barrage on the British positions in and around Bethune. Spearheading the advance on the right, I. R. 3 of SSTK quickly overwhelmed the British defenders in Locon, linked up with units of the Fourth Panzer Division, and then halted to await further orders. On the left, in the sector most heavily defended by the British, the advance of Bertling's I. R. 2 ground to a halt under murderous enemy fire. Eicke's men had begun to pay dearly for the two days respite the German halt order had given the British. In addition, the British units in and around Bethune, the First Battalion of the Royal Scots Regiment, Second Battalion of the Royal Norfolk, and First Battalion of the Eighth Lancashire Fusiliers, knew their delay of the Germans along the canal would let the British and French forces fleeing northward to the channel coast escape encirclement. Consequently, the intensity of the fighting increased throughout the morning and reached its peak early in the afternoon.[21]

The British hung on grimly to every building and defensive position in Bethune. All morning hand-to-hand fighting raged in streets and alleys, darkened buildings, barns and shacks. When ammunition ran out, frenzied soldiers used knives and bayonets or hacked each other to death with entrenching shovels. Shortly before noon, the situation of Bertling's I. R. 2 became desperate. The inept regimental commander overextended himself to the north without adequate flank protection and took heavy casualties by ordering lightly armed infantrymen to charge camouflaged machine-gun nests. As his casualties mounted, the British began chopping Bertling's regiment into separate pockets, and he lost all radio contact with Eicke. At division HQ it quickly became obvious that Bertling was in serious trouble. To relieve the crisis, Eicke ordered Götze's I. R. 3 to halt its forward movement and send one battalion to wipe out the British troops near Le Paradis

[21] BAMA, III SS, 42/2, pp. 141-42; Ellis, pp. 136-37; Stein, pp. 72-73.

and Le Cornet Malo who were pinning down I. R. 2. By 1:00 P.M. the entire Totenkopfdivision had stopped in its tracks as an all-out effort was made to dislodge the British and rescue Bertling.

At Eicke's HQ the scene was total confusion. Contradictory calls and radio messages concerning the uncertain situation poured in as a raging Eicke constantly issued, countermanded, and then reissued conflicting sets of orders to his bewildered staff and unit commanders. In the middle of one of Eicke's tirades, his operations officer, Montigny, suddenly collapsed, unconscious. Brigadeführer Dr. Ernst Grawitz, chief of the SS medical services, who had come forward to observe the performance of SSTK medical units, quickly diagnosed a hemorrhaging stomach ulcer. With Eicke's concurrence Grawitz ordered Montigny evacuated at once to a rear-area dressing station, and then had him flown to a hospital in Germany that same afternoon. This left Eicke without the services of the best military mind in the Totenkopfdivision—a loss he and his men would feel greatly during the remainder of the western campaign.[22]

The gloom surrounding Eicke and his staff after Montigny was carried away by ambulance deepened with the arrival of more bad news. Standartenführer Götze, while leading a battalion from his regiment to rescue Bertling, was killed by a British sniper just outside Le Paradis. Within one hour, Eicke had lost two of his most experienced and capable senior officers. The attack by Götze's battalion, however, succeeded finally in dislodging the British and freed I. R. 2 to resume its advance. By mid-afternoon Eicke had reestablished radio contact with Bertling and had ordered all units in SSTK to resume the attack. Not for some time, however, did Eicke manage to regain control of himself and of the military situation.[23]

[22] BAMA, III SS, 41/8, i, pp. 133-34; 42/2, pp. 141-42; and Ellis, pp. 183-89. For the events at Eicke's HQ and the details of Montigny's illness, see BAMA, III SS, 46/1, Divisions Arzt, KTB No. 2, pp. 4-9; and USDC, SS Personalakte von Montigny, series of letters between Eicke and Himmler and a medical report on the incident written by Grawitz. Montigny recovered from his ulcer sufficiently to be named commandant of the SS Junkerschule at Bad Tölz by Himmler on July 15, 1940. He served in this capacity, however, only until November 8, 1940, when he died suddenly of a massive heart attack during a British air raid.

[23] BAMA, III SS, 41/8, i, p. 133; 42/2, pp. 141-42. To the northwest of Bethune, Eicke's neighbor, the SS Verfügungsdivision, was advancing through

As the Totenkopfdivision resumed its advance, clearing the villages Hinges and Locon of the last enemy snipers, the few remaining British survivors around Bethune withdrew to a new defensive line being formed along the Canal de Lawe between the villages of Lestrem and Vieille Chapelle. Here the retreating soldiers were reinforced by fresh troops from the British Twenty-fifth Brigade, First Battalion of the Royal Irish Fusiliers, and a battery of the Sixty-fifth Antitank Regiment. These British units dug in quickly and prepared to give the Totenkopfdivision another hard fight.

Near the village of Le Paradis, about one mile west of the fortified British defensive line, some 100 members of the Second Royal Norfolk barricaded themselves in a farmhouse to slow down the advance of the SSTK left wing. The farmhouse was surrounded quickly by the Fourteenth Company of the First Battalion/SSTK/I. R. 2—men in Bertling's regiment who had been badly mauled only a few hours before. The company commander was SS Obersturmführer Fritz Knöchlein. British soldiers in the house pinned down his company with rifle and machine-gun fire for nearly an hour, killing and wounding several of his men. Eventually, the British survivors ran out of ammunition and decided that further resistance was useless. After agreeing among themselves to surrender, they showed a white flag, threw their guns onto the ground, and marched out with their hands raised, expecting to become prisoners of war.[24]

The surrender by the men of the Second Royal Norfolk was followed by the most hideous wanton brutality committed during the German campaign of 1940. Knöchlein had the British prisoners assembled, searched, then marched across the road into a barnyard. As a number of SS soldiers gathered to watch, the 100 prisoners were placed against the barn wall and, on Knöchlein's command, cut down in a crossfire from two heavy machine guns. The gunners continued to fire into the sprawled heap of bodies

the thick, tangled Forest of Nieppe and encountering equally stiff resistance. By mid-afternoon on May 27, the Verfügungsdivision had lost nearly every SS officer in two of its battalions (Stein, p. 73).

[24] Stein, pp. 76-77; Reitlinger, *The SS*, pp. 148-49; and Cyril Jolly, ed., *The Vengeance of Private Pooley* (London, 1956), pp. 19-39. This latter work is the memoir, written after the war, of Private Albert Pooley, one of the two British soldiers who survived the massacre at Le Paradis.

until the shrieks of the wounded and all signs of movement ceased. Knöchlein then had a squad of his men fix bayonets and move among the bodies, stabbing or shooting in the head any who showed the faintest sign of life. After an hour of this, Knöchlein was satisfied that all the British soldiers were dead and ordered his company to move out and rejoin the rest of the regiment, which had pushed on toward Estaires.[25]

Miraculously, two of the British soldiers survived all the shooting and, though badly wounded, remained still enough to convince the Germans that they were dead. After Knöchlein's company had left, these two men, Privates Albert Pooley and William O'Callaghan, crawled out from under the bodies of their comrades and hid in a pigsty on a nearby farm for several days. Owing to the seriousness of Pooley's wounds, however, they finally had to give themselves up and surrendered to a medical company of the 251st Infantry Division. Both men subsequently were well cared for. Pooley, the more seriously wounded of the two, eventually was repatriated to England in 1943, while O'Callaghan sat out the war in Germany as a prisoner. After the war, the testimony of these two men was instrumental in having Knöchlein tried by a British military tribunal at Altona near Hamburg, condemned to death as a war criminal, and hanged.[26]

The incident at Le Paradis was more than just an isolated act of individual brutality. The urge to massacre defenseless prisoners seems to have been a natural and logical byproduct of the poisonous climate of fanaticism that had existed in the SS Totenkopfdivision since its creation. The mixture of exhaustive military

[25] See especially the accounts given in Stein, pp. 76-77; Reitlinger, *The SS*, pp. 148-49; Ellis, pp. 191-92; and the chilling recollections of Pooley and O'Callaghan in Jolly, pp. 19-76.

[26] Jolly, pp. 151-232, recapitulates the entire incident and quotes at length from the transcript of Knöchlein's trial. During his trial, several former members of the SSTK sought to place all the blame on Knöchlein and to exonerate the other SS men involved with specious testimony about Knöchlein's unpopularity in the division. The claim was also made that other SS officers in the division, when they learned of the event, had wanted to challenge Knöchlein to a duel. In fact, Knöchlein never fought a duel with anyone in the SSTK. Moreover, it is highly improbable that after years of serving with Eicke in the concentration camps, and performing "police and security measures" in Poland, many officers in the Totenkopfdivision would be morally outraged by the killing of enemy soldiers who had been shedding SS blood. See also Jolly, pp. 159-63, 187-97.

training and thorough indoctrination in Eicke's form of Nazi ideology had produced among the men in SSTK a reckless bravado that hardened into suicidal zeal and ferocity when seared by the intense heat of combat. The hours of training and indoctrination and the qualities of bravery in action, however, had not automatically brought combat success to the Totenkopfdivision—especially in the face of stiff resistance from the determined, courageous British. This failure seems to have genuinely mystified and frustrated Eicke and his officers.

When set against the qualities Eicke's leadership had produced in the SSTK—a reckless contempt for death and a vehement hatred for the enemy—the rage generated by this inexplicable failure to overwhelm all resistance had exploded in the behavior of Knöchlein and his company on May 27. The foolish risks Bertling and his men had taken resulted only in disastrous casualties, while the SS troops' intense anger at seeing so many of their comrades fall found gratified release in the destruction of the responsible enemy. Summarily executing prisoners, of course, was not a wartime practice exclusive to the SS Totenkopfdivision, or to the Waffen SS or the German armed forces. Waffen SS divisions such as SSTK did, however, develop a special and generally well deserved reputation for viciousness and cruelty. In many instances, combat atrocities committed by SS divisions resulted from circumstances similar to those at Le Paradis on May 27, 1940.[27]

Word of the atrocity at Le Paradis spread quickly through SSTK to the neighboring divisions in Sixteenth Panzer Corps, and up the chain of command to Hoepner, who ordered a full investigation. Ugly rumors about the behavior of Eicke's men had been circulating along the front for nearly a week, and Hoepner was determined to have Eicke dismissed if they proved true. In fact, as early as May 24, Hoepner apparently was aware that Eicke's men

---

[27] A similar point is made by Professor Stein, pp. 91-92, in assessing the overall role of the Waffen SS in the battle of France. As a result of the fierce fighting on May 27, SSTK lost 155 dead, 483 wounded, and 53 missing. Eicke claimed that he had inflicted casualties of 300 killed and wounded on the British (BAMA, III SS, 42/2, pp. 141-42; Stein, p. 78). As Professor Stein has suggested, the disparity between Eicke's losses and the British casualties is striking—even when the 100 prisoners shot at Le Paradis are included.

were seriously mistreating prisoners. At that time he had issued a special order warning all officers and men that killing prisoners as a reprisal or punishment would be considered murder by an army court-martial. In addition to the rumors about the murder of prisoners, Hoepner had also received a number of reports that men from the Totenkopfdivision had engaged in extensive plundering in Bethune.[28]

Hoepner's investigation, if it was ever undertaken thoroughly, had no visible effect upon Eicke or the Totenkopfdivision. No charges were brought against Knöchlein, and Eicke apparently suffered only the embarrassment of having to explain away the incident to Himmler —claiming in the process that the British had been using dum-dum bullets against the Totenkopfdivision on May 27. In the heat of the final assault upon the British perimeter at Dunkirk and the reduction of the remaining Allied forces in northern France, interest in the atrocity quickly ebbed and the whole incident seems thereafter to have been quietly forgotten.[29]

In the hours immediately following the massacre on May 27, the Totenkopfdivision regained the momentum of its advance and continued pressing northward against the British rearguard units covering the Allied retreat toward Dunkirk. By sundown the British forces in front of Eicke had withdrawn successfully into yet another defensive line along the Lys Canal between Estaires and Merville. Shortly after dark, Eicke's exhausted riflemen stumbled against the new British positions and withdrew groggily for the night in the face of intensive enemy fire.

While his men rested in comatose slumber, Eicke received orders from Hoepner to attack Estaires in force early on the morning of the twenty-eighth and secure a bridgehead across the Lys Canal. The objective of the Sixteenth Panzer Corps was to force the

---

[28] BAMA, III SS, 41/8, I, pp. 137-39; 46/1, KTB No. 4, p. 36.

[29] Ibid., III SS, 41/8, I, pp. 136-39; Reitlinger, *The SS*, pp. 148-49. The documents examined for this study contained no mention of the atrocity at Le Paradis. Any written communications dealing with a topic so sensitive were, no doubt, eventually destroyed. In the absence of any definite evidence about the aftermath of the incident at Le Paradis, the most plausible assumption would seem to be that Eicke protected Knöchlein from prosecution, and that Himmler, in turn, intervened at the top on Eicke's behalf to quash any official army investigation.

new canal defense line, smash the enemy's resistance, and advance to the northeast to cut off the withdrawal of further Allied forces toward Dunkirk. As the center division in Hoepner's corps, SSTK was to lead the attack.

Eicke's attack began at 8:00 A.M. after a preliminary artillery barrage, and ground forward only with the greatest difficulty during the morning hours. By noon the fighting had reached the intensity experienced the previous day. The heavy casualties, nervousness, and fatigue caused by the fighting on the twenty-seventh began to tell noticeably, and by early afternoon the assault faded out altogether. Eicke's men were forced onto the defensive by fierce British counterattacks in and around Estaires, and were then driven to take cover by a furious, well-placed artillery barrage that set numerous vehicles on fire and caused some casualties. Eicke's units were stuck fast for the remainder of the day, and when the attack finally was called off at dusk, the Totenkopfdivision had advanced less than a quarter of a mile.[30]

Annoyed at Eicke's failure to crack the British line, Hoepner telephoned on the evening of the twenty-eighth and curtly demanded a full resumption of the attack at dawn the following morning. Eicke was directed to shift the main effort of the attack to the west of Estaires, and to make sure that the Totenkopfdivision did not fail a second time. When the attack was resumed the next morning and lead units of engineers, riflemen, and antitank gunners crossed the canal and secured a bridgehead, the British—no doubt to Eicke's great relief—began to withdraw slowly. This withdrawal prompted General Hermann Hoth, Hoepner's superior as panzer group commander, to directly order Eicke to pursue and maintain contact with the retreating British as far as Bailleul, but to halt there and await the units on his flanks.[31]

The Totenkopfdivision's northward attack, however, was stopped cold once again. As the division began assembling in the first grey light, the British opened with fierce, accurate artillery fire from positions north of Estaires and in Bailleul, and drove everyone, Eicke and his staff as well, scurrying for cover. Their withdrawal well screened, the entire British rearguard managed to get away, while the Totenkopfdivision remained immobile and

[30] BAMA, III SS, 42/2, pp. 144-45. [31] Ibid., pp. 145-47.

Eicke repeatedly asked the Luftwaffe to silence the British artillery.

When the Luftwaffe finally arrived in late afternoon, the cannonade ceased and SSTK once again resumed its advance. By early evening, Eicke's men had pushed into the area south of Bailleul; units of SSTK/I. R. 1 had made contact with reconnaissance elements of the Sixth Army, advancing to link up with the Sixteenth Panzer Corps and close the ring around the Allied forces fleeing northward. The link-up came too late, however, as the bulk of the British forces and part of the French First Army had withdrawn safely into the gradually constricting Dunkirk perimeter. Shortly after the juncture of the converging German formations, orders arrived for Hoepner from OKH directing him to halt the Sixteenth Panzer Corps until further notice. As these orders were passed down to Eicke, the Totenkopfdivision's active part in the first phase of the battle of France ended.[32]

The halt orders that Hoepner and Eicke received on May 29 came as a result of Hitler's decision to rest the armored and motorized units along the canal line so they could refit and catch their breath before the coming campaign south of the Somme against the remaining French armies. The führer had been prompted to this decision by the promise of his Luftwaffe chief, Hermann Göring, that the German air force would annihilate the remaining Allied divisions which were being compressed into the Dunkirk area and were beginning to escape via transport across the channel to England.

As a result of these high-level actions, Eicke received orders from OKH on the evening of May 30 that detached SSTK from the Sixteenth Panzer Corps and assigned it to the quiet sector around Boulogne for a period of rest and coastal defense duty. SSTK was to be attached to the Fourth Army Corps until further notice. Eicke and his staff received these orders in the presence of

[32] BAMA, III SS, 46/1, KTB No. 4, pp. 49-52; 42/2, p. 145; Ellis, pp. 201-23; and Taylor, pp. 265-68. The link-up between the two German army groups at Armentieres was affected on May 29 by units of SSTK, the Third and Fourth Panzer Divisions, and by formations of the Twenty-seventh Army Corps of Colonel General Walther von Reichenau's Sixth Army. Trapped in the pocket between them were five divisions of the French First Army. SSTK was not subsequently assigned to help reduce the pocket and collect the prisoners from it.

Himmler, who had called Eicke to a conference in Bailleul and had then come forward in person from his private train to inspect SSTK and review its performance.[33]

No written record of the May 30 conference has survived. If, however, the tone of Himmler's letter to Eicke on May 28 is a reliable indication of his mood at the time, then the meeting between the two men was unpleasant. Himmler was, with some justification, angry with Eicke. Besides the odium cast upon the Waffen SS in military circles as a result of the incident at Le Paradis, Eicke's amateurish performance in the battle of France had presented Himmler with serious manpower and matériel problems. Specifically, Eicke's impetuous, sledgehammer tactics had caused heavy losses in men and equipment that the Reichsführer SS had to make good. In the ten-day period between May 19 and 29, 1940, the Totenkopfdivision had suffered 1,140 casualties. The loss of approximately 300 officers was the most serious problem, as it forced the highly irritated Himmler to give Eicke at once 300 half-trained cadets from the SS Junkerschule at Bad Tölz just to keep the Totenkopfdivision in the field.[34]

The damage to equipment and vehicles was equally heavy. During the fighting, SSTK lost forty-six trucks, a score of antitank guns and motorcycles, eight armored cars, and unspecified quantities of mortars, heavy machine guns and rifles. In addition,

[33] BAMA, III SS, 42/1, KTB No. 1, pp. 25-26; 46/1, KTB No. 2, pp. 10-11. On May 30 Eicke received the Iron Cross, First Class from Hoepner for his role in commanding SSTK during the fighting in northern France. Hoepner undoubtedly made the award with the greatest displeasure, since the army tried to prevent the distribution of any medals to the Totenkopfdivision before an inquiry on the Le Paradis atrocity was complete. After vehement complaints by Eicke and direct intervention by Himmler, however, the army gave in and released the standard allotment of medals to SSTK. See especially, BAKO, NS-19/neu-1668, letter from Eicke to Karl Wolff of June 5, 1940; and BAMA, III SS, 41/3, Anlagenband 2 zum KTB nos. 1-4, pp. 5-7, 9, 11, 19, 51, for additional correspondence about the controversy over the medals.

[34] BAKO, NS-19/new-1668, letter from Himmler to Eicke of May 28, 1940; BAMA, III SS, 43/1, Nachschubdienst, KTB No. 1 mit Anlagen, pp. 10-14; and Stein, pp. 80-82. Himmler refused to send Eicke all the replacements he demanded. Upon investigation, the Reichsführer SS discovered that the SS Totenkopfdivision already had an average of twenty percent more commissioned SS officers than the other armed SS units. Himmler finally agreed to send Eicke 1,140 replacements, but by the beginning of the second phase of the French campaign only 500 had actually arrived (BAMA, III SS, 41/3, pp. 65-67).

hundreds of disabled vehicles were in need of such repair as to make them indefinitely useless. The backlog of maintenance was so great by the time SSTK reached Boulogne that Eicke's mechanics had to work around the clock for a week to make the division fully mobile again. In his anxiety to acquire enough vehicles to keep SSTK fit for front-line duty Eicke reverted to his "requisitioning" techniques, causing Himmler yet additional irritation. Besides confiscating all the French transports he could find, Eicke managed, without Himmler's knowledge or permission to obtain thirty-six trucks from the Death's Head units still stationed in Poland. By the time the Reichsführer SS learned of the matter, Eicke already had the trucks safely in his possession in France. An exasperated Himmler agreed to let SSTK keep them, but rebuked Eicke for taking desperately needed transports from SS units in Poland who performed vital "flying actions" against "partisans and bandits."[35]

During their meeting of May 30, Himmler also informed Eicke that a new operations officer had been found for the SSTK. As of June 1, 1940, SS Brigadeführer Kurt Knoblauch was to join Eicke's staff as Ia. Knoblauch was among Himmler's most trusted subordinates, and his appointment was meant to restrict Eicke's freedom of action as an SS division commander. This was not the first time Himmler had tried to use Knoblauch as a check against Eicke. Earlier in May the Reichsführer SS had made Knoblauch the "inspector of Replacement Units of the SS Totenkopfdivision." The creation of this post separated the replacement units of SSTK from the reserve Death's Head formations, and thus strengthened Himmler's direct control over the reserve SSTV. Eicke realized fully the implications of Knoblauch's posting to SSTK, and greeted Himmler's announcement in stony silence. In the following months that Knoblauch remained with SSTK, Eicke treated him as Himmler's messenger boy and spy, dealt with him only when necessary, and generally made his tour of duty with SSTK as unpleasant as possible.[36]

[35] BAKO, NS-19/neu-1668, Himmler's letter to Eicke of May 28, 1940.

[36] BAMA, III SS, 41/3, p. 65; BAKO, NS-19/neu-1668, Himmler to Eicke, May 28, 1940; BAKO, NS-7/426, "Der Inspekteur der E. Einheiten der SS-T.-Division," dated Dachau, May 8, 1940; and USDC, SS Personalakte Knoblauch, Dienstlaufbahn, and a series of reports and complaints Knoblauch sent to Himmler

At the very time Himmler and Eicke conferred, the war in northern France moved toward its climax. Since Hitler regarded the liquidation of the Dunkirk beachhead as a mopping-up operation that could be left to the Luftwaffe, SSTK and its neighboring divisions were directed to take a brief rest.

Before SSTK reached its assigned area around Boulogne, Eicke issued elaborate instructions that were to serve as guidelines for his SS men in their conduct toward the French populace. Still smarting from the reprimands he had received, Eicke warned his men against any attempts at looting since "we find ourselves under sharp criticism wherever we go." Then, in a clear allusion to Le Paradis, he declared that the experience of the French campaign had shown that the actions of a few would cause untruths to be said about the entire division. This, he concluded, compelled each man to conduct himself in the best manner. The men evidently took Eicke at his word, as there were no major incidents during the time SSTK remained on occupation duty at Boulogne.[37]

This leisurely coastal duty ended abruptly on the morning of June 6, when Eicke received orders to move SSTK south to St. Omer to join the Twenty-eighth Army Corps. Eicke was assigned a reserve role among the formations being concentrated to back up Army Group B during the coming drive across the Somme toward Paris. After moving from Boulogne, SSTK enjoyed another four

---

during the summer and autumn of 1940. Knoblauch remained Eicke's Ia until December 1940, when Himmler gave him command of the Second SS Motorized Infantry Brigade, an independent, mobile strike force subsequently used in Russia to hunt down partisans and round up Jews. Himmler also replaced the fallen commander of SSTK/I. R. 3, Standartenführer Götze, with one of his personal choices, Standartenführer Matthias Kleinheisterkamp—who also found himself on bad terms with Eicke (USDC, SS Personalakte Kleinheisterkamp, summary of the materials in Kleinheisterkamp's SS service records, especially his Dienstlaufbahn and a series of efficiency reports written by Eicke).

[37] Stein, pp. 80-81; BAMA, III SS, 46/1, KTB No. 4, p. 63; 41/3, pp. 45, 53, 59; 44/1, Nachschubdienst, Anlagenband zum KTB No. 1, pp. 73-74; 44/2, p. 254. Eicke had also been incensed by accusations made by the Fourteenth Army Corps that men from SSTK were seen plundering in the village of Cassel on the night of May 31. This could not have been possible, as Eicke correctly argued, since none of the units of SSTK were anywhere near the area at the time (BAKO, NS-19/neu-1668, letters from Eicke to Fourteenth Army Corps and to Himmler denying the charges, both dated June 1, 1940).

days' rest in St. Omer while Tschimpke's supply columns shuttled in additional stocks of gasoline, ammunition, and food for the campaign.[38]

On June 10, OKH transferred SSTK to the command of the Sixth Army and ordered Eicke to move further south to Péronne to stand by for another front-line assignment. Two days later, as German armor everywhere bludgeoned the French army toward its final agony, SSTK was sent forward and attached to General Ewald von Kleist's powerful armored group as part of the Fourteenth Motorized Corps (Ninth and Tenth Panzer Divisions and SSTK). Eicke spread the division along the roads between Château-Thierry and Épernay to the rear of the Ninth and Tenth Panzer, and spent two days moving uneventfully to the south, searching for enemy supply dumps, clearing road junctions of refugees, and occasionally gathering contingents of French soldiers who wished to surrender.[39]

On June 14, the day the Germans took Paris and Hitler ordered full pursuit of the French armies south of the Marne, SSTK was shifted forward to serve as the spearhead of the Fourteenth Motorized Corps, which was ordered to swing to the southwest and advance to Orléans. Fanning out in two battle columns, SSTK led the advance south across the Marne. Encountering only scattered resistance from small French units, Eicke's men sped southward, confidently abandoning codes to send all messages and communications *en clair*. The following day Eicke crossed the Seine at Nogent and fell in echelon once again to the rear to protect the flank of the Ninth Panzer Division. The rapid advance continued without difficulty until mid-afternoon on June 16, with the whole army corps changing direction by moving through the department of Yonne due south toward Clamecy. The objective was to seal off the escape route of the French armies in Alsace by striking for Dijon and Lyon. Trouble developed late in the afternoon, however, as units of the Fourteenth Motorized Corps became hopelessly entangled along the main road with hordes of re-

[38] BAMA, III SS, 41/3, pp. 68-74, 79-84. Tschimpke was awarded the Iron Cross, First Class on June 12 in recognition of the excellent performance of the SSTK supply services during the battle of France. (Ibid., 44/2, 258.)

[39] Stein, pp. 82-83; BAMA, III SS, 44/1, Anlagenband zum KTB No. 1, pp. 77-79, 85-88; 41/3, pp. 169-70, 175; 42/1, KTB No. 1, pp. 28-30.

fugees, abandoned and wrecked vehicles, and bedraggled groups of French soldiers trying to surrender. To clear the jam-up, Eicke was instructed to send two of his battalions and a company of engineers forward to shove or blast everything off the roads. By early evening, the SS troopers had opened a path through the jumble and the advance resumed. The columns of the Fourteenth Motorized Corps raced on through the night, driving deeper into southern France almost unopposed.[40]

By dawn Eicke's units were south of Clamecy and sitting astride the Loire River at Nevers and La Charité. At that point, Kleist's HQ decided to split the combat units of SSTK, leaving one column on the Loire while detailing the other to reconnoiter in force east of Dijon. Two motorcycle companies from Eicke's reconnaissance battalion led the move along the highway from Avallon to Dijon. By this time (June 18), organized French resistance had collapsed and the only attacks against the Germans were those initiated by resourceful individual commanders. The column from the Totenkopfdivision moving on Dijon encountered one such French officer. At a road junction in a wooded area several companies of Moroccan troops armed with antitank guns, mortars, and machine guns ambushed the SS men and inflicted substantial casualties before being driven off into the forest.[41]

The next day, June 19, in the area between Dijon and Lyon, the SSTK reconnaissance battalion and two companies of attached infantry were involved in the sharpest fighting the division experienced after the end of the campaign in Flanders. Once again, determined resistance by the enemy provoked harsh reprisals by Eicke's troops. At the village of L'Arbresle near Dijon, the Fifth Company of the Second Battalion/SSTK/I. R. 2 fought a savage action against Moroccan troops left as rearguards. In this particu-

---

[40] Stein, pp. 82-84; BAMA, III SS, 41/3, pp. 175, 179, 183, 194-97, 201, 212, 214, 218, 222; 44/1, pp. 98-99, 116. Between June 15 and 17, 1940, the Totenkopfdivision took 4,000 prisoners and an enormous quantity of weapons and supplies. Included among the captured foodstuffs were 50,000 fresh eggs taken when an entire French supply column surrendered. During this same two-day period, SSTK suffered casualties of only two killed—both in an air attack by French fighters. By June 17, the advance had become so rapid that Eicke ordered his men to leave behind booty—including armored vehicles—so the division could keep up with the rest of the Fourteenth Motorized Corps.

[41] BAMA, III SS, 41/3, pp. 224-26, 231, 252; 41/4, pp. 57-61.

lar engagement, the Moroccans used their foot-long, razor-sharp knives in hand-to-hand fighting—a tactic Eicke's men found fittingly primitive for soldiers they considered racial inferiors. In clearing out this rearguard position, the SS men refused to take any prisoners and killed every one of the thirty Moroccan soldiers involved in the skirmish.[42]

This was not the only instance during the French campaign in which men from the SSTK fought against nonwhite troops and refused to take prisoners, or summarily shot those whose surrender they had accepted. On June 21 in an engagement near Lentilly, according to the daily report (Tagesmeldung) submitted by the Third Battalion/SSTK/I. R. 1, the Twenty-fourth Platoon of Third Battalion took twenty-four white French prisoners, while twenty-four Negroes (Negern) "fell." The report describes another encounter in which seven Negroes were "put out of action" (nieder zu kämpfen), and concludes with the cryptic comment that the day's fighting yielded "twenty-five French prisoners and forty-four dead Negroes."[43]

Later that day, just before dusk, forward units of the reconnaissance battalion driving toward Villefranche were ambushed and lost a number of men killed or wounded before the French machine-gun nests guarding the road could be silenced. This was the last engagement in the battle of France for units of the Totenkopfdivision. The final days of the war in France were spent rounding up the large groups of French soldiers making their way into captivity. The war diary of the Totenkopfdivision claimed a total of 6,088 prisoners taken between June 17 and 19, and the collection of vast quantities of war matériel—including 230,000 liters of gasoline. Casualties during the last days of fighting were insignificant, totalling only five killed and thirteen wounded.[44]

On the last day of the campaign, SSTK reached the south-

[42] Stein, pp. 86-87; BAMA, III SS, 46/1, KTB No. 4, pp. 105-8; III SS, 41/4, pp. 8-9. Black soldiers in French uniform were not unique in receiving harsh treatment from the Germans during the closing days of the French campaign. Hitler issued orders—which Eicke directed his men to enforce without exception—for the summary execution of all ethnic Germans and Czechs captured while fighting for the French. The SSTK records, however, do not mention the execution of any prisoners in this category (BAMA, III SS, 41/3, p. 285; 44/2, p. 263).

[43] BAMA, III SS, 41/4, Anlagenband zum KTB Nos. 1-4, pp. 2-3.

[44] Ibid., 46/1, KTB No. 4, pp. 106-8; 41/3, pp. 288-91.

ernmost point of its advance by driving through Villefranche to the northern edge of Lyon. Everything Eicke's men saw confirmed the impression of total French collapse. In Villefranche, for example, units of Max Simon's I. R. 1 stumbled upon an abandoned armaments factory still intact with unfinished tank chassis sitting on an assembly line, and thousands of cases of hand grenades stacked and ready for shipment to the front. In the nearby village of St. Sorbin the reconnaissance battalion caught up with a long column of French stragglers, marching aimlessly through the countryside, and accepted the surrender of the 1,300 bewildered officers and men.[45]

As the new French government of Marshal Pétain began armistice negotiations in earnest, the Totenkopfdivision was ordered to halt and regroup, and the following day, June 21, received instructions to rejoin the rest of the Fourteenth Motorized Corps in Orleans. On June 22, the day the armistice was signed at Compiègne, Eicke arrived in Orléans to await reassignment. On June 25, the day hostilities ended officially, SSTK was assigned to occupation duty. Eicke was to follow the Fourteenth Motorized Corps to the area south of Bordeaux and there position SSTK in the strip of territory between the Atlantic coast and unoccupied France. The Totenkopfdivision and the SS Verfügungsdivision together were given responsibility for security in the southernmost portion of the occupied strip, along the Spanish frontier. Eicke arrived at his new HQ in the village of Hostens, twenty-five miles southwest of Bordeaux, on June 30 and began busying himself with the problem of finding quarters for his men and the task of guarding the demarcation line. For Eicke and the Totenkopfdivision, the war appeared to be over.[46]

The campaign in France had presented the Totenkopfdivision with its first crucial test—a challenge that Eicke and his men surmounted in acceptable, though by no means brilliant, fashion.

[45] Ibid., III SS, 41/3, pp. 293, 297; 41/4, pp. 16, 21, 63, 67.

[46] BAMA, III SS, 42/1, KTB No. 1, pp. 31-34; 41/4, pp. 28, 32, 45-52, 124-26. The Fourteenth Motorized Corps HQ were located south of Eicke in the famous resort town of Biarritz. The quantity of French supplies captured by units of the corps in this area was so enormous that the Totenkopfdivision drew its rations for the first two weeks of July 1940 entirely from captured French army food stores.

The most significant aspect of the war in France and Flanders for the SSTK was the experience it provided—experience which welded the division into a combat-hardened, self-confident formation. The performance of SSTK, while not influencing decisively any aspect of the campaign, did at least compel the German generals to agree with Himmler that armed SS units, including those formerly responsible for guarding and running the concentration camps, could fight alongside the army in the most sensitive and important sectors of the front. Casualties could be steep, as the Totenkopfdivision had also shown. In eighteen days of contact with the enemy, including seven days of heavy fighting, SSTK suffered 1,152 casualties—or slightly more than ten percent of its effective combat strength.[47]

In addition, the fighting in France elicited characteristics in the Totenkopfdivision that later became hallmarks of Waffen SS behavior. Fanatical recklessness in the assault, suicidal defense against enemy attacks, and savage atrocities committed in the face of frustrated objectives all were clearly present in the Totenkopfdivision's performance during the western campaign.

Finally, the exigencies of war caused a demonstrable change in Eicke's relations with Himmler. The heady experience of commanding a division in combat magnified Eicke's already inflated sense of self-importance and increased his desire to handle the Totenkopfdivision without interference from the Reichsführer SS.

[47] Ibid., 41/4, pp. 84-85.

CHAPTER FIVE

The Long Interlude: Occupation Duty and Transfer to the East

THE year between the French surrender in the forest of Compiègne on June 22, 1940 and the German invasion of the Soviet Union on the morning of June 22, 1941, was a crucial period in the Totenkopfdivision's history. For Eicke personally, moreover, the full year of military inactivity became one of the most difficult and frustrating phases of his SS career. Myriad problems involving the reorganization, refitting, and finally the large-scale retraining of SSTK for the Russian campaign kept Eicke and his staff busy until the very day "Operation Barbarossa" began. In addition, much of Eicke's energy and attention in the interlude between campaigns was devoted to intrigue and quarreling within the SS hierarchy.

The disputes in which Eicke became involved resulted from the general convulsion caused by the enormous expansion of the Waffen SS that took place between the French surrender and the Russian campaign. With Hitler's permission to increase the armed SS from three divisions to six, Himmler undertook to streamline the command structure of the Waffen SS and to bring its units more directly under his own control. Eicke was a major obstacle in the path to this goal. At the end of the French campaign, Eicke enjoyed a measure of power and influence disproportionate to his official position as an SS division commander. The former concentration camp czar still exercised great personal influence among the SS officers he had left behind in the camp system. Through them, he had managed to collect enormous stockpiles of weapons, vehicles, and supplies, which were stored inside the concentration camps and reserved for exclusive use by the Totenkopfdivision. In addition, Eicke considered and used the reserve Death's Head units as his own personal manpower pool—thus hoarding for the Totenkopfdivision a huge source of replacements. During the last months before the attack in the west, he even designated a number of the reserve SSTV as replacement units for the Totenkopfdivision, and initiated the practice of transferring men back and forth between the reserve SSTV and SSTK when and as he wished.

To bring the entire expanded Waffen SS under his own control, Himmler had to break Eicke's hold on this sizeable private replacement system in order to use the reserve SSTV, their weapons and equipment as replacements for the entire Waffen SS. For assistance, the Reichsführer SS turned to several of Eicke's longtime enemies, who willingly assisted Himmler in carving up the empire of their arrogant colleague. Though Eicke resisted tenaciously, in the end he had to relinquish control of the camp supply dumps and the SSTV reserve units, and to accept a much-reduced role within the expanded Waffen SS.

In the exuberant atmosphere immediately after the victory in France, however, none of these tensions had yet appeared. During the first few weeks after the surrender, the mood among the men in the Totenkopfdivision was one of exultation mingled with the pride and relief that new soldiers feel once they have proven themselves under fire. In their new quarters south of Bordeaux Eicke and his men were in a holiday mood. While most of his officers and men swam in the warm waters of the Bay of Biscay, played soccer on the beach, lolled in sidewalk cafes, and relaxed with excursions into Bordeaux, Eicke and an SS private chosen from the ranks flew by special plane to Berlin at Hitler's personal invitation to attend the gigantic victory celebrations and the Reichstag session of July 19.[1]

During Eicke's absence, which also included several weeks leave with his family in Oranienburg, OKH ordered the Totenkopfdivision transferred from Bordeaux to Avallon. Here, SSTK was garrisoned with the Thirty-ninth Army Corps of General Weichs' Second Army just to the north of the demarcation line. In mid-July the division settled into its new quarters and began routine security assignments with patrols along the demarcation line. The days passed uneventfully as the first contingents of SS soldiers were allowed to return home to Germany on extended

[1] BAMA, III SS, 41/4, p. 110.

leave—the first that most of the men had enjoyed since the previous winter.

The relaxed atmosphere changed somewhat on July 18, when Colonel General Weichs issued detailed orders for SSTK in its relations with the French civilian populace. Knoblauch, substituting in Eicke's absence as division commander, was instructed to have the SS men assist in the return to normal civilian living conditions. Specifically, soldiers from SSTK were to help with the reopening of schools, businesses, and essential public services in the Avallon area. In addition, Knoblauch was warned to keep the Totenkopfdivision completely ready in case the political situation made it necessary to cross the demarcation line and occupy the rest of France. The signal to begin this contingency plan was to be the dispatch of the code-word "Ernte" (harvest). Within twelve hours after receipt of the code-word, SSTK was to move across the demarcation line and advance to the south to occupy Vichy, the capital of Marshal Pétain's government, and the nearby towns of Roanne and Mâcon.[2]

On July 29, shortly after Eicke's return from leave, Colonel General Weichs arrived in Avallon to inspect the Totenkopfdivision. The general especially wanted to see the artillery regiment and the reconnaissance battalion perform in exercises, and also wished to confer with Eicke about a new series of combat training exercises planned for late summer. After spending the morning watching field exercises, Weichs invited Eicke and the entire division staff to a sumptuous luncheon in Avallon. That afternoon he listened attentively for more than an hour to Eicke's detailed proposals for a new training program, then expressed complete satisfaction with what he had seen and with Eicke's plans. Before leaving for his own HQ, Weichs advised Eicke to keep the division in top condition, as it appeared likely that an invasion of the British isles would be mounted in early autumn and the Totenkopfdivision probably would be chosen to cross the channel and go ashore with the lead units.[3]

Throughout the first half of August, Eicke avoided overworking his men and engaged only in field exercises to prepare SSTK

[2] Ibid., pp. 142-49, 157, 227-29, 241-42; III SS, 44/2, p. 275; 41/8, 1, pp. 138-42.
[3] Ibid., III SS, 41/4, pp. 270-71, 281-82.

for the possible invasion of unoccupied France. As the prospects for this action grew dimmer, however, he complied with Weichs' original instructions and put the men in the division to work helping with the harvest around Avallon. The German military authorities were intent on gaining their share of the crops, and sent Eicke detailed instructions on how to harvest corn and grain. At the end of August, he was even given a large detachment of French POWs to help his own men with the work.[4]

While his men were busy in the fields and his officers helped supervise the expropriations from French farmers, Eicke's medical staff worked in a positive fashion to assist the civilian populace in the area where the division was quartered. In a policy initiated by Knoblauch during Eicke's absence, doctors from SSTK units in small villages and hamlets around Avallon assumed responsibility for the medical care of local civilians if no French doctor was available. With the cooperation of local French officials, this practice quickly became popular and resulted in SSTK doctors spending more time treating French civilians than tending to the men in the division. In the entire six-year history of the SS Totenkopfdivision this is the only recorded instance of such behavior by the division in dealing with an enemy civilian population.[5]

The Totenkopfdivision remained in the Avallon area until the end of August 1940. At that time, it was transferred back to coastal defense duty near Biarritz with the German Seventh Army, commanded by Colonel General Eugen Dollmann. This routine, uneventful summer in France culminated on September 2, 1940, when Eicke and Knoblauch received the commander in chief of the German army, Field Marshal Brauchitsch, for an inspection visit at the new division HQ at Dax.[6]

This long summer of inactivity left Eicke ample time to concen-

[4] Ibid., III SS, 44/2, pp. 292-93, 310.

[5] Ibid., pp. 297, 306-8. In occupied France, all Wehrmacht and SS men were forbidden normal contacts with French civilians. German soldiers initially could not buy food from the French and were under strict orders not to attend religious services in French churches. Since SSTK had no chaplains, this meant that any more professing Christians in the division had no chance whatever to attend religious services.

[6] BAMA, III SS, 41/4, pp. 324, 329-31, 341-42; III SS, 41/5, KTB No. 5 mit Anlagenband, 8; and IFZ, *Das Schwarze Korps*, issue for September 28, 1940, picture of Brauchitsch with Eicke during the inspection visit.

trate once again on internal and administrative problems in SSTK—especially the recurring question of poor discipline. During the battle of France, the SSTK court-martial system had remained inactive. Once the campaign ended, however, SSTK tribunals reconvened to face a large backlog of cases that had come to light during the fighting. In addition to the cases already on the docket, the arrival of large numbers of reservists resulted in a new rash of embarrassing incidents that kept the court-martial busy well into the autumn.

In a report written in November 1940, the judge advocate of the SS Totenkopfdivision revealed that the division's courts-martial had dealt with 137 cases since the end of June. Although most of the cases reported concerned serious traffic accidents involving death, injury, or property damage, in 37 instances the charges had involved criminal activity. These were mostly cases of plundering, larceny, rape (or attempted rape), and insubordination—crimes for which a prison sentence and expulsion from the SS was the punishment. Many of the prison sentences for serious crimes—including one case in which a private physically assaulted an NCO—Eicke changed to expulsion from the SS and an indefinite term of forced labor in the penal company attached to the engineer battalion of SSTK. During the entire summer only one officer in SSTK was court-martialed—an SS Untersturmführer convicted of cowardice in the face of the enemy was demoted to private, expelled from the SS, and sentenced indefinitely to the penal company.[7]

The decline in the number of criminal cases and the severity of the sentences imposed on those convicted may be explained by the fact that most of the disciplinary incidents mentioned in the division's records, including the most serious criminal charges, involved acts committed by SS men against French civilians or property. One SSTK private, for example, had been caught by an army major in the act of looting a house near Boulogne on May 31. The SS man was also drunk and had, before entering the house, tried to rape a French woman in front of a group of Ger-

[7] BAMA, III SS, 45/1, SS Richter, "Tätigkeitsberichte in Rahmen der SS-T.-Division," dated November 26, 1940; and III SS, 44/2, pp. 262, 310-11, 318, 319-22, 326, for a listing of the criminal cases tried by the SSTK court-martial.

man soldiers. After being arrested and turned over to Eicke by the army, the SS private was court-martialed on July 1, 1940. His punishment of two years in prison, however, was set aside by Eicke for an equal sentence to the penal company. The same treatment was also applied to another SS private convicted of public drunkenness and the rape and severe beating of an elderly French woman in Laventie.[8] Eicke remained obsessed with the idea of good discipline and strict obedience, but clearly did not regard acts of violence committed against the civilian population as serious offenses against the wartime code or as stains upon the "honor" of the SS.

SS officers who mistreated civilians during the French campaign often received nothing more than an official warning or reprimand from Eicke. Two young lieutenants in the SSTK artillery regiment took a large supply of pocket watches from a Jewish-owned store in Arras during the fighting and distributed them as gifts to their men. When the incident subsequently came to light, Eicke simply reprimanded the officers and had the watches collected by the commander of the artillery regiment and turned over to the Wehrmacht. Even while taking this mild action, Eicke felt compelled to explain to the two SS officers and to the men in the artillery regiment that the watches were being returned not because they had been taken from the shop of a Jew, but because the army had previously laid claim to the shop and all the merchandise in it—thus making the SS officers technically guilty of stealing Reich property.[9]

Eicke also had to devote considerable time during July 1940 to uncovering and dissolving a ring of swindlers operating within the ranks of the division. Early in the month, several SS soldiers were caught trying to pass off as Reichsmarks in French cafes and stores old 1000-mark notes dating from the great inflation of

---

[8] Ibid., III SS, 44/2, pp. 262-63. The seven men who did not have their sentences changed to service in the penal company were sent to concentration camps for their period of imprisonment.

[9] Ibid. In the Totenkopfdivision, Eicke also saw to it that the racial laws of the SS were enforced to the letter. During the summer of 1940, one SSTK soldier was court-martialed and expelled from the SS for associating with a half-Jewish woman after her ancestry had become known to him and his commanding officer had ordered him not to see her again (ibid., III SS, 44/2, p. 310).

1923. An investigation led subsequently to the arrest of three enlisted men in SSTK/I. R. 2, who appear to have been the source of supply for the invalid currency. Among the possessions of the three men were several sacks full of old inflation marks which Eicke promptly ordered burned.[10]

In an effort to relieve the restlessness and boredom in the months after the French campaign, Eicke made careful and elaborate arrangements for having several houses of prostitution in Bordeaux reserved solely for SSTK soldiers. These arrangements included a separate house for officers, regular inspection of the houses by SSTK medical officers, and strict sanitary regulations for all SS men who wished to indulge. In addition, Eicke warned all the men in the division that he would consider venereal infection a racial crime, and would court-martial any SS officer or enlisted man who contracted gonorrhea by neglecting the proper precautions.[11]

To make sure that he would be kept informed on their activities, Eicke ordered all officers and men in SSTK—under pain of court-martial—to report to their unit medical officers periodically for check-ups if they thought they might have contracted venereal disease. He then secretly instructed all the doctors in SSTK to send him the names of any men found to have venereal disease so they could be punished. Apparently, the basic stupidity of this tactic never occurred to Eicke. Virtually all the doctors in SSTK ignored the order and kept secret the names of those they were treating to save them from prosecution. This ridiculous policy epitomized the primitive, narrow pig-headedness that formed the basis of Eicke's personality, and demonstrated graphically his mania for obedience and his obsession for knowing everything that went on in his division.

News of Eicke's "gonorrhea orders" traveled mirthfully up the SS chain of command and eventually got him into serious trouble. In December 1940 the story reached Himmler, who flew into a rage and sent Eicke the stiffest dressing-down of his SS career. In an angry letter sent from Oslo on January 30, 1941, Himmler scathingly informed Eicke that his orders to the doctors in SSTK violated basic German civil laws recognized by the regime, and

[10] Ibid., pp. 262-66.   [11] Ibid., pp. 267, 310, 320.

126

declared bluntly that he was disgusted with Eicke's pettiness in matters concerning the discipline of the troops. Hitting Eicke at his most vulnerable point, Himmler added that he had shamed the entire SS with these crazy (wahnsinnig) orders, leaving Himmler doubtful of Eicke's sanity and fitness to command an SS division. The Reichsführer SS then concluded his lengthy rebuke by ordering Eicke to cease punishing those who contracted venereal disease and by warning that he personally would penalize any doctor in SSTK who revealed the names of men being treated.[12]

This severe rebuke from Himmler was but one in a whole series of clashes between Eicke on the one side, and Himmler and Eicke's senior SS colleagues on the other. Most of the disputes arose as a result of the eccentricities Eicke practiced on his men, or grew out of the arrogant and high-handed tone he assumed when dealing with other SS agencies. Whenever he tangled with his SS colleagues, Eicke appears to have been motivated by several factors. The first was the constant and nagging fear that his enemies, aided by informants within the Totenkopfdivision, were intriguing to undermine his influence with Himmler. Secondly, Eicke was determined to control completely all matters concerning SSTK while retaining his influential ties with the reserve SSTV and the concentration camp system. Finally, and most significantly, he was obsessed with preserving the racial purity of the Totenkopfdivision. At a time when the Waffen SS was undergoing tremendous expansion and the standards of selectivity were beginning to slip, Eicke remained the same fanatic apostle of SS racial elitism he had been in 1936. He was unwilling to compromise the doctrine of racial purity by admitting "inferior elements" as replacements for SSTK, and viewed with alarm the resourceful methods for expanded recruiting dreamed up by the

---

[12] BAKO, NS-19/370, Himmler to Eicke, January 30, 1941. Himmler was also enraged by Eicke's habit of listing the punishments of officers publicly in division orders, and by his practice of disciplining high-ranking SS officers as though they were privates. The Reichsführer's anger was aroused particularly when Eicke ordered Standartenführer Kleinheisterkamp, a regimental commander, confined to quarters allegedly for failing to carry out an order, and then published the news of Kleinheisterkamp's punishment in a special circular to all units in SSTK. See also the account in Höhne, pp. 428-29.

ingenious Gottlob Berger, the powerful chief of the Waffen SS Recruiting Office.

To Eicke, it appeared that the men in charge of the SS selecting and recruiting agencies were trying to curb his own power and build up theirs by inundating the armed SS with unqualified men who would destroy the elitist nature of the SS. In an attempt to halt these supposedly pernicious developments, Eicke became embroiled in a continuous series of disputes during the summer and autumn of 1940.

The first of these clashes occurred when Eicke refused to accept many of the SS replacements sent him during the summer of 1940. When the first groups of reservists arrived in SSTK on June 25, Eicke expressed strong dissatisfaction, complaining to Berlin that many of the young men sent him were criminals and obvious racial inferiors incapable of discipline and unworthy of wearing the SS uniform. Overlooking the fact that many of the reservists came directly from SSTK reserve units in Dachau, Breslau, Radolfzell, Arolsen, and Prague, Eicke accused Berger and the officials in RuSHA (the SS Race and Resettlement Office) of conspiring deliberately to send him unqualified replacements. Consequently, he ordered Standartenführer Dr. Fuhrländer, the division's "racial expert," to conduct racial examinations on all incoming recruits and to reject those whose acceptance would damage the racial purity of the Totenkopfdivision. He also directed his individual unit commanders to screen carefully all arriving replacements and to send back to their respective reserve units any who had criminal records.

Finally, Eicke ordered that incoming reservists be segregated for training together in a group, and directed that they not be assigned to regular units until their training officers were sure their presence would not weaken or disrupt discipline.[13]

To protect himself and SSTK even further during this large-scale personnel shuffle, Eicke forced the first group of older men released from duty with the Totenkopfdivision to sign an oath swearing themselves to complete secrecy about everything they

[13] BAMA, III SS, 41/4, pp. 55, 284-90; BAKO, NS-19/neu-1668, Kommando der Waffen SS, den 27. Juli 1940, "Marschbefehl;" and BAKO, NS-19/neu-1711, Kommando der Waffen SS, den 15. August, 1940, "Auffüllung der SS-V. und SS-T.-Division."

had seen and done while serving with SSTK. This was intended specifically, it seems, to prevent any talk of the Le Paradis atrocity from becoming public gossip. These practices threw the recruiting and replacement system of the Waffen SS into major confusion and touched off such a furor in Berlin that Eicke found himself the target of bitter criticism by several of Himmler's most powerful vassals.[14]

The strongest protest came from Gottlob Berger, who reacted to Eicke's rejection of the recruits by complaining in turn to RuSHA, to SS Brigadeführer Hans Jüttner, the chief of the operations office of the SS (SS Führungshauptamt), and finally to Himmler. It appears, moreover, that Berger's hostility to Eicke and the vigor with which he complained about the latter's high-handed tactics had a direct influence in prompting the Reichsführer SS to crack down on his former concentration camp commander.

Berger's motives were by no means solely the result of jealousy. The gravity of the problems Eicke was creating for Berger may be illustrated by the fact that in mid-September 1940 Eicke had rejected 500 of the 700 replacements he had received since June. The only explanation given Berger was that the men rejected were racial inferiors or "obvious criminal elements." The reserve SS units, which Berger had filled in the meantime with new recruits to replace the men sent to SSTK, consequently found themselves with more men than they could handle. As a result, Berger's office had the problem of trying to keep up with the many SS recruits being shuttled back and forth across the Reich by train from unit to unit as reserve SS commanders attempted to relocate Eicke's rejects.[15]

Eicke's first warning that a major storm was brewing came

[14] BAMA, III SS, 41/4, pp. 289-90. A copy of this release oath is in the records of the Totenkopfdivision. In the oath, the departing SS soldier recognized that "any trashy criticism of my superiors or my unit harms the image of the SS," and swore that he "would not lodge any grievance, or written complaint against my superiors or my SS unit" (ibid., p. 290; and Stein, p. 78).

[15] BAKO, NS-19/neu-1711, "Chef des R.u.S.-Hauptamtes an den Kommandeur der SS-Totenkopf-Division," dated September 16, 1940. The most exasperating stunt Eicke pulled was that of rejecting an entire group of 180 SS recruits sent to him in mid-August 1940. No sooner had the men arrived and Eicke had a look at them, than he sent them all back to the reserve SS Kaserne at Arolson, prompting the bewildered garrison commander to telephone Berlin for instructions as to what to do with the men.

from SS Oberführer Otto Hoffmann, the chief of RuSHA. Hoffmann wrote to Eicke on September 16 to complain about the rejections. Indicating that he had learned from Berger the full details about what was going on, Hoffmann demanded that Eicke cease giving racial examinations to SS recruits who had already satisfied the racial requirements of RuSHA when they joined the SS. Such examinations, Hoffmann complained, were an unwarranted slap at both Berger and the RuSHA. He also warned Eicke that Berger had asked Himmler to prevent the rejection of SS replacements, but declared that the RuSHA was willing to let the matter drop if Eicke would agree to stop racially examining new recruits.[16]

Eicke replied on October 3, denying falsely that he had subjected anyone to a racial examination, and claiming that among the unfit recruits he sent back were men with serious criminal records. Attempting to substantiate this allegation, he enclosed with the letter a copy of the police record of one recruit (relatively weak evidence since the dossier listed only a conviction for petty larceny). Eicke ended his reply by assuring Hoffmann that Berger was in no position to question Eicke's judgment since he had been in the SS much longer than Berger and took orders only from the Reichsführer SS.[17]

One week after replying to Hoffmann, Eicke took his case to Karl Wolff. In a long letter of October 11, he complained of Berger's efforts to destroy Himmler's confidence in him, and assured Wolff that the only men who had been sent back to reserve SSTV units were those who definitely were criminals. Eicke concluded by asking Wolff to suggest to Himmler that a full investigation be made of Berger's recruiting policies, which Eicke claimed were turning the SS into a vast dumping ground for criminals. Wolff, however, knew better than to approach the Reichsführer SS with such twaddle, since Berger's recruiting methods already had met with Himmler's enthusiastic approval.[18]

[16] Ibid. Hoffmann also charged that Eicke had even subjected two SS officers—a company and a battalion commander—to complete racial examinations before accepting them into the Totenkopfdivision.

[17] BAKO, NS-19/neu-1711, Eicke to SS Oberführer Otto Hoffmann, October 3, 1940.

[18] Ibid., letters from Eicke to SS Brigadeführer Hans Jüttner, dated October 3

Berger, who remained silent about the dispute during October, fought back stubbornly a month later, determined to discredit Eicke by having the last word in the matter. In mid-November, he dispatched a long letter to Wolff, describing Eicke as one of the "self-styled princes" of the SS who caused trouble for everyone by placing his own interests above those of the SS. In addition, Berger claimed he had information to prove that Eicke was guilty of mistreating the SS recruits sent to SSTK from the reserve SSTV. The personnel dossiers of the reservists released from the Totenkopfdivision, Berger continued, indicated that over sixty percent had been so dissatisfied with their service in the division that they wanted nothing more to do with the SS. To keep Eicke from getting into serious trouble, Wolff temporarily withheld from Himmler all of the correspondence and the details of the dispute.[19]

The stories of dissatisfaction in the Totenkopfdivision and accounts of Eicke's brutal discipline, however, were by then already common knowledge in the upper echelons of the SS and had provoked criticism of Eicke from other quarters. SS Brigadeführer Hans Jüttner, Eicke's titular immediate superior as chief of the SS Führungshauptamt (SSFHA),[20] had learned, through information supplied by Berger, about the problems Eicke was creating for the Waffen SS. SSFHA had also received direct complaints from officers in the Allgemeine SS who had served briefly with SSTK during the battle of France. As a result, Jüttner made his own inquiries, specifically demanding from Eicke an explanation about the oath of secrecy the men released from the Totenkopfdivision had had to sign. Eicke reacted testily by claiming that the oath was nothing more than a routine security measure. As to the question of alleged dissatisfaction in SSTK, Eicke told Jüttner in no

---

and 11, 1940; and a long letter from Eicke to Karl Wolff written on October 11, 1940.

[19] BAKO, NS-19/neu-1711, letter from Gottlob Berger to Karl Wolff, dated November 13, 1940.

[20] The SS Operations Office (SSFHA) was created officially by Himmler on August 15, 1940 to coordinate all the military activities of the SS. This was done functionally through the main section of the SSFHA designated as the Kommandoamt der Waffen SS. The SSFHA served throughout the war as the SS equivalent of the high commands of the other branches in the German armed forces. See especially Stein, pp. 105-6.

uncertain terms to mind his own business. Bristling with the self-righteousness he always employed in a tight spot, Eicke raged at Jüttner for even questioning his actions as a division commander. He stated further that he considered himself a direct subordinate of the Reichsführer SS, to whom alone he was answerable in SSTK matters. He was not about to tolerate any interference from Jüttner or anyone else at SSFHA who knew nothing about commanding a division. He would, he conceded, be willing to cooperate with Jüttner as an equal and a comrade if the latter would respect his wishes, but he would not take orders from the SSFHA under any circumstances. This was justifiable, Eicke concluded (with a dig at Jüttner) because he himself, unlike the chief of SSFHA, had risen through the ranks of the SS, acquiring in the process the kind of experience in leading men that had earned him the trust and confidence of the Reichsführer SS.[21]

This remarkably insulting and insubordinate letter, which would have garnered an army division commander instant dismissal or worse, gained Eicke a temporary victory in the matter of replacements for SSTK. The rejected SS recruits were replaced by men who satisfied him, and Jüttner made no further inquiries about conditions in SSTK or the oath of secrecy Eicke had imposed upon those who had served under him.

There were several reasons for this unusual outcome. Eicke's status as a member of the SS "old guard," the formidable reputation he had acquired as head of the concentration camp system, and finally the fact that he was one of only three battle-tested SS division commanders, enabled him to get away with a great deal. On the other hand, Jüttner could afford to allow Eicke the temporary luxury of an insulting tirade against the SSFHA. For Eicke was, at that very moment, being brought to heel rapidly on much more important ground—territory on which Jüttner enjoyed the full backing of Himmler against Eicke. This involved the major reorganization and expansion of the Waffen SS that was already underway.

[21] BAKO, NS-19/neu-1668, memorandum prepared by Eicke's adjutant, SS Hauptsturmführer Paul-Werner Hoppe, summarizing a discussion he had with Jüttner in Berlin on October 20, 1940; and a follow-up letter from Eicke to Jüttner, dated October 22, 1940; and Jüttner's reply to Eicke, dated October 24, 1940.

This crucial enlargement of the Waffen SS began on August 15, 1940, when Himmler dissolved the office of inspector of SSTV and ordered the incorporation of the reserve Death's Head units into the active armed SS.[22] All SS officers and men in the inspectorate were transferred to Jüttner's Kommando der Waffen SS (soon to be part of the SSFHA), while all sixteen of the reserve Totenkopfstandarten, the two Death's Head cavalry regiments and the reserve formations of the Totenkopfdivision also were subordinated to the control of Jüttner's office. In addition, Jüttner assumed responsibility for training all replacements for the SS field divisions.[23]

Accordingly, Jüttner set to work quickly reorganizing the reserve system of the Waffen SS, thus breaking the hold Eicke had maintained on the reserve Death's Head formations. This was accomplished by two methods. In September 1940, Jüttner disbanded some of the Totenkopf units designated specifically as reserve formations of SSTK. On September 12, Eicke's motor-training battalion at Oranienburg was dissolved and the older men serving in it released from active SS duty. Less than a month later, Jüttner began disbanding Eicke's reserve motorcycle company at Radolfzell on Lake Constance and transferred the men to the Totenkopfdivision's reserve motorcycle battalion at Ellwangen. Finally, he ordered the consolidation of several more SSTK replacement units and transferred some of their men to other reserve formations and to the concentration camps.[24]

[22] For clarity, it might be well to remember that when he assumed command of SSTK, Eicke's former post as inspector of concentration camps and commander of SS Death's Head units was divided by Himmler into two separate offices. Glücks succeeded Eicke as inspector of concentration camps, while SS Oberführer Alfred Schweder, a Heydrich protégé from the SD, assumed the new job of inspector of the SS Death's Head units.

[23] BAKO, NS-19/374, Kommando der Waffen SS, August 1, 1940, "Auflösung der Inspektion der SS-T.-Standarten;" and ibid., NS-19/neu-1711, circular from Kdo. der Waffen SS, dated August 1, 1940, outlining the organizational changes. See also Stein, pp. 104-7.

[24] BAKO, NS-19/neu-1668; and NS-19/374, a series of circulars and orders dating from the beginning of September to the end of December 1940 and sent from the SSFHA to all Waffen SS units. Among the SSTV incorporated into front-line Waffen SS divisions that autumn was the Eleventh SS Totenkopfstandarte. This was the notorious unit whose sordid behavior in Poland the year before had prompted the written protests by Colonel General Blaskowitz. After the battle of France,

To solidify control of the SSFHA over the Waffen SS reserve system, Jüttner also had to end Eicke's practice of raiding the SS supply dumps in the concentration camps. To do this, Jüttner had to break the personal contacts Eicke had with the camp commandants and other SS officers who had served with him before the war, and who remained in Dachau, Buchenwald and Oranienburg. The methods Jüttner chose were simple. He either transferred Eicke's friends out of the camp system or took disciplinary action against them to break the SSTK monopoly on the war matériel stored in the camps.

Before he moved against Eicke's henchmen in the camps, however, Jüttner offered to settle the matter by compromise. During a long conversation with Jüttner in Berlin in August 1940, Eicke consented to give the Waffen SS Procurement Office all the war matériel his agents had stockpiled in Dachau and Oranienburg. In return, Jüttner agreed to let Eicke keep Buchenwald as an exclusive supply depot for the Totenkopfdivision. This was especially important to Eicke since the camp contained the entire supply of spare parts for all the Opel vehicles in the division. Jüttner soon learned, however, that when Eicke wanted something badly, neither agreements nor orders deterred him.[25]

On the night of October 4, 1940, officers of the Waffen SS Procurement Office by chance caught Eicke's chief "requisitioner," SS Sturmbannführer Weinhöbel, at that time an administrative officer at Buchenwald, trying to bluff his way out of Dachau with a convoy of supplies destined for the Totenkopfdivision. Weinhöbel was arrested and taken to Berlin to face Jüttner. When queried about his pilfering, Weinhöbel would only say that he had been acting on direct orders from Eicke. When word of Weinhöbel's arrest reached Eicke's HQ in France, Jüttner quickly learned the importance of his prisoner and the full details of Weinhöbel's activities as a procurement agent for the Totenkopfdivision.

Himmler transferred the Eleventh SSTV to Holland for occupation duty, and then in November 1940 ordered the entire regiment incorporated into the SS Verfügungsdivision (ibid., NS-19/374, order from the SSFHA dated November 23, 1940; and Stein, p. 107).

[25] BAKO, NS-19/neu-1668, letter from Eicke to Karl Wolff, written on October 9, 1940; and a letter from Jüttner to Eicke, dated October 24, 1940.

After hearing that Jüttner intended to have Weinhöbel court-martialed, Eicke appealed urgently for help from his friend nearest the throne. In a letter to Karl Wolff on October 9, Eicke begged Wolff to intercede with Himmler to rescue Weinhöbel from Jüttner's clutches. In glowing terms Eicke described the herculean feats Weinhöbel had performed in collecting huge stores of weapons and equipment for the prewar Totenkopfverbände. Depicting Weinhöbel as an invaluable asset to the SS and to himself personally, Eicke assured Wolff that the whole "campaign to discredit Weinhöbel" was the result of a vicious conspiracy initiated by the Waffen SS Procurement Office and assisted by Jüttner.[26]

That same day, Eicke fired off an angry letter to Jüttner demanding Weinhöbel's release. In bitter rage, Eicke accused Jüttner and Gärtner (chief of the procurement office) of trying to ruin Weinhöbel so Himmler would believe that they themselves had stockpiled all the war matériel. Furthermore, Eicke fumed, Weinhöbel had been acting under his instructions to let nothing except Himmler's direct order stop him from taking the supplies out of Dachau. Consequently, Eicke concluded, the charges against Weinhöbel should be dropped and placed against Eicke himself. If Jüttner was not willing to press charges against him, Eicke taunted, then Weinhöbel should be released, and he (Eicke) given back *his* concentration camp.[27]

As a follow-up, on October 20 Eicke sent his adjutant, SS Hauptsturmführer Paul-Werner Hoppe, to Berlin to confer with Jüttner. Hoppe's visit occurred as Jüttner's investigation of the "requisitioning" activities ended. Jüttner sent his reply to Eicke with Hoppe. Writing on October 24, he smoothly informed Eicke that the SSFHA knew Weinhöbel had—on Eicke's orders—been

[26] BAKO, NS-19/neu-1668, Eicke to Karl Wolff, October 9, 1940; and Jüttner to Eicke, October 24, 1940. In his letter to Wolff, Eicke claimed that Weinhöbel, as a key staff member of the prewar concentration camp inspectorate, had been responsible for arming the SS guard units at Dachau, Oranineburg, and Buchenwald. In the process, Eicke boasted, such huge quantities of arms and ammunition were collected that the SSTV organized after the Czech crisis had been armed without a hitch.

[27] Ibid., letter from Eicke to Jüttner of October 9, 1940. The emphasis is in the original. The copy of this letter in the Himmler files is Jüttner's, which, aside from this one heavily underlined annotation and his initials, contains no marginal comments about the matter.

sending weapons and supplies secretly to the Totenkopfdivision from the camps for a long time, even after the deal he and Eicke had made the previous August. Furthermore, Jüttner continued, Weinhöbel had been disrespectful and insubordinate when caught, so his court-martial would be carried through. Faced with Jüttner's resolution—and physical possession of Weinhöbel— Eicke had no choice but to admit defeat.[28]

By removing Weinhöbel from Buchenwald, Jüttner eliminated Eicke's most resourceful remaining protégé in the concentration camp system. Eicke continued to use the supply dump in Buchenwald as his own, but was forced to go through the procurement office of the Waffen SS for supplies and equipment, rather than taking what he pleased wherever he could find it. In thus establishing a precedent with the Weinhöbel case, Jüttner severed Eicke's most important link with the concentration camps, strengthening in the process Himmler's control of the expanding Waffen SS.[29]

For Eicke, there was at least one small consolation. In December 1940, he finally got rid of the staff officer in SSTK whom he regarded as the chief spy for Himmler and Jüttner. SS Brigadeführer Knoblauch, Montigny's replacement as SSTK operations officer, returned to Berlin on December 9 for reassignment. By then, relations between Eicke and Knoblauch had deteriorated to such an extent that there was little else Himmler could do. In an attempt to mollify Eicke, the Reichsführer SS permitted him to choose Knoblauch's successor from among the officer corps of SSTK. The man Eicke chose was one of his most trusted subordinates, SS Sturmbannführer Heinz Lammerding, who at that time commanded the engineer battalion of the Totenkopfdivision. Lammerding had been a construction engineer before join-

[28] BAKO, NS-19/neu-1668, memorandum by Hoppe describing his conversation with Jüttner on October 21, 1940; letter from Eicke to Jüttner of October 22, 1940; and Jüttner's reply of October 24. Karl Wolff wisely kept the whole Weinhöbel affair from Himmler, fearing that the revelations of the larcenous activities in the concentration camps might result in Eicke's dismissal from command of the Totenkopfdivision.

[29] Eicke's loss of influence over the concentration camps was a purely personal matter. The extensive functional connections between SSTK and the other Waffen SS divisions and the camp system remained intact and even expanded as the war progressed. (See below, chapter nine).

3. SS Obersturmbannführer Heinz Lammerding, Eicke's protégé and operations officer of the Totenkopfdivision.

ing the SS in 1935, and had been singled out by Eicke early in 1936 as a man with a bright future as an SS officer in the concentration camp system. Being on the staff of Eicke's KZ (concentration camp) inspectorate, Lammerding followed his chief to war in October 1939 to organize and command the engineer battalion of SSTK. In choosing Lammerding for chief of operations, Eicke found a man both competent and obedient, and through whom he could exercise greater personal control over the division.[30]

During the long months he was feuding with other SS agencies, Eicke managed somehow not to neglect affairs in his own command. Between mid-August 1940 and the end of May 1941, a good part of his time was devoted to reorganizing and enlarging the Totenkopfdivision. His objective was twofold. First, he wished to increase the mobility and speed of SSTK. As an initial step toward this goal, he stripped his motorized infantry regiments of the more cumbersome vehicles and the lightly armed infantry that marched with them, then transferred these men and vehicles to the rearward supply columns. Eicke began a concerted effort to find more and faster vehicles—especially trucks. With little hope of obtaining what he needed either from Gärtner or the Wehrmacht, he turned to the nearby vehicle parks crammed with captured French army trucks and armored cars. By the spring of 1941 he had more than enough vehicles for the division, whose columns included Peugeot, Renault, and Citroen cars and trucks, and even a few prized American-made Dodge, Ford, and Studebaker trucks.[31]

Secondly, Eicke sought during the interlude between campaigns to strengthen the offensive striking power of the Totenkopfdivision. This was to be achieved by converting the motorized infantry regiments into powerful, self-contained Kampfgruppen or battle groups, and by increasing significantly the firepower of these reorganized combat formations. A Kampfgruppe was organized around the infantry regiment, and

[30] BAMA, III SS, 41/5, KTB No. 5 mit Anlagenband, vol. 1, pp. 8-10; USDC, SS Personalakte Lammerding, summary of the materials in Lammerding's SS service records, especially his Dienstlaufbahn and a series of efficiency reports written by Eicke in 1938 and 1939.

[31] Ibid., pp. 103, 180-81.

included attached companies (in some instances whole battalions) of engineers, communications personnel, antitank gunners, motorcyclists, plus fully motorized light and heavy artillery and antiaircraft batteries. According to Eicke's new plans the Totenkopfdivision, when deployed for action, would have two Kampfgruppen advancing together behind the screen of the reconnaissance battalion, with the other motorized infantry regiment and the rest of the combat units some distance back, moving along in front of the units from the supply and administrative services. As in the French campaign, Eicke planned to travel into combat in his staff car near the front of one Kampfgruppe.[32]

Eicke's efforts to increase the firepower of the division were equally comprehensive. In December 1940 he obtained from the army a surplus stock of 500 tripod-mounted machine guns, the bulk of which he divided equally among the three infantry regiments and the reconnaissance battalion. Three months later, with help from Himmler, Eicke strengthened the division's muscle even more. In April 1941 the Reichsführer SS authorized the formation of a full-sized Flak battalion for the Totenkopfdivision. To make this unit operational as quickly as possible, Eicke picked trained gunners from his artillery and infantry units and sent them to Dachau, where the Flak battalion was to be organized and its men given their initial training. This battalion subsequently joined the SSTK at the end of May, giving Eicke formidable extra firepower from fully motorized twelve-piece batteries of 20 mm and 37 mm Flak and a four-piece battery of the famous high-velocity 88's.[33]

Finally, in the last weeks before the invasion of Russia, Himmler granted one of Eicke's long-standing wishes. In early June, SSTK received its long-promised allotment of twelve 150 mm heavy-artillery pieces, which Eicke assembled immediately into a separate heavy battalion of the artillery regiment. At the same time, Himmler gave Eicke permission to organize a fully motorized reserve battalion for SSTK from whatever men and

[32] Ibid., 41/4, pp. 312, 319-21; 41/5, vol. 2, pp. 98-99; and BAKO, NS-19/neu-1711, Kommando der Waffen SS, den 15. August, 1940, "Auffüllung der SS-V.-und SS-T.-Division."

[33] BAMA, III SS, 41/5, vol. 2, pp. 53-55, 131-36.

equipment were available. This new battalion would serve as the Totenkopfdivision's primary source of replacements, and theoretically would be trained and equipped well enough to step into front-line duty on the shortest possible notice. Eicke managed to organize the new battalion almost overnight. He simply transferred three experienced infantry companies, along with a hodgepodge of captured French vehicles, to the SSTK reserve battalion at Brno in the Protectorate of Bohemia-Moravia.[34]

The most time-consuming activity Eicke engaged in during the lapse between campaigns was that of supervising the continued combat and political training of his men. He and the members of his staff went over every detail of the division's performance in May and June, and stressed the elimination of past mistakes as the main objective for the regimental-sized exercises conducted along the demarcation line in August and September. Eicke's training techniques and the division's combat performance both were complimented in late July when the army requested that a score of officers and NCOs from SSTK be released temporarily to help direct the training and reorganization of the Third and Tenth Divisions into motorized infantry divisions. In return, the army opened its technical schools to as many SS officers and NCOs as could be accommodated. Eicke took full advantage of the army's new friendliness, and during August and September 1940 sent nearly half the officers in the SSTK artillery regiment in shifts to the artillery school at Jüterbog for intensified training.[35]

As the autumn of 1940 approached and the Luftwaffe failed to destroy the Royal Air Force, plans for the invasion of England were postponed repeatedly and then cancelled quietly. Even before he officially abandoned plans for the invasion, Hitler's fundamental racial and ideological objectives forced a German strategic about-face. By early autumn, Hitler had decided to attack Soviet Russia in the spring of 1941, even before the final capitulation of the British. As a result, there was momentary confusion and inactivity at both OKW and OKH, followed by a period of intense activity during the autumn and winter as the plans for what eventually became "Operation Barbarossa" took shape.[36]

[34] Ibid., 42/2, p. 106; 41/5, vol. 2, pp. 176-81.
[35] Ibid., 41/4, pp. 230, 237, 299-302.
[36] According to General Halder (*Kriegstagebuch*, II, pp. 49-50), Hitler dis-

The shocks caused by this strategic reversal traveled quickly down the military ladder to division level, and may be detected readily in the activities of the Totenkopfdivision between September 1940 and February 1941. At the time Hitler began his complete redirection of the war, the strictest secrecy was observed and the number of those privy to developments remained small. This privileged clique certainly did not include SS division commanders such as Eicke; indeed, not even Himmler knew what was afoot during the first months of planning. Long before he learned officially of the plans for the attack, however, Eicke had guessed where the next campaign would be, and had taken several extra steps to prepare his men accordingly.[37]

The first indication that the war was taking a momentous turn

---

cussed his intention of attacking the Soviet Union before a gathering of generals and admirals at the Berghof on the Obersalzburg on July 31, 1940. Hitler did not finally call off the planned invasion of England until September 17, 1940. See Walter Ansel, *Hitler Confronts England* (Durham, N. C., 1960), p. 299. For details concerning Hitler's change in strategy and the development of plans for "Barbarossa," see especially Andreas Hillgruber, *Hitlers Strategie: Politik und Kriegführung, 1940-1941* (Frankfurt am Main, 1965), a massive work that is the most thorough and reliable guide to the subject. Also valuable are the accounts in Norman Rich, *Hitler's War Aims*, vol. 1, *Ideology, The Nazi State, and the Course of Expansion* (New York, 1973), pp. 204-23; Barry A. Leach, *German Strategy Against Russia, 1939-1941* (Oxford, 1973), esp. pp. 227-41; Larry H. Addington, *The Blitzkrieg Era and the German General Staff, 1865-1941* (New Brunswick, N. J., 1971), pp. 177-212; Walter Warlimont, *Inside Hitler's Headquarters, 1939-1945* (New York, 1964), pp. 104-71; Trumbull Higgins, *Hitler and Stalin: The Third Reich in a Two-Front War, 1937-1943* (New York, 1966), pp. 57-129; and Alfred Philippi and Ferdinand Heim, *Der Feldzug gegen Sowjetrussland: 1941 bis 1945* (Stuttgart, 1962), pp. 19-53.

[37] By the end of January 1941, Himmler had received comprehensive instructions from Hitler concerning the role the SS was expected to play in the administration of the occupied regions of the Soviet Union. On March 3, 1941, Hitler informed General Alfred Jodl, operations chief at OKW, that Himmler in his capacity as Reichsführer SS would be responsible for directing the extermination of the Jewish-Bolshevik ruling class in the occupied Russian territories behind the army's operational zone. A general description of Himmler's "special tasks" in the east was subsequently incorporated into the OKW directive of March 13, 1941 dealing with the political administration of the conquered Russian territories. See especially Höhne, pp. 324-25; and Hillgruber, *Hitlers Strategie*, pp. 523-24.

For the SS Totenkopfdivision, the only break in an otherwise monotonous autumn came with the celebration of Eicke's forty-ninth birthday on October 17. Himmler came to Dax to pay his respects and review the division while enroute to a state visit in Spain (BAMA, III SS, 41/5, vol. 1, KTB No. 5, pp. 6-7; and IFZ, *Das Schwarze Korps*, issue for October 31, 1940, for a story and photographs of Himmler's visit to the Totenkopfdivision).

came in early November 1940. After months without specific orders for combat training, Eicke suddenly received detailed instructions from the Seventh Army for a training program he was directed to begin at once and carry through until the following spring. The main emphasis in the new training was on mobile warfare over much broader and more open expanses of territory than those upon which the German Army had previously fought. Units of the Totenkopfdivision were taught to move up to sixty kilometers in one day, pause for several hours rest, and then move the same distance during the night. The new SSTK field exercises included special drills in assaulting fortified positions, fighting in villages and heavily wooded areas, and practice in developing camouflage techniques for long distance moves through open country. In addition, the SSTK engineer battalion devoted most of its training time to the techniques of rapid bridge building, while the infantry regiments and the tank-destroyer battalion concentrated on the tactics for fighting large formations of tanks at close range. Finally, the Seventh Army training directive stipulated that Eicke's artillery regiment undergo an unusually thorough series of drills designed to increase its speed and accuracy of fire, and its ability to operate in coordination with the Luftwaffe.[38]

Unlike that of the year before in Germany, the weather in southern France during late autumn and early winter presented no problems. Intensive training continued uninterrupted through November in crisp, sunny weather broken only at intervals by cold winds and rain. The good weather held into December and gave

[38] BAMA, III SS, 41/5, vol. 2, pp. 22-40, copy of a long memorandum from the Ia of the Seventh Army outlining the training program the Totenkopfdivision was to follow for the winter and spring of 1940-1941. On the basis of these instructions and widespread rumors concerning Spain's imminent entry into the war, Eicke concluded that Hitler planned to attack either Portugal or Gibraltar, and wrote requesting Himmler to obtain an important role for the Totenkopfdivision in the Iberian operation (BAKO, NS-19/335, letter from Eicke to Himmler, dated November 20, 1940). In the final plans developed by OKW for a dash across Spain and the seizure of Gibraltar—the operation code-named "Felix"—the Totenkopfdivision would be part of the Thirty-ninth Army Corps, and would have the objective of capturing Seville on the Guadalquivir River to provide flank and rear security for the German forces assaulting the fortress of Gibraltar. The standard work on this aspect of Hitler's wartime strategy is Charles B. Burdick, *Germany's Military Strategy and Spain in World War II* (Syracuse, N. Y., 1968), esp. pp. 57, 67, and 70 for the projected role of the Totenkopfdivision in Spain.

Eicke yet another sign that future campaigns would be fought in areas far from France. The unusually favorable climate allowed the units of SSTK to comply with new instructions from the Seventh Army to practice loading and unloading entire battalions and regiments—men and equipment—on and off trains.[39]

When the weather finally became harsh just before Christmas and forced a slowdown in combat training, Eicke was well prepared for a switch to an extensive program of political indoctrination. Materials for this major undertaking had been gathered during the autumn by Fuhrländer, who had also worked out a comprehensive curriculum for the men in the division. With Eicke's approval, Fuhrländer proposed dividing the entire Totenkopfdivision into small discussion-study groups that would meet several times a week under the guidance of experienced SS officers. These discussion groups would follow the schedule and deal with a different subject in the curriculum every month. The list of general topics included "nationality and home" (an examination of the different regions of Germany), the history and geography of German-speaking central Europe, biology (as it pertained to Nazi racial theories), and chemistry and physics. Each general topic, in turn, was divided into specific subtopics for weekly discussion among the study groups.[40] For the period between December 1940 and April 1941, the men were assigned the topics of nationality and home, history, geography, and biology. Eicke and Fuhrländer considered these subjects most important to the proper education of young SS recruits, since they presented most of the basic Nazi racial and political theories.[41]

As a reference and study guide for the discussions during the winter, the SS man could turn to a two-volume mimeographed

[39] BAMA, III SS, 41/5, vol. 2, pp. 42, 59-65.

[40] The study of German history, for example, was divided into periods beginning with "Henry I and the First Reich," and "Henry the Lion and the Germanic Knight Orders." The historical subdivisions then continued down to modern times through "the Vikings and the Hanse," "The Peasants War," "The Hohenzollerns, 1640-1780," "Prussia—the Foundation of the Reich," "War of Liberation of Count Stein," and "Bismarck and the Second Reich." This Nazified version of Germany's history then concluded with sections on "Adolf Hitler and the Third Reich," "The Concept of the Reich since the First Century," and a final section on "The History and Mission of the SS" (BAMA, III SS, 41/5, vol. 2, p. 248).

[41] Ibid.

work compiled by Fuhrländer entitled "Schwert und Pflug" (Sword and Plough). The name of the manual, according to its introduction, honored the two most revered symbols of the SS creed—blood and soil. The sword grasped by the SS man represented the protection of Nordic purity by the elite order of armed knights, while the plow symbolized the virtues of the German peasantry—the foundation of the "racial community" (Volksgemeinschaft) from which many SS men came. These two implements, the sword and the plough, allegedly symbolized the basis of strength in the "Greater German Reich" (Grossdeutschland).[42]

The pages of "Schwert und Pflug" are filled with the stock collection of Nordic nonsense, perverted history, and lurid racist propaganda that formed the core of National Socialist "philosophy." Indeed, long sections of the work are simply block quotations lifted from Alfred Rosenberg's befuddled *Der Mythos des zwanzigsten Jahrhunderts* (The Myth of the Twentieth Century)—the party's official statement of philosophy. In the first of the two volumes of "Schwert und Pflug," Germany's mortal enemies are identified in order of importance as the Jews, Freemasonry, Marxism, and liberalism. The Jews and the churches, moreover, are depicted as partners in a conspiracy to destroy the German family by depriving the peasant of his land. Culturally, according to the book, the "Jewish racial parasite" threatens to dominate the arts, the theater, and the press in order to attack German things. This sinister Jewish cultural activity, moreover, is represented as but one small part of the international conspiracy between Jewish-dominated Marxism and Jewish-run capitalism to encircle and destroy Germany. The first volume concludes with the statement that the German nation, led by the führer and his SS, would not regard this danger lightly nor rest as long as Jews lived in the world.[43]

[42] A copy of "Schwert und Pflug" is contained in BAMA III SS, 41/5, vol. 2, pp. 226-67. Glorification of the peasantry and the identification of the SS man with German soil were themes Eicke felt could not be stressed too strongly or too often. For a further discussion of blood and soil is one of the foundations of SS ideology, see Stein, pp. 121-23.

[43] BAMA, III SS, 41/5, vol. 2, pp. 226-67. In this volume of the training manual, England still appears as Germany's foremost national enemy. It was clearly

The second volume contains more of the same, largely the Nazi version of European history since the fall of the Roman Empire. The section on the history of the Inquisition is especially interesting. In it, Torquemada is described as a practicing Jew in secret who, as part of the conspiracy for mass murder, was directly responsible for the deaths of 30,000 Christians and the torture and maiming of another 97,000. The second volume of "Schwert und Pflug" concludes with a quotation from Alfred Rosenberg to the effect that western civilization really developed out of the northern European "Nordic Peoples," and not from the peoples of the Near East "as taught by the Church and the Jews."[44]

The crucial question on political indoctrination is, of course, that of determining what impact the program had upon the men in the Totenkopfdivision. Within the limitations of this study, it has proven impossible to document specifically just how effective this political and racial indoctrination program was. Given Eicke's fanaticism and his penchant for thorough training, however, it seems reasonable to assume that the men in SSTK were kept on Fuhrländer's schedule and were subjected to a steady diet of this propaganda at least through the winter of 1940-1941. In any event, there is great importance in the simple fact that a Waffen SS division like SSTK had such an indoctrination program, created by an officer who was in effect a political commissar, and supported wholeheartedly by the division commander. Many present-day apologists for the Waffen SS, those who claim that its functions and conduct were strictly military and not political, maintain either that no such training programs existed or that if they did the average SS man did not take them seriously.[45] In the

---

too early for any overt anti-Russian propaganda, although "International Jewish-Bolshevism" is described as one of the most dangerous enemies of the German people. In addition, the glossary of terms "defined" at the end of the second volume lists Marxism as the ally of the Jews and the churches in the conspiracy to destroy Germany (ibid., p. 267).

[44] BAMA, II SS, 41/5, vol. 2, pp. 249-66, 267.

[45] This is a chief theme of much tendentious memoir literature ground out by former Waffen SS generals. See especially Paul Hausser, *Waffen SS im Einsatz* (Göttingen, 1953); Kurt Meyer, *Grenadiere* (Munich, 1957); and two books by Felix Steiner, *Die Freiwilligen: Idee und Opfergang* (Göttingen, 1958), and *Die Armee der Geächteten* (Göttingen, 1963).

Totenkopfdivision such political and racial indoctrination definitely existed. The division's record in France and the reputation it subsequently earned in Russia, moreover, leave the distinct impression that Eicke's men took the lessons of their political training very seriously.

During the weeks of severe weather, Eicke also busied himself with drawing up an SSTK training program for the late spring. Using the guidelines sent down by the Seventh Army, he worked out a program whose emphasis was tailored to the coming campaign in Russia. Combat exercises continued to stress fighting under difficult climatic conditions in forests and small villages, while the engineer battalion spent all its training time in bridge-laying exercises across rivers whose opposite bank was in enemy hands. In addition, to improve the quality of his officer corps, Eicke was permitted by Himmler to send an unusually large contingent of picked NCOs to Bad Tölz and Braunschweig as officer candidates.[46]

Eicke's senior commanders and staff officers also worked quite hard during the winter months. In addition to his regular duties, Max Simon, the commander of SSTK/I. R. 1, planned and carried out a series of exercises that reduced significantly the time needed to deploy a motorized infantry regiment from marching columns into battle formation. After seeing one of the exercises Eicke sent copies of Simon's plans and a description of the exercise to General Rudolf Schmidt, his immediate superior as commander of the Thirty-ninth Army Corps. Evidently impressed, Schmidt visited the Totenkopfdivision at the end of January to participate in one of Simon's exercises. Lammerding, on the other hand, spent most of the winter in the classroom. Ordered by Eicke to master the functions of SSTK operations officer as quickly as possible, Lammerding attended a number of special courses in tactical and logistical problems offered by the army and the SSFHA. Then, beginning in February, Eicke assigned him command of regiment-sized battle groups during field exercises. Finally, in late March, Lammerding received his most crucial test when Eicke sent him to begin representing the Totenkopfdivision at the

[46] BAMA, III SS, 41/5, vol. 2, pp. 67-72, 86-90.

weekly staff conferences held by the chief of staff of the Thirty-ninth Army Corps.[47]

The intensity of the combat training during these months may be gauged from the periodic casualty reports Eicke submitted to Himmler. During January 1941, for instance, SSTK suffered training casualties of 3 dead and 2 wounded, plus 97 cases of varying illnesses requiring hospitalization. Comparable casualties were incurred during February and March, so that by April 1941 combat training had cost the division 10 dead, 16 wounded, and approximately 250 hospitalized. Eicke made no complaints about the casualties. He simply shrugged them off as the price in blood any elite unit had to pay during rugged training. He even encouraged the reckless aggressiveness with which his unit commanders conducted field exercises, theorizing that the fanatical approach to training would lead to exceptional performance in actual combat.[48]

As a result, the grueling pace continued throughout April, while other units of the Waffen SS marched off to fight in the führer's new surprise campaign in Yugoslavia and Greece.[49] The

[47] Ibid., vol. 1, p. 11; vol. 2, pp. 74, 88. Of all the younger SS officers Eicke discovered and launched on successful careers, Lammerding was—at least by SS standards of judgment—among the most capable and talented. In the course of the war, Lammerding rose to the rank of SS Obergruppenführer and served successively as Eicke's operations officer, chief of staff of Erich von dem Bach-Zelewski's antipartisan SS forces in Russia, commander of the Waffen SS division Das Reich, and finally, during the last months of the war, as chief of staff of Himmler's Army Group Vistula. See especially Reitlinger, *The SS*, pp. 400-401, 405, 408; Cornelius Ryan, *The Last Battle* (New York, 1966), pp. 91-92; and USDC, SS Personalakte Lammerding, Dienstlaufbahn.

[48] BAMA, III SS, 41/5, vol. 2, pp. 37-38, 111.

[49] For details of the Waffen SS role in the Balkan campaign, see Stein, pp. 113-18; Bullock, pp. 634-37; Weingartner, pp. 49-57; Reitlinger, *The SS*, pp. 160-61; and Trevor-Roper, ed., *Hitler's War Directives*, pp. 60-63. SSTK had been kept in southwestern France to participate in "Operation Attila," the planned lightning occupation of all France and the seizure of the French fleet at Toulon. In April 1941, this was still the official task for which SSTK remained in southern France. Eicke and Lammerding were summoned by Himmler to Berlin on April 3 and informed of the forthcoming Balkan campaign. It is also likely that during this visit Himmler told Eicke about the military and political plans for "Barbarossa" and assured him that SSTK definitely would be sent to fight in Russia. Himmler was by then engaged in extensive preparations for the police activities to be conducted in the conquered territories, and had already briefed the men chosen to be

Balkan campaign ended on April 30 with the surrender of the Greek army. Immediately thereafter, Hitler ordered the Wehrmacht to resume preparations for "Barbarossa," and to begin in secret the final stages of the massive build-up for invading Russia. Consequently, Eicke received orders from Seventh Army HQ to intensify even further his combat training exercises, and to have the Totenkopfdivision ready to move on a moment's notice. Several days later, he was notified that all leaves would be cancelled as of May 15 and was directed to have all SSTK men who were home on leave back by May 20.[50]

The leave cancellations created an atmosphere of tension and excitement among the men as Eicke put the Totenkopfdivision through a final series of exercises during the first two weeks in May. Finally, at 1:00 A.M. on May 23, 1941, Eicke received a coded, top-secret telegram from Seventh Army HQ alerting him to have the division ready to move by rail from southern France no later than June 3. The following week, an advance party of officers and NCOs from the division staff left secretly by truck for Germany to prepare new quarters for SSTK. At the same time, Eicke issued orders for his men to pack their equipment and prepare all the heavy vehicles for immediate shipment by rail to an undisclosed destination.[51]

At dawn on June 3, 1941, the first of some fifty-five trains to be loaded with the men, vehicles, weapons, and supplies of SSTK slid out of the rail yards at Bordeaux and began the long journey to the east. The security precautions surrounding the division's departure were uncommonly elaborate. During the last three days before the move, Eicke gradually cut off all contact between his men and the French civilian populace—after warning the SS troopers that anyone who even mentioned the division's leaving Bordeaux would be shot as a traitor.

---

his HSSPF in Russia about their coming tasks. (BAMA, III SS, 41/5, vol. 1, pp. 16-18; vol. 2, pp. 118-21; Trevor-Roper, ed., *Hitler's War Directives*, pp. 44-46; Reitlinger, *The SS*, p. 161; and *TMWC*, IV, p. 482.

[50] BAMA, III SS, 41/5, vol. 2, p. 116.

[51] Ibid., vol. 1, p. 21, and vol. 2, pp. 171, 182-87. To conceal the purpose of the growing masses of German troops in Rumania, Hungary, Poland, and East Prussia, the armored and motorized formations of the army and the Waffen SS were not moved to the east until the last possible moment (Stein, p. 119).

4. In the marshaling yards at Bordeaux, France, May 1941, soldiers of the Totenkopfdivision entrain for East Prussia, prior to Barbarossa.

The first units of SSTK were moved one by one during the night into the yards at Bordeaux and loaded on trains a few hours before daylight. Once the huge convoy of trains was underway, precautions became even tighter. On the long trip through France and Germany, the men were virtually sealed in their cars. Only at selected stations that had been cleared of all civilians could the SS soldiers get out of the trains to stretch briefly. No communication with friends or relatives in Germany was permitted during the move; and Eicke gave strict orders to the SSTK postal censors that after the men reached their destination, no letter was to go through with even the slightest hint that the Totenkopfdivision had moved.[52]

For four days and nights the trains departed from Bordeaux, joining as they rumbled through the Reich the thousands of troop, ammunition, supply, and hospital trains steaming toward the east. The transfer proceeded on schedule and without incident—striking testimony to the remarkable efficiency with which the Wehrmacht Transport Office and the German railway system moved enormous amounts of men and materiel quickly over long distances. By evening on June 9, the last of Eicke's trains had deposited its cargo of tired, disheveled men and dust-coated vehicles in the railroad siding near the new SSTK HQ at Marienwerder, East Prussia. Located some forty miles southeast of Danzig, Marienwerder was to serve as a preliminary staging area for SSTK, which had not then been assigned a forward position among the formations of Army Group North massing along the borders of the Baltic States.[53]

Among the SS men who trudged wearily to their new quarters in the muggy East Prussian forest, there probably were very few

[52] BAMA, III SS, 41/5, vol. 2, pp. 173-75; and 42/2, pp. 133, 151-53. As an additional precautionary measure, SSTK was assigned a long, zigzag rail route through France. The trains traveled north from Bordeaux to Tours and Blois to create the impression that German troops were moving toward Normandy. From Blois the rail convoy turned east-southeast through Avallon to Dijon, where the trains switched north again onto tracks that carried them through Neufchateau, Nancy, Metz, and into Germany at Saarbrücken. See especially the map in BAMA, III SS, 48/1, Bildband "Damals," p. 9.

[53] Ibid., III SS, 42/2, pp. 151-53. According to Philippi and Heim, p. 52, the movement of the Wehrmacht to eastern Europe in the period between January and June 1941 required over 17,000 trains.

who perceived the enormous significance of the division's reloca-
tion. Among those who had guessed the reason for their
thousand-mile journey, certainly none foresaw the savagery of the
coming struggle with a system in mortal opposition to the ideology they represented. The entire experience of the
Totenkopfdivision—the legacy of the concentration camps, the
rigorous combat training, and the ethos of fanaticism and racial
hatred—approached conjunction in its supreme test and ultimate
purpose: a war of annihilation with the largest and most powerful
enemy of Nazi Germany.

CHAPTER SIX

The SS Totenkopfdivision and the War in Russia: June 1941-January 1942

T HE transfer of the Totenkopfdivision from France to East Prussia was followed by a hectic period of final preparation for the campaign against the Soviet Union. The nature and intensity of the training in those last days before "Barbarossa" quickly identified the new enemy and left Eicke's men with little doubt about how they were expected to conduct the struggle against bolshevism. On June 9, as the last groups of SS soldiers detrained from their long journey, orders for the Totenkopfdivision's new assignment arrived from the army. The division was to be attached to General Erich Hoepner's powerful Fourth Panzer Group, which would spearhead the drive of the northernmost German armies through the Baltic States toward Leningrad. General Hoepner, however, still retained vivid memories of the Totenkopfdivision's performance in France and refused to designate SSTK for the first attack waves. Consequently, Eicke and his officers and men learned to their disappointment that they would have to wait in reserve during the first phase of the invasion.[1]

The magnitude of the plans for "Operation Barbarossa," however, assured the Totenkopfdivision of eventual combat participation and necessitated a final call-up of SS reservists to fill SSTK units that had remained understrength since the end of the French campaign. Between June 12 and June 18, 1941, more than 900 SS

[1] National Archives of the United States, Washington, D. C., Microcopy T-314, Microfilm Roll 1389, frames 000213-000220, "Kommando der Panzergruppe 4, Aufmarsch- und Kampfanweisung 'Barbarossa' (Studie)," dated May 2, 1941. (Hereafter cited by microcopy, roll, frame numbers, and item identification as NA/T-314/1389/000213-000220, "Kommando der Panzergruppe 4 . . ."). See also, BAMA, III SS, 41/6, vol. 1, Anlagenband zum KTB No. 6, pp. 2-3; III SS, 50/1, SS Totenkopf-Division, Infanterie Regiment No. 3, KTB No. 3, pp. 2-3. The June 9, 1941 entry in the war diary of SSTK's Third Infantry Regiment noted the arrival of a whole truckload of maps of the Soviet Union, thus disspelling the lingering uncertainty about the transfer of the Totenkopfdivision to East Prussia.

recruits arrived from replacement units of SSTK located in Nuremberg, Dresden, Breslau, Prague, and Brno. The majority of the new replacements were assigned to the infantry regiments and the reconnaissance and engineer battalions.[2]

While the new SS men were arriving, Eicke held a series of conferences with his officers to discuss the conduct of the coming war with Russia. On June 14 he presided over a meeting of the regimental and battalion commanders in SSTK and announced officially that war with the Soviet Union would begin within two weeks. The new campaign, he emphasized, would be much different from those conducted in the past. The coming war, Eicke contended, had to be fought as an ideological conflict, a life-and-death struggle between National Socialism and Jewish-Bolshevism—a fact that would demand the most ruthless and uncompromising conduct. As a result, he continued, the führer had ordered that the principal carriers of the enemy ideology, the political commissars attached to Red Army units, were to be killed immediately after their capture or surrender, regardless of the circumstances. Eicke concluded by exhorting his officers to be fanatical and merciless, and by reminding them that the Russians had not signed the Geneva Convention, and therefore could not be expected to wage war in a civilized fashion. The men in the Totenkopfdivision would consequently be expected to fight without mercy or pity in the war in the east—a struggle upon which the fate of the German people depended.[3]

[2] BAMA, III SS, 42/2, pp. 158-61, 163-66. At the beginning of the Russian campaign, the arriving reservists swelled the ranks of the Totenkopfdivision to approximately 17,400 men.

[3] Ibid., p. 160; III SS, 50/1, p. 4. For details concerning Hitler's notorious "Commissar Order," see Krausnick, *Anatomie*, II, pp. 163-97. Eicke's orations on exterminating the "Jewish-Bolshevik Commissars" were more than pep-talk rhetoric or empty repetitions of themes developed by Hitler and Himmler. As a statement of his own views on the coming conflict, they were an individual reflection of the whole racial and ideological basis of Hitler's strategy for waging a war of domination and extermination against the Russians. For Hitler, whose views were shared by Himmler, Heydrich, Bormann, and initially Goebbels, the military conquest of the Soviet Union to acquire Lebensraum (living space) was indissolubly linked with his obsession to exterminate the Jews of Europe. Hitler considered victory in Russia to be contingent upon and thus inseparable from his planned annihilation of the Jews, because he regarded the millions of Jews in European Russia as the biological basis of the Bolshevik system of power. Thus, the complete elimination of the Jews and the Communist hierarchy and the merciless destruction

The announcements made by Eicke on June 14 were repeated several times during the days that followed in conferences among the SS officers and men in every unit in the Totenkopfdivision. At a general meeting attended by all the officers in the SSTK on June 16, Eicke lectured again on the nature of the coming war in the east and reemphasized the need for carrying out Hitler's order to kill every commissar who fell into German hands.[4]

On June 19, Eicke received orders from Hoepner to move the division into the assembly area of Panzer Group Four near Kreuzingen on the frontier between East Prussia and Soviet-occupied Lithuania. The march into the jumping-off positions for the attack began after dark on June 19 and resumed the next night.

---

of the Red Army were seen as necessary preludes to the long-range plans for the ruthless subjugation of the Slavs and the total economic exploitation of Russia west of the Urals. This thesis is comprehensively, convincingly, and brilliantly argued in two works by Andreas Hillgruber, *Hitlers Strategie*, pp. 516-35; and "Die 'Endlösung' und das Deutsche Ostimperium als Kernstück des Rassenideologischen Programms des Nationalsozialismus," *Vierteljahrshefte für Zeitgeschichte*, 20 (April 1972), 133-53. See also, Rich, vol. 2, *The Establishment of the New Order*, pp. 348-52; and Jay W. Baird, *The Mythical World of Nazi War Propaganda, 1939-1945* (Minneapolis, Minn., 1974), pp. 156-57, 164-65, for a description of the radical anti-Bolshevik propaganda in the first phase of the war. The behavior of the Totenkopfdivision throughout the Russian war graphically underscores the thesis of the campaign in the east as a racial and ideological struggle. The tone and substance, even the language and phraseology, of Eicke's speeches to his men conform precisely to a subsequent comprehensive directive Heydrich prepared for the HSSPF in Russia to use in carrying out the elimination of Jews and Communist party leaders (BAKO, R70, Sowjetunion/32, fol. 1-31, "Der Chef der Sicherheitspolizei und des SD, Berlin, den 2. 7. 1941, *Als Geheime Reichssache*." For a more extensive discussion and analysis of the influence of Nazi racial ideology upon the Totenkopfdivision's performance during the Russian war, see Charles W. Sydnor, Jr., "La Division SS 'Totenkopf,' " *Revue d'histoire de la deuxième guerre mondiale*, No. 98 (April 1975), pp. 59-76; and below, chapter nine.

[4] BAMA, III SS, 50/1, p. 4. SS divisions, of course, were not the only German formations ordered to follow these savage guidelines. The records of the Fifty-sixth Panzer Corps, one of the two mechanized corps in Hoepner's Panzer Group Four, contain a general order of June 12, 1941 specifying the most ruthless conduct against "Bolshevik instigators, guerrillas, saboteurs, and Jews." Describing Bolshevism as the mortal enemy of the German people, the order declares that the Communist ideology and its carriers are the objects of the German struggle and must be crushed absolutely. At the same time, the order warns against looting in the strongest language, and stipulates that German soldiers should behave with impeccable correctness toward Russian civilians (NA/T-314/1388/000416-000417, "LVI Pz. Kps., Richtlinien für das Verhalten der Truppe in Russland," dated June 12, 1941).

During daylight hours Eicke complied with the tight security imposed by the Army High Command (OKH) and kept his vehicle columns hidden under camouflage netting in previously chosen wooded areas. By dawn on June 21 all units of the Totenkopfdivision had reached assigned locations to spend a final day of rest in the shade of the East Prussian forest.[5]

Like an atmospheric calm preceeding some great natural calamity, June 21 passed almost serenely as the SS men played cards, smoked, wrote letters, and dozed for the last time in pleasant, uninterrupted slumber. Shortly before 3:00 A.M. on June 22, 1941, Hitler's proclamation to the German troops was read aloud to the Totenkopf soldiers by their unit commanders. A tense interval followed; and then, between 3:05 A.M. and 3:30 A.M., a three-mile-wide strip of territory stretching the length of eastern Europe from the Baltic Sea to the Carpathian Mountains erupted in a torrent of fire and flying steel as German aircraft, artillery, and armor blasted across the Soviet frontier. In the violence of its initial collision, the immensity and ferocity of its subsequent development, and the profligacy of its destruction of human life and resources, the German-Russian conflict transcended anything then in the human experience. To the men of the SS Totenkopfdivision, who were to fight exclusively against the Russians until the end of the war, the campaign became a grim crusade of extermination.[6]

[5] BAMA, III SS, 41/6, vol. 1, Anlagenband zum KTB No. 6, pp. 2-4; vol. 2, Anlagenband 4 zum KTB No. 6, p. 11.

[6] Philippi and Heim, pp. 36-40; and Helmuth Greiner and Percy Schramm, eds., *Kriegstagebuch des Oberkommandos der Wehrmacht, 1940-1945*, vol. 1 (Frankfurt am Main, 1965), p. 417, indicate that the attack began at different intervals along the front. This latter work is the war diary of the High Command of the German Armed Forces (OKW), and is cited hereafter by volume and page number as KTB/OKW.

Although published too late for extensive use in the preparation of this and subsequent chapters, John Erickson, *The Road to Stalingrad: Stalin's War with Germany*, vol. 1 (New York, 1975) is the best and most important recent addition to the literature on the conflict. In its description of the problems and perceptions in Soviet military planning before June 1941, and in its narrative and analysis of the first phase of the war from the perspective of the Russian side, it is the most valuable work that has yet appeared in any language.

In addition to the previously cited work by Philippi and Heim, the diary of General Halder, and the memoirs of General Guderian, other general studies helpful in the development of the remainder of this book include: Alexander Werth, *Russia at War, 1941-1945* (New York, 1964); Alan Clark, *Barbarossa: The Russian-German Conflict, 1941-1945* (New York, 1965); Albert Seaton, *The Russo-*

The disposition of the German armies at the beginning of the Russian campaign represented a much-enlarged version of the previous summer's deployment in the west. The three and one-half million Axis soldiers participating in the invasion were divided into three huge army groups. From staging areas in Rumania, Hungary, and Poland, Field Marshal Gerd von Rundstedt's Army Group South (four German armies, one panzer group, and a Rumanian contingent of twenty divisions) rushed the Soviet frontier and advanced rapidly to overrun the Ukraine and the vital industrial complexes in the Donetz basin.[7] The middle of the German front was anchored by Field Marshal Fedor von Bock's Army Group Center. With two panzer groups and two infantry armies, Bock's massive conglomeration of tanks and men advanced into Russia in the area just north of the Pripet Marshes. The northern and southern edges of this gigantic armored pincer bypassed the Soviet frontier forces concentrated between Grodno and Brest-Litovsk and converged upon Minsk, trapping or destroying the bulk of the Red Army in central Russia.[8]

To the left of Bock, in East Prussia, two infantry armies and

---

German War, 1941-45 (New York, 1970); and two books by Paul Carell, Hitler Moves East, 1941-1943 (Boston, 1965), and Scorched Earth: The German-Russian War, 1943-1944 (Boston, 1970). The standard work on the post-Stalingrad phase of the war is Earl F. Ziemke, Stalingrad to Berlin: The German Defeat in the East (Washington, D. C., 1968). Operations on the northern sector of the eastern front—where the Totenkopfdivision was engaged for so long—are described well in the English edition of Field Marshal Manstein's memoirs, Lost Victories (Chicago, 1958); and graphically from the Soviet side in Harrison E. Salisbury's absorbing The 900 Days: The Siege of Leningrad (New York, 1969). This supersedes the older but still useful study by Leon Goure, The Siege of Leningrad (Stanford, Calif., 1962). General studies that touch upon the political and military role of the SS in Russia include: Alexander Dallin, German Rule in Russia, 1941-1945: A Study of Occupation Policies (New York, 1957); the previously noted volumes by Norman Rich, Hitler's War Aims; Josef Ackermann, Himmler als Ideologue; Gerald Reitlinger, The SS; and Heinz Höhne, Der Orden unter dem Totenkopf. In addition, the books by Stein, The Waffen SS; Hilberg, Destruction of the European Jews; Klietmann, Die Waffen SS; and the recent studies by Lucy S. Dawidowicz, The War Against the Jews, 1933-1945 (New York, 1975); and Reuben Ainsztein, Jewish Resistance in Nazi-Occupied Eastern Europe (New York, 1974), are vital for understanding the comprehensive role assumed by the SS in the Russian war. More specialized studies, from both the German and Soviet sides, dealing with individual battles involving the Totenkopfdivision will be cited below as specific references.

[7] Philippi and Heim, p. 40.   [8] Ibid., pp. 54-57.

Hoepner's panzer group formed Army Group North, which was under the command of Field Marshal Wilhelm Ritter von Leeb. Leeb's objective was threefold. Hoepner's panzer group (which included the Totenkopfdivision) occupied the center of the army group and was to lead the rapid drive toward Leningrad—the primary objective. On Hoepner's left flank, General Georg von Küchler's Eighteenth Army was to advance toward Riga and then wheel north between the Baltic and Lake Peipus, rolling up and destroying the bulk of the Soviet forces in Latvia and Estonia. In the meantime, Ernst Busch's Sixteenth Army was scheduled to move forward on Hoepner's right in pursuit of the third objective—protecting the open flank of the army group and maintaining contact with Bock's left wing as the advance into Russia pulled the army groups in diverging directions.[9]

As the Schwerpunkt of Leeb's advance, Hoepner's Panzer Group Four contained the mass of the armored and motorized units in Army Group North. The left wing of the panzer group was formed by General Max Reinhardt's Forty-first Panzer Corps (First and Sixth Panzer Divisions, and the Thirty-sixth Motorized Infantry Division). The right prong of Hoepner's armored fork consisted of the Fifty-sixth Panzer Corps (the Eighth Panzer, Third Motorized, and 290th Infantry Divisions), a crack, spirited force led by General Erich von Manstein—the ablest field commander in the German army. The SS Totenkopfdivision and the 269th Infantry Division were to be held in reserve for Hoepner and committed to either Reinhardt or Manstein, depending upon which panzer corps advanced more rapidly.[10]

At the first trace of daylight on June 22, Hoepner's two panzer corps smashed into the Soviet frontier positions and quickly overwhelmed the bewildered Red Army units along the border. Once free of the frontier entanglements, the armored units of Panzer Group Four began the headlong dash to capture the vital bridges over the Dvina River—one of the most formidable natural obstacles interposed in the advance toward Leningrad. Manstein's

---

[9] Ibid., pp. 57-59.

[10] Manstein, *Lost Victories*, pp. 178, 186. The assessment of Manstein as the most talented of the German generals during the Second World War was made by B. H. Liddell Hart in *The German Generals Talk* (New York, 1948), pp. 63-67. See also Liddell Hart's introduction to Manstein's *Lost Victories*, pp. 13-16.

Fifty-sixth Panzer Corps quickly set the pace for Leeb's entire army group.[11]

By dusk on June 22, with the war only eighteen hours old, Manstein's armor and motorized infantry had advanced fifty-three miles into Soviet territory and captured the road and rail bridge over the giant Dubisa gorge near the village of Airogola. Less than forty-eight hours later, after encountering only light, scattered resistance, the Fifty-sixth Panzer Corps reached the Dvinsk highway at Wilkomierz—105 miles from the East Prussian border. Manstein covered the remaining eighty miles to Dvinsk in little more than a day. On the morning of June 26, units of the Eighth Panzer Division careened through the city of Dvinsk and across the great road and rail bridges over the Dvina, disarming both the startled Russian sentries and the badly placed explosive charges. Manstein's capture of the Dvina crossings—quickly consolidated by the construction of formidable bridgeheads—was a stunning coup, ranking by comparison with the spectacular seizure of the Belgian fort Eban Emael the previous summer. In little more than four days, Manstein's panzer corps had advanced nearly 200 miles into enemy territory, driven a powerful wedge between the disintegrating Soviet Eighth and Third Armies, spread panic and paralyzing confusion through the rear areas of the Red Army, and unhinged the entire Russian defensive network in the Baltic States. Through his unrivaled mastery of blitzkrieg tactics, Manstein had pushed the Russians' wing in the north to the brink of disaster.[12]

[11] BAMA, III SS, 41/6, vol. 1, Anlagenband zum KTB No. 6, pp. 6-7. Despite the numerous signs that for weeks had pointed to an imminent German attack, the Red Army units in front of Panzer Group Four were taken completely by surprise. Luftwaffe squadrons coordinating with Hoepner's armor destroyed 108 Soviet aircraft during the first six hours of the attack. Eighty-seven of these were caught and knocked out on the ground.

[12] The surprise, confusion, and chaos that overwhelmed the Soviet forces along the frontier on the opening day of the war are graphically described in Erickson, *The Road to Stalingrad*, pp. 101-35; and in Seweryn Bialer, ed., *Stalin and His Generals: Soviet Military Memoirs of World War II* (New York, 1969), pp. 219-60. See also, Manstein, pp. 183, 186; Halder, *KTB*, vol. 3, p. 617, entries for June 22 and 26, 1941; and NA/T-314/1389/000715, 000742-000745, radio message from the Eighth Panzer Division to the Fifty-sixth Panzer Corps describing the capture of the lightly damaged bridges; and the daily report (Tagesmeldung) of the Fifty-sixth Panzer Corps to Panzer Group Four, both dated June 26, 1941.

The speedy advance of the Fifty-sixth Panzer Corps, however, left the rest of Panzer Group Four and the slower infantry divisions of the Sixteenth Army far to the rear. Consequently, Manstein was forced to halt on the Dvina and wait until the rest of the army group caught up with him. In the meantime, Manstein's rapid dash had also compelled Leeb to commit the SS Totenkopfdivision and the 269th Infantry Division to action.

Shortly before dusk on June 24, at approximately the same time that Manstein reached Wilkomierz, Eicke received orders to move the Totenkopfdivision east before midnight, and to proceed forward as quickly as possible to plug the lengthening gap between Manstein's right flank and the left wing of Busch's Sixteenth Army. The first combat assignments, Eicke was told, would involve mopping up isolated groups of enemy stragglers and repairing damaged main roads while moving forward to cover the resumption of Manstein's advance. After crossing the frontier during the night of June 24-25, SSTK spent two days combing the Lithuanian forests around Jurbarkas for remnants of the Red Army units smashed along the borders on the first day of the war. By late afternoon on June 26, Eicke reported that the assignment had been completed and that the units of the Totenkopfdivision were reassembling to move on toward Wilkomierz.[13]

At this juncture, SSTK received fresh orders from Panzer Group Four that corresponded to the situation created by Manstein's advance. The Totenkopfdivision was directed to proceed to Deguciai and to cross the Dvina at Dvinsk on June 29. Getting to Dvinsk proved a bit more difficult than anticipated, however, as the Russians began to recover from their initial paralysis and offered vicious resistance. After extricating his vehicle columns from an enormous traffic bottleneck near the Kedainiai crossroads early on June 27, Eicke led SSTK east through central Lithuania. Here, the SS men ran into serious opposition and had their first taste of what war in the east was like. At one point, the reconnaissance battalion was forced to halt and repel a succession of Russian counterattacks led by a group of tanks. After destroying three

[13] BAMA, III SS, 41/6, vol. 1, pp. 13-14; vol. 2, p. 19; 50/1, p. 6; 41/8, vol. 2, pp. 4-5. General summaries of the Totenkopfdivision's activities in Russia during 1941 may also be found in Klietmann, pp. 110-12.

of the tanks and driving the others off, the SS soldiers were astonished by the Russian infantry's continued suicidal charges. Finally, after three successive assaults, the surviving Soviet soldiers fled into the forest, leaving Eicke's reconnaissance battalion without casualties but shaken by the Russians' fanatical determination.[14]

The following day, units of Max Simon's First Infantry Regiment ran into similar trouble, clashing repeatedly with wandering groups of Soviet soldiers who consistently fought to the death rather than surrender to SS troops. The reaction of Simon's men to this new phenomenon was a mixture of anger, amazement, and mounting fear. To Max Simon, for example, it was incomprehensible that these isolated, hopelessly bypassed groups of Russians should want to fight. The answer, he concluded in an order to his men, was that these units of Russian stragglers were "bandits" who had been organized and whipped into a frenzy by Bolshevik commissars and fanatical Red Army officers. Therefore, Simon ordered that groups of Russian stragglers be dealt with most ruthlessly, and not be given the chance to injure German soldiers. Simon's attitude was certainly shared by Eicke and Lammerding, and it is quite likely that after these first harrowing encounters the units of the Totenkopfdivision shot the majority of the Russian stragglers they encountered, especially those who offered resistance rather than immediate surrender.[15]

[14] BAMA, III SS, 41/6, vol. 2, pp. 29-32, 35-38, 90; vol. 1, pp. 17-19; and NA/T-314/1390/000009, SSTK daily report to the Fifty-sixth Panzer Corps for June 29, 1941, signed by Lammerding. In his report, Lammerding described the Soviet units as bandits armed and organized by fanatical commissars to work behind the German lines with no specific goals or objectives.

[15] BAMA, III SS, 41/6, vol. 2, pp. 59-60, 115-17. Despite the absence of direct evidence to document the large-scale shooting of Russian stragglers, there are several factors indicating that this was probably what happened. Simon's report, and reports of other SSTK units that encountered Russian stragglers during the first days of the war, are all nearly hysterical in describing the enemy as fanatical, inhuman creatures who employed the vilest tricks to kill German soldiers. In a report Eicke forwarded to the Fifty-sixth Panzer Corps on July 6, Max Simon described how a group of 200 Russian soldiers approached units of SSTK/I. R. 1 with hands raised, as if to surrender, then dropped to the ground and opened fire when they were twenty yards from SS positions. In the exchange of fire, the SS soldiers killed every Russian, including those who begged to surrender (NA/T-314/1390/000006-000007, SSTK/I. R. 1 daily report of July 2, 1941). In addition, Eicke's soldiers were undoubtedly motivated by the knowledge that the Russians were

As his men continued to clash with groups of Soviet "bandits," Eicke received further instructions from Hoepner. SSTK was assigned to Manstein's Fifty-sixth Panzer Corps and directed to send one infantry battalion and the tank-destroyer battalion forward to Dvinsk at once to help secure the flank of the Third Motorized Division, which was being subjected to fierce Russian counterattacks designed to wipe out its bridgeheads over the Dvina. In addition, Manstein ordered Eicke to move the rest of SSTK to Dvinsk as quickly as possible so that the advance of the Fifty-sixth Panzer Corps might be resumed. The Totenkopfdivision, however, struggled forward for another three days against stiffening resistance and mounting enemy air attacks before reaching Dvinsk. Just before dark on June 30, Eicke crossed the Dvina River into the bridgehead of the Fifty-sixth Panzer Corps, and the Totenkopfdivision moved into place on the right of the Third Motorized Division as the wing formation of Manstein's Panzer Corps.[16]

At the same time the Totenkopfdivision crossed the Dvina, units of Reinhardt's panzer corps pulled abreast of Manstein to the north and the slower-moving infantry of the Sixteenth Army drew within contact range to the south. With the additional muscle provided by SSTK, and with his flanks protected to Leeb's satisfaction, Manstein was free to resume his advance. Accordingly, at 3:00 A.M. on July 2, Hoepner's entire panzer group attacked the hastily regrouped enemy forces in its path. Reinhardt struck northeast toward Ostrov on the former Soviet-Latvian frontier, while Manstein moved in a diverging direction to the east toward Opochka. Having successfully crossed the Dvina, Hoepner's new objective was to hit the string of fortifications in that portion of the

---

killing, in the most horrible manner, all German soldiers who fell into their hands alive. The Bildarchiv of the Bundesarchiv, Koblenz, PK (Propaganda Kompanie) Sammlung, has photographs of the corpses of hideously mutilated German soldiers—both army and Waffen SS—killed on the northern sector of the Russian front during the early fighting.

[16] BAMA, III SS, 41/6, vol. 2, pp. 48-51, 63-64, 92-98, 104-8, 115-17; vol. 3, Anlagenband 2 zum KTB No. 6, pp. 9-13; Clark, pp. 74-75. The appearance on June 29 of Soviet fighter planes hastily summoned from the Russian interior was an unpleasant introduction for the SS soldiers. The Russian aircraft, arriving while the Luftwaffe was off to refuel, bombed and strafed several units of SSTK, killing ten and wounding thirty of Eicke's men.

"Stalin Line" running south from Lake Peipus along the route Pskov-Ostrov-Opochka. Once through these fortifications, Reinhardt's Forty-first Panzer Corps could drive due north along the eastern side of Lake Peipus toward Leningrad. Manstein's Fifty-sixth Panzer Corps, on the other hand, was to perform the more imprecise and less desirable task of advancing east toward Lake Ilmen to sever road and rail communications between Leningrad and Moscow.[17]

As the southernmost formation of the Fifty-sixth Panzer Corps, the Totenkopfdivision was assigned a dual role by General Manstein. Eicke was to protect the right flank of the panzer corps and at the same time maintain contact with the infantry on the left wing of the Sixteenth Army. To carry out its new assignment, SSTK would have to advance from the Dvinsk bridgehead across Latvia along a route that would carry it through the towns of Dagda, Kraslau, and Skorlopova to Rosenov and Opochka. The terrain lying in the path of Eicke's advance, moreover, was dotted with lakes and densely forested areas traversed only by narrow, unpaved roads. This was extremely difficult territory for operations by a motorized infantry division like SSTK, and an area in which, according to Eicke's sober warnings, the Russians could be expected to resist vigorously.[18]

Deploying into two march columns, the Totenkopfdivision attacked out of the Dvinsk bridgehead just before dawn on July 2 and made excellent progress in its first contacts with opposing elements of the Soviet Twenty-first Armored Group. In the early afternoon, Max Simon sent Eicke an ebullient report on the capture of Kraslau while Kleinheisterkamp's SSTK/I. R. 3 gathered huge quantities of gasoline, guns, and ammunition abandoned by the fleeing Russians. As the day progressed, however, the Russians somehow regained their coordination, and their resistance

[17] KTB/OKW, vol. 1, pp. 424-26; Halder, *KTB*, vol. 3, pp. 33-36, entry for July 2, 1941; Philippi and Heim, p. 58; Manstein, p. 186; and Clark, pp. 74-75. Manstein's willingness to forego the security of protected flanks in order to advance as rapidly as possible was a constant source of worry to Field Marshal Leeb. The latter was especially anxious to prevent any gaps from opening in the German lines as the diverging axes of advance of Army Groups Center and North broadened the operational front in Russia.

[18] BAMA, III SS, 41/6, vol. 1, pp. 29-32; vol. 2, pp. 132-40.

stiffened appreciably. By evening, several of Eicke's units were locked in bloody engagements.[19]

At the village of Dagda, the Soviets dealt the Totenkopfdivision its first sharp setback of the campaign and gave Eicke's soldiers a bitter taste of what lay ahead. Survivors of the badly mauled Soviet Forty-second Rifle Division, which was part of General D. D. Lelyushenko's disintegrating Twenty-first Armored Group, ambushed and halted Max Simon's lead battalion, killing 10 and wounding nearly 100 SS soldiers. By midnight on July 2, moreover, the Russians had managed to call in support from tanks and artillery and had launched a series of counterattacks that forced the entire Totenkopfdivision to go on the defensive. The Russian attacks continued through the night and reached a crescendo just before dawn. The fury of the counterblows forced the division to yield ground, and compelled Eicke to postpone his advance until late afternoon on July 3—after the Luftwaffe arrived to destroy the Russian artillery. Even with the help of Stukas, Eicke found the going sticky, and assault groups from his infantry regiments did not retake Dagda until after 10:00 P.M. that evening. As the exhausted SS men regained their positions of the previous day, the Russians withdrew quietly toward Sebesh and Opochka to regroup in the Stalin Line.[20]

[19] Ibid., vol. 3, pp. 14-17; vol. 2, pp. 180-85, 194-95. Before resuming his advance on July 2, Manstein ordered Eicke to detach the Totenkopfdivision's Second Infantry Regiment and leave it in Dvinsk to serve as a reserve force for the Fifty-sixth Panzer Corps.

Max Simon's glowing report on the SSTK capture of Kraslau was contradicted by an official complaint of the 121st Infantry Division filed with the Fifty-sixth Panzer Corps about the behavior of Simon's Regiment during the attack at Kraslau. According to the report, Major General Lancelle, commander of the 121st Division, had to enter Kraslau on foot to untangle an enormous traffic jam of SS vehicles and to prod the resumption of an SS attack that had become chaotic and disorganized. In Kraslau, the astonished general found a group of SS soldiers gathered in the main street trying fruitlessly to make an ancient Russian gramophone play while other groups of SS infantrymen shattered windows, looted shops, and loaded all available vehicles with booty of every description. Those SS units seriously attempting to clear the town of its Russian defenders, General Lancelle maintained, violated every training rule by foolishly moving in exposed clusters, thereby incurring frightful losses (NA/T-312/548/8157249-7252, "121. Inf. Division, Ia., Bericht über Einsatz des I. R. 407 bei Kraslawa," dated July 5, 1941).

[20] BAMA, III SS, 41/6, vol. 2, pp. 197-203, 205-9, 212-15, 222; vol. 3, pp. 17-19; NA/T-314/1390/000173, radio message from the Fifty-sixth Panzer Corps

The Russian withdrawal was covered skillfully by an artillery barrage that rained shells on Eicke's men until daylight. After a second sleepless night, SSTK resumed its pursuit on the morning of July 4, with orders to advance and cut the Opochka-Ostrov highway. The advance proceeded smoothly as the Soviets withdrew, and at midday Eicke's men took Rosenov. The long columns of trucks, supply wagons, and assorted litter abandoned by the Russians once again created the impression of a beaten, dispirited enemy and led Eicke to the hasty conclusion that enemy resistance was on the verge of collapsing altogether. This euphoric view was dispelled permanently by the events that began the following day.[21]

On the evening of July 5, 1941, Manstein's panzer corps, with SSTK on the right, the Third Motorized Division in the center, and the Eighth Panzer Division on the left, paused briefly to regroup before assaulting the dense system of fortifications in the Stalin Line. The attack was scheduled for dawn on July 6, with the Totenkopfdivision designated to play a major role in Manstein's plan for breaking through the Russian defenses. Eicke's orders called for an advance by SSTK to the southeast along the Sebesh-Opochka road. Once in Opochka, the division would pause long enough to guard against any attempted Soviet counterattack from the south. Eicke then would advance due east, bypassing the southern end of the Soviet defensive line, and swing north behind Opochka to cut off the retreat of the Russian forces being driven back by the Third Motorized and Eighth Panzer Divisions.[22]

Striking southeast from Rosenov before dawn on July 6, the Totenkopfdivision punctured the Stalin Line and became embroiled in the most vicious fighting it had yet experienced. The Russian fortifications, which were much denser in Eicke's sector

---

to Manstein of 5:00 A.M., July 3, 1941, describing the Soviet pounding of Dagda; and Salisbury, pp. 164-65.

[21] BAMA, III SS, 41/6, vol. 1, pp. 40-43; vol. 2, pp. 223-24. The only serious trouble the Totenkopfdivision encountered on July 4 was a succession of unexpected air attacks. Soviet fighters and bombers again arrived while the Luftwaffe fighter squadrons were absent for refueling. On this occasion, the Russians damaged some SSTK vehicles but caused only a few casualties.

[22] Ibid., III SS, 41/6, vol. 1, pp. 44-45; vol. 2, pp. 263-65.

than had been anticipated, were a system of concrete bunkers, camouflaged machine gun nests, entrenched tanks, and minefields and booby traps nearly five miles deep. Progress by the SS troops was measured in yards, as every bunker and position had to be blasted open and the defenders rooted out and killed. The division's advance, which was preceeded by intensive artillery fire, was led by special assault groups of engineers and infantry using flame throwers, high explosives, and hand grenades to blow a path through the Russian defensive network.[23]

The Totenkopfdivision's attack ground forward slowly throughout the day; by nightfall units of engineers had cleared the defensive network and built the first of a series of bridges across the Velikaya River. By then, it appeared that the most difficult obstacles had been hurdled for a quick advance around Opochka to encircle and destroy the remaining Soviet forces in the southern part of the Stalin Line. In reality, the first day's advance proved easy compared to what followed.

With the onset of darkness, the Soviets brought up artillery and started peppering Eicke's positions. Russian infantry, moreover, again refused to allow the SS soldiers any sleep and began their nightly series of desperate counterattacks. The most serious casualty of the day's fighting was Eicke. While returning from the front to his HQ near midnight, his command car ran over an enemy mine and blew up, seriously wounding both Eicke and the driver. Before his removal to a rear-area hospital, Eicke appointed

[23] Ibid., vol. 1, p. 44; vol. 3, p. 22. The fighting on July 6 was so vicious that the Totenkopfdivision failed to take any Russian prisoners. The nature of the struggle in the Russian defensive system was described aptly in several SSTK reports from July 6. SSTK/I. R. 1 spent the entire day in bitter hand-to-hand fighting amidst the bunkers, suffering for the day losses of 50 dead and 160 wounded. In a report on the desperate struggle for a single pillbox, a group of assault engineers claimed that when they finally overwhelmed the defenders in the position "twenty Jews were counted among the forty-two dead Russians." This SSTK clerical euphemism, repeated by Lammerding in the daily report to the Fifty-sixth Panzer Corps, became standard during the Russian campaign. Unusually desperate Russian resistance was attributed to Jews, bandits, partisans, or the sinister influence of commissars. The object was to intensify the SS men's hatred for the enemy by identifying the Russian soldier with the most pernicious and lethal enemies of the Third Reich, who would destroy Germany unless first annihilated (NA/T-314/1390/000414-000416, interim report (Zwischenmeldung) of SSTK/I. R. 1 for July 6, 1941; and NA/T-314/1388/000495, "SS Totenkopf-Division, Ia., an LVI Pz. Kps., Tagesmeldung vom 6. 7. 41").

Matthias Kleinheisterkamp as interim commander of the Totenkopfdivision pending a decision by Himmler on a permanent replacement.[24]

For the next three days the battle for the Stalin Line and
Opochka raged, until the SS soldiers stormed the town on July 11
and overwhelmed the final Russian defensive line. In a desperate
attempt to halt the German drive before Opochka, the Russians
threw in heavy armor and all available infantry reserves. The inhuman savagery of the fighting and the Dantesque background
against which it raged were described vividly in accounts by several SS officers. An SS Obersturmführer in the radio company of
the signals battalion wrote of the struggle that unfolded beneath
the shimmering heat of the July sun, continued uninterrupted
through torrential thunderstorms, and roared on amidst colossal
dust clouds kicked up by the mechanized formations of the two
huge armies. For seventy-two hours, the Opochka sector of the
Stalin Line was transformed into a scenario of countless hand-to-
hand duels as men were incinerated at close range by flame-
throwers, blown to pieces by grenades, shot from ambush by
snipers, or bayoneted in the sulphurous darkness of bunkers and
pillboxes. A specific case was recorded by one group of SS men.

A radio truck from the signals battalion came upon a startling
scene at the edge of a forest. Four dead Russians lay in a semicir-
cle around the corpse of a young officer from the Totenkopfdivision. The lone officer apparently had stumbled upon a sizable
group of Russian stragglers, had shot four of them (three at such

[24] BAMA, III SS, 50/1, Schilderung des Einsatzes des I. R. 3 vom 6. 6. 41 bis
14. 12. 41, pp. 18, 29; III SS, 41/8, vol. 2, p. 12; NA/T-314/1390/000477, transcript of a long-distance telephone call from Lammerding to Himmler of 1:20
A.M., July 7, 1941; and USDC, SS Personalakte Eicke, letter to Himmler from
Eicke's doctor (signature illegible) at the Charité Hospital in Berlin, dated August
4, 1941, describing Eicke's wounds and recovery progress. Eicke's injuries consisted of a shattered right foot and extensive nerve damage in the right leg from
penetration by metal fragments. For almost a year after his recuperation and return
to the division, Eicke hobbled around only with the aid of a cane. One day after
losing Eicke, the Totenkopfdivision suffered two additional damaging casualties.
Max Simon and Walter Bestmann, commander of the reconnaissance battalion,
were wounded on July 8—Simon moderately and Bestmann seriously (BAKO,
NS/19-370, letter from Kleinheisterkamp to Himmler of July 9, 1941; and BAMA
III SS, 41/10, Funkspruche, Fernschreiben und Telegrammen, 1941-1942, vol. 2,
p. 74).

close range that there were large powder burns on their field jackets), and then had killed himself rather than surrender and endure a more horrible death.[25]

For the Totenkopf soldiers, the nights brought no relief. The battle continued without pause by the light of blazing villages and vehicles, following as it progressed the erratic path stenciled across the blackness by flying tracer shells. The climax of the struggle for Opochka came early on July 10, when the storming of the town was preceded by a massive artillery and air attack watched from a distance by the awed soldiers of the Totenkopfdivision. The fighting subsided on the morning of July 11, as units from SSTK and the Thirtieth Infantry Division (the left-flank formation of the Sixteenth Army) entered Opochka and captured the town. The Russian forces engaged against SSTK, mainly the 180th and the 182nd Rifle Divisions, which had been badly mauled during the fighting, slowed the German advance and gained precious time for the organization of fresh Soviet forces in the Lake Ilmen area. The scattered surviving units of the Soviet Twenty-first Armored Group withdrew into the swampy forests east of Opochka to regroup with new Russian divisions and form another defensive line.

For the bone-weary men of the Totenkopfdivision, the capture of Opochka meant a chance for a few hours sleep before resuming pursuit of their elusive enemy. The pause also gave Kleinheisterkamp an opportunity to send Himmler a detailed casualty report for the first weeks of the campaign. According to the figures given Himmler, the Totenkopfdivision in sixteen days of fighting had lost 82 officers and 1,626 NCOs and enlisted men killed, wounded or missing—nearly ten percent of the division's combat

[25] BAMA, III SS, 41/6, vol. 1, pp. 46-48, 51-55; III SS, 41/8, vol. 2, p. 13; and especially III SS, 47/2, Erlebnisberichte einzelner SS Soldaten, pp. 2-4. During this battle, Totenkopf soldiers for the first time encountered Russian tanks in significant numbers. At this stage of the campaign in the northern sector, the Red Army was using the huge, fifty-two-ton KV II tanks. These lumbering mammoths, with their low-velocity 152 mm cannon and thick armor, at first frightened the SS soldiers. Antitank gunners in SSTK, however, quickly learned to disable the KV IIs by shooting off the treads—leaving the helpless giants to be finished off by infantry and engineers. See I. G. Andronikow and W. D. Mostowenko, *Die Roten Panzer: Geschichte der sowjetischen Panzertruppen* (Munich, 1963), esp. pp. 252-54; and BAMA, III SS 41/8, vol. 2, p. 13; III SS, 41/6, vol. 3, p. 24.

strength. This serious casualty rate brought quick criticism from General Manstein, who felt the losses were disproportionate to the relatively modest gains made by SSTK during the first weeks of fighting.[26]

The breach of the Stalin Line removed the last great obstacle between the Germans and Leningrad. Accordingly, OKH ordered Hoepner's panzer group to resume its advance at once. Reinhardt's panzer corps was to strike north between Lakes Peipus and Ilmen and close in on Leningrad, while Manstein was to drive northeast to Novgorod on the north shore of Lake Ilmen to sever the main Leningrad-Moscow highway. As Manstein's Fifty-sixth Panzer Corps moved into action again on July 12, Hoepner detached the Totenkopfdivision and sent it north to Porkhov as part of the panzer group reserve. General Manstein parted with SSTK somewhat reluctantly, and expressed the hope that the division might someday again be under his command. Unpleasant events later fulfilled his wish much more quickly than anticipated.[27]

For three days after it was sent into reserve, the Totenkopfdivision enjoyed a period of relative quiet. The engineer battalion worked at repairing damaged roads and bridges in the Porkhov

[26] BAKO, NS/19-370, Kleinheisterkamp to Himmler, July 9, 1941; complemented by a report on losses suffered at Opochka as of July 11, in BAMA, III SS, 41/6, vol. 3, p. 24; and the Fifty-sixth Panzer Corps casualty figures for its divisions as of the morning of July 9, in NA/T-314/1390/0000030. These latter figures show that SSTK by July 9 had suffered nearly twice the total casualties of the other two divisions—Third Motorized and Eighth Panzer—in the Fifty-sixth Panzer Corps. SSTK casualties were heaviest in the First and Third Infantry Regiments. Owing to the lack of trained SS replacements, these losses were made up by transferring men from the Second Infantry Regiment of SSTK—a process that resulted in the dissolution of SSTK/I. R. 2 a month later. See especially, BAMA, III SS, 41/7, Anlagenbänder zum KTB No. 7, vol. 6, pp. 301-02.

When Manstein learned the full details of the serious and heavy fighting around Opochka, he retracted his criticism of the Totenkopfdivision, insisted that the record show officially that SSTK had captured Opochka by itself, and commended the division for its part in breaching the Stalin Line in a special letter he sent to Army Group North (NA/T-314/1388/0001056, "Generalkommando LVI A. K. (mot.), Ia Op." dated July 20, 1941; and NA/T-314/1388/000542, "Kdo. Pz. Gp. 4, Ia, an Heeresgruppe Nord," dated July 25, 1941).

[27] NA/T-314/1388/000513-514, "Kommando der Panzergruppe 4, Ia, an SS 'T'-Division," dated July 12, 1941; Halder, *KTB*, vol. 3, pp. 65-70, entries for July 11-12, 1941; Carell, *Hitler Moves East*, pp. 225-26; Manstein, pp. 193-94; and BAMA, III SS, 41/6, vol. 1, pp. 59-62, 64-65, 67.

area while the reconnaissance battalion and infantry regiments rounded up bypassed Russian units and probed cautiously into woods north of Porkhov. Enemy contact was slight, with only a few minor SS casualties as the result of the Russians' nightly artillery harassment. Meanwhile, Fifty-sixth Panzer Corps had run into trouble northeast of Porkhov and Manstein was forced to call for help. On July 17, SSTK was pulled out of reserve by Hoepner and reattached to the Fifty-sixth Panzer Corps.[28]

The crisis in Manstein's sector had developed on July 15 as the Eighth Panzer and Third Motorized Divisions attempted to cross the Mshaga River near the village of Zoltsy, some twenty-five miles southwest of Lake Ilmen. The Soviets threw two fresh divisions (the 180th Rifle and 220th Motorized) against Manstein's flank and rear from the southeast and northwest, respectively, disrupted communications within the panzer corps, and cut Manstein's main supply route that ran from Porkhov through Dno to Zoltsy. As a result, Hoepner ordered the Totenkopfdivision into action to help prevent any further delay in Manstein's drive on Novgorod.[29]

Attacking along the Dno-Zoltsy road, SSTK pushed the Russian infantry back to the southeast and sent a battalion to the village of Baranova to help the Third Motorized Division smash a series of armored and infantry attacks that lasted most of the night on July 17-18. The following day, Manstein ordered the Totenkopfdivision into the line on the right flank of the panzer corps to replace the exhausted Eighth Panzer Division, which was sent rearward to Porkhov to rest and hunt partisans. From this reassignment to combat duty the Totenkopfdivision remained committed to the fighting in Russia until its temporary withdrawal from Russia more than a year later after the battle of the Demyansk pocket.[30]

[28] BAMA, III SS, 41/6, vol. 1, pp. 66-69, 72-74; vol. 3, p. 31.

[29] Halder, *KTB*, vol. 3, pp. 88, 93, entries for July 17 and 18, 1941; Manstein, pp. 195-98; Carell, *Hitler Moves East*, pp. 230-32; and BAMA, III SS, 41/6, vol. 1, pp. 75-78, 80.

[30] Manstein, pp. 195-98; BAMA, III SS, 41/8, vol. 2, pp. 25-27; III SS, 41/6, vol. 1, pp. 81-83. Manstein was highly critical of Hoepner's decision to withdraw the Totenkopfdivision from the right flank of his panzer corps after the battle of Opochka. Manstein felt that if the Totenkopfdivision had been left in echelon to protect his right flank, the crisis of July 15 would not have been serious enough to

Coinciding with the division's recommitment to action was the arrival of a new commander, personally selected by Himmler to direct SSTK until Eicke's recovery. Himmler's choice was Brigadeführer Georg Keppler, a senior SS officer who had had a long career as a professional soldier and as a police officer before joining the SS. Prior to taking over the Totenkopfdivision, Keppler had served as a battalion commander in the SS Standarte Deutschland, and had commanded the crack SS Regiment Der Führer in the battle of France. The two months he was to spend with the Totenkopfdivision in Russia were among the most difficult of his long military career.[31]

The first task confronting Keppler was that of protecting Manstein's exposed flank as the German advance resumed on July 21. This assignment was made nearly impossible by the nature of the terrain. The SSTK soldiers found themselves in an almost prehistoric setting of gloomy forests, vast swamps, and dense thickets crisscrossed by a bewildering network of rivers and streams. The entire area southwest of Lake Ilmen, moreover, was poorly mapped and traversed only by narrow, soggy roads unsuitable for use by a motorized division. This environment provided the Soviets with overwhelming defensive advantages. In this hostile and forbidding landscape the special Russian fighting qualities— expertise in camouflage and ambush, preference for close-order fighting, and physical toughness and adaptability to the elements—had an immediate and dramatic effect on the combat. As the motorized columns of the Totenkopfdivision slithered into this stagnant wilderness the SS soldiers began a prolonged and terrible agony.[32]

---

halt his advance on Novgorod. By the time SSTK rejoined the Fifty-sixth Panzer Corps, Manstein had sat immobile while five precious days of perfect campaigning-weather passed. See especially, NA/T-314/1389/000297-298, for Manstein's letter to Hoepner of July 14, requesting retention of SSTK for the Fifty-sixth Panzer Corps; and Hoepner's reply of July 15, refusing on the grounds that Panzer Group Four could not detach forces whose absence would divert the army group from the main objective of Leningrad.

[31] USDC, SS Personalakte Keppler, summary of the materials in Keppler's SS service records, especially his Lebenslauf and Dienstlaufbahn. Keppler had been a company commander during the First World War, and in the years of the Weimar Republic rose through the ranks of the police as an officer and criminal inspector before becoming chief of the Schutzpolizei in Jena in 1930.

[32] BAMA, III SS, 41/8, vol. 2, pp. 28-30, 34-35. An appreciation of the nature

For ten days following Keppler's arrival, the Totenkopfdivision slogged through the swamps west of Lake Ilmen pushing the Soviet forces back to the north. By July 28, the Soviet units opposite SSTK had withdrawn northeast from the Utorgosch-Sakibje area across the Mshaga River into a new defense system hastily constructed by Russian infantry and conscripted civilian laborers from the Novgorod area. New orders drafted by Hoepner called for continued pursuit of the enemy to crack through the Russian fortifications stretching along the Mshaga and Luga Rivers from the western tip of Lake Ilmen to the Gulf of Finland. At the time, this defensive network known as the "Luga Line" was the last man-made barrier between the Germans and Leningrad.[33]

For the coming assault on the Luga Line the Totenkopfdivision received a difficult, dirty assignment. On July 31, Field Marshal Leeb detached SSTK from Manstein's panzer corps and sent it to stiffen the Twenty-eighth Army Corps. This force, commanded by General Herbert Wiktorin and part of the Sixteenth Army, was to attack the Russian positions on Manstein's right at the eastern end of the Luga Line, cross the Luga River, and position itself to the northeast as a blocking force to cover Hoepner's advance on Leningrad.[34]

---

of Russian defensive tactics was summarized in a report compiled by the intelligence staff of the Sixteenth Army and distributed to every division in Army Group North. Enemy snipers had been known to sit motionless for days in trees or thickets for a chance to kill one high-ranking German officer. Groups of Russian soldiers hid in the swamps, let German columns pass them, and then emerged to machine-gun supply columns, field hospitals, and regimental headquarters. As a result, soldiers in SSTK were instructed to advance through the forests in short spurts, spraying the trees on all sides with small-arms fire. All SS units were warned to keep each other in sight at all times, to stay alert for attacks from the rear, and to break every glass vessel they found so the Russians could not use them for making Molotov cocktails (ibid., III SS, 41/7, vol. 2, pp. 101-3).

[33] Ibid., III SS, 41/8, vol. 2, pp. 33-41; KTB/OKW, vol. 1, pp. 448-50; Halder, *KTB*, vol. 3, pp. 127-29, entry for July 28, 1941; Manstein, pp. 199-201; Clark, pp. 114-16; and Salisbury, pp. 200-201.

[34] BAMA, III SS, 41/7, vol. 2, pp. 2-3, 10-12. The Twenty-eighth Army Corps consisted of the Totenkopfdivision and the 121st and 122nd Infantry Divisions. The Totenkopf soldiers did not like being removed from Manstein's command, as they had grown to respect his superior talents as a field commander. Manstein, for his part, praised the division highly on its departure from his panzer corps, and later declared that he considered SSTK the best of all the Waffen SS divisions he had seen (BAKO, NS/19-370, letter from Manstein to Keppler, dated July 30, 1941; and Manstein, p. 188).

The new assignment and the transfer from Manstein's command produced widespread discontent among the officer corps of SSTK, and caused the first recorded case of serious friction between the Totenkopfdivision and the army. Keppler and Heinz Lammerding, the operations officer of SSTK, fell into a sharp dispute with General Wiktorin over alleged insults to SSTK made by headquarters staff members of Twenty-eighth Army Corps. The matter was settled quickly with a formal apology to Keppler from the army after the SSTK commander complained to Karl Wolff, and the latter aired the Totenkopfdivision's grievance at Hitler's headquarters.[35]

The quarrelsome attitude of the senior officers in SSTK also reflected the deteriorating conditions in the division. In a letter to Eicke written on August 8, the day the assault on the Luga Line began, Heinz Lammerding described soberly how the fighting had weakened the Totenkopfdivision. The clashes in the swampy, thickly wooded region, he wrote, had cost SSTK heavy casualties and had resulted in numerous vehicle breakdowns. In addition, the pattern of advancing in the day and repulsing Russian counterattacks all night had exhausted the men. Contact with other units, Lammerding continued, had become erratic and very difficult because of Russian snipers' success in picking off SS motorcycle couriers on the forest roads. Lammerding concluded with a bitter indictment of the army for the allegedly impossible objectives it continued to assign the Totenkopfdivision, and for its unrealistic view of the Red Army as a weakened, beaten force.[36]

At the time Lammerding wrote this gloomy report, the Totenkopfdivision supposedly enjoyed a quiet period in a temporarily inactive sector. The assault on the Mshaga fortifications, originally ordered for August 4, had been postponed until August 10 because of bad weather and supply difficulties. The Russians used

[35] BAKO, NS/19-370, copy of the report on the insult incident sent by Wiktorin to Sixteenth Army HQ on August 2, 1941; and *ibid.*, letter from Wolff to Keppler dated August 7, 1941. See also, Halder, *KTB*, vol. 3, p. 168, entry for August 10, 1941; and NA/T-314/786/0000041-0000043, "Der Oberbefehlshaber der 16. Armee, an XXVIII A. K.," dated August 3, 1941, for the letter of rebuke General Wiktorin received from the commanding general of the Sixteenth Army, Ernst Busch.
[36] BAKO, NS/19-370, "Im Osten, den 8. 8. 1941," an unsigned letter from Heinz Lammerding to Eicke.

the respite to entrench on the south bank of the Mshaga River along a line between the villages of Sakibye and Ugarely, and began harassing the units of the Totenkopfdivision. The Soviets dragged heavy mortars and artillery pieces forward and opened up on the exposed SS soldiers, whose own artillery was bogged down in the swamps miles to the rear. The Luftwaffe, moreover, could not silence the enemy guns because of a momentary fuel shortage and growing exhaustion among the overworked fighter pilots. The result was an increase in Totenkopf casualties and mounting anger among the weary SS soldiers.[37]

The Soviets at this point also began to gain valuable information by tapping the Totenkopfdivision's telephone lines and monitoring its radio messages. This led to attacks by Russian infantry against exposed and weak positions and forced Keppler to tighten the division's defensive posture. Finally, the Totenkopfdivision bore in these weeks the additional menace of large bands of partisans operating in its rear area. Groups of partisans using gasoline bombs, grenades, and small arms attacked columns and isolated units of SSTK moving through the deep forests. Knowing of the developing partisan menace behind them, the men in SSTK grew more uneasy in the face of Russian resistance that was stronger and more vicious with each passing week. The overall effect of the campaign until the beginning of August 1941 had been to weaken, exhaust, and dispirit the Totenkopfdivision. Thus debilitated, the division was expected to play a decisive role in the final German offensive that would demolish the Luga Line, lead to the quick seizure of Leningrad, and end operations in northern Russia before winter.[38]

The onslaught against the Soviet river defenses in the Totenkopfdivision's sector began at 4:30 A.M. on August 10. The course of the assault was a weary repetition of an already familiar pattern. Assault groups of SS infantry supported by Stukas and

[37] BAMA, III SS, 41/7, vol. 2, pp. 39-41, 49-51, 105-15, 127-35, 158-82, 190-93; vol. 6, pp. 279-80; 41/8, vol. 2, pp. 44-47. The Russian defense line along the Mshaga River was manned by the Soviet Seventieth and 237th Infantry Divisions and a mélange collected from a number of different rifle regiments. The Russian fortifications south of the Mshaga ran along the road from Shimsk through Stary-Medved to the wooded hills around the village of Ugorody.

[38] Ibid., III SS, 41/8, vol. 2, pp. 51-52; III SS, 41/7, vol. 2, pp. 136-39, 153-54.

artillery crossed the Mshaga at the village of Sakibye and established a firm bridgehead by dusk of the first day. Russian resistance, however, was suicidal, and Keppler's assault groups had to clear each of the numerous bunkers individually at great cost in hand-to-hand fighting. Once the SS bridgehead was established, the Soviets counterattacked. Fresh masses of Russian infantry, summoned from the Red Army's substantial reserve pool and driven to a frenzy by special rations of vodka and the exhortations of the commissars, charged repeatedly at the entrenched SS throughout the night, inflicting additional casualties that the Totenkopfdivision could ill afford. At daylight the attacks ceased abruptly and the Russians withdrew to regroup in new defensive positions—leaving the Totenkopf soldiers more fatigued and fewer in number.[39]

The same bloody pattern was repeated during the next several days. SSTK struggled forward, probing cautiously against enemy positions by day; and then dug-in at dusk to protect the day's gains against the nightly Russian artillery barrages and infantry counterattacks. On August 13 General Wiktorin suddenly ordered Keppler to swing the division's front to the northeast so as to cover the flank of the Twenty-eighth Army Corps while it continued its assault across the Luga. SSTK in effect was to stand still and absorb the continued punishing counterattacks from the east while the 121st and 122nd Infantry Divisions pursued the Soviet forces retreating northward. Keppler and Lammerding were furious over these orders and protested vigorously to Wiktorin—especially after Luftwaffe fighters strafed Totenkopf units that were shifting position in accordance with Twenty-eighth Army Corps orders. The relegation of the Totenkopfdivision to a role Keppler considered analogous to that of a punching bag did not last long, however, as a new crisis on the northern front forced a quick transfer of SSTK.[40]

[39] Ibid., III SS, 41/7, vol. 6, pp. 23-25; vol. 2, pp. 186, 190-96, 199, 200-203, 217-21; KTB/OKW, vol. 1, pp. 461-65; Halder, *KTB*, vol. 3, pp. 162-63, entry for August 8, 1941; Philippi and Heim, p. 73; and Clark, pp. 114-17. The main German assault on the Luga Line began on August 8, but was postponed in the sector of SSTK by torrential rains.

[40] BAMA, III SS, 41/7, vol. 2, pp. 223-38, 243, 246, 253-58, 263-68, 275; Halder, *KTB*, vol. 3, p. 173, entry for August 12, 1941. Lammerding was espe-

The new threat to Leeb's Army Group had developed on August 14 when the Soviet Thirty-fourth Army, a force consisting of eight infantry divisions and one cavalry corps, moved south from Novgorod around the eastern edge of Lake Ilmen and slammed into the flank of Busch's Sixteenth Army in the Staraya Russa-Demyansk area. Marshal Klementi Voroshilov, supreme commander of the Soviet Northwestern Front, hoped to drive a wedge between the right flank of Army Group North and the northernmost units of Bock's Army Group Center in the Rzhev area. Once he had split open the German front, Voroshilov unrealistically hoped to drive due west to Lake Peipus and cut off from the rear the German armies advancing toward Leningrad. Field Marshal Leeb responded to this challenge by detaching the Fifty-sixth Panzer Corps and the Totenkopfdivision from the Luga Line and sending them to aid the Tenth Army Corps—the German force that took the brunt of the Soviet Thirty-fourth Army's assault south of Lake Ilmen. SSTK was withdrawn from the Mshaga sector on the afternoon of August 14 and sent to Dno to await Manstein's arrival. Owing to a series of unexpected Russian counterattacks and the uncooperative attitude of his neighboring German divisions, Keppler had to withdraw the Totenkopfdivision very slowly from the Mshaga and did not manage to get the bulk of the division to Dno until midday on August 16.[41]

Upon arriving at Dno, Keppler found Manstein hatching a plan for using the motorized strength available (SSTK and the Third Motorized Division) to subdue Voroshilov's infantry and cavalry. While the Tenth Army Corps defended Staraya Russa and stalled the Russian attacks from the east and south, Manstein screened

---

cially irked by the fact that the Totenkopfdivision had been halted only after clearing the most difficult sector of enemy defenses for the Twenty-eighth Army Corps, and that the 121st and 122nd Infantry Divisions received all the credit in the army group communiqués.

[41] KTB/OKW, vol. 1, pp. 466, 469; Halder, *KTB*, vol. 3, pp. 175-80, entries for August 14 and 15, 1941; Clark, pp. 116-17; Salisbury, pp. 200-201; Manstein, pp. 200-201; Carell, *Hitler Moves East*, pp. 234-37; BAMA, III SS, 41/7, vol. 2, pp. 278-79, 281-82, 336, 340, 358, 363-68; III SS, 41/8, vol. 2, pp. 54-56. The Soviet breakthrough caused a minor crisis of nerves at the Führer Headquarters at Rastenburg and prompted Hitler to order the transfer of several units from the central front to help Manstein close the gap (Philippi and Heim, p. 74; KTB/OKW, vol. 1, pp. 467-68).

the concentration at Dno with infantry and quietly prepared SSTK and the Third Motorized Division for an assault against the left flank of the Soviet Thirty-fourth Army. On August 17, the Soviet attack swung north into the area directly east of Dno, exposing the Russian flank and rear directly to Manstein—whose presence at Dno was still undetected by the Thirty-fourth Army. General Manstein waited calmly until the Russians were heavily engaged against the Tenth Army Corps (Thirtieth and 126th Infantry Divisions), then blasted into the Soviet flank with the Third Motorized and SS Totenkopfdivision.[42]

This German counterthrust, which began at 7:00 A.M. on August 19, swiftly turned into the most spectacular operation in which SSTK had yet been involved. The Russians were taken offstride by Manstein's charge and crumbled quickly in confused panic. By late afternoon of the nineteenth, units of SSTK had taken 785 prisoners and captured undamaged ten enemy tanks, nine antitank guns, six heavy mortars, fifty automobiles, a score of horses, and a huge cache of small arms and ammunition. This was the single most successful day the Totenkopfdivision had experienced since the beginning of the Russian campaign. By the end of the day, all signs pointed to an imminent rout of the Soviet Thirty-fourth Army.[43]

The exuberant SS soldiers were not allowed to pause, however, as Manstein ordered immediate pursuit of the fleeing Russians. SSTK was ordered to press on through the night without regard to the situation on its flanks and to reach the Polist River just south of Lake Ilmen. Once there, Keppler was instructed to seize all the bridges he could find to cut off the Russians' escape route to the east. The Totenkopfdivision, therefore, continued on, deployed in

[42] KTB/OKW, vol. 1, p. 471; Carell, *Hitler Moves East*, pp. 236-38; Manstein, pp. 199-201; Salisbury, pp. 200-201; Halder, *KTB*, vol. 3, pp. 184-85, entry for August 18, 1941; and BAMA, III SS, 41/7, vol. 2, pp. 371-75, 388-91, 399-402; III SS, 41/8, vol. 2, pp. 57-62. To reduce the risk of his motorized columns' bogging down in the swamp around Staraya Russa, thus allowing the Russians to slip away, Manstein ordered Keppler to leave all unnecessary vehicles at Dno and to gather from the supply and support units of SSTK every man who could be spared for combat duty BAMA, III SS, 41/7, vol. 2, pp. 407-409).

[43] BAMA, III SS, 41/8, vol. 2, pp. 64-65; III SS, 41/7, vol. 2, pp. 431-39, 447-56, 465-70, 475-76; III SS, 41/7, vol. 6, pp. 57-58; Halder, *KTB*, vol. 3, p. 187, entry for August 19, 1941.

the shape of a wedge with the reconnaissance battalion in the center and the two infantry regiments strung out on either side. The haul in prisoners and booty was even larger on August 20, as all coordinated Russian resistance ceased and the Soviet forces disintegrated under the constricting pressure of the Fifty-sixth Panzer Corps and the Tenth Army Corps. By dusk, SSTK had advanced fifteen miles, captured the village strongpoints of Baranova, Dubrova, and Pikulino, taken over 900 prisoners, and seized vast stocks of food, weapons, ammunition, and gasoline. The shattered remnants of the Soviet Thirty-fourth Army were squeezed into a small triangle bordered on the east by the Polist River, the northwest by the Tenth Army Corps, and in the southwest by Manstein. The only remaining task for SSTK and the other German divisions was to liquidate the encircled army.[44]

After an all-night artillery bombardment of the trapped Russians, SSTK and the Third Motorized Division moved in for the kill early on August 21. Mass slaughter followed. Whole companies and battalions of Russian infantry were blown down by machine-gun fire or ripped apart by artillery as they sought to escape encirclement across the Polist. The SS soldiers advanced at a walk raking the ground ahead with machine-gun fire and destroying with grenades and high explosives every building, bunker, or suspected enemy position in their path. On August 21, SSTK captured more men and enemy matériel than it had at any other time since the closing hours of the battle of France. Keppler's field police gathered over 1,000 enemy prisoners, while other units of SSTK sorted out items that included 23 heavy artillery pieces with attached tractors, 10 trench mortars, 25 fully loaded ammunition trailers, and another 200 horses. In mid-afternoon, General Manstein arrived at Keppler's field headquarters in high spirits and

---

[44] BAMA, III SS, 41/7, vol. 2, pp. 478-87, 497-503, 508-14, 519-21; III SS, 41/8, vol. 2, pp. 67-68. In addition to the prisoners captured on August 20, the Totenkopfdivision claimed the seizure of 500 horses, 100 wagons, 12 artillery pieces, 1,000 liters of gasoline, and 5 fully stocked Russian field kitchens. These figures were given by Lammerding in his daily report to the Fifty-sixth Panzer Corps, and subsequently were confirmed by Manstein (BAMA, III SS, 41/7, vol. 3, pp. 50-55, a copy of the report sent by the Fifty-sixth Panzer Corps to Army Group North describing the action of August 19-20 in the Polist sector).

praised the Totenkopfdivision for its key role in the destruction of the Soviet forces along the Polist River.[45]

By nightfall on August 21 all Russian troops west of the river had been killed or captured, and only a few scattered small units had slipped through the German ring and escaped across the Polist into the swamps. Voroshilov's plan to outflank the army group and take Hoepner in the rear had been thwarted. Manstein's brilliant counterthrust, however, was at best only a limited victory. He had eliminated the temporary threat to Leeb's flank and rear (and destroyed eight Soviet divisions in the process). It had, however, taken him five days to do it. During these five days most of the army group had remained at a standstill, awaiting the outcome of Manstein's counterthrust. The Soviets had used this precious respite to stiffen their defenses before Leningrad and to deploy additional reserves of infantry, armor, and artillery in the outskirts of the city.

The sacrifice of the Thirty-fourth Army left the Soviet northwestern front in a stronger rather than a weaker position. In this lengthening war of attrition, as the example of the Totenkopfdivision illustrated so well, German strength was beginning to ebb markedly in the face of the Russians' numerical superiority and their willingness to attack regardless of losses in order to kill German soldiers. Although not then apparent, the offensive initiative in northern Russia was passing permanently to the Soviets. The exertions endured by the Totenkopfdivision during the following weeks provided dramatic evidence of how decisively, even at that early date, the tide of war in northern Russia was turning against the Germans.[46]

---

[45] BAMA, III SS, 41/7, vol. 3, pp. 7-11, 16-17, 25-30, 44, 56-60, 64-68; III SS, 41/7, vol. 6, pp. 75-79, 90-93. In his daily report to Keppler on August 21, Kleinheisterkamp inadvertently mentioned that his soldiers had shot a captured commissar during the day. This was a slip-up, as it violated Eicke's express orders not to include such information in written communications (ibid., III SS, 41/7, vol. 3, p. 60.

[46] According to the figures compiled by the Sixteenth Army, 33,140 Russian prisoners, 498 cannons, 275 tanks, 1,131 machine guns, 930 motor vehicles, 209 mortars, and 72 antitank guns were captured in the Polist sector as a result of Manstein's destruction of the Soviet Thirty-fourth Army. General Manstein, however, calculated that by August 22 the Soviets had made good these losses by moving three new armies into the area south of Lake Ilmen and opposite the Sixteenth

The pursuit of the remaining Soviet forces across the Polist resumed at midday on August 22. Manstein spurred his divisions eastward toward the Lovat and Pola rivers to prevent the Russians from regrouping for a major counterattack along these parallel natural barriers. The rapid advance of SSTK and the Third Motorized Division was for several days almost unopposed, and by the time both units reached the Lovat they had rounded up additional groups of Russian stragglers and hundreds of tons of war matériel. Upon reaching the river, however, the weary German troops found the Russians already dug in and prepared to hand out more punishment. Unusually intense activity by the Red Air Force over the area between the Lovat and Pola Rivers also greeted the arrival of Manstein's divisions. The absence of German fighter cover (a result of the reconcentration of the Luftwaffe to support Hoepner's renewed advance on Leningrad) finally forced SSTK and the Third Motorized to halt completely on the twenty-fifth and to take cover in the woods west of the Lovat.[47]

The Totenkopfdivision was ordered to attack again on the morning of August 26 and to keep going until it had thrown the Russians back across the Pola. This assignment proved unrealistic in view of the new Russian strength. The attack was finally called off when several squadrons of Soviet fighters appeared and began methodically blasting the assembled SSTK vehicle columns with rocket and cannon fire. Repeated calls by Keppler to the Luftwaffe for help brought no response, and the SS men were

---

Army (BAMA, III SS, 41/7, vol. 3, pp. 251-52; Manstein, pp. 201-2). By contrast, the German casualty and replacement situation at the end of August had become serious. In a report to Army Group North written on August 21, General Busch claimed every division in the Sixteenth Army had suffered at least forty percent total casualties since June 22. Among the divisions in the Fifty-sixth Panzer Corps, SSTK had the highest rate of losses with over 4,000 total combat casualties. In the case of the Totenkopfdivision, Busch declared, these losses reduced the division's combat effectiveness even more sharply because of the unusually high number of SS officers killed, wounded, or missing (NA/T-312/548/8156867-6869, "A. O. K. 16, Ia, Gefechtskraft der Div., An Heeresgruppe Nord," dated August 21, 1941).

[47] BAMA, III SS, 41/7, vol. 3, pp. 115-46, 202-3, 212-18, 240-47, 281, 287; vol. 6, pp. 109, 112-14. For the week of August 17-24, 1941, the Totenkopfdivision claimed the capture of 5,586 prisoners, 41 tanks, 5 armored cars, 67 artillery pieces, 1,088 horses, 311 baggage wagons, 98 trucks, 14 field kitchens, and 10,000 liters of gasoline.

forced to huddle against the ground without air cover for the rest of the day. Gathering thunderclouds just before dusk finally forced the Soviet fighters home, leaving the Totenkopfdivision with a number of casualties and wrecked vehicles.[48]

With the reappearance of the Luftwaffe the following day the advance resumed in earnest, and the reconnaissance battalion of SSTK reached the Pola near the village of Vasilyevschina at 9:30 that evening. A sudden temperature drop after sundown brought a torrential downpour that lasted all night and turned the Totenkopfdivision's sector of the front into a slimy quagmire. Despite the heavy rains and the exhaustion of the troops, Manstein ordered Keppler to cross the Pola on August 28 and annihilate the Russian units on the other side. Before the Totenkopfdivision could move into action, however, the Soviets attacked with several battalions of infantry. Consequently, SSTK spent all of the twenty-eighth and most of the twenty-ninth repulsing these charges and clearing Russian stragglers and snipers out of the woods on the German-held side of the river. Throughout this time the heavy rains continued, and by the evening of August 29 the narrow forest roads under the Totenkopfdivision had become impassable. Even the tracked vehicles of SSTK were stuck fast.[49]

Manstein, however, was determined not to allow the adverse weather to give the Russians additional time to dig in, and issued new orders for an attack across the Pola by the Fifty-sixth Panzer Corps on August 30. These instructions elicited a strong protest from Keppler and caused a rare instance of friction between General Manstein and the Totenkopfdivision. At a conference at Keppler's headquarters at 5:00 P.M. on August 29, the Totenkopf commander told Manstein bluntly that the debilitated condition of SSTK made any further advance out of the question. He also asked that Manstein intercede with Army Group North at once to

[48] Ibid., III SS, 41/8, vol. 2, pp. 73-74; III SS, 41/7, vol. 3, pp. 340-41, 346-54, 357-58. The Flak batteries of SSTK were kept busy all day on August 26, and claimed at the end of the day to have shot down five Soviet fighters.

[49] BAMA, III SS, 41/7, vol. 3, pp. 398-99, 403, 419-25, 459-63, 465-66. The size of the Soviet build-up east of the Pola worried Manstein, and he warned Keppler on August 27 that the Totenkopfdivision would probably encounter heavy Russian resistance from at least one fresh infantry division (the 192nd Rifle Division), which had been moved into the front opposite SSTK and alongside the Soviet Thirty-third Rifle Division.

have the Totenkopfdivision withdrawn from the front for a rest. According to Keppler, his SS soldiers were so exhausted and their bodily resistance so weakened that the cases of sickness had become almost too numerous to handle. In addition, heavy casualties (4,854 dead), insufficient replacements, and the worn out state of the vehicles and equipment had reduced the Totenkopfdivision's effectiveness as a line unit. Keppler concluded by urging Manstein to call off the attack scheduled for the next day, since it was obvious that the Soviets had amassed great strength beyond the Pola and had the advantage in this sector of the front. Manstein was won over by Keppler's argument and agreed to postpone the attack until the weather cleared. While it rained, the Totenkopfdivision could sit and rest in its positions along the river. In addition, Manstein promised Keppler he would do everything possible to have the Totenkopfdivision relieved in the immediate future.[50]

The Russians, however, were not so agreeable as Manstein, and denied the Totenkopfdivision its much-needed respite. From the few remaining bridgeheads they still held on the Pola, the Soviets launched a series of strong counterattacks on the morning of August 30 and forced SSTK and the Third Motorized Division to fight desperately to hold their positions. When the last attack had been beaten off in late afternoon, Russian artillery opened up to keep Manstein's divisions pinned down and awake throughout

[50] Ibid., III SS, 41/7, vol. 3, pp. 468-69, 472; vol. 6, pp. 292-95; BAKO, NS/ 19-370, letter from Keppler to Eicke of August 30, 1941, describing the conference with Manstein and the overall condition of the Totenkopfdivision. In his letter to Eicke, Keppler wrote that exhaustion, soggy rations, and the bad weather had caused an epidemic of dysentery in the division. Keppler also claimed that casualties among the SS officers and NCOs in SSTK were so high that if qualified replacements were not sent forward immediately the division would be leaderless.

Manstein was alarmed by Keppler's remarks and shocked by the obvious physical deterioration of the SS men he reviewed. Immediately after returning to his HQ from the conference with Keppler, Manstein wrote to Busch urging that both SSTK and the Third Motorized Division be detached from Sixteenth Army to rest and refit. Unless such respite were granted immediately, Manstein claimed, the men and matériel in both divisions would break down completely. In his reply of August 30, Busch dismissed Manstein's alarm with the observation that SSTK was no more tired than any other formation on the eastern front, and ordered the Fifty-sixth Panzer Corps to proceed with its advance into the Demyansk area (NA/T-314/1389/0000329-0331, 0000332-0333, Manstein to Busch, August 29, 1941; and Busch's reply of August 30, 1941).

the night. The following morning the Russians attacked again in even greater strength and, to the consternation of Keppler's men, managed to get several tanks across the river and into action against SSTK.[51]

The situation became especially tense in the sector occupied by Kleinheisterkamp's Third Infantry Regiment, where the enemy armored and infantry attacks became the strongest. During the morning the Soviets managed to overrun part of the area held by the First Battalion of the Third Infantry Regiment, and their tanks narrowly missed penetrating all the way through the Totenkopfdivision's front. The Russian attacks finally were stopped and their tanks destroyed by the individual initiative of a few SS officers, who exposed themselves constantly to enemy fire to direct the defense and personally led the reckless charges that knocked out the Russian tanks.[52]

After the heavy fighting on August 31, a temporary lull settled over the Pola front as heavy casualties, exhaustion, and the uninterrupted rain took their toll on the Russian side. The Soviets, however, still clung to the west bank of the Pola at the villages of Rykalova and Staraya Gorki. From these bridgeheads they continued to harass the Germans with artillery and heavy patrol activity. On September 4, the rain let up enough for Manstein to order renewed preparations for an attempted German crossing on September 5. That same day, the engineers in the Totenkopfdivision began tearing down all civilian dwellings in the area to use the wood for bridge-building materials. The following morning, under a bright, sunny sky, two battalions from Kleinheisterkamp's regiment forded the Pola at Romanovo and established a tentative bridgehead. Their position improved during the after-

[51] BAMA, III SS, 41/7, vol. 3, pp. 475, 479-80, 495-500, 503-4, 508-18, 528-29. On the basis of information gained from Soviet prisoners, SSTK intelligence officers by August 30 had identified parts of eight Russian divisions—six infantry and two motorized—in the Pola sector opposite the Fifty-sixth Panzer Corps.

[52] Ibid., pp. 520-22; vol. 6, pp. 129-32. The tanks that crossed the Pola on August 31 were Soviet KV IIs. The standard—if risky—SS procedure for engaging a KV II was to disable it by shooting off a tread. A lone SS man (often an officer) would then dash forward and stuff a live grenade into the muzzle of the tank's cannon, or place a double-satchel charge on the hull of the tank where the turret joined the deck.

noon when General Manstein ordered the Army's 503rd Infantry Regiment across the river into the bridgehead. By the evening of September 5, the Fifty-sixth Panzer Corps had one foot planted firmly on the east bank of the Pola—after a delay of eight days.[53]

This belated success was soon compromised by the caprice of the elements and the ubiquitous resiliency of the Russians. It began raining hard again just after dark on September 5, causing the vehicles of the Totenkopfdivision to sink helplessly once again into the muck. As expected, the Soviets took advantage of the worsening weather and renewed their pressure on the Germans with strong infantry assaults during the night and heavy air attacks on Romanovo the following morning. Gradual clearing on the afternoon of the sixth enabled Keppler to enlarge the bridgehead by ferrying engineers, more infantry, and part of the artillery regiment across the river. At the same time, the Third Motorized Division finally secured a crossing, and by evening the pressure against the Totenkopfdivision's foothold at Romanovo had eased considerably.

The return of warm, dry weather and the rapid improvement in road conditions in the Pola sector enabled Manstein to cross the river in force on September 7 and to order an attack by the Fifty-sixth Panzer Corps for the eighth. With the simultaneous resumption of offensive operations by Manstein's neighbors (Second and Tenth Army Corps) the Russians once again were forced into a general retreat. The immediate objective of the Sixteenth Army was to encircle and destroy the Soviet forces withdrawing from the Pola. Manstein's superior Colonel General Busch hoped as a result to take possession of the Valdai Hills and establish a continuous German front between Lake Ilmen and Lake Seliger.

The Russians, however, had taken care to mine and booby trap nearly every yard of all the roads east of the river, so that the Germans were able to advance no faster than the pace at which the army and SS engineers cleared the minefields. Moreover, Russian

[53] BAMA, III SS, 41/8, vol. 2, pp. 76-77; III SS, 41/7, vol. 4, pp. 4-5, 13, 75-92, 100-101, 111-19. General Manstein's difficulties in this sector were compounded by the numerous loops and bends in the course of the Pola River. The high, densely wooded banks along the shore provided the Russians with excellent defensive cover, while the river's meandering course made the shoreline on both sides too long to hold as a continuous front.

skill at concealing mines and booby traps caused some casualties and a good deal of damage to vehicles in the Totenkopfdivision. The slow advance and the absence of consistent air cover also left SSTK and the Third Motorized Division especially vulnerable to Russian aircraft. Soviet fighters appeared in relays throughout the day, bombing and strafing the units of the Totenkopfdivision from treetop level.[54]

By September 10, the renewed German drive had full momentum. The large groups of Russian prisoners and tons of weapons and supplies that Manstein's divisions hauled in once again evoked the image of a broken and fleeing enemy. The Soviets, however, had merely withdrawn behind rearguard protection to regroup for another series of counterattacks. Strengthened by fresh reserves, the Russians lashed back with such strength in the Demyansk area on the eleventh and twelfth that the Germans had to abandon offensive operations and entrench in a permanent defensive network to protect the extreme right wing of Leeb's army group. In vicious fighting during these two days, the Totenkopfdivision and the Third Motorized Division managed to halt the Russian attacks along the Demyansk-Staraya Russa highway and to stabilize this sector of the German front.[55]

The Sixteenth Army's change to a defensive posture on September 12 coincided with orders from OKH for General Manstein's transfer to assume command of the Eleventh Army with Army Group South. Keppler received accompanying instructions

[54] Ibid., III SS, 41/7, vol. 4, pp. 142-45, 171, 219-20, 245-52; III SS, 41/8, vol. 2, p. 80; Clark, pp. 122-23. The absence of German fighter cover on September 8 was owing to the transfer of the Luftwaffe's entire Eighth Air Fleet to duty with Army Group Center. This was done in anticipation of renewed offensive operations to capture Moscow. As a result, Army Group North had to give up all the aircraft it could spare, and after September 7 had fewer than 300 operational planes for supply and combat missions. Thus, at the very moment the German formations south of Lake Ilmen were exhausted and losing the initiative to the Russians, Hitler withdrew their air cover. When the Russians launched their powerful counteroffensive several weeks later, this coincidence proved nearly fatal for the Totenkopfdivision.

[55] BAMA, III SS, 41/7, vol. 4, pp. 278-80; KTB/OKW, vol. 1, p. 630; and NA/T-312/549/8158339-8340, 8158354, reports submitted by the Fifty-sixth Panzer Corps to the Sixteenth Army on September 13, and the Sixteenth Army to Army Group North on September 15, confirming the SSTK figures for prisoners captured and war matériel taken.

reassigning SSTK to the Second Army Corps for duty in clearing the remaining enemy units out of the forests north of Demyansk.[56]

On Monday, September 15, 1941, soldiers of the Totenkopfdivision began building bunkers and shelters in the blackened ruins of villages with names like Kirilovschina, Grutiki, Chilkovo, and Lushno. Facing the Totenkopf soldiers was a similar Russian defensive network on the other side of the Pola. At certain points along the winding river, German and Russian bridgeheads remained on either enemy's bank. This situation placed the Totenkopfdivision in acute peril, as it prevented the establishment of an airtight front and allowed the Russians to filter through the swamps and probe the area to Keppler's rear.

The senior officers in the Totenkopfdivision, however, were not unduly worried about the gaps along their front, nor were they especially anxious to hasten the work on the division's fortifications. The majority of the unit commanders, in line with the official view put forward by OKH, seemed convinced that the heavy fighting and adverse weather had hurt the Russians more than it had themselves. Many SS officers were certain that the Red Army had already lost most of its best-trained, top-quality troops, and were left with only undisciplined, inferior reserve units. The consensus of the Totenkopfdivision staff, despite mounting evidence to the contrary, was that the Russians were beaten and that all Soviet resistance would collapse before the end of winter. For those Totenkopf soldiers who shared this view, the shock of the next few weeks was unusually traumatic.[57]

Signs of what lay ahead were evident as early as September 18. SS construction parties found themselves harassed constantly with deadly artillery fire, and men in the forward observation posts began hearing engine noises generated by large numbers of vehi-

[56] BAMA, III SS, 41/7, vol. 4, pp. 299-300, 308-18, 322; vol. 6, pp. 324, 339-41; III SS, 41/8, vol. 2, pp. 81-83. Manstein's departure from the Totenkopfdivision was a parting based on mutual esteem. Before leaving for southern Russia, Manstein thanked Keppler personally for the Totenkopfdivision's "exceptional performance" while part of the Fifty-sixth Panzer Corps.

[57] Halder, *KTB*, vol. 3, pp. 232-33, entry for September 15, 1941; BAMA, III SS, 41/7, vol. 4, pp. 363-66, 375-77, 397-99, 405-8, 425-26; III SS, 41/8, vol. 2, pp. 85-86; BAKO, NS/19-370, action report of the First Infantry Regiment of SSTK, dated September 17, 1941.

cles moving around in the woods beyond the river. The following day, Russian aircraft again appeared in dense formations over the Pola and forced a halt to all construction activity as the Totenkopf soldiers were driven to whatever cover they could find. The artillery fire and air attacks continued throughout the day. When they ceased at dusk, the first infantry assaults began. These attacks caught many units of SSTK in unfinished defensive positions and were repulsed only with great difficulty and at heavy cost. Shortly before midnight the infantry charges ceased abruptly, and an ominous silence fell over the Pola sector as a dense, bone-chilling fog rolled in from Lake Ilmen and shrouded the combatants from each other's view.[58]

For the next two days the sector held by the Totenkopfdivision remained very quiet, with little or no movement and noise observed in the enemy defensive positions. Into this quiet but tense atmosphere, Eicke returned on September 21. After a four-hour briefing by Keppler and Lammerding, he assumed active command of the Totenkopfdivision once again and Keppler reported to Himmler for reassignment. Eicke was shocked by the physical condition of his men, and wrote immediately to Karl Wolff protesting. In a tone as close as he ever came to compassion, Eicke complained that the exertions suffered by his men were far beyond the limits of human endurance. Describing his soldiers as emaciated wrecks in rotten, soggy clothing, he requested Wolff to intercede at once with Hitler so the Totenkopfdivision could be given a rest. In stronger language, he demanded that Jüttner release a number of NCOs who had been sent home on leave from the Totenkopfdivision, but in the interim had been transferred to other SS agencies. This, Eicke concluded, was especially urgent, since the division was suffering from an acute shortage of SS officers and NCOs.[59]

[58] BAMA, III SS, 41/7, vol. 5, pp. 11-18, 47-59, 103, 107, 109-16, 122. Some of the Russian attacks on September 19 were led in person by commissars, several of whom were captured and immediately shot by SS officers (ibid., III SS, 41/7, vol. 5, pp. 110-11).

[59] BAKO, NS/19-370, Eicke to Karl Wolff, September 21, 1941. The undertone of hostility to the army in Eicke's letter to Wolff, and the hints that the generals somehow were to blame for the condition of the Totenkopfdivision, were totally unjustified. In a conference at Sixteenth Army HQ on September 19, the

Eicke's return to command the Totenkopfdivision was both timely and crucial. During his absence SSTK had been deprived of the benefits normally gained through his formidable aggressiveness in dealing with the SS supply and support agencies. While Eicke was home convalescing, moreover, his rivals converged upon his abandoned preserve. Other SS organizations had grabbed his seasoned officers and NCOs who had been wounded and sent home to recuperate; Jüttner and the SS Führungshauptamt took advantage of his absence to seize completely the reserve units of the Totenkopfdivision. Finally, the quality and quantity of replacements and equipment sent to SSTK declined markedly during the months Eicke was absent. In resuming command, he moved quickly to halt these developments and to improve the general condition of the Totenkopfdivision.

Furthermore, Eicke's return was crucial because it came on the very eve of the greatest crisis the Totenkopfdivision had faced. The confidence his presence inspired and the catalytic effect that his fanaticism had among the ranks proved invaluable in pulling the Totenkopfdivision through the Soviet counteroffensive that began two days later.[60]

Eicke's first warning of what the Russians intended came on the morning of September 22. At that time, the Second Army Corps notified the Totenkopfdivision that three new Red Army brigades had been identified along the Pola, and that the Russians were stepping up patrol and reconnaissance activity. Eicke immediately alerted all his units and ordered increased patrols to prevent

commander in chief of the army, Field Marshal Brauchitsch, took special note of the severely weakened state of SSTK, and recommended to Busch that the division be entrenched behind a heavily mined sector south of Lake Ilmen and committed to action only in the event of serious Russian attacks. Brauchitsch also noted that SSTK was short 2,800 replacements (NA/T-314/548/8157268-7271, typed copy of the minutes of the meeting between Brauchitsch and Busch on September 19, 1941).

With Eicke's return there was renewed emphasis upon racial and ideological indoctrination. These activities had been drastically curtailed by the more subdued and less fanatical Keppler during the period in which SSTK was so heavily engaged in combat (BAMA, III SS, 41/7, vol. 6, p. 329).

[60] BAKO, NS/19-370, "Auflösung des Feldersatz Bataillons der SS-T. Division," dated August 7, 1941. This was a circular order from Jüttner dissolving the remaining reserve battalions of the Totenkopfdivision and transferring their personnel, arms, and equipment to the jurisdiction of the SS Führungshauptamt.

enemy infiltration of the Totenkopfdivision's defenses. During the morning of September 23 the positions held by SSTK once more received intense air attacks and artillery fire. By noon Russian infantry had begun to probe along the northern or left wing of the Totenkopfdivision—especially against the sector held by the Second Battalion of Kleinheisterkamp's Third Infantry Regiment. In this heavily wooded area, between the villages of Suchaya-Niva and Lushno, there was a slight gap in the German line between the left flank of the Totenkopfdivision and the right wing of the neighboring Thirtieth Infantry Division. By probing, the Russians discovered this weak spot and made it the focal point of their furious attacks during the days that followed.[61]

Russian air attacks continued at two-hour intervals throughout the day, while reports filtered in to Eicke from forward posts describing large troop concentrations and assembled formations of Russian tanks east of the river. In late afternoon two Russian deserters told their startled SS interrogators that a massive attack was planned for noon on September 23. The object of this attack, they said, was to rip open the German front south of Lake Ilmen so that the Soviet forces along the Pola could drive into the flank and rear of the German armies besieging Leningrad. This disquieting information was passed along immediately to every unit in the Totenkopfdivision and a full alert was ordered to begin at dark. That night the shivering soldiers of the Totenkopfdivision experienced an additional unpleasant sensation. The temperature dropped below freezing for the first time in the Russian campaign and a thick frost covered the ground—a prophetic gesture by the elements.[62]

Promptly at noon on September 24 the Russians attacked the SS Totenkopfdivision with shattering impact. Eicke's infantry regiments were literally engulfed by human tidal waves. Whole regi-

[61] Philippi and Heim, p. 81; KTB/OKW, vol. 1, p. 653; BAMA, III SS, 41/7, vol. 5, pp. 162-67, 170-77; III SS, 47/2, pp. 5-6; BAKO, NS/19-370, Eicke to Karl Wolff, September 30, 1941. On September 23, the Totenkopfdivision was strung out facing northeast along a fifteen mile front between Lushno in the north and Plemevizy in the south. Max Simon's First Infantry Regiment was deployed in the southern half of the defensive network, while Kleinheisterkamp's Third Infantry Regiment occupied the northern part of the Division's front which terminated at Lushno.

[62] BAMA, III SS, 41/7, vol. 5, p. 184; vol. 6, pp. 166-67; III SS, 47/2, pp. 6-7.

ments of Soviet infantry in marching formation charged out of the forests, swarmed across the Pola River and fell upon the SS soldiers. Simultaneously, the Red Air Force appeared, raking Eicke's units with machine-gun and rocket fire. By mid-afternoon the situation had become chaotic. A flood of confused telephone calls and radio messages requesting orders, information, ammunition (and help) poured in upon Eicke's headquarters. By 3:00 P.M. the Russians had penetrated deeply into the division's defenses at several points, and had surrounded and isolated a number of individual SSTK units and strongpoints.[63]

At Lushno, where the initial attack was the strongest, two regiments of Russian infantry charging behind a screen of twenty tanks crashed into the Second Battalion of the Third Infantry Regiment and scattered the SS men in confused retreat. Only quick action by antitank gunners and individual batteries of Eicke's artillery regiment saved the situation at Lushno. Gunners from the Second Company of the tank-destroyer battalion engaged the Soviet armor at close range, fired until their ammunition was gone, and knocked out nine enemy tanks in less than an hour. Batteries of SSTK artillery deployed behind Lushno, some of them firing over open sights, blasted entire platoons of Russian infantry into bloody heaps of raw flesh and splintered bone. Gradually, as the afternoon waned, the units of the Totenkopfdivision stiffened, and with precise and methodical fire repulsed the suicidal enemy charges. As the division regained its balance, Eicke ordered a counterattack to recapture Lushno and warned all his units to be prepared for continued massive enemy assaults. By dusk, Totenkopf infantry and engineers had dislodged the Russians from Lushno and forced them to withdraw into the forest east of the village.[64]

[63] Ibid., III SS, 41/7, vol. 5, pp. 203-10; vol. 6, pp. 167-78; III SS, 47/2, pp. 7-11. The SS radio company at Lushno lost all its vehicles and equipment to fire from Soviet tanks on the afternoon of September 24, disrupting for several hours all communications between Eicke's headquarters and the Toteknopf units in the area most heavily attacked.

[64] BAMA, III SS, 41/7, vol. 5, pp. 210, 212-24. The massive Russian air attacks on September 24 were the most devastating the Totenkopfdivision had experienced. The Flak batteries of SSTK counted 225 Soviet aircraft during the afternoon, and reported that damage to vehicles, communications equipment, and to the supply and ammunition dumps was extensive.

The lull, as Eicke had expected, was only a short one; at 5:00 A.M. on September 25 the Russians stormed out of the woods toward Lushno in an attempt to break through the Totenkopfdivision's flank. The forces employed in this assault on Lushno were much stronger than those that had attacked the day before. The Russian infantry moved forward behind a screen of thirty tanks (including several brand new T-34s). Once again the Russians penetrated the SS defensive positions and hand-to-hand fighting raged. This time, however, the Totenkopf soldiers were prepared and held their ground firmly while slaughtering the enemy infantry with coordinated artillery, machine gun and small arms fire. The Soviets kept up their attacks at half-hour intervals all day, and by evening the open spaces in front of the SS positions were heaped with corpses. In their desperation to break through the Totenkopfdivision's defenses, the Russians on September 25 employed what were, even for them, novel tactics. In mid-afternoon a company of startled SS engineers, dug in behind a minefield south of Lushno, repulsed an attack led by a herd of pigs. To clear a path through the minefield without suffering casualties, the Russians gathered all the hogs they could find and stampeded the frightened, squealing animals through the mines and into the German positions. Eicke's soldiers, however, seemed prepared for any eventuality and turned back even this assault with heavy losses to both the Russians and the pigs.[65]

The Soviet counteroffensive on the Pola reached its high point on September 26-27. In a series of attacks beginning just after midnight of the twenty-sixth, the Russians committed all their reserves in a continuous forty-eight-hour assault along the entire length of the Totenkopfdivision's front. Once more, the weight of the Russian blow fell upon the vulnerable junction in the German front at Lushno; and once more the SS soldiers in the Third Infantry Regiment of the Totenkopfdivision refused to crack under the tremendous onslaught. Decimated by heavy casualties, weakened

---

[65] Ibid., pp. 244-50, 254. During the counteroffensive at Lushno, the Russian infantry were emboldened with an extra ration of vodka, and in some cases literally staggered toward the German lines. One battery in the artillery regiment of SSTK reported that enemy soldiers on September 25 ran straight at the entrenched SS heavy guns without taking cover. The few who survived the heavy shelling then charged aimlessly about in the field of fire until killed or exhausted.

from three days without food deliveries, and hampered by a growing shortage of ammunition, the SS defenders gradually and grudgingly gave ground at Lushno in furious fighting. By evening on September 26 every SS officer in the Second Battalion of SSTK/I. R. 3—including four successive battalion commanders —had been killed, and the unit had less than 150 survivors still in action. Despite these incredible conditions, this same battalion actually managed to launch a counterattack after dark on September 26, and retook the village of Lushno.[66]

Elsewhere along the front, other units of SSTK were locked in desperate struggles. The situation grew so critical on September 27 that Eicke ordered every available man from the supply and support units into the front line, armed himself and his staff officers with rifles, and moved in behind the line at Lushno to serve as a last-ditch reserve. The fighting raged continuously all day with an intensity never before and seldom afterward experienced by the Totenkopf soldiers. The Russians threw over 100 tanks and the numerical equivalent of three infantry divisions against the battered Totenkopfdivision on September 27 and still failed to crack the SS defenses. Under conditions that defy description, the fanatical survivors of this remarkable Waffen SS formation summoned their last reserves of energy and determination and smashed the Russian forces besieging them.[67]

[66] Ibid., pp. 259-79; III SS, 41/7, vol. 6, pp. 166-78; III SS, 50/1, SS-T. K. Div. I. R. 3, KTB v. 6. 6. 41 bis 14. 12. 41, "Darstellung der Ereignisse," pp. 76-79, for a meticulously detailed, hourly account of the Russian attacks on September 24-26. See also, KTB/OKW, vol. 1, pp. 662, 664; BAKO, NS/19-370, letter from Eicke to Karl Wolff of September 30, 1941, describing the Soviet counterthrust on the Pola; NA/T-312/584/0000730-0732, "A. O. K. 16, Lage am 27. 9. 1941," a detailed situation map of the sector of the front south of Lake Ilmen; and NA/T-312/549/8158298-8306, the evening and interim reports (Abend- und Zwischenmeldungen) sent to the Sixteenth Army by the Second and Tenth Army Corps describing the savage armored and infantry attacks against the Totenkopfdivision's positions at Lushno on September 25 and 26, 1941.

The SS defenders of Lushno were forced out of the village on the morning of September 27, and the ruins subsequently changed hands three more times before the Russians withdrew for good late on the twenty-eighth. OKH did not become worried about the situation in Eicke's sector until September 27. At the time, everyone in the German High Command and those at Hitler's HQ were preoccupied with the end of the great battle of encirclement at Kiev. See especially Halder, KTB, vol. 3, pp. 255-56, entry for September 27, 1941.

[67] BAMA, III SS, 41/7, vol. 5, pp. 311-21, 335-37; BAKO, NS/19-370, Eicke to Karl Wolff, September 30, 1941.

The major factor contributing to the division's success in the face of such overwhelming odds was undoubtedly the fighting quality of the individual Totenkopf soldier. The years of constant political and racial indoctrination, the long periods of strenuous training and physical conditioning, and the intensive cultivation of elitism had produced an SS fighting man superbly suited for the unique rigors of the Russian war. Inured to hardship, contemptuous of death, and obsessed with a fanatical hatred of the "Jewish-Bolshevik" enemy, these products of Eicke's tutelage fought with a tenacity that earned them the unqualified respect of such first-rate professional soldiers as Manstein and Busch. Good examples of the fighting qualities Eicke's soldiers possessed may be seen in the performance of two SS men (an officer and an enlisted man) during the battle for Lushno.

To counter the possibility of a breakthrough by the new Russian T-34 tanks—against which the Totenkopfdivision's antitank guns were ineffective—Eicke created special "tank annihilation squads." These units consisted of two SS officers and ten men armed with bags of satchel charges, mines, grenades, and gasoline bombs. They were ordered to attack on foot individual Russian tanks that penetrated through the defensive line, and to destroy or disable the machines as quickly as possible with their variety of explosives. One such group was led by SS Hauptsturmführer (captain) Max Seela, a company commander in the engineer battalion of the Totenkopfdivision. At Lushno on September 26, Seela's squad destroyed seven Russian T-34s in this fashion. To set an example for his men and demonstrate the proper finesse in hand-to-muzzle combat with armor, Seela destroyed the first Russian tank (which had halted momentarily) by crawling right up to it, placing a double-satchel charge against the turret and detonating the explosives with a grenade. He then personally led his men as they tackled the remaining six tanks in the same manner. After disabling or setting the armored monsters ablaze, Seela and his SS squad shot down the Soviet crews as they struggled to escape from their doomed vehicles.[68]

[68] BAMA, III SS, 41/7, vol. 5, p. 341; vol. 6, pp. 183-96. Eicke's men had found that their 37 mm antitank guns would not pierce the T-34 armor and that their 50 mm guns were effective only at ranges under 500 yards. Seela's men also

5. SS Hauptsturmführer Max Seela, Totenkopfdivision tank-killing specialist.

6. SS Sturmmann Fritz Christen wearing the Knight's Cross he
was awarded for heroism in the battle of Lushno.

SS Sturmmann (corporal) Fritz Christen, a gunner in the Second Company of the SSTK tank-destroyer battalion, provided an even better example of how the individual Totenkopf soldier fought under extreme pressure. Christen's battery was located just north of Lushno on the morning of September 24, and took the full brunt of the first Soviet armored assault. During that initial engagement every SS soldier in the battery except Christen was killed. He stayed with his gun and kept firing feverishly until he had knocked out six Russian tanks and driven off the others. For the next two days Christen remained alone in the emplacement with his 50 mm cannon and repeatedly drove back Russian infantry and tank attacks while exposed to a constant hail of artillery, mortar, and machine gun fire. Cut off completely from the rest of his unit and the division, without food or water, Christen hung on grimly and refused to abandon his post—a lone breakwater around which the Russian tide surged and receded. During the hours of darkness he carried shells to his gun from the disabled batteries around him and blazed away at enemy tanks and infantry by dawn. When the Totenkopfdivision's counterattack finally drove the Russians out of Lushno on September 27, Christen's astonished SS comrades found him still crouched behind his anti-tank cannon. The field in front of the gun emplacement he had held alone for nearly three days was littered with corpses and the blasted wreckage of Russian tanks. In seventy-two hours Fritz Christen by himself knocked out thirteen Soviet tanks and killed nearly 100 enemy soldiers. For this astonishing feat of individual heroism, Eicke awarded Christen the Iron Cross, First Class and recommended him simultaneously for the Ritterkreuz (Knight's Cross to the Iron Cross). Christen was subsequently flown to Rastenburg and decorated personally by Hitler as the first enlisted man in the Totenkopfdivision to receive this prestigious, coveted medal.[69]

---

discovered that the tank turret could be blown loose from the deck and immobilized only by using a double-satchel charge (weighing about fifteen pounds). These explosives were detonated either with hand grenades or with a five-second flare fuse. Consequently, in addition to the hazards involved in attacking a tank on foot, the SS men in Eicke's special squads ran the extra risk of being blown up by their own explosives before they could leap to safety.

[69] BAKO, NS/19-370, Eicke to Karl Wolff, September 30, 1941; ibid., NS/

The initiative and bravery shown by Seela and Christen at Lushno were typical. There were dozens, probably even hundreds, of Totenkopf soldiers who fought with equal courage, tenacity, and fanaticism on the Pola, but who did not live to be decorated or to have their individual heroics recorded. Their collective anonymity as casualty statistics was, in the final analysis, what made the difference between rout and the success of the Totenkopfdivision. The SS man's ability to remain calm in the face of disaster, his willingness to fight on against impossible odds, his lust for killing Russians, and most important, his readiness to perish rather than retreat and appear weaker than his racial enemy were all qualities that proved crucial throughout the war in retrieving hopeless situations; they became hallmarks of the Totenkopfdivision's performance wherever it fought.[70]

The heavy casualties and enormous losses in equipment caused by the Totenkopfdivision's murderous resistance on the Pola finally forced the Russians to break off their attacks at dusk on September 27. The following morning, they were able to mount only a few company-sized infantry assaults and one probing raid with their last serviceable KV IIs. Both of these feeble efforts were easily checked with only slight SS losses. On the morning of September 29, the badly weakened Soviet forces broke off their offensive and withdrew to the northeast to regroup. This move was spotted at once by the Germans and, as the good news spread quickly along the line, the jubilant and relieved gunners in the

---

19-370, "Kurze Begründung und Stellungsnahme der Zwischenvorgesetzen," an undated report on the incident sent to Himmler by Eicke; and BAMA, III SS, 41/7, vol. 6, p. 336. Both Christen and SSTK (though neither was identified specifically) were the subject of a special broadcast by Berlin radio on September 30, 1941, describing the fighting in the area south of Lake Ilmen. In the period September 24-29, the Totenkopfdivision was credited with destroying fifty-one Russian tanks. See the official figures in KTB/OKW, vol. 1, p. 666; and the report in NA/T-312/549/8157499, "A. O. K. 16, Ic, an Heeresgruppe Nord, Abendmeldung vom 29. 9. 1941."

[70] BAKO, NS/19-370, Eicke to Karl Wolff, September 30, 1941. The Second Battalion of Eicke's Third Infantry Regiment (the unit at Lushno) suffered 889 casualties during September 24-29, but was never thrown back more than a few hundred yards and did not allow a single Russian unit or tank to break through its sector of the front. The survivors of this battalion were relieved on September 30 and sent to the rear to form the nucleus of a new battalion.

SSTK artillery batteries opened up with devastating accuracy on the retreating Russian columns.[71]

The Totenkopfdivision's key role in repulsing the Soviet counterattacks south of Lake Ilmen was a significant contribution to German operations on the northern sector of the Russian front. In the months before the battles on the Pola the division had, on occasion, participated in important offensive actions involving Manstein's Fifty-sixth Panzer Corps. The Soviet thrust on the Pola, however, put Eicke and his men to the real test—forcing them to endure a prolonged period of defensive fighting under extremely adverse conditions. The ability to withstand the shock of repeated mass enemy onslaughts and at the same time retain its fighting spirit helped prepare the SSTK for the even more severe tests ahead.

The defensive success on the Pola, on the other hand, cost the Totenkopfdivision enormous casualties, seriously depleting the ranks at a time when the SS soldiers had already been weakened physically to the brink of collapse. In his letter to Karl Wolff of September 30, Eicke detailed how serious the situation had become. As of September 29, he wrote, the Totenkopfdivision had suffered 6,610 casualties. As replacements, however, he had received only 2,500 SS reservists, so there were still large gaps in the division's ranks. Most of the Totenkopf soldiers, moreover, were weak and exhausted, their uniforms in rags, and their weapons, equipment, and vehicles worn out or broken down. In short, Eicke concluded, the division urgently required not only a prolonged rest but also large quantities of men, guns, transport, and the assurance of regular supplies. Otherwise, there could be no guarantee that the Totenkopfdivision would remain an effective combat unit. Unfortunately for the Totenkopf soldiers, the exigencies of the Russian war and the meager reserves of men and equipment then available to the Waffen SS precluded the possibil-

[71] BAMA, III SS, 41/7, vol. 5, pp. 347-55, 358; BAKO, NS/19-370, Eicke to Karl Wolff, September 30, 1941. The army attempted belatedly to help Eicke by giving him the Twenty-seventh Infantry Regiment early on September 28. By then, however, the crisis had passed and the Army replacements who moved in to share bunkers and trenches with the Totenkopf soldiers were ordered to help rebuild the SSTK defensive positions in anticipation of another Russian attack (BAMA, III SS, 41/8, vol. 2, p. 93).

ity of rest or the prospect of fortifying the division. The Toten-kopfdivision had to remain committed to the fighting in northern Russia as its men became fewer and weaker, and as the weather grew steadily colder.[72]

Three days after the Russians withdrew from along the Pola, Hitler announced in a bombastic proclamation that the "last great decisive battle of the year" to smash the remaining Soviet armies had begun. This decree was timed to coincide with the October 2 beginning of an offensive by Army Group Center to capture Moscow (and theoretically end the war) before the onset of winter. As this massive German operation on the central front ground forward during the first weeks of October, its momentum pulled Busch's Sixteenth Army forward once again onto the offensive. The huge holes torn open in the Russian front by the armor on Bock's northern wing forced the German divisions in the area south of Lake Ilmen to stretch their line out further east and south to protect the northern flank of Army Group Center.

By October 8, Army Group Center had broken through the Russian defenses north and south of Smolensk and encircled huge masses of infantry at Vyazma and Bryansk in the first of a series of concentric pincer operations designed to converge eventually on the Soviet capital. This turn inward by the panzer divisions on Bock's northern wing drew the Sixteenth Army into action to keep a gap from opening between Bock and Leeb.[73] Early on Oc-

[72] BAKO, NS/19-370, Eicke to Karl Wolff, September 30, 1941; BAMA, III SS, 47/3, Erfahrungsberichte vom 7. Oktober 1941 bis 9. Mai 1942, pp. 8, 15-16, 19-21, 24-30. Eicke was most emphatic in his demand for the return of convalescing officers and NCOs who were being snatched by other SS agencies while home from the front. Their return was crucial, he maintained, because their experience was needed to help the ill-trained SS replacements survive long enough to learn how to fight against the resourceful Bolsheviks. To prevent any more of his NCOs from being administratively kidnapped, Eicke established his own convalescence section (Genesenden Abteilung) at nearby Demyansk. Men expected to recover from their wounds within four weeks were sent there to recuperate so their return to SSTK would be assured (BAMA, III SS, 41/7, vol. 6, p. 349).

[73] BAMA, III SS, 41/7, vol. 6, pp. 338-39, contains a leaflet copy of Hitler's October 2 proclamation. For details concerning the shift in offensive initiative to Army Group Center and the development of "Operation Typhoon," the German push toward Moscow, see KTB/OKW, vol. 1, pp. 673-74; Halder, KTB, vol. 3, pp. 264-65, entry for October 2, 1941; Philippi and Heim, pp. 83-87; Clark, pp. 145-83; Seaton, pp. 171-91; and especially, Klaus Reinhardt, Die Wende vor Moskau: Das Scheitern der Strategie Hitlers im Winter 1941/42 (Stuttgart, 1972),

tober 8, Colonel General Busch ordered the Second and Tenth Army Corps (the latter containing SSTK and the Thirtieth Infantry Division) to advance east from the Pola in pursuit of the Soviet forces withdrawing into the Valdai Hills. The Totenkopfdivision was ordered to move east to the line formed by the villages of Syechova, Muiry, and Yablonka, to halt there, entrench defensively, and reconnoiter the new front in an attempt to take prisoners, maps, and charts for army intelligence.[74]

For the next week, SSTK and the Thirtieth Infantry Division probed cautiously along the forest roads, combing the dense woods and swamps for partisans and stragglers and destroying the minefields and booby traps left by the retreating Russians. On October 16, in the hilly region around Samoshye—about ten miles due east of Lushno—Eicke's men ran into a new Russian defensive network imbedded securely in the dense forest. Aerial reconnaissance indicated that the complex of fortifications was nearly six miles deep and laced with entrenched tanks, artillery, minefields, and wire obstacles. Once again, the Totenkopfdivision faced the task of assaulting another formidable defensive system manned by a skillful, stubborn enemy. This raised the prospect of additional heavy casualties and an even further weakening of the men, although the Tenth Army Corps sent Eicke an optimistic report stating that in view of the heavy Russian losses the Totenkopfdivision could count on meeting only light resistance in the defensive network.[75]

The attack by the Totenkopfdivision and the Thirtieth Infantry Division, which began early on October 17, stalled almost immediately in the face of very stiff resistance. By evening, the Totenkopfdivision had gone over to the defensive and during the night

---

pp. 49-101, 123-43, for an exhaustive treatment of the autumn campaign on the central front. Among the formations dispatched to add muscle to the Moscow offensive was Hoepner's entire Fourth Panzer Group, which was withdrawn from the outskirts of Leningrad at the end of September and inserted on the central front between Roslavl and Bryansk.

[74] BAMA, III SS, 41/8, vol. 2, p. 102; Halder, *KTB*, vol. 3, pp. 265-74, entries for October 2 through 8, 1941; KTB/OKW, vol. 1, pp. 686-87.

[75] BAMA, III SS, 41/8, vol. 2, pp. 105-13. On October 15, 1941, as Eicke's soldiers crept forward looking for the enemy, ten inches of snow fell—the first of the coming winter, as the war diary of the Third Infantry Regiment noted cryptically (ibid., III SS, 50/1, p. 87).

fought off a series of Soviet counterattacks. During the next several days, heavy fighting continued as the Germans tried vainly to crack the Russian defenses. With the exception of a few local successes, which altered only the contour of the front, the attacks gained nothing. By this time, the German units along the front south of Lake Ilmen were simply incapable of mounting further successful attacks. This was especially true in the case of the Totenkopfdivision, whose soldiers were now too few and too feeble to overwhelm the entrenched enemy. On October 24, Eicke's unit commanders warned him that the only task the Totenkopf soldiers had the strength for was defensive fighting from fixed positions—and that it was uncertain how much longer they would remain fit even for this. There were for the first time, moreover, signs of an appreciable drop in morale; in some cases the SS men were so listless that only prolonged pep talks by their officers revived their ebbing strength sufficiently to repulse the Russian assaults. The situation of the Totenkopfdivision, in short, was beginning to look desperate.[76]

During the first week of November 1941, as the German offensive toward Moscow began to falter, the Sixteenth Army's front stabilized along a line facing northeast between Lake Ilmen and Lake Seliger. The backbone of this sector of the front (and the hinge on the extreme right flank of Army Group North) was formed by the heavily wooded Valdai Hills. In this thick forest, units of the Sixteenth Army began constructing an elaborate defensive system in which to sit out the cold weather. Along the northern edge of the Valdai Hills, the bedraggled soldiers of the

[76] Ibid., III SS, 41/8, vol. 2, pp. 115-17, 121, 124-26; III SS, 50/1, p. 91; and BAKO, NS/19-370, letter from Eicke to Karl Wolff, dated October 28, 1941. The strain of the fierce fighting along the Pola also exacerbated relations between Eicke and his SS colleagues. On October 27, he relieved Matthias Kleinheisterkamp of his command and sent him home for an indefinite leave. The reason given was that Kleinheisterkamp's nerves had been shattered by the fighting on the Pola and that he needed a lengthy rest. Eicke's real reason was probably personal, since he intensely disliked Kleinheisterkamp. In any event, his act violated a standing order by Himmler forbidding the transfer of any senior unit commander in the Waffen SS without his express approval. When he learned of what had happened, Himmler sent Eicke a stiff written reprimand, accusing him of disobeying orders just to satisfy his own jealousy and spite. Eicke was warned—for the last time, Himmler said—that such actions would have serious repercussions (USDC, SS Personalakte Eicke, Himmler to Eicke, November 28, 1941).

Totenkopfdivision also dug in. As they labored in the lengthening November chill, Eicke's soldiers undoubtedly realized that in the months to come they would have to face the Russian soldier and his two powerful new allies—the partisans and winter.[77]

Partisan bands behind the front of the Totenkopfdivision became especially menacing with the arrival of cold weather. By the second week of November, partisan attacks on SSTK supply columns, field hospitals, and other rear-area services had become so frequent that Eicke had to send detachments taken from the front and from construction work into the dense woods for extensive combing-out operations. The thoroughness and brutality with which these "cleansing actions" were conducted reflects how serious this danger had become and how violently the SS soldiers hated and feared the stealthy bands of irregulars roaming freely behind their lines. For the first time during the Russian campaign, the Totenkopfdivision's records mention the shooting of civilians, and indicate that when SSTK units encountered groups of partisans or suspects no prisoners were taken.[78]

[77] BAMA, III SS, 41/7, vol. 6, pp. 226-33, 241-47. The Russians attempted to deny Eicke's soldiers winter shelter by burning down nearly every dwelling and village in the sector held by SSTK. Those buildings that could not be destroyed by Russian infantry were set ablaze with phosphorus bombs dropped by planes, or with incendiary shells fired by Russian artillery. The problem of constructing shelters for the units of SSTK was complicated further by the sub zero weather, which froze the ground to such a depth by mid-November that bunkers and shelters could be dug only by using powerful explosive charges (ibid., III SS, 50/1, p. 99).

[78] Ibid., III SS, 50/1, pp. 100, 102, 109; III SS, 41/7, vol. 6, p. 233; KTB/OKW, vol. 1, pp. 733-47. There were, however, exceptions. On November 28 a company from the tank-destroyer battalion of SSTK found the bodies of three SS men in the forest. In a nearby thicket they uncovered an earthen bunker inhabited by four Russian civilians. Instead of summarily shooting the civilians, an SS officer and a squad of men took the Russians to a nearby village, where the mayor vouched for their identity. The four Russians had been in the bunker when a partisan band killed the three SS men, but had been too frightened to reveal themselves or come out afterward. The four were subsequently released by the SSTK unit.

The extent of the Soviet partisan menace in the area behind the Totenkopfdivision, and the ruthlessness with which the army, SS and police units dealt with it, are meticulously documented in two extraordinary statistical collections. Among the reports compiled by the intelligence officer (Ic) of the German Sixteenth Army were a series of weekly collective reports (Sammelmeldungen) tabulating the number of commissars, partisans, Soviet civilians, spies, and saboteurs who had been executed, and the villages burned down as reprisals by the different divisions of the Sixteenth Army. Between June 22 and December 31, 1941, Sixteenth Army units killed 57 commissars, 2,639 partisans, and 53 Soviet civilians, and destroyed

The most serious clash between Totenkopf units and partisans operating south of Lake Ilmen occurred during the night of November 27-28. The incident was typical of the skillful hit-and-run tactics used by Soviet guerillas and the devastating effect that their raids had upon German morale. After combing the forest all day in subfreezing temperatures on November 27, an SSTK combat group bedded down for the night in the undamaged village of Ilomlya. The SS men shared their billet with a convoy from the Thirtieth Infantry Division, and with two companies of riflemen from the 503rd Infantry Regiment. Total German strength in the village was equal to that of a battalion. The senior SS officer present personally inspected the double-strength ring of sentries and was satisfied that the security arrangements for the night were adequate.

Shortly after 10:00 P.M. the sleeping Germans were jolted awake by a series of explosions. A group of Soviet partisans, armed with Tommy guns and grenades, had filtered silently and undetected through the ring of guards and into the center of the village. At a given signal, they began blowing up trucks, cars, and supply trailers, and hurling grenades and gasoline bombs through windows and doors of the buildings where the Germans were sheltered. Another group of Russians positioned themselves to cover the exits and shot down the German soldiers who ran into the street. Illuminated by burning vehicles and buildings, the struggle continued for an hour before the partisans vanished sud-

---

13 villages in retaliation for Soviet guerrilla actions. These totals were determined by this writer on the basis of a hand count of the Sammelmeldungen for each week during this period. These reports form a significant part of the materials contained in NA/T-312/Roll 549, "Ic/A. O., Nebenakte 9-12z, Tätigkeitsberichte u. Meldungen der AK's vom 22. 6. 41 bis 21. 12. 41;" and T-312/Roll 567, "A. O. K. 16, Ic/A. O., Anlagenband z. Tätigkeitsberichte, Abendorientierungen und Beuteunterlagen, Morgen- und Abendmeldungen, Januar bis März, 1942."

In addition, the exhaustive, chilling reports kept by the SD Einsatzgruppen charged with liquidating partisans, Jews, and spies are deposited in BAKO, R58/217, fol. 1-472, Der Chef der Sicherheitspolizei und des SD, Meldungen aus den besetzten Ostgebiete, Ereignismeldungen aus der UdSSR. The weekly SD reports in this collection for November 1941 contain extensive information on the large-scale antipartisan sweeps conducted in the immediate rear of the Totenkopfdivision's sector.

denly into the darkness. The attack cost the Germans four dead, twelve seriously wounded, and a sleepless night of dousing fires and reorganizing defenses.[79]

Fortunately for the Totenkopfdivision, the Red Army units across the lines made no attempt to match the harassing activities of the partisans, and a general lull settled along the entire front of the Sixteenth Army. In lieu of attacking each other the exhausted contestants broadcast propaganda across the front with loudspeakers, and reconnaissance planes dropped thousands of leaflets into the opposing German and Russian positions. For the next several weeks, neither side engaged in anything more serious than an occasional patrol or artillery barrage. The period of inactivity was a welcome change to the exhausted men in SSTK, who had been in action continuously since the first week of the campaign.

Eicke took advantage of the lull to compile for his superiors a long memorandum outlining in detail the desperate, and critically weakened state of the Totenkopfdivision. On the basis of figures compiled by his medical units, Eicke claimed that since June 24, 1941 the Totenkopfdivision had suffered 8,993 casualties—nearly fifty percent of the division's ration strength at the beginning of the campaign. Moreover, Eicke maintained, less than half of these losses had been replaced, and those reservists the Totenkopfdivision had received were markedly inferior soldiers to those whose places they filled. This was especially true, he continued, in the case of the reserve SS officers. Many of them were killed in their very first exposure to combat or fell prey to the ruthless and cunning Russians while leading their first reconnaissance patrol. This fact, Eicke argued, forced him to fight using untrained men led by untrained officers. The inevitable results were frightful casualties and a corresponding decline in the morale and fighting

---

[79] BAMA, III SS, 41/7, vol. 6, pp. 235-37. The tactics used by the partisans in this specific attack corresponded precisely with a Soviet directive of October 4, 1941, which contained detailed instructions for strikes at night. The Soviet directive claimed that such assaults would succeed because German sentries were inattentive and often slept while on duty. Eicke obtained a copy of this directive and had it translated and distributed to all units in the Totenkopfdivision with an accompanying warning to learn its lessons (ibid., pp. 343-45).

7. Himmler visits the Totenkopfdivision in Russia, December 1941.

spirit of the troops. Hence, the replacements he had been sent, according to Eicke, were weakening rather than strengthening the Totenkopfdivision.[80]

In addition to the problems caused by inexperienced officers, Eicke complained, the division was weakened further by the inferior physical quality, laziness, and political ignorance of the newly arriving SS replacements. This was most notable, he claimed, among the ethnic German (Volksdeutsche) recruits. They seemed to Eicke weaker physically, more susceptible to illness and prone to cowardice than SS reservists who were true Reich Germans. Self-inflicted wounds, Eicke asserted, were common among the Volksdeutsche recruits, as were incidents of cowardice and sleeping on guard duty. In general, the new SS recruits were not physically tough enough to endure the primitive conditions and severe weather of the Russian war. To remedy the situation, Eicke suggested that Waffen SS training programs include exposure to severe weather for lengthy periods under combat conditions, and that the SS trainees be denied any food or shelter while they were left outside. Only a drastic revision of the Waffen SS training program, Eicke insisted, could prepare the SS man adequately to fight and survive in Russia.[81]

The worst thing about the new SS recruits, in Eicke's estimation, was their "lack of political training and National Socialist indoctrination." Men sent into the harsh crucible of Russia after only eight weeks of training, he lamented, were politically ignorant and did not arrive at the front as convinced Nazis. Therefore, Eicke claimed, many new SS men lacked the fanatical determina-

[80] BAKO, NS/19-370, "Erfahrungen über den Nachersatz," a memorandum sent by Eicke to the SS Führungshauptamt on November 15, 1941; and BAMA, III SS, 41/7, vol. 6, pp. 271-73. Eicke complained again that most of his experienced officers and NCOs who were home on convalescent leave were being grabbed by other SS agencies. Though he did not specify which SS organizations he was accusing, Eicke almost certainly meant the concentration camp commanders.

[81] BAKO, NS/19-370, "Erfahrungen über den Nachersatz," dated November 15, 1941. This is the first mention of ethnic Germans in the ranks of the SS Totenkopfdivision. A Volksdeutscher, or ethnic German according to the SS definition, was a person of German language and culture who was not a citizen of the German Reich in 1938. As a racial purist and an arch advocate of SS elitism and selectivity, Eicke was resolutely opposed to admitting even ethnic Germans into the ranks of the Waffen SS. The best discussion on recruiting ethnic Germans and other foreign nationals into the Waffen SS is in Stein, pp. 168-96.

tion necessary for the struggle against bolshevism, and did not know the political realities of the Russian front. To correct this as quickly as possible, Eicke urged the SS Führungshauptamt to use more of the training period to indoctrinate the young SS men in the importance of the struggle.[82]

The tone of his pessimistic memorandum indicated Eicke doubted whether the weakened physical condition and low morale of his men would permit them to survive another prolonged period of heavy fighting. The dilemma of the Totenkopfdivision at the end of 1941 was largely self-imposed. Eicke's division—like the other Waffen SS formations then fighting in Russia—was the victim of its own elite image. The typical Totenkopf qualities of reckless courage and fanatical determination had caused enormous casualties when met by skillful and equally fanatical Russian resistance. On the other hand, these Waffen SS traits had provided the extra punch needed for a local victory, or had (as at Lushno) been the margin of difference between a Russian breakthrough and the retention of a stable German front. Because of its dependability, especially in defensive fighting, the Totenkopfdivision by late November 1941 had become one of the key formations of Army Group North—a division whose presence in the area south of Lake Ilmen was crucial to the security of Leeb's right wing. This fact was grudgingly recognized by many senior officers at the corps, army, and army group levels. Despite their private dislike for Eicke and his former desperadoes from the concentration camps, the army commanders in the northern sector clearly appreciated the special value of the Totenkopfdivision in a struggle like the Russian war. Consequently, as the shorter days and lengthening chill stung the weakened, shivering soldiers of Army Group North, Eicke's superiors exerted every effort to prevent even a temporary withdrawal of the Totenkopfdivision.[83] The raw

[82] BAKO, NS/19-370, "Erfahrungen über den Nachersatz," November 15, 1941.

[83] The last time any of Eicke's superiors at the corps, army, or army group level tried to have the Totenkopfdivision withdrawn from the front to rest and refit was early November 1941. In a letter to Colonel General Franz Halder, the chief of the army general staff, Field Marshal Leeb requested that OKH consider giving Eicke's division a short rest in a quiet sector so it could recuperate from the long weeks of heavy fighting in the swampy and forested region south of Lake Ilmen.

east wind that blew steadily in early December and plunged the thermometer to thirty-four degrees below zero carried the faint but unmistakable scent of disaster.

Implicit in the tone and title of Leeb's letter is the assumption that SSTK would be reinforced before the onset of winter, and left under the command of Army Group North (NA/T-312/548/8157008-7013, "Heeresgruppe Nord, an OKH, Die Abwehr im Winter und der Kräftebedarf," dated November 4, 1941, and signed by Leeb).

CHAPTER SEVEN

The Soviet Counteroffensive: Encirclement in the Demyansk Pocket, January-October 1942

DURING the first dreary days of December 1941 the great German assault against Moscow ground slowly and inexorably to a standstill. Driven to the brink of prostration by six months of continuous fighting, horrendous weather, and mounting casualties, Army Group Center spent itself in a final series of desperate, spasmodic attacks on the outskirts of the Soviet capital. By the morning of December 5, 1941, offensive operations had ceased altogether and Bock's armies lay exhausted and immobile in the snow. Then the Russians struck. On the night of December 5-6 the armored and infantry divisions of Army Group Center, already benumbed by the icy blast of the winter's first blizzard, found themselves locked in the deadly embrace of the first major Soviet counteroffensive of the war.

Attacking along a 500-mile front from Kalinin in the north to Yelets in the south, twelve Russian armies under the overall command of Marshal Georgi Zhukov hacked the entire front of Bock's army group into isolated splinters. Fresh divisions shuttled into European Russia by train from Siberia and outfitted with the best winter equipment cracked into the reeling Germans behind massed formations of T-34 tanks. Under the weight of this overwhelming and unexpected assault Army Group Center began to disintegrate. During the first days of the crisis, while panic and paralysis gripped the army group at every level, Hitler prevented a rout by issuing over Bock's head a series of categorical "no retreat" orders calling upon the German soldier to stand where he was and fight without regard to the consequences. During the next weeks field commanders who disobeyed this directive, regardless of rank or reputation, were cashiered and packed off into professional oblivion. By mid-January 1942 the combination of Hitler's fanatical orders and the remarkable fighting qualities of the Ger-

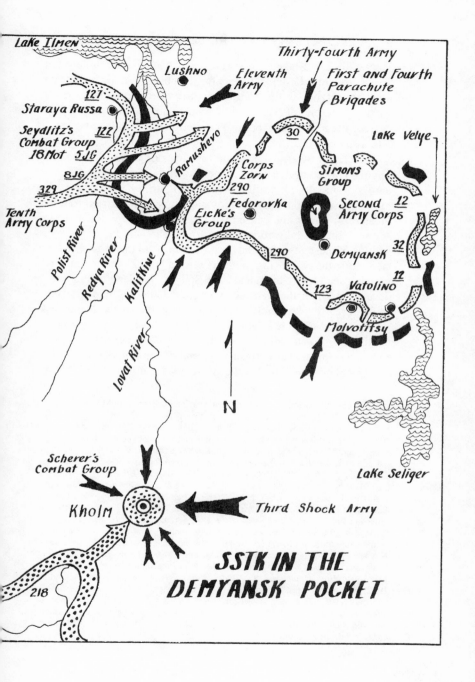

SSTK IN THE DEMYANSK POCKET

man soldier had taken the steam out of Zhukov's counteroffensive, and Army Group Center's front stabilized along a line running from Rzhev in the north through Vyazma to Bryansk in the south. At the end of January the Soviet attacks on the central front ceased altogether, and both exhausted armies sank temporarily into a stupor of inertia.[1]

The crisis of German arms in the winter of 1941-1942 was not confined to central Russia alone. Like the ripples that spread across a smooth pond after a huge rock strikes the surface, the momentum generated by Zhukov's counterthrust carried to other areas of the front and caused the Germans a succession of sharp setbacks that lasted well into the spring of 1942. One of the most serious of these reverses occurred in January in the most sensitive area along the right wing of Army Group North—the wooded region between Lake Ilmen and Lake Seliger. The lengthy crisis that developed when the Red Army encircled the German divisions in this area (subsequently known as the battle of the Demyansk pocket) was mastered largely because of the gritty resistance of the SS Totenkopfdivision. In a grueling series of defensive engagements between January and the end of October 1942, the Totenkopfdivision was the nucleus of a mixed force of sur-

---

[1] The best discussion of the great German winter crisis before Moscow is Klaus Reinhardt, *Die Wende vor Moskau*, esp. pp. 198-213, 234-54, for a thorough examination of the Soviet conduct of the counteroffensive; 216-33, for details on the leadership crisis in Army Group Center and the motives for Hitler's "halt" orders; and 255-61, for an assessment of the Soviet offensive and the psychological and material shape of the German army in the aftermath. Good accounts are also in Seaton, pp. 224-41; Clark, pp. 172-83; Carell, *Hitler Moves East*, pp. 176-91; in KTB/OKW, vol. 1, pp. 805-72; and in the terse but graphic daily comments in Halder, *KTB*, vol. 3, pp. 327-78, entries for December 5, 1941 through January 8, 1942. Adequate only is the narrative in Alfred W. Turney, *Disaster at Moscow: Von Bock's Campaigns, 1941-1942* (Albuquerque, N. M., 1970), pp. 92-162. For the Soviet side, see especially the long account by the major architect of the counterthrust, Georgi K. Zhukov, *The Memoirs of Marshal Zhukov*, trans. Novosti Press Agency (New York, 1971), pp. 320-61; the excellent versions in Erickson, *The Road to Stalingrad*, pp. 249-96; and the same author's earlier study, *The Soviet High Command: A Military-Political History, 1918-1941* (London, 1962), pp. 628-66; and the account in Werth, pp. 261-73. German generals who resigned or were dismissed in December and January included the commander in chief of the army (Brauchitsch), all three army group commanders (Leeb, Bock, and Rundstedt), two panzer group leaders (Guderian and Hoepner), and a score of corps and division commanders.

rounded army and waffen SS formations that hung onto the Valdai Hills, prevented a major Russian breakthrough, and stabilized the weakened right flank of Army Group North. In the process, however, the Totenkopfdivision suffered such severe losses that it had to be rebuilt rather than reconditioned when it finally was withdrawn from Russia in the autumn of 1942.

The first hint that the Soviets planned a major counteroffensive in the Lake Ilmen area came within twenty-four hours of Zhukov's assault on Army Group Center. Eicke's forward observation posts detected a sharp increase in enemy construction activity and noted uncomfortably that Russian patrols were growing more aggressive in their probing and in their efforts to take German prisoners. Simultaneously, German spotter aircraft observed heavy troop and vehicular movement into the area around Bolgoye on the former Leningrad-Moscow railroad line. In conjunction with additional warnings issued by the Second Army Corps and the Sixteenth Army, Eicke alerted his men to entrench and be prepared to repel strong and continuous enemy attacks. For the remainder of December, the Totenkopfdivision stayed on full alert while work continued on the network of bunkers and trenches that were to serve as shelter and defensive positions for the winter. The Russian activities SSTK and its neighboring divisions had observed, however, were only the prelude to an enormous Russian build-up beyond the Valdai Hills. For the next several weeks, the front remained relatively calm, with only occasional probing attacks by small groups of Russian infantry.[2]

[2] BAMA, III SS, 41/8, vol. 2, pp. 99-100; KTB/OKW, vol. 1, pp. 791-872, the daily action summaries for this period entered under the heading "Heeresgruppe Nord"; and NA/T-312/548/8156769, "A. O. K. 16, Lage am 13. 12. 1941"; and NA/T-312/548/8157155, "II A. K., an A. O. K. 16, Tagesmeldung vom 18. 12. 1941," in which the commander of the Second Army Corps, General Graf Brockdorff-Ahlefeldt warned Busch that all the signs pointed to an imminent and powerful Russian offensive—a situation the weakened and bedraggled divisions south of Lake Ilmen could not handle.

Much of the construction work on the winter quarters for the Totenkopfdivision was done by groups of Russian prisoners pressganged from the prisoner-of-war transit camps behind the lines. Russian prisoners evidently were at a premium in the Totenkopfdivision's sector during December and January. Eicke squabbled constantly with the Tenth Army Corps and with neighboring divisions over who was to use how many prisoners and for how long. Beginning in January 1942, Eicke was required to send a monthly report to Sixteenth Army with information

For the weakened army and Totenkopf units this period of combat inactivity proved a welcome but all too brief respite. During the night of January 7-8, 1942, in the midst of a blizzard and with the temperature at forty degrees below zero, the Russians launched a massive offensive against the right wing of Army Group North. Along the front of Sixteenth Army between Lakes Ilmen and Seliger three Russian armies, the Eleventh, Thirty-fourth, and the First Shock Army, tore into the German defensive positions and quickly broke through along the southern shore of Lake Ilmen and in the woods just north of Lake Seliger. Simultaneously, the Soviet Third Shock Army swept around the southern edge of Lake Seliger, on the extreme right of the Sixteenth Army, and swung to the northeast along an arc intended to carry it far into the rear area of Busch's army. The Russians hoped to encircle and destroy the Sixteenth Army, unhinge the entire right wing of Leeb's army group, and open a yawning gap between the northern and central sectors of the German front. During the crucial weeks that followed, the Red Army came perilously close to achieving these objectives.[3]

The area immediately southeast of Lake Ilmen, where the Totenkopfdivision was entrenched, was the region through which the northern prong of the Russian attack sliced on January 8. The initial enemy blows glanced along the Totenkopfdivision's front and smashed with full force into the 290th and Thirtieth Infantry Divisions, Eicke's neighbors on the left. Within twenty-four hours the Soviets achieved a major breakthrough, destroyed most of the 290th Infantry Division, and drove nearly twenty miles into the rear of the Tenth Army Corps. On January 9, units of the Soviet Eleventh Army reached Staraya Russa and wheeled south into the rear of both the Second and Tenth Army Corps. At the

about the physical condition of the POW's, the number that had been shot, had escaped, or had been turned over to the Einsatzkommandos of the SD for "special handling" (BAMA, III SS, 41/10, vol. 2, pp. 470-79; III SS, 42/2, pp. 184-85).

[3] Halder, *KTB*, vol. 3, pp. 377-78, entries for January 8-9, 1942; Philippi and Heim, pp. 112-14; Carell, *Hitler Moves East*, pp. 342-66. The attack against the Sixteenth Army coincided with an offensive by the Soviet Twenty-second and Fourth Shock Armies into the area southwest of Lake Seliger. The object of this operation was to widen the breach between the two German army groups by driving into Bock's flank in the Vitebsk area northwest of Smolensk.

same time, units of the Soviet First Shock Army, attacking westward from Lake Seliger, turned northward along the Lovat River and began to push toward a link-up with the Eleventh Army that would trap the bulk of the Sixteenth Army in a huge bag. As the outlines of this disaster rapidly took shape, the Sixteenth Army detached units from the Totenkopfdivision (over Eicke's vehement objections) and sent them to stiffen sectors of the front to the north, west, and south that were in danger of collapsing.

Five battalions from the Totenkopfdivision, including the reconnaissance and engineer battalions and part of the artillery regiment, were hurried to Staraya Russa late on January 9 with orders to hold that vital rail and road junction at all costs. Several days later, Eicke was also compelled to send two additional battalions southeast to Demyansk to bolster the southern flank of the Sixteenth Army against increasing Russian pressure. As the atmosphere of crisis intensified, the corps and division commanders in the Sixteenth Army appealed with increasing urgency for help from units of the Totenkopfdivision.[4]

By the afternoon of January 12, the situation in the area held by the Sixteenth Army had become critical. Judging that encirclement of Busch's army was imminent, Field Marshal Leeb requested permission from Hitler to withdraw the Second and Tenth Army Corps behind the Lovat River to form a new front before they were surrounded and cut to pieces. Hitler rejected the request out of hand, and issued orders to the Sixteenth Army to stand and fight where it was. At this the angry and shaken Leeb requested and received his release from command from Army Group North. His successor, appointed by Hitler on January 17, was Colonel General Georg von Küchler—the former commander of the Eighteenth Army.[5]

In the interval between the exchange of commanders the situation west of the Valdai Hills grew worse. Slowly but relentlessly

[4] Philippi and Heim, pp. 112-13; KTB/OKW, vol. 2, pt. 1, pp. 209-13, 216, 219, 222; BAMA, III SS, 41/9, Lageberichte und Meldungen aus Kessel Demyansk, pp. 89-95.

[5] Philippi and Heim, pp. 112-13; Halder, *KTB*, vol. 3, pp. 381-82, 386-87, entries for January 12, 16, and 18, 1941. Küchler's replacement as commander of the Eighteenth Army on the Leningrad front was General Georg Lindemann. See also, Seaton, pp. 244-47.

the powerful Soviet forces pressed the Second and Tenth Army Corps into a constricting pocket centered around the town of Demyansk. On January 20, all land communication with the rest of the Sixteenth Army were cut and the Luftwaffe began air drops of supplies and ammunition to the German divisions east of the Lovat. West of the Lovat River at Staraya Russa, meanwhile, the units of the Eighteenth Motorized Division and SSTK that were pinned down in and around the town continued to hold out, inflicting heavy casualties on the Red Army formations besieging them. Staraya Russa quickly developed into a major breakwater in the path of the Red Army's advance. Continued resistance by the army and SS soldiers there threw a serious kink into the enemy offensive and forced the Soviet Eleventh Army to wheel southward prematurely rather than westward into the rear of the Sixteenth Army.[6]

Despite the determined resistance offered by the German divisions in the Valdai region, Russian strength was such that, given Hitler's orders, the encirclement of a major portion of the Sixteenth Army was only a matter of time. Heavy fighting continued for another three weeks, as the Soviets gradually closed the ring. Finally, on February 8, units of the Russian Eleventh and First Shock Armies linked up on the Lovat River about twenty-five miles west of Demyansk. Trapped inside this Demyansk pocket were two German army corps (the Second and Tenth) containing

[6] Carell, *Hitler Moves East*, pp. 349-52; Seaton, pp. 244-45; and NA/T-312/ 567/8180592, Sixteenth Army situation map bearing the heading "Feindlage vor 16. Armee, stand vom 24. 1. 1942." The Germans held Staraya Russa mainly because of the stubbornness of the Totenkopf units deployed there. Max Seela, who had distinguished himself in the battle at Lushno, emerged as one of the heroes of the long siege of Staraya Russa. A combat group led by Seela fought for just over a month east of Staraya Russa in the village of Dipovitzy. There Seela and his SS men endured repeated Russian ground attacks and air strikes without surrendering the village or the adjacent bridge over the Lovat River. As a result, Eicke recommended Seela for the Ritterkreuz, which the latter subsequently received in May 1942. See BAKO, NS/19-345, "Kurze Begründung und Stellungsnahme der Zwischenvorgesetzten," an undated recommendation for the Ritterkreuz signed by Eicke; and Ernst-Günther Krätschmer, *Die Ritterkreuzträger der Waffen SS* (Göttingen, 1953), p. 111. Hitler awarded Eicke the Ritterkreuz by radio on January 15 in recognition of his role in slowing the Russian offensive south of Lake Ilmen. See especially the long article in IFZ, *Das Schwarze Korps*, issue for January 22, 1942, which describes Eicke as one of the founders of the Waffen SS; and Krätschmer, pp. 16-22.

214

most of the units of six divisions (Twelfth, Thirtieth, Thirty-second, 123rd, and 290th Infantry Divisions, and the SS Toten-kopfdivision). Against this exhausted and severely weakened German force, the Russians pressed in from all sides with the equivalent of fifteen fresh, well-equipped infantry divisions and an assortment of armored and ski battalions. Since the Luftwaffe (Göring) assured Hitler that the 95,000 men and 20,000 horses inside the pocket could be supplied by air, the führer repeated his orders forbidding any attempt to break out to the west. The trapped German divisions were instructed to hold fast until a new front was built west of the Lovat and a relief attack launched to rescue them.[7]

For Eicke and his SS men, there was no questioning Hitler's directive to stand and fight to the last man. This was the kind of order the hard-bitten Totenkopf soldiers understood best, and the

[7] NA/T-312/556/8166491, "A. O. K. 16, Ia, Tagesmeldung," for February 3, 1942; ibid., T-312/556/8166425-6426, transcript of a telephone conversation between Busch and Brockdorff of February 11, 1942, discussing Hitler's orders for the divisions trapped inside the pocket; and ibid., T-312/556/8167267-7288, copy of a lengthy teleprinter message from Busch to OKH of February 10, 1942, describing the completion of the Soviet encirclement, the condition of the German units in the pocket, and Busch's estimation of the minimum tonnage—177 per day—needed via air supply for the forces trapped in the Demyansk pocket. See also Halder, KTB, vol. 3, pp. 397-400, entries for February 8 through 14, 1942; and Philippi and Heim, p. 113. Hitler's rationale for ordering the Second and Tenth Army Corps to remain encircled was that they would tie down the bulk of the Soviet forces south of Lake Ilmen and prevent a further advance into the German rear. Göring's promise to keep the encircled garrison supplied merely confirmed Hitler's resolve to have "Fortress Demyansk" hold out until relieved. For the first two weeks of the air supply operation the Luftwaffe managed to deliver more than the daily minimum tonnage calculated by Busch, achieving peak deliveries of 182 tons in 110 flights on February 22, and 286 tons in 159 flights into the pocket on February 23. Thereafter, the weather, Soviet fighters, flight crew exhaustion, and a shortage of aircraft caused the deliveries to drop off to a daily average of less than half the minimum requirements for the trapped German forces. NA/T-312/556/8167219-7261, contain the daily tonnage summaries of supplies air-delivered by the Luftwaffe to the Demyansk field during February. In the opinion of Higgins (pp. 250-52), Seaton (pp. 245-47), and Carell (Hitler Moves East, pp. 397-400), the success of the Luftwaffe and the survival of the Demyansk pocket mortgaged future German strategy. When the same situation arose at Stalingrad, Hitler insisted on a similar action—hold-out by the trapped garrison and air-supply by the Luftwaffe. The facts of the Demyansk experience indicate that the survival of the trapped divisions was due more to the toughness and endurance of the soldiers of the army and the Waffen SS than to any great success by the Luftwaffe in aerial supply.

type of assignment for which they had few peers on the eastern front. At the time of the Russian encirclement on February 8, the Totenkopfdivision and the other trapped units were subordinated formally to the Second Army Corps of General Count Walter Brockdorff-Ahlefeldt. This had resulted when the Tenth Army Corps staff and HQ had been pushed west of the Lovat, and thus out of the closing pocket, in late January. As Soviet pressure against all sides of the pocket increased after February 8, Count Brockdorff separated the Totenkopf units remaining under Eicke's command into two regimental Kampfgruppen and deployed them in the two most hard pressed areas inside the cauldron.

Eicke kept command of the larger of the two mixed SS and army battle groups, which moved into line between the surviving units of the 290th Infantry Division at the western tip of the pocket. Eicke's group had the vital task of defending the network of villages and connecting roads against Russian attacks from the west. Count Brockdorff ordered Eicke to hold this line at all cost in order to prevent any widening of the gap between the encircled divisions and the new German front beyond the Polist River. The other Kampfgruppe of army and SSTK soldiers was placed under Max Simon's command and spread along the northeastern side of the pocket, where unusually severe pressure by the Soviet Thirty-fourth Army threatened to collapse the German front. During the weeks that followed, determined resistance by both of these SS battle groups proved crucial to the survival of the Demyansk pocket.[8]

During February and early March, 1942, in an uninterrupted series of savage engagements, units of the Totenkopfdivision repeatedly beat back strong Russian infantry attacks and refused to

[8] Carell, *Hitler Moves East*, pp. 397-400; BAMA, III SS, 41/10, vol. 3, pp. 29-35, 134, 141; and BAKO, NS/19-345, "Abschlussmeldung über die Abwehrkämpfe des II A. K. vom 8. 1. 42—8. 2. 42," a report from Eicke to Jüttner dated February 9, 1942. The two SS battle groups were so short of men that on February 9 Eicke ordered all the wounded men in the SSTK convalescent center at Demyansk to return to duty with his battle group, regardless of their physical condition. An additional gleaning of the remaining supply and administrative services helped bring the total strength of Eicke's Kampfgruppe to 4,100 men. The activities of Simon's Kampfgruppe during the battle of the Demyansk pocket are summarized in BAMA, III SS, 41/9, pp. 2-3, 89-95, "Lagebericht," a memorandum written by Max Simon on September 12, 1942 summarizing the events of the previous winter.

be dislodged from their assigned positions. In the few instances in which the Russians did overrun SS positions or penetrate the front, it was only after every Totenkopf soldier had been killed. In the burned-out villages of Tscherentizy, Vasilyevschina, and Kobylkina, for example, two companies of Eicke's Kampfgruppe held out for over a month in chest-deep snow and temperatures that averaged thirty degrees below zero. On several occasions, the survivors were dislodged and retreated to a new defense line where they regrouped, counterattacked, and retook the villages. Repulsing the continuous Russian attacks was made even more difficult for these SS men by the erratic performance of the Luftwaffe. German transports frequently missed their drop zones and hit Russian positions, and in at least two cases German fighters strafed Eicke's positions while JU-52 transports simultaneously dropped their supply cargo into the hands of grateful Soviet units.[9]

In one respect, however, the soldiers in SSTK fared much better during the winter months than did their army comrades. As a result, the Totenkopf units probably were able to fight more effectively in the severe weather. In early January 1942, SSTK began receiving ample winter clothing from SS supply sources. Part of the shipments came from the huge SS warehouse of confiscated goods in Riga controlled by the HSSPF for Northern Russia,

[9] BAMA, III SS, 41/10, vol. 3, pp. 51-53, 58, 67, 76, 86, 91, 108-14, 128-35, 151-62, 167-70, 176-93, 196-210, 216-24, 241-53, 301-21, 328-36; III SS, 42/2, pp. 201-2; NA/T-312/556/8166262-6279, 8166293-6511, for the morning, interim, and evening reports of the Sixteenth Army to Army Group North describing the situation in the pocket in February and March; and NA/T-312/567/8181115-1445, for the morning and evening reports of the Second Army Corps (which included SSTK) for February and March 1942. In late February, two more of Eicke's officers received the Ritterkreuz for heroism in the Demyansk pocket. SS Sturmbannführer Karl Ullrich, commander of the SSTK engineer battalion, and SS Sturmbannführer Franz Kleffner, commander of the SSTK reconnaissance battalion, received confirmation of their awards by radio from Hitler's headquarters (BAMA, III SS, 41/10, vol. 3, pp. 172, 186, 362). In April 1942, Eicke also recommended SS Sturmbannführer Otto Baum, commander of First Battalion/SSTK I. R. 1 for the Ritterkreuz for Baum's personal role in holding the villages and supply roads in Eicke's flanks and rear during the entire battle of the Demyansk pocket (USDC, SS Personalakte Baum, "Kurze Begründung und Stellungsnahme der Zwischenvorgesetzten," undated copy of the recommendation signed by Eicke).

8. Trapped in the Demyansk pocket, February 1942, Totenkopf soldiers unload badly needed supplies.

Friedrich Jeckeln, who had served with SSTK during the battle of France. By mid-January, most SSTK soldiers had been issued fur-lined parkas, boots and gloves, and wool socks and long underwear. Subsequent reports sent to Eicke complained only that the winter clothing was too bulky and thus reduced the mobility of the wearer. The big parkas, according to many Totenkopf soldiers, restricted head movement and visibility, while the fur-lined gloves prevented sufficient finger dexterity to handle light weapons, and tended to absorb moisture and freeze in the severe cold. Despite these complaints, the soldiers in the Totenkopfdivision suffered a great deal less from the elements than the men in neighboring army units; frostbite was rare in SSTK after mid-January 1942.[10]

During the last week of February 1942 the Russian effort to an-

[10] BAMA, III SS, 42/2, pp. 193-99, 205-6; III SS, 41/10, vol. 3, p. 469; III SS, 47/3, pp. 63-72, 74-81, 89-91. Totenkopf units in the pocket suffered less and were supplied better than their army counterparts largely because of efforts by SS Sturmbannführer Hans Ulmer. An ingenious, resourceful supply officer, Ulmer had the foresight to acquire winter clothing and equipment before the Soviet encirclement, and coordinated the aerial drops with the Luftwaffe during the entire Demyansk battle. He established the cargo priorities for these drops and worked out a series of drop schedules among rotating locations, which baffled the Russians. See especially USDC, SS Personalakte Ulmer, "Vorschlag für die Verleihung des Deutschen Kreuzes in Silber," December 30, 1943, signed by SS Obergruppenführer Paul Hausser.

Sheltering the SS men was the most serious dilemma during January and February. The Russians tried to burn villages with artillery and air strikes, and the Red Air Force habitually dropped incendiary bombs on any SSTK bunkers or shelters that could be detected. The long winter ordeal of SSTK in the Demyansk pocket is described graphically by SSTK veteran Wolfgang Vopersal in seven articles, "Südlich des Ilmensees, Aus dem Kampf der SS Totenkopf-Division," pts. 1-7, Der Freiwillige (May-December 1974). See especially September through December.

The battle of the Demyansk pocket and the condition of the SSTK units in the cauldron also were discussed in an interview between this writer and Herr Otto Baum in Stetten bei Hechingen, West Germany on July 7, 1972, and recorded in a memorandum Herr Baum prepared for the author on October 15, 1973 (hereafter cited as Baum interview and/or Baum memorandum). A battalion commander in SSTK during the struggle for the Demyansk pocket, Baum subsequently became one of the most brilliant field commanders in the Waffen SS. He rose to the rank of SS Brigadeführer (brigadier general) at the age of thirty-three and commanded the SS divisions Götz von Berchlingen and Sixteenth SS Panzergrenadierdivision Reichsführer SS during the last years of the war. One of Eicke's favorite subordinates, Baum also became one of the most highly decorated German soldiers of the Second World War, earning the Ritterkreuz with Oak Leaves, Swords and Diamonds.

219

nihilate the encircled German forces reached its zenith. Along the western edge of the pocket, the Soviets pounded Eicke's Kampfgruppe ceaselessly with heavy artillery. At the same time, the tempo and size of the Russian infantry and armored assaults increased to such an extent that the defensive points held by the SS battle groups became isolated, and Eicke's front was cut into a string of small, individual pockets. Casualties among the SS combat groups soared correspondingly. During the third week of February Eicke became so frustrated over the apparent hopelessness of the situation that he abandoned all procedures for communication through proper channels and appealed directly to Himmler via radio for reinforcements, supplies, and better support from the Luftwaffe. As the situation deteriorated further, his radioed appeals to the Reichsführer SS included bitter denunciations of the Luftwaffe and barbed criticism of the allegedly inept combat performance of neighboring army units.

Himmler was at first unable to help Eicke. The Reichsführer SS could not immediately scrape together any replacements for the Totenkopfdivision; when he finally did, the Luftwaffe did not have enough available transport to fly them into the pocket. Any other direct effort Himmler may have exerted on Eicke's behalf at Hitler's HQ produced no discernible change in the drastic condition of the Totenkopf units trapped in the pocket.[11]

The Russians engaged against the SS battle groups seemed to sense a weakening of the German front at the western end of the pocket, and so threw in fresh reserves in an attempt to overrun the positions held by Eicke. The Red Army units fought with such determination that their attacks could be repelled only when the Totenkopf soldiers wiped out the attackers. The ferocity of the fighting may be gauged from the fact that during the second half of February 1942 units in the Kampfgruppen of both Eicke and Simon—though attacked repeatedly every day—took fewer than 100 Russian prisoners. The increased intensity of the Soviet assaults, however, had their intended effect. By the third week of February 1942 Eicke's entire battle group (which was defending an eight-mile front) consisted of 36 officers, 191 NCOs, and

[11] BAMA, III SS, 41/10, vol. 3, pp. 270-78, 287, 293-95, 426-28; Baum interview of July 7, 1972.

1,233 enlisted men. To the dwindling number of SS men in the Demyansk pocket, Eicke offered only a repetition of the order to stand and hold. Echoing Hitler's admonition that fanatical resistance and superior will would break the back of the Russian counteroffensive, Eicke drove the surviving men in his command past the point of conceivable human endurance.[12]

By the end of February the front on the western side of the pocket was so fragmented and Russian penetrations so deep that Eicke could no longer evacuate the wounded to the SS hospital at Demyansk. The sick and badly injured were made as comfortable as possible, while those with only slight wounds remained in their foxholes and firing-pits in the front lines. In a radio dispatch to the Second Army Corps late on February 28 Eicke said that he had lost all contact with his neighboring units and admitted that the situation along his front looked hopeless.

Once again, however, the individual soldier of the SS Totenkopfdivision proved more than equal to the crisis. For another ten days, the SS defensive strongpoints somehow withstood the unabated fury of the enemy's infantry attacks. The Russian armies besieging the Demyansk pocket committed all of their reserves during the last days of February in a final effort to destroy the encircled Germans before the spring thaw turned the frozen terrain into an impassable bog. To bolster the ebbing strength of Eicke's Totenkopf units during these crucial days, Himmler finally managed to round up 400 reservists and by direct intervention by Hitler's headquarters succeeded in having the Luftwaffe free enough transports to fly them into the pocket on March 7. In addition, the slight improvement in the weather during the first week of March, as Eicke noted with relief, improved the Luftwaffe's accuracy in dropping supplies. Therefore, the SS Kampfgruppe acquired large quantities of desperately needed food, medicine, ammunition, grenades, mines, and automatic weapons.[13]

---

[12] BAMA, III SS, 41/10, vol. 3, pp. 328-36, 339-43, 371-83, 391-96, 405-19.

[13] NA/T-312/567/8181219-1220, "A. O. K. 16, Ic, Morgenmeldung vom 6. 3. 42"; NA/T-312/556/8166513-6752, "II A. K., Taktische Befehle und Meldungen," for February and March 1942; BAMA, III SS, 41/10, vol. 3, pp. 423-25, 430-36, 442-46, 448-55, 479; Halder, *KTB*, vol. 3, p. 402, entries for February 17-18, 1942; and Carell, *Hitler Moves East*, pp. 398-400. The survival of the Totenkopf units in the pocket hinged upon the ingenuity of Eicke and his SS offi-

During the second week of March 1942 the attacks against the sides of the pocket subsided. The Russians were exhausted by their winter effort, and many Red Army units had been bled white by the repeated suicidal charges against the entrenched German positions. On March 20, the last day of winter (with the temperature still at minus thirty degrees), Russian assaults against Eicke's SS battle group ceased temporarily and the front fell silent for the first time in over two months. According to reports later prepared by intelligence officers in the Totenkopfdivision, during the period between February 3 and March 20, 1942, Eicke's Kampfgruppe fought Red Army formations that included the crack Seventh Guards Division, the Fourteenth, Fifteenth, Forty-second, and Fifty-second Guards Brigades, the 154th, 203rd, 204th, and 205th Ski Battalions, the 272nd Ski Regiment, and the 154th Soviet Naval Rifle Brigade. From among these Soviet forces, the Totenkopfdivision claimed the infliction of 22,279 casualties—including 12,000 dead and wounded (virtual annihilation) in the Soviet Seventh Guards Division. Losses in the Totenkopfdivision, however, were equally disastrous. Figures compiled by the SS Führungshauptamt and the army indicated that the SSTK, which began the Russian campaign with 17,265 men, by March 20, 1942 had suffered 12,625 casualties. Of this total, approximately half—6,674 dead, wounded, missing, or sick—were incurred between January and April 1942 in the battle of the Demyansk pocket. During this same period, moreover, Eicke received only 5,029 replacements. At the end of March 1942, SSTK had altogether 9,669 men scattered throughout the pocket and stationed with the army at Staraya Russa. As the Soviet winter offensive drew to a close, it was obvious to Eicke and his SS

---

cers in improvising to master the ordnance and manpower shortages. Without German heavy weapons, captured Russian tanks, artillery pieces, and antitank guns were employed with great effect. To circumvent the army's refusal to send the SSTK reconnaissance battalion from Staraya Russa into the pocket, Eicke shrewdly secured the transfer of individual key SS officers and NCOs from Staraya Russa to Demyansk. By mid-March when the Tenth Army Corps discovered what was afoot and halted the transfers, Eicke had already moved many of the battalion's most experienced officers and NCOs into the pocket (BAMA, III SS, 41/10, vol. 3, pp. 459, 462, 470-78, 484-86, 492-93).

superiors that the surviving and weakened members of the Totenkopfdivision had to be withdrawn from Russia at the first opportunity to avoid the prospect of annihilation.[14]

The withdrawal of the Totenkopfdivision, however, could not
be considered until the German units in the pocket broke out to the
west or were liberated by a renewed German offensive against the
Valdai Hills. Since Hitler still categorically forbade withdrawal
from the region, the only hope was for a relief attack by units of
the Tenth Army Corps then sitting along the Polist River, approximately twenty-five miles from the western edge of the pocket. At
the beginning of March 1942 such a relief attack had been planned
and significant reinforcements shuttled into the Staraya Russa area
to carry it through. Hitler entrusted the operation to Lieutenant
General Walter von Seydlitz-Kurzbach, who received command
of the Tenth Army Corps and its specially beefed-up force consisting of the Fifth and Eighth Jäger Divisions, and the 122nd, 127th,
and 329th Infantry Divisions. Seydlitz's attack against the Soviet
forces between the Tenth Army Corps and the pocket was scheduled for 7:30 A.M., March 21.

To help achieve a quick junction with the beleagured units in
the pocket once the relief expedition began, Hitler consented to a
simultaneous attack toward Seydlitz's advancing divisions by the
units on the western side of the pocket. Since his battle group occupied the area at which the relief attack was aimed, Eicke's

[14] BAKO, NS/19-363, "Gruppe Eicke, Abt. Ic, Bericht über die vor der
Gruppe Eicke in der Zeit vom 3. 2-20. 3. 42 angesetzten feindlichen Einheiten," a
report sent by Eicke to Himmler on March 25, 1942; NA/T-312/567/8181791-
1794, an undated intelligence chart prepared by the Ic of the Sixteenth Army,
indentifying the individual Russian formations and their dispositions around the
Demyansk pocket; NA/T-312/567/8181772-1773, "II A. K., Artilleristische
Feindlage (bis einschl. 10. 3. 42)," dated March 10, 1942. SSTK casualty figures
are listed in BAKO, NS/19neu-1520, a comparative casualty table for all Waffen
SS divisions as of March 24, 1942, signed by Jüttner; and in NA/T-312/570/
8184229, "II A. K., Stärkemeldung vom 10. 4. 42"; and T-312/570/8184173,
"Anlage 2 zu A. O. K. 16, Ia No. 386/42, g. Kdos. vom 11. 4. 1942." Given the
size of the Soviet forces engaged against the pocket, the ferocity of the fighting,
and the Russians' willingness to expend lives profligately, the figure of 22,000
enemy casualties claimed by Eicke does not seem exaggerated. The Second Army
Corps claimed infliction of 60,000 Russian casualties (dead and wounded) between January 8 and April 20, 1942 (NA/T-312/570/8185195, "Abschlussmeldung, Die Verteidigung der 'Festung Demyansk.' " dated April 20, 1942).

combat-hardened Kampfgruppe was to spearhead the breakout assault.[15]

To assist Eicke's men in launching "Operation Gangway" (Fallreep), the code-name for the breakout attack, Second Army Corps concentrated units from the Thirtieth, Thirty-first, 123rd, and 290th Infantry Divisions in the western tip of the pocket. According to the plans prepared for "Gangway," the units inside the pocket were to wait until Seydlitz's offensive had smashed through the Russian lines and reached the Lovat River at Ramushevo. At that point, the units inside the pocket would attack in full force toward the west.

The offensive by the Tenth Army Corps to link up with the pocket began precisely on time under cover of the largest concentration of German aircraft on the northern sector since the previous summer. For two days Seydlitz's divisions made excellent progress, driving the Russians back from the Polist with heavy losses in men and matériel. On March 24, however, Soviet resistance stiffened appreciably as the Red Army units fell back into prepared defensive positions built during the winter along both sides of the Lovat River at Ramushevo. On March 28, Seydlitz's offensive stalled in the face of heavy resistance, and the Tenth Army Corps was forced to tackle the Russian strong points one at a time. This costly, time-consuming process slowed the advance considerably, and caused repeated postponements of "Operation Gangway" from inside the pocket.[16]

The reduction of the Russian defensive network west of the Lovat took Seydlitz another two weeks. The spearheads of the

[15] BAMA, III SS, 41/10, vol. 3, pp. 509-26; III SS, 41/9, pp. 89-96; NA/T-312/570/8184130-4144, "A. O. K. 16, Ia, KTB Nr. 5, Teil IV, Kartenband Brückenschlag," a series of situation maps from March and April 1942 detailing the progress of Seydlitz's attack to link up with the forces in the pocket. See also, Halder, *KTB*, vol. 3, pp. 408-11, entries for March 2-8, 1942; Seaton, p. 246; and Carell, *Hitler Moves East*, pp. 403-5. The account in Carell is confusing and in places inaccurate. Moreover, it ignores almost completely the decisive role played by Eicke's Kampfgruppe in the successful operation to break the Russian ring around the Demyansk cauldron.

[16] NA/T-312/570/8184291-4294, 8184296-4367, a series of radio messages between the Sixteenth Army and Second Army Corps concerning the slow progress of the desperate attacks by Seydlitz's formations toward the Lovat and Ramushevo. See also, Philippi and Heim, p. 119; and Halder, *KTB*, vol. 3, pp. 417-18, 422, entries for March 21, 25, and 30, 1942.

Eighth Jäger Division could not force their way into Ramushevo until April 12; and then did not secure the town, mop up the last of the Russian snipers, and occupy the west bank of the Lovat until two days later. Throughout this time, the units inside the pocket waited impatiently, conserving their last reserves of energy and ammunition for the anticipated attack. When Seydlitz finally radioed on April 14 to announce the capture of Ramushevo, Second Army Corps ordered "Gangway" to begin, and the troops under Eicke's command finally went to the offensive.[17]

The SS and Wehrmacht soldiers of Second Army Corps attacked at 11:00 A.M. on April 14, falling upon the weakened Soviet units opposite them with frenzied vengeance. The repeated postponements of "Gangway," however, caused Eicke's breakout assault to coincide with the first full spring thaw. The German units in the pocket had to struggle along muddy roads and slog through chest-deep swamps that only two weeks previously had been frozen and easily traversible. Consequently, the hand-to-hand fighting took on an extra dimension of savagery, with heavy losses on each side and no quarter given by either contestant. For the next six days Eicke's battle group pushed toward Ramushevo, averaging little more than a mile per day in its advance. Finally, on April 20, a company from the SSTK tank-destroyer battalion broke through the last Soviet defensive ring and reached the east bank of the Lovat at Ramushevo.

The following day, additional units fought through to the flood-swollen river (at that point more than 1,000 yards wide) and helped clear out the remaining Soviet strongpoints. On April 22, seventy-three days after the encirclement of the German

---

[17] NA/T-312/570/8184384-4389, 4391, 4396, radio messages between Eicke and Second Army Corps, April 13 and 14, 1942; Baum interview; and Halder, *KTB*, vol. 3, pp. 423-26, entries for April 2-12, 1942. To strengthen his own army and SS units for "Gangway," Eicke transferred many men from Max Simon's Kampfgruppe, prompting Simon to protest that the men he had left—2,177 as of March 31—were far too inadequate and thinly strung out to protect the northeastern wall of the pocket (BAMA, III SS, 41/9, pp. 2-3, Simon to Eicke, April 10, 1942). The Second Army Corps also interceded with the Luftwaffe in Eicke's behalf to have 500 SS replacements belonging to SS Freikorps Dänemark flown into the pocket beginning on April 17, providing critically needed muscle (NA/T-312/570/8184368, 8184398-4399, 8184459, radio messages between Second Army Corps and Sixteenth Army concerning air transport of the men from Porkhov).

forces around Demyansk, the bridgehead was secure enough for Seydlitz to begin ferrying supplies across the river by barge; the siege officially ended.[18]

In battering down the Russian defenses between the pocket and Ramushevo, thus completing the relief offensive, the weakened units from the Totenkopfdivision that fought under Eicke's command in the pocket contributed significantly to the successful winter defense in the Lake Ilmen sector. Eicke's Kampfgruppe had served as the driving element among the German units that completed the breakout and thus reestablished a continuous front for the right wing of Army Group North. Hitler recognized the contribution of the Totenkopfdivision in mastering the winter crisis, evidenced by the decorations and personal praise he lavished upon ·Eicke and his men.

To complement the Ritterkreuz he received on January 15, Eicke was awarded the Oak Leaves to the Knight's Cross on April 20, 1942, and promoted to SS Obergruppenführer. In the formal award ceremony subsequently held at Rastenburg on June 26, Hitler praised Eicke and the Totenkopfdivision in the presence of Himmler and an assembled group of army and SS dignitaries, courtiers, and adjutants. In recognizing the exceptional performance by SSTK during the battle for the Demyansk pocket, the führer declared that he considered Eicke and his men primarily responsible for the fact that the pocket had held out through the winter and for the successful breakout that had liberated the pocket. In addition to the recognition given Eicke, eleven other officers and men in the Totenkopfdivision received the Ritterkreuz from Hitler for heroism during the winter crisis of January-March 1942. This represented the most of such distinguished medals then given to any Waffen SS division over such a short period of

[18] NA/T-312/570/8184411, radio message from Second Army Corps to Sixteenth Army, describing the difficulties of Eicke's Kampfgruppe in the swollen swamps on April 14; NA/T-312/570/8184505, radio message from Seydlitz to Second Army Corps, April 20, 1942, confirming the link-up at Ramushevo; BAMA, III SS, 41/10, vol. 3, pp. 527-51; III SS, 41/9, pp. 89-95; KTB/OKW, vol. 2, pt. 1, pp. 320, 326; and Halder, *KTB*, vol. 3, p. 432, entry for April 22, 1942. The first unit from inside the pocket to contact men of the Eighth Jäger Division on the Lovat was a company from the SSTK tank-destroyer battalion commanded by Max Seela (Baum interview/Baum memorandum).

9. At Hitler's headquarters, the Wolfschanze, Eicke poses after receiving the Oak Leaves to his Knight's Cross. In the foreground, left to right, are Karl Wolff, Eicke, Field Marshal Keitel, and Julius Schaub, Hitler's personal adjutant.

10. SS Obergruppenführer Theodor Eicke at the peak of his prestige as first wartime commander of the SS Totenkopfdivision.

time, and provided striking testimony to the immense prestige the Totenkopfdivision had earned in Russia.[19]

The price of this formidable reputation, however, had nearly proved fatal. In a summary report on SSTK casualties prepared for Himmler at the end of May, Eicke claimed that the total strength of the Totenkopfdivision (which was then still in action south of Lake Ilmen) had dwindled to 6,700 men. Considering the division's staggering losses, Eicke wrote, there were only two possible courses of action that could save SSTK from eventual destruction. The Reichsführer SS, he suggested bluntly, must either send up the 10,000 replacements that were needed or see to it that SSTK was withdrawn from Russia at once for a lengthy period of rest and refitting. In any event, Eicke concluded, something had to be done soon since the units of the Totenkopfdivision simply were too weak to resist the Russians much longer.[20]

The depressing statistical picture painted in Eicke's intemperate communiqué was overshadowed by even gloomier medical reports describing the shocking physical state of the SS soldiers who

[19] USDC, SS Personalakte Eicke, Dienstlaufbahn; and ibid., front-page articles clipped from the Berlin edition of the *Völkischer Beobachter*, issues for January 16 and April 21, 1942. Both articles carry prominent pictures of Eicke. See also, IFZ, *Das Schwarze Korps*, issue for April 23, 1942, which contains a full-page story about Eicke's exploits during the battle of Demyansk; and BAMA, III SS, 41/10, vol. 3, pp. 172, 186, 458; III SS, 41/9, pp. 101-7, letter from Eicke to Max Simon sent from Hitler's headquarters on July 5, 1942; and Krätschmer, pp. 55-61, 82-84, 88-89, 90, 92-94, 99, 106-21, for accounts of those in SSTK who received the Ritterkreuz and the actions for which the awards were given.

[20] BAKO, NS/19-345, "Aktennotiz für den Reichsführer SS," a report signed by Eicke, dated May 30, 1942. Eicke's evaluation of his soldiers' condition in the pocket was underscored in an equally grim report Count Brockdorff, commander of the Second Army Corps, sent to Colonel General Busch on April 19. Count Brockdorff warned Busch that the Totenkopf units in the pocket were much weaker in the wake of "Operation Gangway" than they had been at any other time during the winter, and declared that Eicke's was the one Kampfgruppe in the pocket most in need of immediate withdrawal from the front (NA/T-312/570/8185189-5193, "Generalkommando II Armeekorps, Dem Armeeoberkommando 16," dated April 19, 1942).

Eicke's curt language to Himmler in the letter of May 30 was a sign of the lingering bad relations between the two. Himmler grew exceptionally cool to Eicke after their row over Eicke's dismissal of Kleinheisterkamp the previous autumn. Eicke felt that Himmler had not acted decisively with Hitler and OKH in protecting the interests of the Totenkopfdivision (USDC, SS Personalakte Eicke, letter from Himmler to Eicke of November 28, 1941; and Baum interview of July 7, 1972).

had survived the winter. The most revealing of these was a lengthy memorandum sent to Max Simon on April 7, 1942, by SS Hauptsturmführer Dr. Eckert, the physician of the Second Battalion of Simon's First Infantry Regiment. Eckert's report outlined the results of extensive physical examinations he had conducted in late March and early April. Eighty-eight of the 281 Totenkopf men he had examined were, even by army standards, unfit for further military service. Some of them, he continued, were in such bad physical shape that they resembled concentration camp inmates he had seen during his tour of duty in the camp system (a most revealing comment in several respects). The rest of the men examined had lost an average of twenty pounds and were weak and listless. The main reasons for the weight loss and weakness, Eckert asserted, were lack of sufficient food, the intense cold, and the inadequate winter shelter that had been provided for the men.[21]

Dr. Eckert concluded that at least thirty percent of the men in the battalion were unfit for continued duty. The other seventy percent, he felt, had been weakened to such an extent that they required at least a short period of rest before they were recommitted to action. Medically, Eckert judged the entire battalion to be incapable of continued combat effectiveness without rest and recuperation.[22]

In a letter accompanying Eckert's medical report the commander of the battalion, SS Sturmbannführer Hellmuth Becker, informed Simon that he agreed completely with the observations and conclusions of the SS doctor. Even worse than the decline in the troops' physical condition, Becker added, was the deterioration in morale and discipline that had occurred since the beginning of the Soviet counteroffensive. Since the end of November, he claimed, there had been a marked increase in cases of theft, sleep-

[21] BAKO, NS/19-320, II./SS-Totenkopf Inf. Reg. 1 (mot), Truppenarzt, "Ärztlicher Bericht über den Gesundheits—und Kräftezustand der in der vorderster Linie eingesetzten Teile des Bataillons, den 7. 4. 1942."

[22] *Ibid*. Eckert could not resist the temptation to speculate on the racial and political deficiencies of the new SS recruits, especially the Volksdeutsche who had arrived during the winter. Echoing Eicke's long-familiar theme, the doctor concluded that greater racial selectivity and more-thorough political indoctrination among new SS recruits would produce tougher soldiers better fitted to fight in Russia.

ing on guard duty, self-inflicted wounds, and acts of cowardice in battle. In February, when the situation was most desperate, there had even been three known cases of desertion to the enemy—a phenomenon extremely rare among Waffen SS units. Such developments, Becker concluded, were dramatic evidence of the overall decline in the effectiveness of the Totenkopf soldiers—a process that would grow worse unless the troops were relieved immediately.[23]

The conditions described by Becker and Eckert epitomized the physical state of the overwhelming majority of SSTK soldiers in the Demyansk pocket. When these reports were subsequently forwarded to Himmler, however, they elicited only a callous and typically unrealistic response. The Reichsführer SS angrily rejected them as the products of exaggerated fantasy. In a tart letter to Eicke written on April 30, Himmler testily replied that the reports contained nothing new, since everyone knew the winter had been harsh. In any event, Himmler asserted, the return of warm weather and the availability of fresh vegetables would quickly restore the physical vigor of the Totenkopf soldiers! Turning to the subject of morale and discipline, the Reichsführer SS insisted that he did not need a doctor to tell him about the obvious ideological deficiencies in SS troop training. One had to recognize also that a war was in progress, and in wartime one could not be as selective as in peacetime. Given the present circumstances, Himmler admitted, he was forced in his recruiting to compromise quality for the sake of needed quantity. Assuring Eicke that he was well aware of conditions in the Totenkopfdivision and that he would look after the division's best interests, the Reichsführer SS closed by categorically forbidding any further such medical examinations and reports as those compiled by Dr. Eckert and Sturmbannführer Becker.[24]

[23] BAKO, NS/19-320, Becker to Max Simon, April 7, 1942. The same letter may also be found in IFZ, as Nuremberg Document NO-1731. Becker also was highly critical of the Volksdeutsche recruits, many of whom he felt had been dragooned most unwillingly into service with the Totenkopfdivision. Consequently, Becker told Simon that he favored greater selectivity by SS recruiters to preserve the racially elite status of the SS, and hence the physical toughness of its soldiers.

[24] BAKO, NS/19-320, Himmler to Eicke, April 30, 1942. Himmler admitted that losses among Waffen SS units had been so high in 1941 that he was forced to

Himmler's letter of April 30, filled with a typical mixture of prissy naïvete and nutritional nonsense, ignored the stark facts confronting Eicke and his men. The otiose suggestions contained in the Reichsführer's response were based upon a gross miscalculation. This erroneous impression, which Hitler shared, placed the Totenkopfdivision in an ironic dilemma during the coming months. The successful conclusion of the battle of the Demyansk pocket convinced Himmler, and more importantly Hitler, that the Totenkopfdivision's presence was crucial to the continued stability of the German front south of Lake Ilmen. Ignoring the debilitating effect that the winter had had on Eicke's soldiers, the führer and Himmler regarded the Totenkopfdivision as one of the most reliable units in the German armed forces; as one whose record in defensive fighting was among the most illustrious on the entire eastern front. Consequently, during the spring and summer of 1942 Hitler repeatedly refused to allow SSTK to withdraw from Russia for rest and refitting. The result was the piecemeal decimation of the remaining units of the Totenkopfdivision.[25]

While refusing SSTK the respite it needed to survive, Hitler did authorize the organization of new SS units in Germany that were to be sent to join the Totenkopfdivision once they had been equipped and trained. Raising these new formations, however, was expected to take at least three months. By the time they actually were ready for service in Russia in October 1942, the SSTK units around Demyansk were so small and the men so sick and exhausted that Eicke and his surviving senior unit commanders were left the task of building a completely new Totenkopfdivision.[26]

---

send inadequately trained replacements to the front. The war, he declared, had become a contest of improvisation; whoever improvised best would win. Himmler also defended the Volksdeutsche recruits, insisting that they had to be reliable or Germany would otherwise be unable to depend upon the twelve million ethnic Germans throughout the world.

[25] BAMA, III SS, 41/9, pp. 101-7, Eicke to Simon, June 26, 1942; III SS, 41/9, pp. 108-11, Simon's reply of July 8. Details of the division's combat activities in the summer and autumn of 1942 may be found in the daily exchange of radio messages, telegrams, and letters among Eicke, Simon, Jüttner, and Himmler in this same volume.

[26] BAKO, NS/19-345, "Neuaufstellung und Umgliederung von Teilen der SS-T. Div.," a circular order from the SS Führungshauptamt of June 24, 1942.

The final ordeal for the units of the Totenkopfdivision in the Demyansk salient began immediately after Seydlitz's successful relief operation. After April 24, land contact with the Tenth Army Corps was firmly reestablished by means of a three-mile-wide corridor whose center was the Staraya Russa-Demyansk road. This thin connecting artery transformed the Demyansk pocket into a salient that protruded into the body of Soviet-held territory south of Lake Ilmen. Since Hitler still forbade any withdrawal or shortening of the front, the sides of the salient and the narrow landneck had to be reinforced and protected against constant Russian attempts to cut the road and encircle the German forces once again. To keep open the supply artery and shore up the salient for the summer campaign Hitler directed that all the army and SS units in the western side of the salient be placed under Eicke's command as a corps. Eicke then received instructions from Hitler's HQ via the army to entrench, hold open the corridor, and not be dislodged under any circumstances.[27]

The "corps" Eicke received on May 5, 1942 consisted of fewer than 14,000 survivors from the six divisions that had been badly mauled in the Demyansk pocket. These sick and exhausted men were expected to defend a front forty-five miles long, a task even Eicke's army superiors admitted was impossible unless large numbers of fresh reserves were sent into the salient. On May 3 Colonel General Busch traveled through the corridor for the first time since the end of the winter crisis and visited at length with Eicke in the latter's headquarters in the village of Kalitkino. Eicke was extremely pessimistic about the situation and implored Busch either to send in replacements or to withdraw the units of the Totenkopfdivision from the salient so it could be saved to recuperate and rebuild. Impressed by Eicke's arguments and shocked by the physical condition of the SS men he saw, Busch penned an un-

[27] BAMA, III SS, 41/9, pp. 89-95; BAKO NS/19-345, Korpskommando Eicke, "Korpsbefehl," dated May 17, 1942. Eicke's corps was designated simply Korpskommando Eicke by the Sixteenth Army, and consisted initially of surviving units from the 290th Infantry Division, SSTK, and the 105th Artillery Command. These units had previously been designated as a corps under the command of Major General Hans Zorn. Until Zorn left the salient on May 4, the corps command at the western end of the pocket carried his name (NA/T-312/570/8184683, radio message from Sixteenth Army to Second Army Corps announcing Zorn's departure and Eicke's appointment as of May 5, 1942).

233

precedented letter to Himmler upon his return to Sixteenth Army headquarters the following day.[28]

The colonel general began by praising the Totenkopfdivision effusively and by assuring Himmler that the reopening and relief of the Demyansk pocket had been due mainly to Eicke's energetic leadership. Since the führer considered it essential to keep SSTK in the Demyansk salient, Busch continued, it was absolutely necessary that Eicke receive at least 5,000 replacements immediately. If these troops were sent forward at once, he promised, Sixteenth Army would have the newly arriving reservists and all other Totenkopf units in the salient withdrawn temporarily to be reorganized and placed under Eicke's command. The result, Busch pointed out, would be an overall strengthening of SSTK and a corresponding improvement of the situation within the salient. This was the first and only recorded occasion during the war in which an army commander attempted to intervene directly with Himmler in support of Eicke and on behalf of the Totenkopfdivision. In every other documented instance, communications between Eicke's tactical superiors in the field and the SS hierarchy involved some complaint; or, as the Russian campaign dragged on, more frequently contained praise for the Totenkopfdivision for its exceptional performance in some individual action.[29]

Himmler, however, was both unwilling and unable to comply

[28] NA/T-312/570/8185223-5226, "Generalkommando II Armeekorps, Dem Armee-Oberkommando 16.," dated April 27, 1942, a long letter from Graf Brockdorff to Busch warning of the perilous state of the exhausted and disease-wracked German units in the salient, and of the impossibility of holding out against future Russian attacks without massive reinforcements; and NA/T-312/570/8184663-4666, long radio message from Second Army Corps to Sixteenth Army describing the units under Eicke's command as so weak and spread across such a broad front as to have only the effective strength of sentries in the forward trenches. See also, BAKO, NS/19-345, "Der Oberbefehlshaber der 16. Armee, An den Reichsführer SS," dated May 4, 1942. At the time of Busch's letter, all units of the Totenkopfdivision in the Lake Ilmen area, except Max Simon's SSTK/I. R. 1 deployed northeast of Demyansk, were under Eicke's direct command and grouped at the western edge of the salient where the land corridor to Staraya Russa began. Simon's regiment also remained under Eicke's authority in his capacity as commander of the Totenkopfdivision.

[29] BAKO, NS/19-345, Busch to Himmler, May 4, 1942. No copy of Himmler's reply to Busch was found among the documents examined for this study.

fully with Busch's recommendations. The Totenkopfdivision subsequently did receive 3,000 ill-trained reservists from Germany, a few Danish SS volunteers, some Volksdeutsche recruits from other SS divisions, and the return of its own reconnaissance battalion (much weakened) from Staraya Russa. As Himmler was already looking ahead to building a new Totenkopfdivision in Germany, he refused to send further replacements or even sufficient quantities of vehicles and heavy weapons to Demyansk. By withholding these valuable instruments of war from men outnumbered by an enemy liberally equipped with tanks and artillery, Himmler in effect sentenced the SSTK units at Demyansk to death—as the coming months proved. The powerful Russian forces ringing Eicke's corps on three sides recovered quickly from their winter exertions and launched infantry assaults against the supply corridor in May that were repulsed only with serious difficulty. By early June, the signs of a major Soviet build-up to destroy the German forces in the salient were unmistakable. Russian attacks against Eicke's positions grew stronger and more frequent, forcing an emergency reorganization of the remaining army and SS units in the corridor in anticipation of a coming crisis. As the weeks passed with no sign of any effort by Himmler to rescue the remnant of the Totenkopfdivision from its Demyansk dilemma, Eicke's despondency and irritation turned to rage over the impossible situation he and his men faced.[30]

During the second week of June, Eicke received a unique op-

[30] NA/T-312/570/8185279-5283, "Generalkommando II Armeekorps, Abt. Ia, Verteidigung der Festung Demyansk gegen die russische Frühjahrsoffensive," dated June 5, 1942. This is a report Second Army Corps sent Sixteenth Army describing the Soviet build-up during early May, and the constant, strong assaults against the western side of the salient. The report claimed that the Russian artillery bombardment and air attacks preceding the first assault on May 3 surpassed in intensity anything the most seasoned German troops had previously experienced. The Russian attacks, which continued until May 24, were conducted by young, strong, fresh infantry supported by masses of tanks, flame throwers, and assault engineers. See also, BAKO, NS/19-345, SS Totenkopf-Division, Kommandeur, "Wiederordnung der Verbände gemäss Führerbefehl," of May 27, 1942; a copy of this is also in IFZ, Microfilm Collection, roll MA-284. frames 2520978-0979; and KTB/OKW, vol. 2, pt. 1, pp. 340, 343, 345, 347, 350, 357, 359, 362, 364, 367, 377-79, 381, 393, 407, 417; Halder, *KTB*, vol. 3, pp. 437, 445, entries for May 5 and 20, 1942; and Baum interview/Baum memorandum.

portunity to carry his case for the reinforcement or relief of SSTK to the highest level. Orders arrived from Himmler instructing Eicke to report home for a period of leave and a series of consultations. The Reichsführer SS directed Eicke to relinquish command of the division to Max Simon, leave Russia aboard a special plane being sent for him, and go directly to spend a few days with his family at Oranienburg. When his leave ended, Eicke was to present himself at Hitler's HQ to receive the Oak Leaves to his Ritterkreuz.[31]

At noon on Friday, June 26, 1942, Eicke rode through the security rings of smartly saluting SS sentries into the "Wolf's Lair" (Wolfschanze)—the code-name for Hitler's HQ near Rastenburg, East Prussia—to be decorated by the führer. Just after the ceremony, Hitler invited Eicke to his private study for a chat. For twenty minutes he questioned Eicke closely about the Totenkopfdivision, its strengths, weaknesses, and needs. According to Eicke, Hitler then listened intently while the former described in the bluntest possible language the weakened condition of the men, and the acute shortages of weapons and vehicles. Eicke ended the audience with a plea that Hitler withdraw the Totenkopfdivision from Russia at the first opportunity. The führer allegedly seemed impressed by the arguments and agreed to transfer the Totenkopfdivision to France in August if the situation south of Lake Ilmen remained stable. In addition, Hitler promised Eicke that new units for SSTK, including a tank battalion, would be organized, trained, and fully equipped by the autumn of 1942.[32]

At the end of his private talk with the führer, as he shortly wrote Max Simon, Eicke came away with the impression that Hitler's promise to relieve the Totenkopfdivision was unalterable and his desire to rebuild SSTK to its pre-campaign strength genuine. Eicke's hopes were raised even higher during lengthy discussions with Himmler that same day. After inquiring about the needs of the division, the Reichsführer SS ordered Eicke to

[31] BAMA, III SS, 41/9, pp. 97-99, Simon to Eicke, July 3, 1942, and pp. 101-7, Eicke to Simon, July 5, 1942. Official notice of Eicke's visit to the Wolfschanze is in KTB/OKW, vol. 2, pt. 1, p. 451.

[32] BAMA, III SS, 41/9, pp. 101-7, Eicke to Simon, July 5, 1942; BAKO, NS/ 19-345, "Aufstellung einer Panzer-Abteilung für die SS-T. Div.," dated May 20, 1942; and BAKO, NS/19-345, "Neuaufstellung und Umgliederung von Teilen der SS-T. Div.," dated June 24, 1942.

11. Max Simon, Eicke's immediate successor as commander of the SS Totenkopfdivision.

remain home on leave for a few more weeks until SSTK was removed from Russia.[33]

In the meantime, plans for the reorganization of SSTK on the basis of Hitler's orders took shape rapidly. The first contingent of SS officers for Eicke's new tank battalion arrived at Buchenwald to organize facilities and a training program; while Heinz Lammerding, fresh from a three-week leave, was ordered by Himmler to begin training SS recruits for Eicke's new infantry regiments at the SS Kaserne at Sennelager bei Paderborn in Westphalia. By the first week of July, Lammerding had made all the necessary preparations, and, as the first new SS recruits arrived, wrote to Max Simon in Russia asking when to expect the first convoys of Totenkopf soldiers from the East.[34]

About the time Lammerding wrote, however, events in the Demyansk salient were moving quickly to seal the fate of the SS Totenkopf units deployed there. In the weeks following Eicke's departure, the Soviets completed their build-up around the bulge south of Lake Ilmen under the convenient cover of unseasonably heavy rain. Then on July 2, as the great German summer offensive in southern Russia rolled through the Crimea and toward the Don River and the Caucasus, the Red Army formations around Demyansk resumed their pressure against the salient and its narrow supply corridor. By July 7 the Russian attacks had become most intense against the sectors held by the remaining SSTK units. The overwhelming contrast between Soviet strength and the SS weakness led Max Simon to anticipate an immediate breakthrough and to begin frantic appeals for the relief of the Totenkopfdivision.[35]

---

[33] BAMA, III SS, 41/9, pp. 101-7, Eicke to Simon, July 5, 1942.

[34] Ibid., III SS, 41/9, p. 137, Lammerding to Max Simon, July 7, 1942.

[35] NA/T-312/583/8201625-1628, "Fahrt des Oberbefehlshabers am 4. 7. 1942 zum II A. K.," which contains a summary of the conversation between Simon and Busch during the latter's visit to Simon's HQ on July 4; and NA/T-314/131/ 000110-111, 113, 137, 217-18, 260-61, 271, 352, for the morning and evening reports of SSTK and Second Army Corps for the first week of July describing the Soviet attacks and the situation of Simon's troops. See also, BAMA, III SS, 41/9, pp. 97-99, 108-11, 112-14, letters from Simon to Eicke of July 3, 8, and 9, 1942; and the accounts of the renewed Russian onslaught south of Lake Ilmen in KTB/ OKW, vol. 2, pt. 1, pp. 469, 479; and in Halder, *KTB*, vol. 3, pp. 465, 471, entries for June 25 and July 3, 1942. Max Simon's desperation of early July was in

As the ferocity of the Russian attacks grew, Simon's appeals to Eicke and Himmler also included unrestrained denunciations of the army's operational conduct in the Lake Ilmen area. The interim SSTK commander complained that on several occasions the Second Army Corps had ordered him to attack objectives his units were much too weak to capture. In every instance, Simon argued, the result had been the same: the assaults had failed and the SS units involved had suffered heavy casualties. The Russians had then counterattacked in overwhelming strength with tanks and artillery and inflicted additional casualties on the SSTK units, which had held their original positions only with extreme difficulty. These senseless attacks, according to Simon, had accomplished nothing and had cost SSTK casualties of 20 officers and 776 NCOs and enlisted men. If they continued, he concluded, the annihilation of the Totenkopfdivision was a mere question of time.[36]

Even worse than the army's stupidity, Simon raged, was the obvious disinterest of the Second Army Corps in the fate of the remaining SS men in the salient. The commander of Second Army Corps, Count Brockdorff-Ahlefeldt, was so determined to

stark contrast to his unlimited confidence of early May about the Demyansk situation. During a visit by Busch to his HQ on May 9, Simon had fatuously claimed that the Russians were beaten, since his troops were capturing only old men and young boys dressed in rags, ill-equipped and badly trained. He was, he assured Busch, so convinced that the Russian forces in the area were finished, he was sure increasing the loudspeaker propaganda broadcasts across the lines would enormously increase enemy desertions (NA/T-312/570/8185298-5299, "Fahrt des Oberbefehlshabers zum II Korps," with a summary of the conversation between Busch and Simon on May 9, 1942).

[36] BAMA, III SS, 41/9, pp. 108-11, 112-14, 138-39, Simon to Eicke of July 8 and 9, 1942, and Simon to Lammerding, July 8, 1942; NA/T-314/131/000271, "Korpsarzt des II A. K., and A. O. K. 16, Meldung über personelle Verluste am 7. 7. 42," shows that for one day (July 7) SSTK units in the salient lost twenty-one killed, ninety-one wounded, and thirty-eight missing; while NA/T-314/131/000520, SSTK interim report for July 8, describes the heavy Russian counterattacks and their growing effectiveness against the weakly held villages of Vasilyevschina, Omychkino, and Novo Ramuschevo. Even before the resumption of the Russian attacks at the beginning of July, Simon had protested to Eicke that the army always gave SSTK the dirty assignment of mounting local attacks during rainstorms or other adverse circumstances, but consistently refused to share army supplies and ammunition with the understrength SS units. Friction between SSTK and its army superiors and neighboring units became sharper than at any other time during the war in the midst of the Demyansk crisis of July and August 1942.

239

keep SSTK in the line, Simon claimed, that he had blocked attempts to send key unit commanders and officers home on leave so they could be transferred individually to Sennelager. On July 8, the army ordered Simon not to send any more SS officers or men on leave, and to make certain that he did not—so Simon claimed—tightened controls on all trains and passengers leaving for Germany from the Lake Ilmen area. Simon's erroneous and unfair conviction that the army intended to keep SSTK in the salient until it was destroyed prompted him to urge Eicke to transfer all the men from the Totenkopfdivision then home on leave to Sennelager rather than send them back to Russia to face certain and senseless death. To expedite the transfers, Simon sent an accompanying letter to Heinz Lammerding at Paderborn with the names and addresses of all the SSTK soldiers then in Germany on leave.[37]

Simon's gloomy report on the conditions in the salient angered and depressed Eicke, who once again took advantage of his temporary access to Hitler and Himmler to urge the immediate transfer of the entire Totenkopfdivision to France. On July 13 and 14, 1942, Eicke was present at Rastenburg for a series of conferences on Waffen SS matters. In a private conversation with Eicke on the afternoon of July 13, Hitler modified his earlier promise. Since the Russians had recovered their strength in the Demyansk area, the führer told Eicke, the Totenkopfdivision would have to remain in the line until an attack by Lieutenant General Otto von

---

[37] BAMA, III SS, pp. 41/9, 108-11, 138-39, Simon to Eicke, and Simon to Lammerding, both of July 8, 1942. Simon's attitude and accusations provide one of the best examples of the tendency of many Waffen SS commanders to impute sinister motives to the army's simple desire to utilize fully the tough, dependable Waffen SS divisions at its disposal. Simon's grossly unjust charges of callousness on the part of Count Brockdorff are refuted by NA/T-312/583/8200832-0833, a letter from Count Brockdorff to Busch of July 6, 1942, in which the former urged Busch to remove the remainder of SSTK from the salient before it suffered complete annihilation; and by NA/T-314/131/000549, typed copy of a teleprinter message from Second Army Corps to Sixteenth Army of 10:25 P.M., July 8, 1942, in which Count Brockdorff underscored Simon's analysis of the desperate situation, verified the serious SSTK casualty figures, and requested the immediate dispatch of substantial replacements for the SS units in the salient. The Reichsführer SS took Simon's complaints seriously. Himmler's own suspicions about the army's treatment of his SS divisions prompted him to send the Totenkopfdivision a special radio truck with a powerful transmitter so Simon could communicate directly with the SS Führungshauptamt in Berlin without using the army's facilities.

Knobelsdorff's newly reorganized Tenth Army Corps widened the supply corridor and straightened out the front in the salient. Owing to the shortage of SS replacements, Hitler concluded, the attack could not take place until the end of August. SSTK simply would have to dig in and hold until then.[38]

After Hitler dismissed him with this unpleasant news, Eicke conferred again with Himmler, who sought vainly to lift the SSTK commander's sagging spirits. The Reichsführer SS assured Eicke that the Totenkopfdivision would eventually be withdrawn from Russia. Hitler had only denied this temporarily, Himmler intoned, because of his appraisal of the course of the war and his consideration of all factors involved. What Himmler actually meant was that the German summer offensive in southern Russia was stretching the Wehrmacht to the limit. All available reserves from the Reich and from other fronts were being funneled to the army groups advancing across the Ukraine toward Stalingrad and the Caucasus. Until the completion of this offensive, Hitler intended to leave the other areas of the Russian front to get along as best they could. Units engaged in sensitive or contested sectors simply would have to stick it out regardless of their condition.[39]

At the time Eicke wrote to Simon informing him of Hitler's decision, the Soviets were completing preparations for a renewed offensive against the salient and the supply corridor. The massive attack began at 1:30 P.M. on July 17, and completely stunned the Germans with the sheer force of its intensity. Russian infantry supported by T-34 tanks achieved local breakthroughs in the sector held by SSTK and were stopped and thrown back only at a prohibitive cost in casualties. Fierce fighting continued throughout the night all around the salient, and on the morning of July 18 the Russians captured the village of Vasilyevschina—a vital strongpoint just north of the Staraya Russa-Demyansk road. The two companies of Totenkopf soldiers in the town were wiped

[38] BAMA, III SS, 41/9, pp. 115-23, letter from Eicke to Max Simon, dated July 15, 1942.

[39] Ibid., Eicke to Simon, July 15, 1942. For details concerning the summer offensive as seen from Hitler's headquarters, see KTB/OKW, vol. 2, pt. 1, pp. 456-502; Halder, *KTB*, vol. 3, pp. 470-93, entries for July 2-30, 1942. During his second visit to Rastenburg, Eicke received orders from Himmler to continue his leave at least until the end of July. Eicke's leg and foot wounds from the previous summer were acting up and subsequently required additional surgery.

out—fighting to the last man rather than surrender this key defensive position. With the loss of Vasilyevschina, the way was open for the Russians to push further south and cut the supply road—thus trapping the Second Army Corps once again.[40]

To close the gap in the German front the commander of the Second Army Corps, Count Brockdorff, called on Simon to counterattack immediately to retake Vasilyevschina. For the first time in the more than two years the SS Totenkopfdivision had been fighting under the direction of the army, an SSTK commander categorically and absolutely refused to obey an order from his army superior. In blunt language, Simon informed Second Army Corps that the Totenkopfdivision had suffered 532 casualties in dead and wounded since the afternoon of July 17 and was no longer in shape to attack anything. If the army wanted Vasilyevschina retaken, Simon blustered, it could find one of its own units to do the job. At the same time he declined to obey Count Brockdorff's orders, Simon informed Himmler of his own insubordination by radio, complaining again that the army was destroying SSTK by assigning it the heaviest, dirtiest, and most difficult fighting.[41]

Simon's insubordination went unchallenged, and Count Brockdorff assigned the recapture of Vasilyevschina to units of the Eighth Jäger Division. Their counterattack, however, which was supported by Stukas and fifty tanks, failed to dislodge the

[40] NA/T-314/131/000829, interim report (Zwischenmeldung) of SSTK to Second Army Corps of July 17, 1942; NA/T-314/131/000835, 838, 840, 862, 865, series of radio messages from Second Army Corps to Sixteenth Army during the afternoon of July 17; and NA/T-312/580/8198118-9139, "A. O. K. 16, KTB Nr. 5, Teil IV, Ein- u. Abgehende Fern- und Funksprüche, vom 6. 6. 42 bis 28. 12. 1942," for the radio and teleprinter traffic documenting the renewed crisis in the Demyansk salient during the summer and autumn of 1942. Simon's description of the paralyzing Russian attacks and his own insubordination are in BAMA, III SS, 41/9, pp. 5-9; and BAKO, NS/19-345, transcript of a radio message from Simon to the SS Führungshauptamt, relayed by Jüttner to Himmler at Rastenburg on July 18, 1942.

[41] BAKO, NS/19-345, Simon to SSFHA via radio, July 17, 1942. Another SS company defending a road junction called Velikoye Selo was annihilated on July 21, bringing total SSTK losses since the beginning of the Russian assault to 13 officers and 667 men (BAKO, NS/19-345, radio message from Simon to Eicke via the SSFHA, dated July 21, 1942; and NA/T-314/131/000912-913, 0001304-1331, daily reports of Sixteenth Army to Army Group North, and Second Army Corps to Sixteenth Army for the period July 18-21, 1942).

Russian infantry—a development Simon noted exultantly in a radio message to Eicke. The struggle for the supply corridor continued for another five days without any significant change in the configuration of the front. The combination of heavy rain and stubborn German defense denied the Russians the quick encirclement they sought and exhausted their infantry in a bloody series of frontal attacks. On July 30, the Russians suspended their attacks against the Demyansk salient, and the sectors held by the shrunken remnants of the Totenkopfdivision temporarily fell silent.[42]

Although the Russians failed to pinch off the supply corridor to Demyansk, they did manage to inflict what Max Simon considered a mortal wound on the Totenkopfdivision. The condition of the surviving SS units appeared so desperate that Simon took the unusual step of appealing directly to Field Marshal Küchler, commander of Army Group North, to permit an immediate evacuation of what was left of SSTK. At a conference with the field marshal in Demyansk on July 29, Simon claimed that SSTK had lost 40 officers and 1,945 men since July 17 and that the three battle groups engaged along the northern side of the corridor and salient had only 51 officers and 2,685 men to defend a front forty-one kilometers long. The remaining men, he told Küchler, had been standing in the swampy forests for so long that nearly all were ill. The intense fighting and long exposure to the elements without dry clothing, adequate food, or proper shelter had resulted in numerous cases of pneumonia, dysentery, spotted fever, nervous breakdowns, and kidney disorders. Under such conditions, Simon stated flatly, his SS men could hardly be expected to have enough strength left to stand up, much less repel Soviet infantry assaults for an indefinite time.[43]

[42] NA/T-314/132/000054, 110, 125, 271, 302, 303, 401, 402, morning, interim, and evening reports of SSTK to Second Army Corps, and Second Army Corps to Sixteenth Army on the progress of the fighting and the condition of the units along the walls of the corridor into the salient; and BAMA, III SS, 41/9, 8-10, 15-18, 20-22, 24-25. Simon was especially gratified that following his own insubordination Count Brockdorff threatened the commander of the Eighth Jäger Division with a court-martial when that division's counterattack at Vasilyevschina failed. Simon had a very low opinion of the Eighth Jägers and considered its senior officers especially weak and indecisive.

[43] BAMA, III SS, 41/9, pp. 23, 26-29. Simon was particularly disturbed that

The field marshal, however, was unmoved. Though he expressed sympathy for the plight of Simon's SS units, Küchler had just returned from a morale-boosting visit to Hitler's headquarters (during which he had, in fact, been promoted to field marshal), and consequently was optimistic about the prospects of future operations in the Demyansk area. Parroting Hitler's earlier exhortation to Eicke, Küchler would only offer Simon the possibility that SSTK might be relieved once the supply corridor had been widened and the front stabilized. With Küchler's firm and final refusal, all hope of the Totenkopfdivision's escaping complete destruction seemed to vanish, plunging Simon into abject despair.[44]

In a secret letter sent by courier to Eicke on August 2, Simon informed his long-time chief that the annihilation of the Totenkopfdivision could be anticipated in the immediate future. Pouring out his soul in what he imagined might be his last opportunity, Simon railed against the stupidity and short-sightedness of the army. His only consolation, he claimed, was the knowledge that he had managed under various pretexts to smuggle 170 key SS officers and NCOs out of Russia for the new units of SSTK training at Sennelager. At the end of his letter, Max Simon confessed that for the first time since the beginning of the war he had lost hope. The hardships of the Russian campaign, and the unbelievable suffering and sacrifices of the men, he wrote, had simply become more than he could bear. Moreover, he concluded, Eicke should inform the Reichsführer SS at once that the pitiful remnants of the once-powerful Totenkopfdivision could not endure much longer.[45]

---

even though Sixteenth Army had been given five more divisions to strengthen the salient, Küchler considered it essential to keep the meager remnants of SSTK in the line (ibid., pp. 189-95).

[44] Ibid., pp. 33-36, 124-28; and Halder, *KTB*, vol. 3, pp. 468-69, entry for June 30, 1942. At the time von Küchler visited Hitler, the commander of the Second Army Corps, Count Brockdorff, also was summoned to Rastenburg to receive a private pep talk from the führer. Upon his return to the front, Brockdorff, too, lacked sympathy for the Totenkopfdivision in its plight.

[45] BAMA, III SS, 41/9, pp. 124-28, Simon to Eicke, August 2, 1942; NA/T-314/132/000067-068, "Generalkommando II. Armeekorps, *Betr.*, Kampfwert der Divisionen," dated July 25, 1942; NA/T-314/132/000361-364, and 000650-653, for similar reports by Second Army Corps of August 1 and 8, 1942 detailing the strength and the casualties of the German units in the salient. By August 8, Second Army Corps calculated that the number of SS soldiers belonging to SSTK (as distinguished from army men attached to or under the command of SSTK temporari-

Eicke was shocked and enraged by the conditions Max Simon described and immediately wrote to Jüttner requesting permission to rejoin his men in Russia. In language he knew would (and eventually did) reach Hitler, Eicke expelled every ounce of his long-simmering hatred for the army and his complete contempt for its officer corps. Claiming that the army would hold Demyansk to the last drop of SS blood, he implied that the Totenkopfdivision's plight was but part of a larger plot by the army to destroy the Waffen SS. Count Brockdorff's attitude toward SSTK, his impossible demands upon the division, and his personal treatment of Simon proved, Eicke charged, that the army hoped for the annihilation of the Totenkopfdivision to eliminate the remaining witnesses to its ineptitude during the winter fighting. Eicke pleaded with Jüttner to intercede immediately for the division's relief, claiming that if SSTK were not pulled out within three weeks there would be nothing left upon which to build a new division. If the Totenkopfdivision were destroyed, Eicke concluded, the SS would emerge from the war as an institution too weak to resume its former tasks and serve the führer in its intended capacities.[46]

Eicke's dramatic appeal to return to Russia and so perish with the last of his men was rejected by Hitler personally; to discourage more such outbursts Himmler extended Eicke's convalescent leave indefinitely. In the meantime, relations between the Totenkopf and army units and the physical condition of Simon's surviving men both deteriorated rapidly as the Russians resumed opera-

---

ly) inside the salient constituted the numerical equivalent of five battalions. These figures also included all SSTK noncombatants in the salient—supply, transport, administrative, postal, and medical personnel.

In trying to transfer men from the front to the new units of the Totenkopfdivision in Germany, Simon encountered as much difficulty from the SS as he did from the army. On August 2 he wrote Eicke that it had become impossible to get wounded men returned to the division in Russia since the SS Personnel Office assigned most of them to guard duty in the concentration camps for the period of their convalescence. Once these soldiers were in the camps and fully recuperated, Simon complained, the camp commandants invariably refused to give them back to the Totenkopfdivision.

[46] BAKO, NS/19-345, copy of letter from Eicke to Jüttner, dated August 5, 1942. The fact that Eicke's appeal for immediate reassignment was directed to Jüttner, not Himmler, showed that Jüttner's long struggle to bring Eicke formally under the jurisdiction of the SS Führungshauptamt had finally succeeded.

tions against the Demyansk salient. On August 5, the eve of the renewed Soviet offensive, Simon conferred again with Küchler and raised again the issue of the Totenkopfdivision's relief. The field marshal became angry at Simon's persistence, and in the acrimonious exchange that ensued blamed Himmler for the deplorable condition of the Totenkopf soldiers. In the future, Küchler demanded, Simon was to refrain from mentioning the subject of withdrawal and was to direct all his other communications through proper channels.[47]

Shortly after Küchler's departure from Simon's headquarters, the Russians attacked the Demyansk supply corridor from both north and south. Once again heavy enemy pressure was concentrated on sectors held by Simon's SS men, and once again the Totenkopf units suffered heavy casualties. For the next two weeks the Soviet Eleventh Army and First Guards Corps pounded the irregular front of the Demyansk bulge without interruption. Fresh masses of Russian infantry, supported by tanks, artillery, and Katayusha rocket launchers, daily hurled themselves against the steadily weakening SS units, while overhead squadrons from the Red Air Force drove off the Luftwaffe and bombed and strafed the German positions freely. In the intervals between attacks, Soviet artillery and Katayushas maintained such intense and accurate fire that Simon's men had to stay under cover. Consequently, evacuating the wounded and receiving supplies was for long periods impossible. Because Second Army Corps could spare no replacements for SSTK, Max Simon was forced during the second week of August to comb out the remaining supply and administrative units one final time and order virtually every SS man in the salient into combat. As of August 12, Simon later wrote, the Totenkopfdivision units in the salient had absolutely no one to replace those killed or wounded.[48]

[47] BAMA, III SS, 41/9, pp. 37-40; and ibid., pp. 134-36, letter from Eicke to Max Simon dated August 23, 1942.
[48] NA/T-312/580/8198135-8136, "II A. K. an A. O. K. 16, Tagesmeldung," dated August 10, 1942; NA/T-314/132/000730, 731, 732, 739-740, 743, 767-768, 773-774, 819, 862-870, 893-897, and 936-998, for the morning, interim, evening, and daily reports of SSTK and Second Army Corps describing the Russian attacks against the salient between August 10-16, 1942. See also BAMA, III

Just when it appeared that the resistance of the Totenkopf units would collapse altogether, the weather broke and forced a temporary halt in Soviet operations against the salient. Terrific thunderstorms dumped torrential rains on August 15 and 16, suspending all aerial operations. This gave the hard-pressed Germans time to rest and strengthen their defenses. Despite the abominable road conditions in the area, vital supplies arrived during the downpour and replenished the depleted stocks of guns and ammunition. With sufficient artillery and mortar shells available at last, German heavy guns began dispersing Russian troop concentrations and pulverizing the enemy's vehicle and tank parks. By August 19, the bad weather had enabled the army and SSTK units around Demyansk to catch their breath just as the Russian offensive again lost momentum. As a result, all the Soviet infantry assaults during the period August 20-28 were repulsed successfully.[49]

SS, 41/9, pp. 42-43, 47-58, 62-66, for the SSTK action summaries for the same period.

During the August crisis, SSTK officers in the salient were just as suspicious and critical of the Luftwaffe as they were of the army. In a blistering letter sent to the HQ of the First Air Fleet (Luftflotte 1) on August 17, Sturmbannführer Rudolf Schneider, the SSTK supply officer, bitterly criticized the Luftwaffe for its ineptitude during the Russian assault against the salient. Schneider claimed the Red Air Force bombed and strafed at will SSTK positions, while additional Russian fighters protected the Soviet supply columns so well from the weak attacks of the Luftwaffe that Russian truck convoys delivered huge quantities of supplies to the forces attacking the salient unmolested by German fighters. Schneider also wrote that the constant pounding the SS soldiers were taking from the Red Air Force was beginning to have a disastrous effect upon morale (NA/T-314/132/001031, "SS-T. Div., Ib, an Luftflottenkommando, Luftflotte 1," dated August 17, 1942).

[49] NA/T-314/133/000127, 213, 150, 231-285, 427, 489, for the daily reports of SSTK and Second Army Corps between August 20 and 28, 1942; and BAMA, III SS, 41/9, 57-66, for the SSTK situation reports for the same period. Despite the temporary easing of the situation after August 15, Max Simon's distrust of his army superiors intensified. On August 18, he radioed Eicke that the daily reports of the Second Army Corps were deliberately distorted to minimize the seriousness of the situation at Demyansk—an unfounded charge, as the records themselves show. Simon urged Eicke to inform Himmler immediately so the Reichsführer SS could defend SSTK in the event the front collapsed and the army tried to shift the blame (BAKO, NS/19-345, copy of a teleprinter message from Eicke to Himmler via the SS Führungshauptamt of August 19, 1942). Himmler subsequently ordered that copies of all SSTK reports sent to the army be forwarded simultaneously to the SSFHA daily (NA/T-312/580/8198281, copy of a teleprinter message from Himmler to Simon, sent via Army Group North on August 28, 1942).

To Max Simon, however, the new lull in the fighting appeared at best no more than a temporary reprieve—one that would only prolong the final suffering of his men. In lengthy messages to Eicke on August 19 and 21, Simon described the Totenkopfdivision's situation as desperately critical. Between July 1 and August 20, Simon reported that SSTK units had lost 51 officers and 2,686 NCOs and enlisted men. This left Max Simon commanding fewer than 7,000 men (most of them noncombat personnel in supply, administrative, and medical units) to defend positions that had not been adjusted or reinforced to correspond with the weakened condition of the SS battle groups. Many of the Totenkopfdivision's combat formations had simply been destroyed, while others had been incorporated into different formations. The core of SSTK, the First and Third SSTK Infantry Regiments, as of August 20, 1942, possessed a *combined* strength of 31 officers and 928 men. As a result, Simon argued, the rebuilding of the Totenkopfdivision around a core of experienced infantry, even if the remainder of the division were withdrawn immediately, seemed impossible. The Totenkopf units remaining in Russia, in short, could be written off completely since there was so little left at that late hour worth saving. When given command of SSTK as Eicke's replacement, Simon concluded, he had been convinced that the division's assignment was worthwhile and that the remaining SS men would be relieved. Since then, he wrote, it had become obvious that the Totenkopf soldiers in the salient were being sacrificed in a meaningless struggle to hold strategically worthless swamps. In his final disillusionment, Simon requested Eicke to return to his command to preside over the final phase in the senseless destruction of the SS Totenkopfdivision.[50]

[50] BAKO, NS/19-345, teleprinter message from Eicke to Himmler, August 19, 1942; BAMA, III SS, 41/9, pp. 130-33, letter from Max Simon to Eicke of August 19, 1942; and III SS, 41/9, pp. 70-71, a memorandum sent by Max Simon to Second Army Corps on August 24, 1942. Simon's figures for SSTK losses and the strength of the remaining SS units in the salient correspond with those compiled by Second Army Corps in NA/T-314/132/000862, "Fehlstellenberechnung der Divisionen der II A. K.," dated August 10; and in NA/T-314/133/000041, "Übersicht über eingetretene Verluste . . . vom 1. 7.-15. 8. 1942." The latter report shows that as of August 15, 1942, both the Eighth Jäger and 290th Infantry Divisions had far higher total casualties than SSTK. Throughout the summer, however, both these army divisions had received replacements regularly, whereas SSTK had not.

With great embarrassment and a lengthy attempt at self-justification, Eicke replied that Himmler—seconded by Hitler—still denied his requests to return to Russia. The Reichsführer SS allegedly issued the final veto with the claim that the führer planned to pull the Totenkopfdivision out of action in the near future. In a feeble attempt to encourage his successor, Eicke added that he was in daily communication with Himmler and Karl Wolff, and assured Simon that he had forwarded all radio messages from SSTK directly to Himmler at the führer's headquarters. As a final tonic to his troubled deputy, Eicke affirmed that Hitler was fully aware of the situation at Demyansk and would have SSTK pulled out in due course—since the führer was "greatly interested in the speedy reconstruction of the Totenkopfdivision."[51]

Eicke's letter of August 23 reached Max Simon just as the Russians again attacked the Demyansk salient in force. On the morning of August 25, the beleagured survivors of SSTK were forced anew to repel suicidal infantry charges. In three hours of furious hand-to-hand fighting, Simon's SS battle groups suffered 96 more casualties. With such an average daily loss, Simon wearily reported, the Totenkopf units continued to defend their positions and to stage the required counterattacks to win back what the Russians had gained.

Consequently, by the end of August SSTK was much weaker—a fact Simon was unable or unwilling to blame upon Himmler for his refusal to send SS reinforcements into the salient.

In one respect, Simon's exasperation with Second Army Corps was partially justified. The demands Second Army Corps placed upon the supply services of the Totenkopfdivision prevented Simon from moving additional SS men from the rear-area services into the front lines. Besides its own soldiers, SSTK had to supply 6,000 men in adjacent or attached army units, which led Simon to claim with some exaggeration that any further reduction in the size of the Totenkopf supply units might collapse part of the Second Army Corps' support system.

[51] BAMA, III SS, 41/9, pp. 134-36, letter from Eicke to Max Simon of August 23, 1942. Simon's message of August 19 prompted Eicke to write a highly emotional letter to Himmler blaming the army's temerity and stupidity for the predicament of the Totenkopfdivision and begging the Reichsführer SS to allow him to perish with the last of his men in Russia (USDC, SS Personalakte Eicke, Eicke to Himmler, August 19, 1942, with Himmler's marginal comment for forwarding to Hitler). This letter, with its undertone of heroic suicide, worried Himmler, who made certain Hitler saw the message. Hitler categorically rejected Eicke's request to return to Demyansk.

Along the south side of the landneck leading into the salient, the pressure against SSTK-held sectors was unusually intense. The Soviet First Shock Army threw in the revamped Seventh Guards Division, the 129th, 130th, 364th, and 391st Infantry Divisions, and the Thirty-seventh Rifle Brigade. The staggering blows delivered by these massed formations quickly cut the SS battle groups into isolated pockets. By August 26, the situation appeared so serious that Simon ordered all SS mechanics in the area into action as infantry to shore up the thinning front line. As on previous occasions, however, the Russians proved unable to break through the Totenkopfdivision's lines. Even against five-to-one superiority, the courage and fanaticism of these few surviving SS soldiers and the mechanics, clerks, field policemen, and medical orderlies pressed into action with them proved more than a match for the larger, healthier, and better-equipped Russian units. Although the division suffered over 1,000 more casualties, Simon and his men helped stem this third major Soviet offensive of the summer, which subsided for good on September 4. The Totenkopfdivision, however, was left with the combat strength of a single infantry battalion. Simon's SS battle groups had survived, only by fighting so viciously as to mortgage any chance of enduring a similar crisis in the future.[52]

Luckily for these remaining Totenkopf soldiers, the persistent lobbying by Eicke, Wolff, and Himmler finally prompted Hitler to

[52] NA/T-314/133/000601-0623, 0637-0656, 0776-0777, for the series of morning, interim, evening, and daily reports by SSTK to Second Army Corps, and Second Army Corps to Sixteenth Army detailing the resumption of Soviet assaults between August 25 and September 4; and NA/T-312/583/8201670, "Besprechungsnotizen und Reisen des O. B.," notes kept by Busch during a conference with von Küchler on September 2, 1942; BAMA, III SS, 41/9, pp. 72-74, 78-87, 89-95; and Baum interview/Baum memorandum, for the size and condition of SSTK as of September 1, 1942. See also, KTB/OKW, vol. 2, pt. 1, pp. 636-81, for the official daily summaries of the fighting in the Lake Ilmen sector of the northern front.

Eicke's sympathy for Max Simon's plight did not prevent him from trying to tell Simon how to run the Totenkopfdivision. The latter's use of trained mechanics as infantry angered Eicke, who counted upon the rescue of the SS units in the salient and regarded the survival of skilled mechanics as crucial for the reconstruction of SSTK. When instructed by Eicke to remove the mechanics from the front line, the exasperated Simon offered to resign rather than take orders from both Eicke and Second Army Corps. Faced with such blunt resistance, Eicke let the matter drop (BAMA, III SS, 41/9, pp. 75-77).

issue a directive on August 28 for the complete reconstruction of the Totenkopfdivision. The decision was one of the most important in the division's history. It agreed to the withdrawal of the remaining Totenkopf units from the Demyansk salient (at a time to be decided by Hitler), and provided for the reorganization of SSTK as a Panzergrenadier division. To Max Simon and the human skeletons he commanded in the swamps around Demyansk, Hitler's decision was an eleventh-hour reprieve.

According to instructions drafted by Hitler, the newly organized reserve SS Standarte Thule, the tank battalion at Buchenwald, and the new units being organized at Sennelager were to be sent to France as the nucleus of the new Totenkopfdivision. An additional 6,000 SS men on temporary duty in the Reich Labor Service were ordered released for transfer to SSTK, and Himmler was permitted to draw upon the other SS agencies as he saw fit to fill the division's personnel shortage. The führer also gave in and allowed Eicke to return to the Totenkopf units in Russia, but insisted that he also supervise the reorganization of the Totenkopfdivision. To perform both tasks, Eicke had to travel weekly between Germany and the Russian front until his units were moved out of the Demyansk salient in October.[53]

The removal of SSTK from Russia did not begin until the middle of October 1942, after a series of German counterattacks along the corridor pushed back the Soviet lines north and south of the supply road—making it possible for traffic to move in and out of the salient beyond the range of Russian artillery. During these six weeks between the end of the Soviet offensive on September 4 and the division's relief on October 16, scattered fighting continued along the front south of Lake Ilmen and further exhausted the survivors of SSTK. By the time the remaining Totenkopf units were transported out of the salient by truck to Staraya Russa to entrain for France, most of the once-formidable SSTK combat formations had been reduced to company strength.[54]

[53] BAKO, NS/19-345, "Aktenvermerk," dated August 28, 1942, and signed by Himmler. A copy is also in USDC, SS Personalakte Eicke. Himmler at this time estimated the total strength of the Totenkopf units at Demyansk as 5,000 men— considerably more than Simon calculated.

[54] Accounts of the autumn fighting in the salient and the continued weakening of the Totenkopf units during September and early October are in NA/T-314/133/

A revealing indication of how narrowly the Totenkopfdivision escaped destruction, and the reasons why its survivors blamed the army for the calamity, are contained in a long memorandum written by Max Simon in mid-September 1942. In assessing the events of 1942 and the prospects for the Totenkopfdivision in 1943, Simon blamed indecision at corps and army levels for the absence of a successful German offensive to clear up the salient before the units around Demyansk had been decimated. This command uncertainty and lassitude, he complained, infected the troops as the best weeks of campaigning weather passed, and enabled the Russians to retain possession of the best terrain for operations during the coming winter. The defensive tactics of holding undesirable country and indefensible positions simply to avoid a temporary loss of prestige, Simon argued, was an irresponsible command policy that had nearly destroyed the Totenkopfdivision.[55]

By mid-September 1942 the combined total of all Totenkopf units left in Russia was 6,400 men. This figure, as Simon meticulously explained, was greatly misleading, since two-thirds

---

001067-1070, "Oberstleutnant i. G. Praefcke, II A. K. Ia, Nr. 476/42, g. Kdos, den 11. 9. 42"; NA/T-314/133/001123-1125, letter from Count Brockdorff to Busch of September 12, 1942; T-312/580/8197965-7969, "A. O. K. 16, Planung für die nächste Zeit und den Winter," dated October 6, 1942; and NA/T-312/580/8197264-7295, "A. O. K. 16, KTB Nr. 5, Teil III, vom 1. 10. 42 bis 15. 11. 42." See also, BAMA, III SS, 41/9, pp. 89-95; and USDC, SS Personalakte Eicke, letter from Himmler to Eicke of October 8, 1942, with instructions for Eicke to have SSTK ready for immediate transport, and orders for Eicke to come at once to the Wolfschanze to report personally to Hitler on the progress of the new Totenkopf units in Germany.

[55] BAMA, III SS, 41/9, pp. 89-95. Simon's charges had some merit. Throughout the summer, Field Marshal Küchler conferred with Busch and the corps and division commanders involved in directing the German defense of the salient. The surviving notes of these conferences have a tone of unreality, as senior German field commanders fussed and squabbled, dabbled and procrastinated in planning small, local attacks to improve defensive positions they knew were unimprovable. A good example is NA/T-312/583/8201649-1650, "Besprechung mit Komm. General II. A. K.," notes of a conference Busch held with Count Brockdorff and division commanders from inside the salient on August 5, 1942. By autumn, Field Marshal Küchler was convinced that continued defense of the salient was useless. When he timidly broached the subject of withdrawal to Hitler and was sharply rebuffed, however, he dropped the matter and refused to press Hitler on the point again (Halder, *KTB*, vol. 3, p. 509, entry for August 23, 1942; and Ziemke, pp. 101-2, 111-13.

of the SS men around Demyansk were noncombatants (cooks, drivers, mechanics, radio operators, couriers, medical personnel, and assorted orderlies). The total figure also included the sick and hospitalized, and the unevacuated wounded. Moreover, casualties among the infantry and artillery regiments, the reconnaissance, motorcycle, engineer, and antitank battalions averaged eighty percent. The seasoned personnel essential for rebuilding an effective Waffen SS division, Simon concluded, were dead, badly wounded, or had been snatched by other SS agencies while home on leave or recuperating from wounds.[56]

Simon's penetrating and astute *tactical* criticism of the conduct of operations in the Lake Ilmen area was fundamentally correct. In blaming the army, however, he was completely off the mark. Hitler—not the field commanders of Army Group North—was responsible for the "no retreat" orders that led to the encirclement at Demyansk and the relief operation that created the expensively defended salient. It was Hitler, not OKH or Simon's tactical superiors, who kept the Totenkopfdivision engaged in vicious fighting far beyond the point of endurance. Most importantly, it was the Totenkopfdivision's own style of fighting and its reputation for dependability that inspired the führer's unequivocal confidence in its ability to perform the impossible. This had been the decisive factor prompting Hitler to insist that SSTK stay in the line.

The most remarkable feature about Max Simon's candid criticism, however, was the fact that he got away with it. At a time when the growing crisis at Stalingrad and the generals' increasing criticism of Hitler's personal conduct of the war was causing a second mass-exodus from the German High Command, the insubordinately blunt memoranda written by Simon and given by Eicke to Himmler and Hitler went unchallenged and unpunished. Hitler's contempt for the talents of his generals and his intolerance of their criticism did not apply to his Waffen SS commanders, whose judgment be respected and whose contrary opinions he still encouraged. Finally, the frictions caused by the Totenkopfdivision's ordeal in 1942 indicated that even fanatical SS generals like Eicke and Simon could retain sufficient critical objectivity and in-

[56] BAMA, III SS, 41/9, pp. 89-95.

dependence of mind to question openly (and to disobey occasionally) disagreeable orders sent down from the highest level.

After nearly eighteen months in action on the eastern front, the
remnants of the Totenkopfdivision returned to Germany to rest.
At the end of October, the men from these units reassembled at
Sennelager bei Paderborn for the train trip to southwestern
France. There they joined the new formations of the Toten-
kopfdivision already training under the stern tutelage of Theodor
Eicke.

CHAPTER EIGHT

Perpetual Crisis: The Führer's Firemen, 1943-1945

BETWEEN November 1, 1942 and the end of January 1943, the SS Totenkopfdivision was completely rebuilt according to plans drawn up during the previous summer. Many of the specific details concerning the reconstruction of SSTK Hitler examined and approved personally, insisting that the division be lavishly equipped with the latest heavy weapons and converted as quickly as possible into a Panzergrenadier division. To make certain the work of reconstruction accorded with his intentions, Hitler summoned Eicke to the Wolfschanze three times during October 1942 for progress reports on the planning and preparations. Hitler's keen interest in the Totenkopfdivision resulted mainly from his appreciation for its performance during the lengthy struggle around Demyansk. In the ferocious winter fighting south of Lake Ilmen SSTK had demonstrated that it possessed in abundance a quality Hitler considered indispensable to Germany's chances of eventually destroying the Bolshevik colossus. Despite the terrific punishment, the enormous casualties, and the prolonged suffering it had endured, the Totenkopfdivision had kept its fighting spirit and resisted fanatically to the end—refusing through sheer willpower, as Hitler saw it, to admit defeat or surrender to a radically inferior enemy.[1]

Dazzled by the prospects of what might be accomplished with a corps—or even a whole army—made up of such formations, Hit-

---

[1] This is also noted by Stein, pp. 197-99. For Hitler's own comments about the performance of the Waffen SS in Russia during the winter fighting of 1941-1942 see, *Hitler's Secret Conversations, 1941-1944* (New York, 1961), pp. 177-78. Additional details on the rebuilding of the Totenkopfdivision are in BAKO, NS/ 19-345, "Umgliederung der SS-T. Div. in SS Panzer-Grenadier-Division 'Totenkopf,' " a circular from the SS Führungshauptamt dated November 16, 1942. German Panzergrenadier divisions were completely mechanized formations whose infantry rode in eight-ton halftrack armored personnel carriers (Stein, pp. 200n, 201-3).

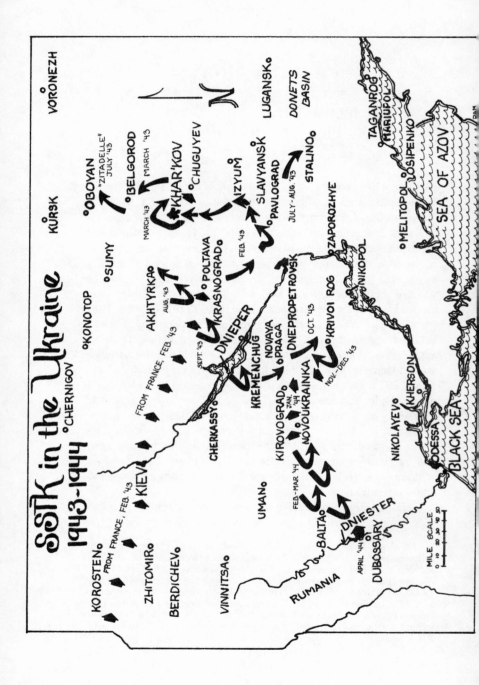

ler not only ordered the immediate reconstruction of SSTK and the refitting of the other SS divisions engaged in Russia, but also authorized Himmler to expand the Waffen SS by creating four new divisions. During the last two years of the war, after the strategic initiative had slipped permanently from his hands and the Wehrmacht was forced onto the defensive, Hitler came to rely increasingly on these SS divisions as emergency "fire brigades" and to use them singly or severally to deal with the frequent crises that threatened to rupture the German fronts in Russia, the Balkans, Italy, and France. Wherever the situation was the most serious and the prospects of German recovery seemed least likely, there the elite divisions of the Waffen SS nearly always were found—in most instances mastering temporarily the crisis of the moment by vicious counterattacks that blunted the enemy offensive. As one of the oldest and toughest of the armed SS formations, the Totenkopfdivision consistently received some of the most difficult of the "firefighting" assignments during the last years of the war. Except for the short intervals required for transit between crisis points in different sectors of the front, the SS Totenkopfdivision spent the entire period from February 1943 until May 1945 fighting desperately to stem the inexorable Russian advance toward the frontiers of the Reich. The result of the suicidal resistance offered by SSTK (and the other Waffen SS divisions) was a significant slowing of the enemy's offensive operations and a corresponding postponement of the military collapse of the Third Reich.[2]

The actual reconstruction of the Totenkopfdivision began in May 1942—when it became obvious that the casualties of the winter fighting were so great that SSTK would have to be rebuilt rather than reorganized. At that time, Hitler ordered the creation of a tank battalion (Panzer Abteilung) for the Totenkopfdivision. This new unit, which was to be organized and trained on the grounds of the Buchenwald concentration camp, would have two

[2] See especially Stein, pp. 197-208, 288-89. Comprehensive summaries of the movements and engagements of the Totenkopfdivision during the last years of the war are in BAMA, III SS, 41/11, Zusammenstellung der Kämpfe der SS Totenkopf-Division, 1939-1943; and in Klietmann, pp. 108-15.

companies of light tanks (PzKw IIIs), one company of medium tanks (PzKw IVs), and a tank-maintenance platoon. Most of the officers and men for this armored formation came eventually from the SS Wirtschafts- und Verwaltungshauptamt and from the guard detachments in the concentration camps.[3]

One month later, on June 24, 1942, Hitler issued more comprehensive orders for the rebuilding of SSTK. Eicke received instructions to organize two new infantry battalions, six motorized rifle companies, an assault-gun battalion of ten platoons, a whole new engineer battalion, a new tank-destroyer battalion of mixed 50 mm guns and antitank rifles (Panzer-Büchsen), two motorcycle companies, and a new heavy bridge-construction company. After conferring with Eicke at Rastenburg, Hitler took the further step of assigning SS Infantry Regiment No. 9 (renamed Thule) to the new SSTK. Orders sent to Eicke on July 10, 1942, called for the conversion of Thule into a "fast regiment" consisting of two motorcycle battalions, and motorized reconnaissance and heavy machine-gun companies. The men for all these new Totenkopf formations subsequently came from among the 6,000 transfers from the Labor Service, 1,500 SS reservists in Warsaw, and the 500 survivors of SS Infantry Regiment No. 9.[4]

On August 4, 1942, just as the German summer campaign in Russia was reaching its peak, Hitler ordered the dispatch of additional heavy weapons to Eicke for the reorganization of the Totenkopfdivision's antiaircraft batteries and tank-destroyer battalion. The antiaircraft battalion (Flak Abteilung) was provided with enough guns to equip three batteries—one each of 88 mm, 50 mm, and 37 mm pieces—and a twelve-piece battery of light 20 mm guns. In addition, the tank-destroyer battalion was given another two companies of 50 mm pieces (eighteen guns in all) and one company (nine guns) of the highly prized 75 mm heavy anti-

[3] BAKO, NS/19-345, "Aufstellung einer SS Panzer-Abteilung für die SS-T. Div.," May 20, 1942; Stein, p. 202. The PzKw III carried a 40 mm gun, while the PzKw IV had a long-barreled 75 mm high-velocity gun that was fairly effective against the Soviet T-34 tank (*Handbook on German Military Forces, 1 September 1943* [Washington, D.C., 1943], pp. 113-17).

[4] BAKO, NS/19-345, "Neuaufstellung und Umgliederung von Teilen der SS-T. Div.," June 24, 1942; and ibid., "Aufstellung des schnellen Regiments der SS-T. Division," July 10, 1942. See also Stein, p. 203.

tank cannons. The old 37 mm guns, which were useless against the Soviet T-34, were discarded.[5]

These plans for expanding the Waffen SS and equipping its divisions with the finest and most recent heavy weapons naturally aroused resentment and resistance in the army, which moved before summer's end to block the distribution of tanks to the Totenkopfdivision. At the end of July, OKH (the Army High Command) notified Jüttner that the creation of the armored battalion for the Totenkopfdivision would have to be postponed indefinitely since the replacement demands of the army's panzer divisions in Russia and Africa had first priority. As the monthly production of tanks, according to OKH, was not even keeping abreast of the rate of loss and breakdown in these two theaters, it was simply out of the question for the army to give Eicke any tanks.[6]

The army's determined stand, however, resulted only in a temporary delay in the organization of Eicke's tank battalion. As the summer campaign lengthened indecisively into autumn and confronted Germany with the prospect of an indefinite and even more bitter conflict, Hitler overrode the army's arguments against giving tanks to the Waffen SS. Brushing aside the vehement objections of OKH, Hitler conferred with Eicke in mid-October and then issued instructions to enlarge the proposed tank battalion for the Totenkopfdivision into an armored regiment. Besides the three companies of tanks promised him during the summer, Eicke was to have supplementary motorized companies of tank repairmen and engineers, and another battalion (Abteilung) of self-propelled assault guns. The most valuable armored addition, however, was the company of brand-new heavy "Tiger" tanks that Hitler promised to send Eicke straight off the assembly lines. The personnel necessary to fill out the new SSTK tank regiment were to be drawn from the SS mountain division Nord, and from an additional gleaning of the various SS agencies—including the guard detachments of the concentration camps.[7]

[5] BAKO, NS/19-345, "Umgliederung der Flak- und Panzer-Jäger Abteilung der SS.T. Division," a circular from the SS Führungshauptamt dated August 4, 1942; and *Handbook on German Military Forces*, pp. 246-48, for the technical specifics about the antiaircraft and antitank weapons.

[6] BAKO, NS/19-1629, letter from Jüttner to Himmler of July 23, 1942.

[7] BAKO, NS/19-345, "Aufstellung von Panzer- und Sturmgeschütz-Einheiten

On the basis of promises and directives he had received from Hitler and Himmler, Eicke could anticipate commanding a completely reorganized and vastly strengthened Totenkopfdivision. By the beginning of November 1942, when he and his staff moved SSTK headquarters to Bordeaux for the reorganization, the Totenkopfdivision possessed—at least on paper—the personnel, firepower, and mobility to make it one of the most powerful formations in the German armed forces. Enthusiastic over the challenge of his new task and invigorated by the experience of his repeated personal contacts with Hitler, Eicke arrived in southwestern France only to discover that the promises and orders from Rastenburg bore very little relation to the actual conditions of his new command.

The handful of SS reservists, concentration camp guards, former SSTK veterans, and survivors of Demyansk that Lammerding had assembled at Paderborn during the summer were the only SS men then in the division with any military training or experience. Fully three-fourths of the men assigned to the new SSTK would have to be trained completely. Moreover, Eicke at first considered the quality of these new arrivals to be low. Most of the recruits who detrained at the SSTK exercise grounds in November were seventeen- and eighteen-year-old draftees from the

---

für die SS-T. Division," October 14, 1942; "Aufstellung einer schweren Panzer-Kompanie für das Pz. Reg. der SS-T. Div.," November 13, 1942; and "Umgliederung der SS-T. Div. in SS Panzer-Grenadier-Division 'Totenkopf,' " November 16, 1942. See also Stein, p. 203. On November 16, 1942 the name of the SS Totenkopfdivision was changed officially to SS Panzer-Grenadier-Division "Totenkopf," and remained such until October 19, 1943, when the name was changed again to the Third SS Panzer Division "Totenkopf," pending its reorganization into a completely armored division. For the sake of clarity and continuity, the designation for the remainder of this study will continue Totenkopfdivision, or SSTK.

The Tiger tanks Hitler promised Eicke were the Henschel models of sixty-five tons and carried long-barreled, high-velocity 88 mm cannon. Though designed and built as a heavy tank to provide fire support for medium armor and infantry assault teams, and though heavier, slower, and less maneuverable than the formidable Russian T-34, the Tiger in the hands of Eicke's crews effectively rivalled the T-34. For the rest of the war, the tank crews of the SS Totenkopfdivision consistently destroyed as much Soviet armor as any German formation on the eastern front. For more details on the development and characteristics of the Tiger tank, see especially Seaton, p. 357 n. 14, 363, 402 n. 37; Guderian, pp. 215-20; and *Handbook on German Military Forces 1943*, p. 118.

Labor Service and older volunteers who seemed less than out-standing physical specimens. To mold this human material into a crack Waffen SS division, Eicke insisted, would require a long period of intensive training.[8]

More serious than the manpower problem was the acute short-age of virtually everything needed to arm and equip the Toten-kopfdivision. At the beginning of November, Eicke had fewer than half the vehicles the division needed, and not enough gasoline to conduct the exercises necessary to train his drivers and tank crews. Even as late as the first week of January 1943 SSTK had received less than half of the tanks earmarked for the armored regiment, and none of the coveted Tigers—whose production was snarled by wrangling and indecision in the Army High Command, by technical difficulties in the factories, and by confusion result-ing from the attempt by Hitler's friend, Professor Ferdinand Porsche of the Krupp works, to steal the design from the Henschel firm and create a rival Tiger. In addition to the dearth of vehicles and tanks, there were insufficient stocks of weapons and ammuni-tion with which to train, and not enough radios, telephones, and other signals equipment to maintain effective communications within SSTK and with other units in the field. All of these shortages, Eicke complained, made it impossible for him to have the Totenkopfdivision combat-ready according to Hitler's time-table.[9]

The most serious delay in rebuilding the Totenkopfdivision, however, was caused by the events in the western Mediterranean that began the whole strategic reversal of the war. On November 8, 1942, an Allied armada sailed into the Mediterranean and suc-

[8] USDC, SS Personalakte Eicke, handwritten letter from Eicke to Himmler of December 19, 1942; BAKO, NS/19-345, copy of a lengthy teleprinter message from Eicke to Himmler, dated January 2, 1943; Baum interview/Baum memoran-dum; and Klietmann, p. 108.

[9] BAKO, NS/19-345, Eicke to Himmler via teleprinter, January 2, 1943; and Baum interview/Baum memorandum. When Eicke visited the Wolfschanze on Oc-tober 13, 1942, to discuss the reconstruction of SSTK, Hitler ordered him to have the division ready for service again in Russia by no later than January 10, 1943. The difficulties encountered in France and the delays in tank deliveries, however, subsequently made it impossible for Eicke to meet this deadline, and SSTK did not return to Russia until February 1943. The delays in Tiger tank production during these months, partially the result of Hitler's interference by constantly changing the armament and firepower specifications, are well described in Guderian, pp. 215-22.

cessfully landed sizeable forces in Algeria and French Morocco. The Allied landings in North Africa prompted an immediate response by Hitler, who ordered the execution of "Operation Attila," the planned invasion and occupation of Vichy, France by the German divisions stationed along the demarcation line. The most important objectives envisaged in "Attila" were the seizure of the French naval squadrons at Toulon and Marseille and the securing of the French Mediterranean coast. Accordingly, Eicke received special orders on November 9 directing him to lead the Totenkopfdivision across southwestern France via Toulouse to the Mediterranean coast. All training activities were suspended and the SS men loaded into what transport was available for the dash to the Mediterranean. The move took nearly four days and consumed all the fuel and supplies Eicke and his staff had carefully accumulated in the short time since their arrival in France.[10]

After reaching the Mediterranean on November 13, SSTK moved into defensive positions between Beziers and Montpellier and remained on coastal watch duty until late December. During this entire period, Eicke was able to conduct only limited training exercises since what heavy weapons and equipment the division had received before "Attila" had been left behind when SSTK moved. On December 18, 1942, after repeated requests from Eicke for the division's release from coastal security duty, the army finally found a reserve infantry division to take the Totenkopfdivision's place and Eicke was allowed to return to Bordeaux and resume training.[11]

By that time, the SSTK training plans were so far behind schedule and the general conditions in supply, transport, and communications so chaotic that Eicke frantically appealed to Himmler for a postponement of the division's return to action. In an urgent teleprinter message dispatched on January 2, 1943, Eicke begged the Reichsführer to countermand orders the Totenkopfdivision had already received to entrain at Bordeaux on Janu-

[10] The text of "Operation Attila," which Hitler originally issued as Directive No. 19 on December 10, 1940, may be found in Trevor-Roper, ed., *Blitzkrieg to Defeat*, pp. 44-46. See also BAKO, NS/19-345, Eicke to Himmler via teleprinter, January 2, 1943; and Klietmann, p. 108.

[11] BAKO, NS/19-345, Eicke to Himmler via teleprinter, January 2, 1943; Klietmann, p. 108; and Baum interview/Baum memorandum.

ary 8 for shipment to Russia. The unexpected activities of the late autumn and the critical shortages of vehicles and weapons, Eicke claimed, would prevent him from having SSTK ready for combat until March. To expedite a decision on his request, Eicke suggested that Himmler either arrange an interview for him with Hitler or make the appeal himself on behalf of the Totenkopfdivision. Eicke's tone was urgent because SSTK still had not received any of its Tiger tanks and less than half of the consignment of light and medium armor Hitler had promised. To send the half-trained and poorly armed men of SSTK to face the furies of a winter campaign in Russia without sufficient transport or proper armored support, Eicke warned, would only result in disaster. If the orders he had received were not countermanded, Eicke concluded, then the Reichsführer SS could expect the complete destruction of the Totenkopfdivision.[12]

For once Himmler took his unpredictable subordinate at his word. The Reichsführer had worked diligently to persuade Hitler to expand the Waffen SS, and had no intention of allowing his most prized divisions to be flung unprepared into the eastern cauldron and ground to bits piecemeal as cannon fodder. Consequently, Himmler traveled the short distance from his headquarters train to the Wolfschanze, sought an immediate audience with Hitler, and persuaded the führer to postpone sending SSTK back to the eastern front until the beginning of February. In a teleprinter message to Eicke on January 3, Himmler warned that the extra four weeks he had secured for SSTK were the only reprieve he could guarantee, since the critical situation in Russia necessitated an early return of the division.[13]

With the extra month of grace granted him by Himmler, Eicke was able to pay what in the long run amounted to a bonanza dividend. For the next four weeks he drove himself and everyone in the Totenkopfdivision relentlessly in an around-the-clock effort to whip the division into shape. Every day from dawn until nearly midnight the SS recruits went through a rigid routine of calisthenics, rifle practice, fire-coordination drills, and a barrage of lectures, drills, and exercises designed to familiarize them with

[12] BAKO, NS/19-345, Eicke to Himmler, January 2, 1943.
[13] Ibid., Himmler's reply to Eicke via teleprinter, January 3, 1943.

techniques of camouflage, the use of different kinds of light and heavy weapons, and the basic tactical problems involved in mechanized warfare. To acquaint new recruits with the enemy they would face, Eicke drew upon the experience of officers and men who had served previously in Russia. SS officers and NCOs regularly lectured on the qualities and weaknesses of the Russian soldier, Soviet techniques of assault and camouflage, and dwelt at great length on the nature of Russian armored tactics and the characteristics of the T-34 tank.

Eicke also proved during these weeks that he had not lost his touch in the refined art of requisitioning. With the assistance of his redoubtable and ingenious supply officer, Hans Ulmer, he tapped once again his numerous sources among the various SS agencies and enterprises inside the Reich and throughout Europe to acquire the vehicles, weapons, ammunition, medical supplies, communications equipment, and winter clothing SSTK desperately needed. To make certain the division would not return to Russia with inadequate transport, Eicke sent armed raiding parties to scour the French countryside for any available cars and trucks. Finally, by remaining in France for another month, SSTK obtained more than half its alloted Tiger tanks and trained the crews briefly before departing for the eastern front.[14]

Therefore, when Eicke received his marching orders and the units of SSTK began entraining at Bordeaux on January 30, 1943, the division had been rehardened into an acceptable state of combat-readiness. The return trip from France to Russia was in marked contrast to the Totenkopfdivision's earlier journey from Bordeaux to the eastern front in June 1941. The increase in the number and size of vehicles and heavy weapons and the addition of the armored regiment necessitated the use of 120 trains to move the entire Totenkopfdivision across Europe. Allied bombing and the heavy rail traffic flowing to and from the eastern front,

[14] USDC, SS Personalakte Eicke, copies of radio messages exchanged between Eicke and Himmler on January 21, 1943; Baum interview; and USDC, SS Personalakte Ulmer, "Vorschlag Nr. 3 für die Verleihung des Deutschen Kreuzes in Silber," dated December 30, 1943, and signed by SS Obergruppenführer Paul Hausser, contains a lengthy description of the organizational, supply, and transport problems Ulmer had to contend with while SSTK was in France in the autumn of 1942 and immediately after the division returned to Russia in February 1943.

moreover, produced delays and tie-ups that kept the shivering Totenkopf soldiers cooped up in their unheated boxcars for nearly
two weeks. On February 14, 1943, the last elements of the Totenkopfdivision clambered out of their trains in the Wehrmacht rail
yards at Kiev in the Ukraine—the main terminus for German reinforcements sent to the southern sector of the Russian front. From
trainside the units of SSTK moved immediately to their vehicles,
which were assembled into marching columns that proceeded,
one after another, through the city, across the Dnieper River, and
onto the vast plain stretching east to the horizon. As the bone-
chilled SS soldiers jolted over the frozen ruts that were the main
highway between Kiev and Kharkov, they undoubtedly sensed the
atmosphere of acute crisis that hung over the eastern front. From
the rumors and gloomy official news about the fighting in Russia
during January, Eicke's men were aware that their transfer to
southern Russia was due to the great disaster at Stalingrad and the
startling reversal in the course of the Russian war that had followed.

The ably planned, well-coordinated, and devastatingly powerful Soviet counteroffensive that led to the encirclement of Colonel
General Friedrich Paulus's Sixth Army at Stalingrad in November
1942 had been followed by strong Soviet attacks that pushed the
German front back from the Volga to the Don River and frustrated
all attempts to relieve Paulus. Then, on January 12, 1943, the Red
Army launched a great winter offensive that ripped open a 200-
mile gap in the German front between the city of Voronezh and
the great bend in the Don. From mid-January to mid-February
1943, an enormous juggernaut of Soviet tank and infantry armies
poured through this huge breach and into the Ukraine.

On February 13, the German retreat west from Stalingrad had
carried nearly 300 miles, enabling the Russians to overrun the
whole area between the Volga and the Donetz basin. Pausing
along the Donetz River only long enough to regroup, the Russian
armies continued at an irresistible pace. By February 15, powerful
Soviet forces had crossed the Donetz on a broad front and captured Kharkov—the rail, industrial, and communications hub of
the eastern Ukraine. From bridgeheads on the Donetz southeast of
Kharkov two Soviet armies, the Sixth and First Guards, then

265

struck southwest toward the Dnieper and deep into the flank and rear of the German armies in southern Russia. The Russian objective was to capture the cities of Dnepropetrovsk and Zaporozhye (the latter being the HQ of German Army Group South), and then to roll the German armies back against the Black Sea and destroy them.[15]

The Totenkopfdivision had been summoned from France by Hitler's direct orders to help with its muscle in the emergency attempt to halt the Soviet winter offensive. In Kiev, Eicke received orders to proceed east immediately to Poltava and link up with the SS divisions Leibstandarte SS Adolf Hitler and Das Reich, which had already been brought together under the command of SS Obergruppenführer Paul Hausser as the First SS Panzerkorps. Hausser's SS Panzerkorps was the German force that had yielded Kharkov to the Russians on February 15, and Hitler quickly wanted, in adding SSTK to Hausser's command, an armored corps powerful enough to recapture Kharkov and give Germany a much-needed prestigious victory.[16]

The commander in chief of Army Group South, Field Marshal Erich von Manstein (Eicke's former patron and corps commander), however, disagreed with Hitler's intended use of the SS Panzerkorps to recapture Kharkov. Manstein was planning a great pincer attack that would converge upon and destroy the Soviet armies as they approached the Dnieper. To ensure the success of his proposed counteroffensive, Manstein wanted to wait until SSTK joined Hausser and then use the SS Panzerkorps as the northern prong of the pincer, striking southeast from Poltava into the rear of the Soviet Sixth and First Guards Armies. To assist the

[15] For details, see especially Ziemke, pp. 81-94; Carell, *Scorched Earth*, pp. 115-54, 173-86; Clark, pp. 277-302; Seaton, pp. 306-47; Major General F. W. von Mellenthin, *Panzer Battles: A Study of the Employment of Armor in the Second World War* (Norman, Okla., 1956), pp. 187-206; and Friedrich Wilhelm Hauck, "Der Gegenangriff der Heeresgruppe Süd im Frühjahr 1943," *Wehrwissenschaftliche Rundschau*, 12 (August 1962), pp. 452-68.

[16] Hauck, "Der Gegenangriff der Heeresgruppe Süd," pp. 467-71; Manstein, p. 424; Carell, *Scorched Earth*, p. 185; Ziemke, pp. 91-92; and Mellenthin, pp. 206-8. Hitler had authorized the creation of an SS Generalkommando (SS army corps headquarters) in May 1942 and had personally selected Hausser to command it. Hausser had then organized his corps staff during the summer and moved to Russia in the late autumn to assume command of the Leibstandarte SS Adolf Hitler and Das Reich divisions as his SS Panzerkorps (Stein, p. 202).

SS Panzerkorps in crushing the Russian winter offensive, Manstein planned to move General Hermann Hoth's still-powerful Fourth Panzer Army, which had countermarched all the way from Taganrog to the Dnieper, due north toward Kharkov. If the operation went according to Manstein's calculations, Hausser's SS divisions would link up with Hoth's armor in the vicinity of Pavlograd, trapping the Soviet Sixth Army in the jaws of a powerful mechanized vise that could crush it before the spring thaw suspended further operations.[17]

Hitler, however, did not share Manstein's enthusiasm for the planned counterstroke and continued to insist on the SS attack to recapture Kharkov. On February 17, the führer even flew out to Manstein's headquarters at Zaporozhye to order the immediate execution of Hausser's offensive. During the afternoon of the seventeenth and then again on the morning of the eighteenth Hitler and Manstein argued over the merits of their respective plans. The führer remained adamant, but just when it appeared that the field marshal would have to give in and accede to Hitler's wishes, a stupid blunder by Eicke 150 miles to the north compelled Hitler to abandon his momentary obsession with the recapture of Kharkov and enabled Manstein to proceed with his plan to destroy the Soviet Sixth Army.[18]

Motoring east from Kiev toward Poltava, Eicke became impatient with the slow progress the Totenkopfdivision was making. On February 17, when the temperature was well below freezing and the ground apparently frozen hard, Eicke ordered his motorized columns off the primitive road and onto the rolling plain in order to speed the pace. During the night, a warm front lifted the temperature above freezing. When the sun rose in a cloudless sky on the eighteenth and the thermometer continued to climb, the ground thawed completely and the entire Totenkopfdivision sank with a loud gurgle into the axle-deep morass. Eicke radioed Hausser that SSTK was stuck fast some twenty-five miles from the SS Panzerkorps, and the message was relayed immedi-

[17] Manstein, pp. 408-22, 424-25; Ziemke, p. 92; Seaton, p. 348; Philippi and Heim, pp. 201-6; and Carell, *Scorched Earth*, pp. 182-89.

[18] Manstein, pp. 424-25; Hauck, "Der Gegenangriff der Heeresgruppe Süd," pp. 469-70; Seaton, pp. 347-48.

ately to Zaporozhye. Hitler then reluctantly agreed to cancel the attack on Kharkov since Hausser's SS Panzerkorps could not hope to succeed without Eicke's division.[19]

With a green light to begin his own counteroffensive, Manstein immediately set about making final preparations. General Otto von Knobelsdorff's Forty-eighth Panzer Corps (Sixth and Seventeenth Panzer Divisions) moved into position east of Dnepropetrovsk, quickly seized bridgeheads over the Samara River, and prepared to move due north into the rear of the exhausted Soviet Sixth Army. At Poltava Eicke's soldiers, helped by Hausser's maintenance crews, hauled the SSTK vehicles and tanks out of the mud, and on the morning of February 19 the Totenkopfdivision finally joined the SS Panzerkorps just east of Poltava. After the arrival of SSTK, Manstein's armored trap was complete. In mid-afternoon that same day, the field marshal ordered Hoth and Hausser to attack.[20]

Along the line between the bend in the Dnieper and Dnepropetrovsk and the Donetz at Slavyansk, Hoth's armored and motorized divisions slammed into the spearheads of the Soviet Sixth and First Guards Armies and knocked them staggering into a panicky retreat to the north. At the same time the cream of the Waffen SS, divisions Totenkopf and Das Reich, advanced southeast from Poltava and bore down upon the rear of the exhausted (and doomed) Soviet Sixth Army.[21] As Hausser and Hoth con-

[19] Carell, *Scorched Earth*, p. 185; Ziemke, p. 92; Manstein, pp. 424-25; and Hauck, "Der Gegenangriff der Heeresgruppe Süd," p. 470.

[20] Manstein, pp. 428-29; Hauck, "Der Gegenangriff der Heeresgruppe Süd," pp. 470-71; Seaton, p. 349; Ziemke, pp. 92-94; Clark, pp. 303-6; Mellenthin, pp. 206-9; and Carell, *Scorched Earth*, pp. 187-92. Unfortunately, almost none of the Totenkopfdivision's records for the period after 1942 survived the war. These documents, and other priceless Prussian and German military materials, were destroyed in the great fire that swept the Heeresarchiv in Potsdam in February 1945 after an Allied bombing raid. In an effort to compensate for the absence of SSTK records after 1942, much of the remainder of this study is based on records of the SS Panzerkorps, the army corps, and armies to which SSTK was attached between 1943 and May 1945; on pertinent correspondence and memoranda scattered throughout the Himmler files; and on important information gleaned from the personnel dossiers of key personalities, staff officers, and unit commanders who served with SSTK between the spring of 1943 and the end of the war.

[21] The stunning, successful German counterthrust near Izyum, on the right and to the northeast of the Fourth Panzer Army, is well described in Carl Wagener, "Der Gegenangriff des XXXX Panzerkorps gegen den Durchbruch der Panzer-

verged on Pavlograd, SSTK and SS Das Reich swung left to the east, then wheeled back north again running parallel to the Russian divisions fleeing from Forty-eighth Panzer Corps. What ensued was a turkey shoot.

Rumbling over the frozen steppe at 25 mph, Eicke's tanks and motorized columns drew alongside the retreating Russians at distances of twenty to thirty yards, machine-gunning at will the trucks crammed with infantry. Whole companies of T-34s ran out of fuel, coughed to a standstill, and were pounced upon and blasted to pieces by Eicke's zealous tank crews. By February 24, the Russians had abandoned most of their vehicles and equipment and were trying to escape on foot. Their exit, however, was sealed off tightly by the SSTK First Panzergrenadier Regiment, commanded by SS Obersturmbannführer Otto Baum. Early on the twenty-fourth Baum's regiment turned on a right angle to the southeast, stretched out to a link-up with units of SS Das Reich, and methodically cut down the panicked herds of stampeding Russians fleeing to the north. Twenty miles to the southwest, the remaining tanks and infantry of SSTK crisscrossed unmolested through the miles-long columns of wrecked and burning vehicles, taking potshots at anything that moved. For four days Eicke's grenadiers, supported by low-flying Stukas, fanned out across the steppe to kill or capture as many Russians as possible. On March 1, all enemy resistance ended and the weary SS soldiers paused briefly to rest.[22]

In one week of fighting, Hausser's SS Panzerkorps and Hoth's

---

gruppe Popow im Donezbecken, Februar 1943," *Wehrwissenschaftliche Rundschau*, 7 (January 1957), pp. 21-36.

While SSTK and Das Reich went over to the attack on February 19, the Leibstandarte SS Adolf Hitler remained behind as a blocking force. On February 20, the Leibstandarte deployed between Poltava and Baranovka to act as the anvil against which Hoth's and Hausser's armor could crush the remnants of the Soviet forces trying to escape northward (Carell, *Scorched Earth*, p. 187).

[22] USDC, SS Personalakte Baum, "SS Panzer-Grenadier-Division 'Totenkopf,' " a five-page report written subsequently by SSTK commander Hermann Priess recommending Baum for the Oak Leaves to the Knight's Cross, and dated July 14, 1943. See also, Carell, *Scorched Earth*, pp. 187-93; Hauck, "Der Gegenangriff der Heeresgruppe Süd," pp. 475-77; the daily summaries of the progress of the offensive in KTB/OKW, vol. 3, pt. 1, pp. 146, 148, 150, 154, 160, 176-77; and the account in the memoirs of the commander of the SS Panzerkorps, Paul Hausser, *Waffen SS im Einsatz* (Göttingen, 1953), pp. 87-88.

Fourth Panzer Army destroyed the bulk of two Soviet armies and forced a sudden, dramatic temporary reversal of the war in Russia. The Soviet Sixth Army, against which SSTK operated, lost two infantry corps (the Fourth and Fourteenth)—the equivalent of three German divisions—and the Twenty-fifth Tank Corps—roughly the size of an enlarged German panzer division. According to the German figures, total captured or destroyed enemy equipment included 615 tanks (almost all T-34s), 400 howitzers and artillery pieces, and 600 antitank guns. The lack of supporting infantry prevented the Germans from closing the ring tightly, therefore only 9,000 prisoners were taken—although Army Group South claimed an actual count of 23,000 enemy dead. By crushing so substantial a Soviet force Manstein's brilliant counterstroke stabilized the German front in southern Russia and provided the Wehrmacht with precious time to refit, rest, and plan renewed offensive operations for the coming summer.[23]

For the SS Totenkopfdivision, which had been such a crucial factor in the success of Manstein's plan, the operation against the Soviet Sixth Army was a spectacular and very important enterprise. The enormous haul of Russian tanks, trucks, weapons, fuel, and food that SSTK was credited with capturing stood second only to the huge cache amassed during the great victories in the opening weeks of the Russian war. The prestige of the Totenkopfdivision was, moreover, enhanced markedly by its participation in Manstein's stunning triumph—as was the stature of the Leibstandarte and Das Reich—and in the months that followed Hitler several times expressed virtually unlimited confidence in both the military and political reliability of his Totenkopf soldiers.[24]

The great victory in the Ukraine, however, was not won cheaply; and for the SSTK the cost was especially dear. Though

[23] Manstein, pp. 432-33; Ziemke, pp. 93-97; Seaton, pp. 348-49; Clark, pp. 304-6; Philippi and Heim, pp. 202-6; and Hauck, "Der Gegenangriff der Heeresgruppe Süd," p. 478; and KTB/OKW, vol. 3, pt. 1, pp. 214-16, for the German claims for matériel and prisoners.

[24] See especially Helmut Heiber, ed., *Hitlers Lagebesprechungen: Die Protokollfragmente seiner militärischen Konferenzen, 1942-1945* (Stuttgart, 1962), "Besprechung des Führers mit Feldmarschall von Kluge am 26. Juli 1943," pp. 370-71. (Hereafter cited as Heiber, ed., *Lagebesprechungen*).

losses among the officers and men were light and the amount of equipment destroyed or damaged was negligible, the Totenkopfdivision suffered the most important single casualty in its history as the operation drew to a close. On the afternoon of February 26, 1943, as Eicke's armored and infantry units spread out over lengthening distances in pursuit of the enemy, a long radio silence from the SSTK armored regiment, which failed to respond to repeated transmissions, had caused uneasiness among those at division headquarters. Therefore, Eicke ordered up his single-engine light plane (the commonly used Fieseler Storch) and took off from SSTK field headquarters to see from the air what his units were doing.

At about 4:30 P.M. Eicke's pilot spotted a company of the SSTK panzer regiment in a tiny village called Michailovka. Unseen by those in the plane, the Russians were dug-in less than half a mile away in the adjoining village of Artelnoye. As the aircraft approached Michailovka to land, it dropped to an altitude of 300 feet in a long turn that carried it directly over the Russian positions. An intense fusillade of small arms and antiaircraft fire instantly tore the Fieseler Storch apart in midair. It crashed and burned fiercely on the open ground between the two villages. SS soldiers in Michailovka tried repeatedly to reach the burning plane but were beaten back by heavy Russian machine-gun fire. With darkness coming, the effort to recover the bodies of the plane's occupants was abandoned and a call was issued for reinforcements to try again later as word spread through the division that Eicke had been killed. At 5:15 the next morning a strengthened group from the SSTK panzer regiment consisting of two assault guns, three tanks, and a company of motorcyclists attacked Artelnoye under artillery cover, drove the Russians out of the village, and recovered the charred, mutilated bodies of Eicke, his adjutant, and the pilot.[25]

[25] The account given here is based upon materials in USDC, SS Personalakte Eicke, especially two memoranda sent to Himmler describing in detail how Eicke was killed: "Bergung der Leiche des SS Obergruppenführers Eicke," a report sent to Max Simon by SS Hauptsturmführer Lino Masarie, the commander of the assault group that recovered Eicke's body; and Simon's own "Bericht über den Flugzeugabsturz des SS Obergruppenführers und General der Waffen SS Eicke," written on March 1, 1943 and sent to Himmler via Jüttner. Sketchy secondary ac-

12. Eicke's body is transferred to an ambulance early on the morning of February 27, 1943.

During the night, word of Eicke's death spread rapidly through the SS Panzerkorps and up the chain of command to Hitler's "Werewolf" field headquarters at Winniza in the Ukraine. Hausser notified Himmler by telegram at 10:50 P.M. on February 26 that Eicke had been killed in action, and the Reichsführer SS, in turn, immediately informed Hitler personally. Public announcement of Eicke's death was withheld until March 1, to give Himmler time to study the reports of the plane crash and to have a laudatory obituary prepared for release to the German press. The official announcement itself came from Hitler's HQ. In recognition of the "exceptional and unique" services to the Reich of the fallen SS Obergruppenführer, Hitler in his eulogy renamed the panzer regiment of the Totenkopfdivision "Theodor Eicke."[26]

In the wake of the public announcement, while the German press extolled Eicke as one of the original founders of the Waffen SS, Himmler was deluged with telegrams and letters of condolence from many leading personalities in the party and the army who had known or worked with Eicke. With few exceptions, these messages are written in the pompous, verbose hyperbole characteristic of official communications in the Third Reich, and betray a barely concealed insincerity in their tone. Among his colleagues in the SS, the army, and the Nazi party, there were doubtless many who genuinely regretted the loss of a man with Eicke's leadership and organizational talents. On the other hand, there were very few outside the Totenkopfdivision who seemed honestly to mourn Eicke's death in sincere friendship. Except among

counts may also be found in Reitlinger, *The SS*, p. 193; Krätschmer, p. 61; Hausser, *Waffen SS*, p. 88; and Weingartner, p. 75.

[26] BAKO, NS/19-neu-334, radio message from the Führerhauptquartier to the SS Totenkopfdivision of March 1, 1943; USDC, SS Personalakte Eicke, "Auszug aus Heeres- Verordnungsblatt, Teil C, Blatt 12, 'Nachruf,' " signed by Hitler and dated April 16, 1943. Eicke was buried on March 1 with full millitary honors in the nearby village of Otdochnina. In September 1943, with the German army in full retreat in the Ukraine, Himmler had Eicke's body moved to the Hegewald cemetery at Zhitomir in a vain attempt to keep the gravesite permanently out of enemy territory. When the Russians overran the western Ukraine in the spring of 1944, Eicke's corpse was left behind, entombed in the soil of the state and system he hated so genuinely and fanatically (USDC, SS Personalakte Eicke, series of letters exchanged between Himmler and Frau Eicke during October 1943).

the men he had commanded, the grief over Eicke was largely ceremonial and official.[27]

The elements in Eicke's personality that had failed to endear him to the SS hierarchy were the very facets of his nature that made him an effective SS division commander and earned him the respect and admiration of his Totenkopf soldiers. During the years he commanded SSTK, Eicke's style of leadership differed little in practice from the methods he had used to administer the prewar concentration camp system. The most consistent feature of his approach to the practice of field command was his fanaticism, which overrode the pragmatic and the logical in nearly all matters. To Eicke, successful tactics boiled down to a simple matter of fanatical determination and utter ruthlessness, whether in the attack or on the defensive. He considered the extermination of the enemy to be the main objective of warfare, and regarded the Totenkopfdivision as his own creation, private preserve, and personal instrument for accomplishing that purpose. As a result, he demanded the absolute and constant loyalty of all his officers and men, and insisted that they enhance the status of SSTK through repeated success in combat.

In the last year of his life, Eicke even became a moderately competent field commander. What he lacked in formal training, imagination, and finesse, he attempted to overcome through diligence, energy, and a constant effort to master the baffling technical intricacies of mechanized war. He developed the ability to

---

[27] IFZ, *Das Schwarze Korps*, issue for March 11, 1943, which contains a full-page story with photos devoted to Eicke's SS career and exploits as commander of the Totenkopfdivision; and USDC, SS Personalakte Eicke, clippings from the *Völkischer Beobachter* (Berlin edition) issue of March 4, 1943, containing a long story about Eicke's SS career and death on the eastern front. The letters and telegrams of condolence received by Himmler are all in USDC, SS Personalakte Eicke. Among the messages of sympathy are: a letter from the Italian ambassador, Dino Alfieri, expressing the personal condolences of the duce; an unintentionally comic memorial from the chief of SS antipartisan operations, Obergruppenführer Erich von dem Bach-Zelewski, declaring that Heydrich and Eicke (who in life hated each other fiercely) would live on together as guiding spirits for the SS; telegrams from numerous Gauleiters (including Eicke's old enemy Josef Bürckel); the written sympathy of three German field marshals—Manstein, Busch, and Rundstedt; and a note from Frau Heydrich comparing Eicke's heroic death at the front with her own husband's martyrdom at the hands of assassins on the streets of Prague.

remain calm under intense pressure in combat, and in Russia performed at his very best when fighting defensively under orders to hold at all cost.

Most importantly, to his men Eicke was a soldier's general. Habitually near or in the thick of fighting, he shared as an example all his men's hardships, and exacted as much from himself as he did from the youngest SS private. During the terrible ordeal in the swamps and snow around Demyansk, he ate the same meager rations, wore the same soggy, ragged clothes, and slept in the same frozen dugouts as the most exposed of his riflemen. The only crime in war Eicke recognized was cowardice, and his severity in punishing officer and enlisted man alike for this weakness was balanced by a disarming personal intimacy with the proven SS officer and the combat-hardened Totenkopf private. As a result, the Totenkopfdivision evinced an extraordinary élan in both victory and defeat, and Eicke commanded a near-religious devotion from his men, who both feared and revered him.

Despite the close personal nature of Eicke's relationship to his men, his loss—though serious—was not tactically or psychologically crippling to the Totenkopfdivision. At the time he was killed, the officer corps and ranks of SSTK contained many protégés, subordinates, and tough SS veterans whose careers Eicke had molded in the years they had served under him. In the hands of these men, SSTK during the remaining two years of the war more than lived up to the reputation it had earned under Eicke as one of the most spirited, potent, and ruthless formations in the German armed forces. This very fact was irrefutable testimony to the success with which Eicke, through the power of his personality and the style of his command, stamped the Totenkopfdivision with the indelible imprint of his own character.[28]

Eicke's career also had a wider and more fundamental value for

[28] This impact of Eicke's personality and character upon his men was confirmed independently to this writer during the Koblenz interviews with the enlisted veterans of SSTK, and was reiterated by Otto Baum during the course of his interview. An earlier version of these observations appeared in the previously cited article, Sydnor, "La Division SS 'Totenkopf,' " pp. 73-75.

The three men who commanded the Totenkopfdivision for the remainder of the war were among Eicke's closest protégés and personal friends. His immediate successor, Max Simon, remained in command of SSTK until October 16, 1943,

the Third Reich—a special significance Hitler recognized and attested to at the time of Eicke's death. In his official eulogy, Hitler described Eicke's services to Nazi Germany as "unique."[29] The choice of words was highly significant. As the architect of the German concentration camp system and the creator of the SS Totenkopfverbände, Eicke had provided Hitler with the institution and personnel essential to the successful operation of the Third Reich's terror apparatus. By building the detention centers for the confinement of Hitler's political and racial enemies and by creating an absolutely reliable corps of SS men to guard and if necessary destroy these adversaries, Eicke contributed markedly to the development of an authoritarian National Socialist State. With the coming of the war, Eicke took the cadre of these same SS guard detachments and transformed them successfully into the nucleus of a crack SS field division utterly reliable in the crusade against the foreign enemies of Nazi Germany. These achievements earned Eicke great respect from both Himmler and Hitler, and may well have been at the back of Hitler's mind when he commented on Eicke's death.[30]

Above all, Eicke represented a very special genre of men who held crucial, though often inconspicuous, posts in the institutional structure of the Nazi State. One might call them "actualizers"— the brutal and ruthless administrators in the SS, the party, the army, and the bureaucracy who were genuine zealots capable of

---

when he transferred to command of the Sixteenth SS Panzergrenadierdivision Reichsführer SS and turned over command of SSTK to SS Brigadeführer Hermann Priess. Priess commanded SSTK until July 13, 1944, when he assumed command of the Leibstandarte SS Adolf Hitler and was succeeded by SS Oberführer Hellmuth Becker, who led the division until the end of the war (USDC, SS Personalakte of Max Simon, Hermann Priess, and Hellmuth Becker, Dienstlaufbahn of each).

[29] Quoted from BAKO, NS/19-neu-334, radio message sent by Hitler to the SS Totenkopfdivision on March 1, 1943.

[30] In response to a questionnaire prepared by this writer on the subject of Hitler's relationship with Eicke, Albert Speer offered several interesting observations. Speer wrote that he remembered seeing Eicke occasionally in Hitler's chancellery apartments in Berlin before the war. From his own observations and recollections of remarks Hitler made, Speer's impression was that Hitler respected and admired Eicke, though Speer himself at the time was not impressed by Eicke and did not regard him as an important personality (Speer letter to the author of October 26, 1971).

translating Hitler's political, racial, and military policies into concrete form, and of carrying them through to the end with absolute obedience. Eicke typified the "actualizer"; though he never rose in rank and status even to the ministerial level, he personally endowed both the concentration camp system and the Waffen SS with qualities that led the Nuremberg tribunal to brand the SS a criminal organization. Had Eicke survived the war, he doubtless would have occupied a prominent place in the defendants' dock.

Theodor Eicke was killed on the very eve of the Totenkopfdivision's most spectacular victory—its participation in the recapture of Kharkov in March 1943. Immediately after the Russian Sixth Army was throttled at the end of February, the Soviet High Command moved additional armored strength (one corps of the Third Tank Army) into the area south of Kharkov to block a further German advance on the city. Because of Hausser's capable maneuvering, this reserve Russian tank corps walked straight into an open trap. Concentrating the SS divisions Totenkopf and Das Reich as if for an immediate move on Kharkov, Hausser lured the Soviet tank corps forward, then sent the Leibstandarte Adolf Hitler circling around to the northwest into a blocking position behind the Russians. With considerable skill, Hausser then closed the jaws of the armored trap before the Russians realized what was happening. In the process, between February 28 and March 3, SSTK and Das Reich completely enveloped the Soviet force and slammed its armor and infantry back against the Tiger tanks and assault guns of the Leibstandarte. Hausser's well-executed pincer operation not only cost the Russians additional tanks, men, and supplies, but also knocked out the last remaining obstacle between the Germans and Kharkov.[31]

[31] USDC, SS Personalakte Baum, "SS Panzer-Grenadier-Division 'Totenkopf,'" report written by Hermann Priess on July 14, 1943 recommending Baum for the Oak Leaves to the Knight's Cross; USDC, SS Personalakte Häussler, "Vorschlag Nr. 5 für die Verleihung des Deutschen Kreuzes in Gold, Begründung und Stellungsnahme der Zwischenvorgesetzten," dated March 22, 1943 and signed by Lammerding, Simon, and Hausser. SS Hauptsturmführer Ernst Häussler was then acting commander of the First Battalion of the SSTK motorcycle regiment "Thule," and the recommendation describes his battalion's role against the Russians in early March 1943. See also Hauck, "Der Gegenangriff der Heeresgruppe Süd," pp. 520-39, esp. 521-23; KTB/OKW, vol. 3, pt. 1, pp. 181-83; Carell, Scorched Earth, pp. 195-99; and Hausser, Waffen SS, pp. 87-89. In

Consequently, on March 5, 1943, the Totenkopfdivision and SS Das Reich joined Hoth's Fourth Panzer Army for a large-scale offensive to recapture the city. Because of the continued hard freeze, Manstein and Hoth decided to try to take Kharkov quickly by a wide enveloping move from the west and north. This would, they felt, avoid any repetition of the heavy street fighting that had taken such a toll among Paulus's panzer divisions at Stalingrad. The task of encircling Kharkov from the west and north was assigned to the SS divisions Totenkopf and Das Reich, which at that moment formed the active bulk of Hausser's SS Panzerkorps and the extreme left wing of the German forces moving in upon the city from the south.[32]

Lead units of SS Das Reich reached the western outskirts of Kharkov on March 9 after meeting only light resistance. At this juncture, the entire SS Panzerkorps should have continued its advance on an arc that would have carried both SSTK and SS Das Reich around the northern edge of the city and then east to the Donetz River. Hausser, however, could not resist storming right into the city to achieve a great victory quickly. He ordered SS Das Reich to halt and regroup in the western suburbs, and sent the Totenkopfdivision skirting around the northern edge of Kharkov to cut off any Russian withdrawal from the city. Then on March 11, in violation of specific orders from Colonel General Hoth, Hausser detailed one battalion from SSTK to join SS divisions Das Reich and Leibstandarte SS Adolf Hitler in retaking Kharkov by direct assault. This led to three days of vicious and costly street fighting in which, by Hausser's own account, units of the three SS divisions suffered altogether about 11,500 casualties.[33]

---

serving as the anvil against which Hausser pulverized the Russian tank corps, the Leibstandarte was knocked a bit groggy and paused for one day before resuming its part in the offensive against Kharkov.

[32] KTB/OKW, vol. 3, pt. 1, pp. 186-94; Ziemke, pp. 96-97; Seaton, p. 349; Manstein, pp. 433-35; and Hauck, "Der Gegenangriff der Heeresgruppe Süd," pp. 523-26.

[33] Further details on the recapture of Kharkov are in KTB/OKW, vol. 3, pt. 1, pp. 196, 198-99, 202, 204, 206, 209, 214, 216, 219, 223; Manstein, pp. 434-37; Stein, pp. 206-9; Weingartner, pp. 74-76; Ziemke, pp. 96-97; Hauck, "Der Gegenangriff der Heeresgruppe Süd," pp. 526-29; Clark, pp. 299-306; and Carell, *Scorched Earth*, pp. 198-201. Casualty figures for the SS Panzerkorps are given in Hausser, *Waffen SS*, p. 95.

While the fighting in Kharkov raged, the bulk of the Toten-kopfdivision achieved what was—as originally envisaged by Manstein and Hoth—the most important objective of the operation against the city. Between March 11 and 15, 1943, the Toten-kopfdivision enveloped Kharkov from the north, and advanced southeast to capture the vital bridge crossings over the Donetz River at Chuguyev. With this maneuver, SSTK not only sealed the exits from Kharkov, but also trapped the remainder of the Soviet forces trying to flee northeast across the Donetz from the fatal clutches of Hoth's Fourth Panzer Army. In fierce defensive fighting around the Chuguyev crossings the Totenkopfdivision destroyed the bulk of the crack Soviet Twenty-fifth Guards Rifle Division, which struggled desperately for several days to break out of the German trap before being cut to pieces.[34]

The culmination of the spectacular German counteroffensive in the Ukraine followed rapidly in the wake of the Kharkov victory. On March 17, Hoth ordered Hausser's entire SS Panzerkorps to regroup north of Chuguyev for a further advance against Belgorod, a city lying astride the Donetz thirty miles northeast of Kharkov. If the Russians retained Belgorod, the German hold on Kharkov would be tenuous at best, since the Soviets could threaten the city at any time from their bridgehead over the Donetz. Consequently, on March 18 the entire SS Panzerkorps, SSTK, Das Reich, and the Leibstandarte, raced north to Belgorod, cleared the Donetz crossings there of the Russian units holding bridgehead positions, and secured the city firmly in German hands. As they did, the spring thaw finally permeated the

---

[34] USDC, SS Personalakte Baum, Priess' lengthy report of July 14, 1943 recommending Baum for the Oak Leaves to the Knight's Cross. The Chuguyev crossings were all seized in a swift and daring attack by Baum's SSTK First Panzergrenadier Regiment and an attached battalion from the SSTK armored regiment on the evening of March 13 (Baum interview/Baum memorandum; with additional details in Hauck, "Der Gegenangriff der Heeresgruppe Süd," pp. 529-30; Carell, *Scorched Earth*, pp. 200-1; and Hausser, *Waffen SS*, pp. 90-95).

In avoiding the heavy street fighting inside Kharkov, the Totenkopfdivision suffered far fewer casualties than either SS Das Reich or the Leibstandarte, and subsequently was in much better shape for the operation against Kursk the following July. The beating taken by the Leibstandarte in Kharkov's apartment-complex death-traps is vividly described in Weingartner, p. 76.

eastern front, bringing with it a much-needed respite for both sides.

The recapture of Kharkov and Belgorod by the SS Panzerkorps worked like a tonic to revive the flagging spirits of Hitler and his immediate entourage. Nazi propaganda trumpeted the recapture of Kharkov as one of the decisive battles in the war; and in a bouncy mood of renewed optimism Hitler expressed unlimited confidence in the political and military qualities of his three elite Waffen SS divisions.[35]

The improvement in Hitler's morale, moreover, enabled him to turn his full attention to the planning of yet another summer offensive in the east. After more than a month of intensive staff work at OKH, and numerous conferences with his military advisers, Hitler completed these preparations in a directive of April 16, 1943, which set down the general objectives for "Operation Zitadelle"—the code-name for the planned assault against the huge Russian salient around Kursk that penetrated into the German front at the junction of Army Groups Center and South. The general plan for Zitadelle was simple. Two powerful panzer armies would be concentrated at the northern and southern hinges of the salient—Orel and Belgorod—and would attack toward each other along a north-south line leading them to converge eventually at Kursk in the very center of the Russian bulge. Hitler expected the outcome would be the destruction of the Soviet armored and infantry forces in central Russia.[36]

[35] KTB/OKW, vol. 3, pt. 1, pp. 228, 263; Carell, *Scorched Earth*, p. 201; and Weingartner, pp. 76-77. As of April 1, 1943, the Totenkopfdivision was assigned officially to garrison duty in Belgorod for an indefinite period, and remained posted in the vicinity in an inactive capacity until the start of the German summer offensive of 1943.

[36] A copy of the directive "Operationsbefehl Nr. 6 (Zitadelle) vom 15. 4. 1943," is reprinted in KTB/OKW, vol. 3, pt. 2, pp. 1425-27. There is a substantial and growing literature devoted to the various phases of the German offensive at Kursk. This is owing partly to some historians' belief that the failure of Zitadelle reversed permanently the course of the war in Russia, and partly to the fascination that the unprecedented, massive collision of German and Soviet armor holds for other writers. To date, Ernst Klink, *Das Gesetz des Handelns: Die Operation "Zitadelle" 1943* (Stuttgart, 1966), is the most solid, comprehensive study of the whole operation. Important also is the series of three articles by Gotthard Heinrici and Friedrich Wilhelm Hauck, "Zitadelle," *Wehrwissenschaftliche Rundschau*, 15 (August-October 1965), pp. 463-82, 529-44, and 582-604; and Joseph E.

The most serious flaw in the plan for Zitadelle was that its merits were as obvious to the Soviet High Command as they were to Hitler. Consequently, as serious German preparations got under way in May, the Soviets began a corresponding build-up opposite the concentration areas at Orel and Belgorod. The prospects for a German victory were weakened further by the repeated delays ordered by Hitler during May and June to allow the armament factories to produce enough new heavy tanks and assault guns for the panzer divisions earmarked for Zitadelle.

By late June 1943 the army and Waffen SS divisions in Russia had received enough new Tiger, Panther, and Ferdinand model tanks to convince Hitler that the operation would succeed. The German dictator fixed the date for the beginning of the Kursk offensive at July 5, 1943, and ordered that all final preparations for the great assault be completed. The German forces concentrated to smash the Kursk bulge from north and south were the most powerful Hitler had been able to deploy for a single operation on so narrow a front. In the Orel sector, on the northern wing of the Kursk salient, the German striking force consisted of Colonel General Walter Model's Ninth Army. To demolish the northern wall of the bulge, Model had three panzer and two infantry corps—a total of nineteen seasoned, first-line divisions.[37]

The southern half of the Zitadelle pincer was even more powerful. In the area just west of Belgorod, Colonel General Hermann Hoth's Fourth Panzer Army disposed of two panzer corps (Forty-

---

Thach, Jr., "The Battle of Kursk July 1943: Decisive Turning Point on the Eastern Front," Diss. Georgetown 1971. Reliable discussions of the German planning for Zitadelle in the spring of 1943 may be found in Klink, pp. 51-197; Ziemke, pp. 119-34; Seaton, pp. 353-58; Guderian, pp. 241-47; Clark, pp. 322-27; Philippi and Heim, pp. 208-11; and Carell, *Scorched Earth*, pp. 19-49.

[37] The Soviet view of the strategic situation in spring 1943 and military planning in response to the obvious German offensive build-up against the Kursk bulge are described in the memoirs of three key Russian participants: Marshal Zhukov, pp. 432-50; Sergei M. Shtemenko, *The Soviet General Staff at War, 1941-1945*, trans. Robert Daglish (Moscow, 1970), pp. 148-68; and Konstantin K. Rokossovsky, *A Soldier's Duty*, trans. Robert Daglish (Moscow, 1970), pp. 184-206. During the Kursk campaign Zhukov served as the on-site representative of the Soviet Supreme Command (Stalin), Shtemenko was chief of the operations section of the Red Army General Staff, and Rokossovsky commanded the Russian forces opposite Model's Ninth Army in the Orel sector.

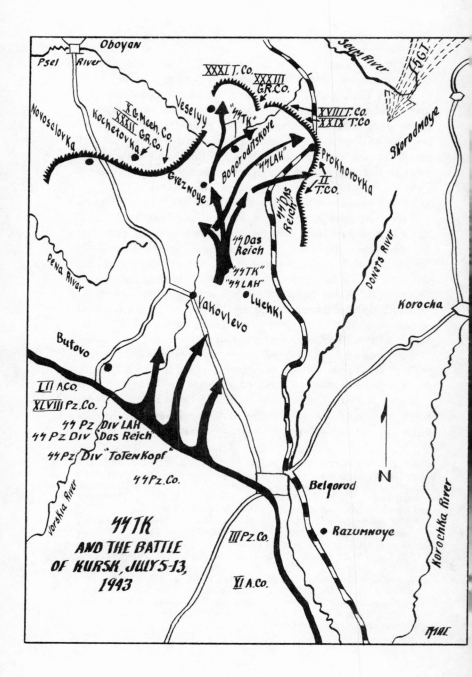

SS TK AND THE BATTLE OF KURSK, JULY 5-13, 1943

eighth and Hausser's redesignated Second SS Panzerkorps) and the Fifty-second Infantry Corps to protect its left flank. To the south of Belgorod, the wing of the German front was anchored by Army Detachment Kempf with the Third Panzer and Eleventh Army Corps. Compressed into a twenty-eight-mile front, nine of the finest divisions in the German armed forces were under Hoth's command, the Third, Sixth, Seventh, Eleventh, and Nineteenth Panzer Divisions, the elite armored division Grossdeutschland, and the three best formations in the Waffen SS—Leibstandarte SS Adolf Hitler, SS Das Reich, and the SS Totenkopfdivision.

The Soviet forces deployed at key points inside the salient, however, were even more impressive. In the southern sector alone, Hoth faced three Soviet infantry armies (the Sixth and Seventh Guards, and the Sixty-ninth) and the crack First Tank Army, plus the massive Fifth Guards Tank Army which was being held in reserve near Voronezh for eventual commitment to the southern sector. Possession of this potent reserve and its timely dispatch by the Soviet High Command ultimately tipped the scale against Hoth by blunting the advance of the Waffen SS divisions just as they verged on breaking through the Russian defenses in the south.[38]

When Zitadelle began at 3:15 A.M. on July 5 with simultaneous German assaults from the north and south, SSTK occupied the crucial slot of wing division on the extreme right flank of Hoth's Fourth Panzer Army. In this position, SSTK was expected not only to keep pace with the northerly advance of the SS Panzerkorps but also to screen the flank of the Fourth Panzer Army

[38] Hausser's SS Panzerkorps was demoted a notch and renumbered the Second SS Panzerkorps after the battle of Kharkov when Hitler agreed to create an additional SS army corps built around his own Leibstandarte (Stein, pp. 212-14; Weingartner, pp. 77-78; and Klietmann, pp. 114-15). The Totenkopfdivision's participation in Zitadelle is documented closely in BAMA, RS 2-2/1 bis 31, Bestand Generalkommando SS Panzer-Korps, ab Juni 1943 II. SS Panzer-Korps, in particular RS 2-2/13, "Generalkommando I. SS Panzer-Korps, An Oberkommando 4. Panzerarmee, Angriffsplan," a comprehensive plan with the operational objectives of the SS divisions in the south prepared by Hausser on May 31, 1943. The strength of the opposing forces, the final German preparations, and the opening phase of the attack are described in Heinrici and Hauck, "Zitadelle," pp. 537-42, and pp. 584-90; Seaton, pp. 359-61; Ziemke, pp. 135-37; Thach, pp. 246-69; Manstein, pp. 443-49; Clark, pp. 322-29; Mellenthin, pp. 212-16, 218; Phillippi and Heim, pp. 208-11; and Carell, *Scorched Earth*, pp. 19-51.

against any possible Soviet penetration from east of the Donetz until supporting infantry arrived. Opposite the three SS divisions on July 5 were mixed armored and infantry formations from the Soviet First Tank and Sixty-ninth Armies, entrenched in the densest and most elaborate network of fortifications any SS soldier had ever seen.

Within an hour after the assault began, the divisions of the Second SS Panzerkorps were involved in the heaviest fighting in the most crucial sector of the southern front. Despite intense Russian resistance and great casualties, all three SS divisions made excellent progress the first day. The Totenkopfdivision crashed head-on into the Fifty-second Guards Division and began grinding its way methodically through the first network of Russian defenses. By evening, the lead assault companies of SSTK, cooperating with groups of Tiger and Panther tanks, had penetrated the second line of Russian defenses and captured the village of Yakhontovo—an important forward command post for the Soviet Sixty-ninth Army. Progress the following day was equally encouraging. While the Leibstandarte and Das Reich continued to blast their way forward one yard at a time, SSTK shook free of the Soviet flank defenses and penetrated twenty miles to the north. By dusk on July 6, SSTK had crossed and cut the Belgorod-Oboyan highway and halted for the night astride the Belgorod-Kursk rail line.[39]

On the morning of July 7, the situation in the sector of the SS Panzerkorps—as seen by Hoth and Manstein—looked most promising. The Totenkopfdivision had advanced nearly thirty miles from its original jumping-off positions and had cut the main road and rail links to the Russian rear. The Leibstandarte and Das

[39] BAMA, RS 2-2/17, Gen. Kdo. II. SS Panzer-Korps, "Darstellung der Ereignisse," entries for July 5 and 6, 1943; USDC, SS Personalakte Baum, description of events in Baum's regiment July 5-6 written by Hermann Priess on July 14, 1943; USDC, SS Personalakte Häussler, "Vorschlagsliste Nr. 8 für die Verleihung des Ritterkreuzes zum Eisernenkreuz," dated July 20, 1943, and signed by Priess as acting SSTK commander in place of the wounded Max Simon. This recommendation details the techniques used by an assault group commanded by Häussler in clearing the Russian minefields, tank traps, and pillboxes on July 5 and 6. See also, Klink, pp. 217-19; Thach, pp. 269-74, 277, 289-90; and the general summaries in KTB/OKW, vol. 3, pt. 2, pp. 1619-24; Ziemke, pp. 135-37; Mellenthin, pp. 220-30; Seaton, pp. 361-62; and Weingartner, p. 81.

Reich, meanwhile, were having a stickier time beating off enemy counterattacks while clearing a path through the first two Soviet defense systems. As they chopped their way forward against tough resistance, the SS divisions left an immense junkyard of wrecked Soviet armor and heavy weapons; Hausser's SS field police units herded thousands of dazed and bewildered Russian prisoners toward the German rear. By the evening of July 7, these previously unmistakable signs of disaster created the impression that the Second SS Panzerkorps was poised for a decisive breakthrough which would roll up the southern front of the Kursk salient.[40]

Under similar circumstances in the summer of 1941 and 1942 this conclusion might have been valid. In July 1943, however, it bore no relation whatever to the actual situation on the southern sector of the Kursk front. During the night of July 7-8, the SS divisions were only beginning to encounter what proved to be the real Russian opposition. Instead of having destroyed the bulk of the Soviet armor in the forward fortifications, as the weary German soldiers thought, the SS Panzerkorps did not face it until July 8 in the form of the First Tank Army. In the advance since July 5, moreover, the Waffen SS divisions had far outdistanced their neighbors on the left, who were still grappling with the first Soviet defense line. The Russians quickly applied pressure against this gap on Hausser's left flank and forced the Leibstandarte to hold back units to cover the rear of the SS Panzerkorps' advance. On Hausser's right flank, meanwhile, the Totenkopfdivision remained tied down all day on July 8 waiting for the 167th Infantry Division to advance and relieve it of responsibility for guarding the right flank of the SS Panzerkorps.[41]

[40] BAMA, RS 2-2/17, Gen. Kdo. II. SS Panzer-Korps, "Darstellung der Ereignisse," entry for July 7, 1943; Seaton, pp. 362-63; Klink, pp. 219-21; and Carell, *Scorched Earth*, pp. 62-73. Part of the success achieved by the SS panzerkorps was due to a novel tank-killing technique developed by the Luftwaffe and used for the first time during Zitadelle. Hans-Ulrich Rudel, the famous Stuka ace, hit upon the idea of mounting a 37 mm antitank cannon under the fuselage of the German dive bomber. Armed with this new weapon, whole squadrons of Stukas flew in support of the SS divisions at Kursk. Swooping down upon the Russian armored columns from behind, they destroyed numerous T-34s with direct hits to the engine-housing—the most vulnerable spot on the tank's chassis (Carell, *Scorched Earth*, pp. 59-62).

[41] BAMA, RS 2-2/17, Gen. Kdo. II. SS Pz. Kps., "Darstellung der Ereig-

Hausser's advance, moreover, concerned the Soviet High Command enough to prompt the dispatch of the first contingent of Russian reserves. On July 8 General Vatutin, commander of the Soviet Voronezh front, ordered the Second Guards Tank Corps, which was deployed to the northeast of Belgorod, to attack the right flank and rear of the SS Panzerkorps. Fortunately for the Totenkopfdivision, which lay directly in the path of the Second Guards Tank Corps' attack route, the Luftwaffe spotted the Russian armored columns from the air and demolished most of the T-34s with flying antitank cannons before the Soviet Corps was in range of SSTK.[42]

When supporting infantry relieved SSTK, Hausser was able on July 9 to throw the full weight of the SS Panzerkorps against the last Soviet defense line. Exhorted by their commanders to spare nothing in this final heave against the Russian front, the weary assault groups of the Leibstandarte SS Adolf Hitler, SS Das Reich, and the Totenkopfdivision hurled themselves into the maze of antitank positions, machine-gun nests, bunkers, and trenches. The sheer fury of the SS assault was enough to overcome even the most stubborn resistance, and on the tenth the Russian defense began crumbling. That afternoon the Third Battalion of the Totenkopfdivision's First Panzergrenadier Regiment, commanded by Standartenführer Karl Ullrich, cleared the last Russian bunkers in its sector and forded the Psel River—the only remaining natural obstacle between the Fourth Panzer Army and Kursk. Ullrich's SS grenadiers then established a bridgehead on the north bank of the Psel, after a frustrating wait for the arrival of heavy bridging equipment, and captured the villages of Vasilyevka, Koslovka, and Krasny Oktybar. This, the northernmost German penetration of the southern front of the salient, put the Totenkopfdivision in an ideal position from which to wheel left into the Russian rear on the eleventh.[43]

---

nisse," entry for July 8, 1943; Klink, p. 222; Thach, p. 306; and Carell, *Scorched Earth*, pp. 68-73.

[42] BAMA, RS 2-2/17, Gen. Kdo. II. SS Pz. Kps., "Darstellung der Ereignisse," entries for July 8 and 9, 1943; Baum interview; Carell, *Scorched Earth*, pp. 74-77.

[43] BAMA, RS 2-2/17, Gen. Kdo. II. SS Pz. Kps., "Darstellung der Ereignisse," entries for July 9, 10 and 11, 1943; Klink, pp. 224-26; Baum interview; and Thach, pp. 306.

13. Two of the division's best soldiers—Otto Baum (left) and Karl Ullrich (right), photographed during the battle of Kursk.

The alarming progress made by Hausser's SS divisions on July 10, however, provoked the Soviet High Command to commit its huge armored reserves for action on the southern front. Early on the eleventh, Vatutin ordered General Nikolai Rotmistrov's Fifth Guards Tank Army out of its staging area east of Kursk and sent it south to crush the SS Panzerkorps. To make certain the SS divisions were halted (an indication of how highly the Russians regarded them), the worried Vatutin received at his request additional armored reserves of two tank corps from the neighboring Soviet Steppe front. Thus as the three Waffen SS divisions mopped up remaining resistance in the field fortifications on the eleventh and confidently regrouped to deliver the Russians a knockout blow, this unseen armored juggernaut bore down upon them from the northeast at full speed.[44]

The Second SS Panzerkorps and the Soviet Fifth Guards and Fifth Guards Tank Armies collided at mid-morning on July 12 in a fitting climax to the battle of Kursk. The clash between the SS divisions and the Soviet guards formations (the cream of the tank contingents on each side) materialized in a small triangular area bordered by the village of Vesely on the west, Prokhorovka on the north, and the Belgorod-Kursk railroad embankment on the east. Against the 273 tanks and assault guns of the SS Panzerkorps the Russians threw a total of seven corps (Fifth Guards Mechanized, Thirty-second and Thirty-third Guards Rifle, and the Second, Eighteenth, Twenty-ninth, and Thirty-first Guards Tank Corps) with a complement of over 850 T-34 tanks and SU-85 self-propelled assault guns.[45] The fierce day-long engagement that resulted was the largest single armored battle in the history of land warfare.

The sudden compression of so many tanks into such a small area—roughly three miles square—caused the commanders on

[44] Heinrici and Hauck, "Zitadelle," pp. 594-96; Klink, pp. 240, 243-44; Seaton, pp. 363-64; and Thach, p. 311.

[45] Heinrici and Hauck, "Zitadelle," pp. 597-98, for the most reliable tank estimates for the SS Panzerkorps; and Zhukov, pp. 460-61, for the official Soviet armored strength figures. BAMA, RS 2-2/17, Gen. Kdo. II. SS Pz. Kps., "Darstellung der Ereignisse," entries for July 11 and 12, 1943, describe developments leading to the armored clash at Prokhorovka. See also, Klink, pp. 243-44; Seaton, p. 364; Carell, *Scorched Earth*, pp. 77-82; and Clark, pp. 335-38.

both sides to lose control of their armored companies almost at once. In consequence, the battle quickly became a confused free-for-all in which every tank and crew fought individually amidst the chaotic jumble of German and Russian tanks driving and firing frantically in all directions. For eight hours on July 12 this enormous armored brawl raged unabated, slashing the orchards and churning the lush, green cornfields of the upper Donetz River valley into a blackened inferno of exploding tanks, burning vehicles, and charred corpses—drenched intermittently by downpours from violent thunderclouds.

In the sector of the Totenkopfdivision, on the left flank of the SS Panzerkorps, some of the most vicious fighting of the day occurred. SSTK had been on the move in mid-morning when it ran into Russian tank reserve. Before noon, Totenkopf soldiers found themselves under attack by two Soviet corps (the Thirty-first Guards Tank and the Thirty-third Guards Rifle)—the equivalent of four divisions—and forced onto the defensive in savage close-quarter fighting among tanks and infantry. Once on the defensive, however, SSTK refused to yield ground. The armored duels intensified so much that SS Tigers and Panthers and Soviet T-34s blazed away at each other point-blank—and resorted to ramming when their ammunition gave out. Under such circumstances and at such short distances the massive armor of the German tanks offered no protection against T-34s; many Russian direct hits struck with such force that some SSTK tanks simply blew up, tossing their splintered turrets into the air.[46]

[46] BAMA, RS 2-2/17, Gen. Kdo. II. SS Pz. Kps., "Darstellung der Ereignisse," entries for July 12, 13, and 14, 1943, with the entry for July 12 claiming a total of 244 Soviet tanks knocked out during the day; and ibid., RS 2-2/18, Gen. Kdo. II. SS Pz. Kps., "Anlagenband A vom 1. 6. 43 bis 2. 8. 43, Meldungen und Befehle," contains the SSTK daily report for July 12—a document whose tone of terse urgency eloquently underscores the awesome magnitude of the armored duel at Prokhorovka. Additional information about the experience of SSTK at Prokhorovka was drawn from the Baum interview; Thach, p. 316, quoting Rotmistrov's first-hand observation of the struggle; Weingartner, pp. 81-82, for the Leibstandarte's role in the engagement; Carell, *Scorched Earth*, pp. 77-83; and Shtemenko, p. 170, for an independent Russian view of July 12 at Prokhorovka as the crisis and climax of Zitadelle. The official Soviet version of the battle of Kursk in Hans-Adolf Jacobsen and Andreas Hillgruber, eds., *Die Sowjetische Geschichte des Grossen Vaterländischen Krieges, 1941-1945, von Boris Semjonowitsch Telpuchowski*, (Frankfurt am Main, 1961), pp. 233-42, contains no details or useful specifics about the battle of Prokhorovka.

Though outnumbered four-to-one in both tanks and infantry, the Totenkopfdivision managed successfully throughout the twelfth, the thirteenth, and into late afternoon of the fourteenth to contain the two Soviet corps and prevent any penetration into Hausser's flank. In the process, however, SSTK absorbed terrific punishment, and by the time the Russians broke off their attacks at dusk on July 14 Totenkopf had lost over half its tanks and vehicles and had taken heavy casualties among all its combat units. When added to the losses suffered during the first week of the Zitadelle operation, the cost at the battle of Prokhorovka debilitated the Totenkopfdivision. For several weeks after the battle of Kursk SSTK had to remain out of the line recuperating while some additional reserves and a few extra tanks and assault guns were scraped together to stiffen the thinned ranks. Even with the limited time for rest and refitting, however, the Totenkopfdivision—like many of the army's crack panzer divisions—did not regain anything resembling its offensive capability prior to Zitadelle. The experience of the Totenkopfdivision in Zitadelle mirrored well the irreversible weakening that German armored forces suffered in the great tank battles at Kursk of July 1943.[47]

For the three divisions of the SS Panzerkorps the end of their role in the southern sector of Zitadelle came with merciful swiftness after the terrible experience at Prokhorovka. The dispatch of Russian reserves to the Belgorod sector had been timed to coincide with an attack into the flank and rear of Model's Ninth Army by powerful Soviet forces deployed north of Orel. These twin counterthrusts blunted the German advance in both sectors and induced Hitler—who was also troubled by the successful Allied landings in Sicily on July 10—to cancel Operation Zitadelle on

---

[47] BAMA, RS 2-2/18, Gen. Kdo. II. SS Pz. Kps., "Meldungen und Befehle," daily report of SSTK for July 13, and the Second SS Panzerkorps for July 14 and 15; ibid., RS 2-2/17, "Darstellung der Ereignisse," entries for July 13 and 14; Baum interview; USDC, SS Personalakte Baum, description of the events on July 12 and 13 in the Priess recommendation of Baum for July 14, 1943; and USDC, SS Personalakte Becker, "Vorschlagsliste Nr. 10 für die Verleihung des Ritterkreuzes des Eisernen Kreuzes, den 25. 8. 1943," signed by Hermann Priess. At the time of Prokhorovka, Hellmuth Becker commanded the SSTK Panzer Regiment "Theodor Eicke," and fought with it in the very thick of the action along the Psel between July 10 and 15, 1943. Nearly all panzer and motorized divisions used in Zitadelle lost about half their men and equipment. See especially, Carell, *Scorched Earth*, pp. 291-303; and Ziemke, pp. 138-44.

July 13. He ordered the German armies pulled back to their original jumping-off positions so that the front could be shortened and German divisions withdrawn from Russia for transfer to Italy.[48]

Interestingly enough, Hitler's confidence in his three elite Waffen SS divisions rose to an even higher level after the disaster at Kursk than it had in the wake of the SS Panzerkorps' recapture of Kharkov the previous March. The fact that the SS Panzerkorps had made the deepest penetration of the salient yet did not buckle under the immense pressure of the Russian armored counterattack enabled the three senior SS divisions to emerge from this decisive defeat with their reputations intact and their prestige enhanced. In the atmosphere of increasing recrimination and bitterness that pervaded Hitler's military conferences after the battle of Kursk, the führer repeatedly abused his generals and the Wehrmacht by singling out the SS divisions (including SSTK) for their leadership and fighting capacity, which Hitler alleged the army formations lacked. Where true, such conditions resulted largely from the preferential treatment Hitler gave SS divisions in matériel and manpower replacement after 1943. Moreover, as the tide of war turned unmistakably against Germany after Zitadelle, and as the Russians began to hammer relentlessly against the entire weakened eastern front, Hitler began relying almost exclusively upon Waffen SS formations to shore up the most dangerous weak spots and halt for a time the inexorable Soviet march westward. It was in this capacity as crisis-retrieval specialists that the soldiers of the SS Totenkopfdivision spent the remaining twenty months of the Second World War.[49]

Four days after his abrupt termination of the Kursk offensive, Hitler ordered Hausser's SS Panzerkorps withdrawn from the front for transfer to Italy. While the exhausted SS divisions en-

---

[48] Between July 12 and 18, the four Soviet fronts anchoring the bulge between Orel and Belgorod—the western, Bryansk, central, and Steppe fronts—received the green light from Zhukov to pass over to the offensive, beginning an uninterrupted series of Soviet assaults that were to last into April 1944. Otto P. Chaney, Jr., *Zhukov* (Norman, Okla., 1971), pp. 254-55; Heinrici and Hauck, "Zitadelle," pp. 600-1; Manstein, pp. 448-49; Clark, p. 337; and KTB/OKW, vol. 3, pt. 2, pp. 773, 776-79, 781-87, for the development of Hitler's plans for countermeasures in Sicily and Italy using formations withdrawn from Russia.

[49] See especially, Heiber, ed., *Lagebesprechungen*, "Besprechung des Führers mit Feldmarschall von Kluge am 26. Juli 1943," pp. 369-83; Stein, pp. 206-8; Seaton, p. 375; Clark, pp. 351-62; and Ziemke, p. 139.

joyed a short respite in the comparative quiet of Kharkov waiting for their train convoys, the Russians launched the first in a powerful series of their own summer and autumn offensives. Potent, fresh forces commanded by General Rodion I. Malinovsky attacked the German front on the lower Donetz on July 25 and overwhelmed Manstein's positions along the Mius River. To seal off the Russian breakthrough, Hitler sent the SS divisions Totenkopf and Das Reich and Third Panzer Corps (Sixteenth and Twenty-third Panzer Divisions) south to Stalino, where they were thrown into the breach on July 30 with orders to halt the Russian offensive regardless of the cost. After three days of fierce defensive fighting, the two Waffen SS formations and their sister panzer divisions succeeded in halting Malinovsky's advance and in stabilizing the front temporarily.[50]

With this crisis mastered for the moment, Hitler turned again to the question of sending the Leibstandarte, SS Das Reich, and the Totenkopfdivision to Italy, where Mussolini had been overthrown and arrested on July 25 and a military government established under Marshal Pietro Badoglio. Before he could finally decide however, another major Soviet offensive shattered a wide sector of the German front and settled the issue of where the crack SS divisions were to be used. On August 3, the Russians attacked in the area between Orel and Belgorod and tore huge gaps in the German lines. To deal simultaneously with the crisis in Italy and this new threat on the Russian front, Hitler divided the three SS divisions. The Leibstandarte was ordered to entrain for Italy, while SSTK and Das Reich were rushed north from Stalino to reinforce the hard-pressed German formations at Kharkov struggling to prevent the disintegration of Manstein's left wing.[51]

The Soviet offensive against Belgorod was launched by the combined forces of the Voronezh and Steppe fronts—five armies with a six-to-one superiority in tanks and guns over the German

[50] Seaton, pp. 369-70; Carell, *Scorched Earth*, pp. 87-88, 93, 298; Mellenthin, pp. 229-30; Stein, pp. 213-14; and Klietmann, pp. 114-15.

[51] Seaton, p. 370; Thach, p. 364; Clark, pp. 350-51, 363; Ziemke, pp. 149-56; Mellenthin, pp. 235-37; and Stein, pp. 213-14. For a discussion of the crisis in Italy that prompted Hitler to contemplate sending his best SS divisions there, see F. W. Deakin, *The Brutal Friendship: Mussolini, Hitler and the Fall of Italian Fascism* 2nd ed. (New York, 1966), pt. 1, pp. 420-78; and Charles F. Delzell, *Mussolini's Enemies: The Italian Anti-Fascist Resistance* (Princeton, N. J., 1961), pp. 223-34.

formations opposite them. The brunt of the Russian assault fell upon Hoth's Fourth Panzer Army and the Army Detachment Kempf (Armee Abteilung Kempf, a mixed force of armored and infantry divisions commanded by General Werner Kempf), and quickly dislodged them from their pre-Zitadelle positions. On August 5, the Russians captured Belgorod and succeeded in opening a thirty-mile gap in the front at the junction between the Hoth and Kempf forces. In the days that followed the Soviets widened the breach, through which General Vatutin, the overall commander, hurled all the tanks and infantry he had. The Red Army formations streaming westward between the Fourth Panzer Army and Army Detachment Kempf bypassed Kharkov on the north and swung to the southwest making straight for Poltava. Vatutin's objective in this rapidly enlarging full-scale offensive (code-named by the Soviets "Operation General Rumyantsev") was to drive a powerful armored prong deep into Manstein's rear and cut off Army Group South by capturing the crossings over the Dnieper River between Kiev and Zaporozhye.[52]

Manstein correctly interpreted the Soviet objective and ordered the SS divisions Das Reich and Totenkopf—the nucleus of his fire brigade—into the area west of Kharkov. SSTK and Das Reich were given the twofold task of halting the Russian drive toward the Dnieper and preventing the Soviet armor from wheeling south, enveloping Kharkov from the west, and surrounding Army Detachment Kempf—which was holding out inside the city upon express orders from Hitler. In accordance with Manstein's directive, the Totenkopfdivision dug in west of Kharkov just south of the town of Akhtyrka and braced for the armored avalanche that descended from the north and east. For one week SSTK and Das

---

[52] Manstein, pp. 454-55; Shtemenko, pp. 177-84; Seaton, p. 370; Carell, *Scorched Earth*, pp. 298-303; Ziemke, pp. 149-55; Clark, p. 363; and Philippi and Heim, pp. 212-14. The unprecedented violence of the Russian offensive, the exhaustion and growing despair of the average German infantryman, and the unparalleled suffering and hardship of the last two years of the war are described in Guy Sajer, *The Forgotten Soldier*, trans. Lily Emmet, (New York, 1971), esp. pp. 169-273. This is the most powerful memoir by any soldier who fought in and survived the German-Russian conflict. Sajer was a seventeen-year-old Alsatian volunteer in the Grossdeutschland Division, an elite formation that fought a number of rearguard actions with the Totenkopfdivision during the great German retreat from the Ukraine in autumn 1943.

Reich acted as a breakwater and successfully repulsed all Russian attempts to break through to the southwest toward the Dnieper. In the meantime, however, the situation at Kharkov became untenable. Soviet pressure against the city from the west and north forced General Kempf on August 13 to issue preliminary orders for evacuation. Hitler personally countermanded these orders and directed that Kharkov be held at all costs. When this proved impossible and Kempf was forced to withdraw from the city on August 22 to escape encirclement, Hitler forced Manstein to dismiss Kempf. Army Detachment Kempf was then redesignated Eighth Army, placed under the command of General Otto Wöhler, and given the task of rebuilding the German front west of Kharkov.[53]

The fact that Wöhler accomplished this feat so quickly under such difficult circumstances was due partly to the yeoman service performed by the Totenkopfdivision and SS Das Reich. All during the German withdrawal from Kharkov they counterattacked and held firm against mounting Russian pressure from the north. In a local counteroffensive between August 15 and 20, SSTK led the encirclement and destruction of the spearheads of Vatutin's forces trying to envelop Kharkov from the west, and linked up near Akhtyrka with units of the Seventh Panzer Division—thus reestablishing firm contact with the shaken but still intact Fourth Panzer Army. Having served as the key to the successful counterthrust that halted the Russian attempt to reach the Dnieper and encircle Kharkov, the SS divisions gave Manstein the extra bonus of covering the German retreat and screening the redeployment of the Eighth Army. Once more, SSTK and Das Reich had helped avert a major disaster with their skill and tenacity and had given Manstein precious time to regain his balance.[54]

[53] NA/T-312/54/7569773-7570029, "Kriegstagebuch Nr. 2. Bd. 2, Armeeoberkommando 8, Abt. Ia., vom 1. 8. 43-31. 8. 43," contains detailed daily information about the movement and combat activity of SSTK during August 1943. See also, Shtemenko, pp. 179-83; Ziemke, pp. 155-56; Manstein, pp. 455-58; and Carell, Scorched Earth, pp. 303-12.

[54] NA/T-312/54/7569900-9942, war diary of the Eighth Army with daily entries for August 15-21, records the step-by-step progress of SSTK in the counteroffensive and credits the division with the destroying three Soviet rifle divisions, an armored brigade, and capturing 1,611 prisoners. General accounts of the fighting in late August are in Ziemke, pp. 155-56; Manstein, pp. 455-58; Carell, Scorched Earth, pp. 303-12; and Shtemenko, pp. 181-83.

During the short breathing spell after the evacuation of Kharkov, Manstein concluded that his army group could no longer hold the Donetz line in southern Russia, and that an immediate but orderly withdrawal to the natural defense line of the Dnieper River was essential. After several inconclusive meetings with Hitler at Rastenburg and Zaporozhye in late August and early September 1943, Manstein finally secured Hitler's tentative agreement on September 15 for the withdrawal of the Fourth Panzer and Eighth Armies to the Dnieper. To cover this gradual retreat, Manstein attached SSTK and Das Reich to the Eighth Army and put them to work again as rearguards. By the time Hitler gave in and agreed to the withdrawal, however, the Russians had already resumed strong pressure against the northern and southern wings of the army group. The retreat had to be hurried, and SSTK and Das Reich had a sticky time protecting Wöhler's formations as they withdrew toward the vehicle-jammed crossing points over the Dnieper. In fighting that raged throughout September, Wöhler's two SS divisions—supported by Grossdeutschland—held off the Russians while much of the Eighth Army (with most of its heavy weapons and equipment) safely crossed the Dnieper over the bridge and ferry installations at Kremenchug.[55]

[55] NA/T-312/54/7570032-0239, "Kriegstagebuch Nr. 2, Armeeoberkommando 8, Abt. Ia., vom 1. 9. 43-30. 9. 43," traces the daily movements and engagements of SSTK while it fought with the rearguard of the Eleventh Army Corps and Forty-eighth Panzer Corps during September 1943; while NA/T-313/64/ 7300593-0643, 0684-0689, 0703-0729, "Pz. AOK 1, Ia., Tägliche Lagekarten, Anlage zum KTB Nr. 12," consists of the daily situation maps pinpointing the withdrawal route of SSTK to the Dnieper. Additional details on the bitterness of the fighting during the retreat are in USDC, SS Personalakte Priess, long teleprinter message from Manstein to SSTK of September 5 praising SSTK for the destruction of seventy-two Russian tanks on September 2. See also, Manstein, pp. 458-70; Ziemke, p. 156; Philippi and Heim, pp. 215-18; and Carell, Scorched Earth, pp. 312-23. The difficulties of evacuating Kharkov and withdrawing to the Dnieper led the Germans to indulge in what the Soviets claimed was wholesale brutality against the Russian civilian populace. According to the Soviet charges, SSTK directly committed savage atrocities. A Russian tribunal that convened at Kharkov in December 1943 executed as war criminals several army and SS officers and NCOs who had been captured during the German retreat from the city. This same tribunal condemned Max Simon to death in absentia for the Totenkopfdivision's alleged participation in the murder of 10,000 Russian civilians in the Kharkov area during late summer 1943. See Heiber, ed., Lagebesprechungen, "Mittagslage vom 22. Dezember 1943 in der Wolfschanze," p. 460n; TMWC, vol. 21, p. 352; Stein, p. 273; and Weingartner, p. 129. The Russians never sub-

For the weary men of Totenkopf and Das Reich, however, the Dnieper offered neither respite nor safety. Yet another crisis further south along the river compelled Manstein during the first week of October to shift his reliable Waffen SS divisions to the new danger point on the army group's front. The trouble arose from heavy Soviet pressure against the German forces holding along the great bend in the Dnieper between Kremenchug and Zaporozhye. Trying to surround and annihilate the Wehrmacht formations in the river bend, the Russians exerted every effort to force their way across the river at several points. In the first week of October, Red Army units overpowered the thin German garrisons holding the crossing points around Kremenchug and Zaporozhye and established firm bridgeheads at these two vital crossings. Then, on October 15, 1943, the newly organized Soviet Second Ukrainian Front, commanded by Marshal Ivan S. Konev, attacked out of the Kremenchug bridgehead with six armies and punched a gap in the German front between the right flank of Wöhler's Eighth Army and the left wing of General Hans Valentin Hube's First Panzer Army. Once into the hinterland west of the Dnieper, the long Russian armored columns turned due south and roared straight for Krivoi Rog, the communications, supply, and rail center for Army Group South. Loss of the enormous supply and ammunition dumps at Krivoi Rog, not to mention the considerable number of locomotives and quantities of rolling stock, would have dealt a severe blow to Army Group South's continued powers of mobility and resistance.[56]

By October 18, it appeared that this lucrative prize was within easy reach of Konev's armies. On that day the Russians bowled over the exhausted Fifty-seventh Army Corps, cut the rail line between Dnepropetrovsk and Krivoi Rog, and pulled within striking

---

stantiated these charges, nor did they press for the extradition of Max Simon after the war. In view of SSTK's constant, heavy engagement in combat away from the immediate vicinity of Kharkov in the summer and autumn of 1943, the Soviet allegations appear groundless.

[56] NA/T-313/64/7300819-0825, Pz. AOK 1, Ia., "Tägliche Lagekarten," situation maps for October 16-18, 1943, showing the progress of the Soviet breakthrough and the movement of SSTK to the south in response to it. See also, Manstein, pp. 471-82; Ziemke, pp. 181-84; Philippi and Heim, p. 221; and Carell, *Scorched Earth*, pp. 371-83. A good general account of Army Group South's retreat to the Dnieper in autumn 1943 is in Mellenthin, pp. 241-46, and 247-75.

distance of the latter city. Anxious to keep Krivoi Rog at any cost, Manstein immediately began shuttling in what reserves he had to slow the Soviet advance until he could scrape together enough armor for a strong counterattack sufficient to halt the Russians. The force Manstein rapidly mustered to stop Konev's armies consisted of General Ferdinand Schörner's Fortieth Panzer Corps (the SS Totenkopfdivision, and the Fourteenth and Twenty-fourth Panzer Divisions), plus the remnants of the Ninth and Eleventh Panzer Divisions and the Sixteenth Panzergrenadier Division— six weakened armored formations to blunt the offensive of six enemy armies! On October 27, Fortieth Panzer Corps—led by SSTK—attacked Konev's force in the right flank from positions north of Krivoi Rog; in the week that followed the Totenkopfdivision spearheaded a counterthrust that rolled up and smashed two Soviet armored corps and the bulk of nine rifle divisions. The bloody defeat inflicted upon Konev, who lost over 300 tanks and 5,000 prisoners, threw the Russians back half the distance to the Dnieper and stabilized temporarily the situation along the right-center of Manstein's front. Moreover, when the Russians finally forced the evacuation of Krivoi Rog four months later, the end of February 1944, the Germans were able to take with them most of the supplies, ammunition, vehicles, and rolling stock that otherwise would have fallen into Soviet hands. In its key role during the brief counteroffensive by Fortieth Panzer Corps, the Totenkopfdivision again helped rescue the German position in southern Russia from acute peril.[57]

[57] NA/T-313/63/7299074-9075, 7299050-9053, 7299024-9025, teleprinter messages from Army Group South to the Eighth and First Panzer Armies of October 16, 17, and 18, 1943, outlining Manstein's plans for the deployment of SSTK and Fortieth Panzer Corps in the path of the Soviet advance; NA/T-313/63/ 7298984-8981, 7298978, 7298945, 7298936, 7298928, 7298891, 7298836, 7298738, teleprinter messages from Army Group South to First Panzer Army of October 19, 20, 22, 24, 26, and 28, 1943, discussing the progress of SSTK and Fortieth Panzer Corps against the Soviet forces. USDC, SS Personalakte Becker, "Vorschlag für die Verleihung des Eichenlaubes zum Ritterkreuz des Eisernen Kreuzes, Kurze Begründung und Stellungnahme der Zwischenvorgesetzten," dated September 4, 1944, contains a summary of the successful SSTK action at Krivoi Rog, giving Becker as commander of SSTK credit for the destruction of most of Konev's armor; and ibid., copy of a teleprinter message from Wöhler to Fortieth Panzer Corps of October 30, 1943, praising SSTK for smashing the Russian forces west of the Dnieper. NA/T-313/63/7298677-8682, 7297505-7509,

In the dreary, disaster-filled months that followed the local counteroffensive at Krivoi Rog, the Totenkopfdivision continued to serve as an all-purpose fire brigade, trudging back and forth between the threatened sectors of the southern front in Russia. Throughout November and December 1943, SSTK remained with Hube's First Panzer Army, fighting continuously in the desperate struggle to hold Krivoi Rog and the Dnieper bend. Continued German possession of the city and region was vital, since Hitler insisted that the Seventeenth Army retain its positions in the Crimea. Loss of Krivoi Rog then would have enabled the Russians to cut all rail and communication lines between Army Group South and the German forces in the Crimea, and at that juncture conceivably could have caused another encirclement on the scale of Stalingrad.

The Russians also realized this and acted accordingly. During the first two weeks of November, Konev built up sizable forces northeast of Krivoi Rog, and on November 14 attacked the weakest point in the entire front of the First Panzer Army, the sector held by the 384th Infantry Division; a wide gap was torn in the German lines. Hube responded by detailing SSTK to restore the situation. On November 15, Totenkopf counterattacked the surprised Russians near Bairak and halted the Soviet advance long enough to dig in firmly for repulsing the massive enemy tank attacks that followed between November 18 and 21. In the process, SSTK claimed the destruction of 245 T-34 tanks.

After a short pause to regroup, the Russians on November 25 renewed their effort to plough through SSTK and capture Krivoi Rog. For three days and nights Soviet armor and infantry surged against the thinning ranks of an exhausted SSTK. The expertise of the SS grenadiers and gunners, however, overcame the Russians' numerical superiority. The practiced Totenkopf veterans calmly allowed the T-34s to roll over their forward positions as they concentrated their precise, methodical machine-gun fire to chop down

---

contains the daily reports (Tagesmeldungen) of the First Panzer Army to Army Group South for October 28-November 1, 1943, with tallies of the Russian matériel and manpower losses attributed to the Totenkopfdivision. See also, Manstein, pp. 481-86; Ziemke, pp. 181-84; Seaton, pp. 385-86; and Philippi and Heim, pp. 218-24.

the Russian infantry following. SSTK tank-killer crews in the second line then tackled the unaccompanied T-34s, while entrenched heavy guns and artillery in the third line finished off stray enemy tanks which managed to penetrate that far.[58]

The one-week lull that followed the last attacks on November 28 was only a consequence of yet another Russian build up. At dawn on December 5, 1943, the Soviets renewed their offensive by crushing the remnants of the 384th Division in a swift, overpowering attack against the extreme left wing of the First Panzer Army at the village of Fedorovka, northwest of Krivoi Rog. On December 6, the Russian armor wheeled south into open country, threatening to cut the rail lines into Krivoi Rog while enveloping the city from the northwest. Late on December 6, General Hube ordered SSTK out of its entrenched line between the villages of Spasovo and Novo Praga and into the crisis sector south of Fedorovka, where the SS grenadiers again counterattacked so vigorously that they stunned and for a time halted the Russians. On December 12, Hube shifted the Totenkopfdivision to the Fifty-seventh Corps, which he had ordered to prepare for a large-scale counterattack. On December 19, Hube hurled his SS fire brigade and the Eleventh and Thirteenth Panzer Divisions into a surprise counterthrust whose violence stopped the Russians once

[58] NA/T-313/63/7299441-9448, 7299651-9656; 7299674-9675, 9682, 7299694-9706, 7299764-9766, 7299787-9788, 7299836-9837, 7299869-9870, 7299899-9900, 7299919-9927, 7299934-9939, 7299944-9946, for the morning, interim, evening, and daily reports of the First Panzer Army and the Fifty-second Army Corps (to which SSTK was attached), for the period November 15-28, 1943; and NA/T-313/62/7297510-7517, 7297522-7523, 72977530, 72977549, 72977563-7568, 72977572-7578, 72977583-7587, 72977591-7596, 72977598-7604, 72977615-7626, 72977627-7643, for the radio, telephone, and teleprinter messages exchanged between Army Group South and the First Panzer Army for the same period detailing the step-by-step progress of the Soviet assaults and the vicious, bitter resistance from the units of the Totenkopfdivision.

The successes achieved by SSTK in the Dnieper bend flowed largely from the regularity with which it received replacements of men, supplies, weapons, and equipment. As of November 22, SSTK was one of the strongest divisions in the First Panzer Army, containing three full battalions of panzergrenadiers, one weak (40 percent effective) battalion of tanks, 75 percent of its artillery, 75 percent of its Flak component, 55 percent of the engineer battalion, and nearly full strength supply and support units (NA/T-313/63/7299815, Pz. AOK 1, "Kampfwert der Divisionen, Wochenmeldung," dated November 21, 1943).

more, and again temporarily restored the German front—with Krivoi Rog still beyond the Soviets' grasp.[59]

During the first week of January 1944 Manstein withdrew SSTK from action and sent it north with the elite Grossdeutschland division to attack the southern flank of the Soviet forces trying to envelop Kirovograd. As on previous occasions, the sharp, vicious attacks delivered by Totenkopf units momentarily knocked the Russians off balance, enabling Wöhler to withdraw from Kirovograd in relatively good order and to establish a cohesive front southwest of the city. Working with the still-powerful Grossdeutschland division, SSTK had helped salvage a drastic and potentially disastrous situation.[60]

The Totenkopfdivision remained with the Eighth Army during January and February 1944 as the great Russian winter offensive continued to push the Wehrmacht back toward the western frontiers of the Soviet Union. As had been the case during the retreat to the Dnieper in autumn 1943, General Wöhler chose SSTK to help in the extremely difficult task of covering the Eighth Army's withdrawal southwest from Kirovograd. The objective of Wöhler's planned retreat was to establish another natural defense line along the Bug River. To hold off the Russians until the army could entrench on the Bug for a renewed stand, SSTK during February 1944 fought a continuous series of quick, sharp engagements between Kirovograd and the Bug. In this instance, the disparity between Soviet strength and German weakness was simply too great. The Totenkopfdivision and the other rear-guard units were unable to slow the Russian drive effectively, and the Eighth

[59] NA/T-313/64/7300112-0141, Generalkommando LII A. K., Abt. Ia., K. H. den 15. 1. 1944, "Gefechtsbericht des LII A. K. über die Abwehrschlacht im Raume Nowaja Praga- Werblujushka- Nowogorodka vom 5. 12.-21. 12. 1943"; and NA/T-313/64/7299980-9981, 7300035-0039, 7300052-0068, 7300070-0078, 7300089-0093, 7300229-0237, 7300251, 7300274, 7300328, 7300346, 7300363, 7300393, 7300441, and 7300567 for the morning, interim, evening, and daily reports of the First Panzer Army for the period December 5-21, 1943; and NA/T-313/62/7297650, 7297667-7672, 7297675, 7297687-7688, 7297690, 7297698-7699, and 7297701 for the radio and teleprinter messages between Manstein and Hube concerning the attacks. See also, Ziemke, pp. 226-27.

[60] NA/T-312/64/7581600-1643, "Kriegstagebuch Nr. 3, AOK 8, Ia., vom 1. 1.- 31. 1. 44," for the daily entries tracing SSTK's role in the battle for Kirovograd between January 1 and 7, 1944. See also, Ziemke, pp. 226-27; Seaton, pp. 412-13; Carell, *Scorched Earth*, p. 395; and Mellenthin, pp. 267-74.

Army proved far too weak to hold a continuous front on the Bug.[61]

Therefore, Army Group South was forced during the first week of March 1944 to plan an immediate staged withdrawal further west to the Dniester River—the border between Rumania and the Soviet Union. To insure a solid defensive front on the Dniester, General Wöhler on March 11 had the combat units of SSTK loaded into Luftwaffe transports and airlifted across the Bug to Balta where they were to form the center of the army's defense line along the river. SSTK, however, could only briefly hold Balta and protect the army's approaches to the Dniester. The converging First and Second Ukrainian Fronts of Marshal Malinovsky and General Fyodor I. Tolbukhin were too much for the tottering divisions of the German Sixth and Eighth Armies; the Dniester line was blasted open by the Russians before it could be established. During the first week in April 1944 the armies of Malinovsky and Tolbukhin crossed the Dniester on a wide front and pushed into Rumania. Serving once again as a rear-guard, SSTK during these weeks struggled constantly to escape encirclement while fighting its way westward. On March 30, SSTK began crossing the Dniester in order to deploy on the west bank and protect the withdrawal of German formations over the Dubossary bridge. On April 5, Eighth Army attached SSTK to the Forty-seventh Panzer Corps, the armored rear-guard bearing the brunt of the continued Russian pressure, and for the next three weeks the Totenkopfdivision repeatedly blunted Russian attacks while covering the general withdrawal through Balti to Roman, and thence across the Sireth River to Targul Frumos in the foothills of the Carpathian mountains, where the division entrenched on May 1 in anticipation of yet another Soviet assault.[62]

---

[61] NA/T-312/66/7584797-4900, 7585257-5491, "AOK 8, Ia., Morgen-u. Abendmeldungen der Korps und Armee, Ic- Morgen- Abend- u. Tagesmeldungen d. Armee, sonst. takt. Meldungen unterstellter Verbände, vom 1. 2.- 15. 2. 44, und vom 16. 2.- 29. 2. 44," for the repeated blows SSTK dealt the pursuing Russians. More general discussions of the entire operation are in Ziemke, pp. 282-85; Seaton, pp. 422-23; Clark, pp. 376-79; and Klietmann, pp. 114-15.

[62] NA/T-312/64/7581967-2178, "Kriegstagebuch Nr. 3, AOK 8, Ia., vom 1. 3.- 31. 3. 44," and 7582182-2335, "Kriegstagebuch Nr. 3, AOK 8, Ia., vom 1. 4.-30. 4. 44"; and NA/T-312/66/7585494-5979, "Anlage zum KTB, AOK 8 /Nr.

By this time the Soviet winter and spring offensives had run their course, and both armies, succumbing to fatigue, sat down to rest in the deep mud of the spring thaw. Throughout May and most of June 1944 the Totenkopfdivision experienced a relatively quiet period, broken only by local Russian attacks and by patrols probing the division's defenses. During the two-month lull Himmler managed to find enough replacements and sufficient tanks, guns, and vehicles to cover part of the serious losses the Totenkopfdivision had incurred during the winter of defensive fighting and retreating. Among the 6,000 men sent to Rumania to join the division in May and early June were 1,500 Totenkopf soldiers who had been home on leave or recuperating from wounds, and 4,500 new recruits that Himmler ordered transferred from the then recently formed Sixteenth SS Panzergrenadierdivision Reichsführer SS. The simultaneous arrival of new consignments of tanks, assault guns, artillery pieces, and various types of vehicles also helped restrengthen the Totenkopfdivision for the anticipated renewal of the Russian offensive in June.[63]

To insure the full recovery of SSTK, Wöhler on June 9 pulled the division out of the front line and sent it into reserve for a complete rest during the final stage of refitting. Unfortunately for Wöhler, OKH was equally eager to acquire the services of reliable fire brigades for crisis employment, especially in view of the prevailing uncertainty as to where the next Russian blow would fall. Hitler believed that the main Soviet offensive for the summer of 1944 would be directed against the southern flank of Army Group

---

3) Ia., Morgen- u. Tagesmeldungen der Korps u. Armee, Ic- Morgen- Abend- u. Tagesmeldungen der Armee, sonst. takt. Meldungen unterstellter Verbände vom 1.- 31. 3. 1944"; with good secondary accounts in Ziemke, pp. 282-85, 289-91; Philippi and Heim, pp. 230-34, 238-42; and Seaton, pp. 422-23. The special value General Wöhler placed upon SSTK may be gauged from comments attributed to him. Wöhler reportedly described Totenkopf as a "lightning sword of retribution" and a division that fought with "unshakable fortitude" (Stein, p. 216).

[63] BAMA, III SS, 41/11, "Aktennotiz über Besprechung am 16. April 1944, betr.: Auffrischung der 3. SS-Panzer Division 'Totenkopf' und Fertigstellung der 16. SS-Panzer-Grenadier-Division 'Reichsführer SS.' " The dispatch of 6,000 replacements to SSTK brought the division's ration strength up to approximately 12,000 men. NA/T-312/64/7582413-2477, "Kriegstagebuch Nr. 3, AOK 8, Ia., vom 1. 5.- 31. 5. 44," and 7582481-2592, "Kriegstagebuch Nr. 3, AOK 8, Ia., vom 1. 6.- 30. 6. 44," for the combat activity and refitting of SSTK in the Carpathians in May and June 1944.

Center in Galicia and would be aimed in a northwesterly direction—toward East Prussia and the Baltic coast. Such an offensive was imminent, Hitler insisted, because if successful it would trap both Army Groups Center and North, causing the whole German theater in the east to collapse. Based upon this estimation of Soviet intentions, OKH began extensive unit transfers in June to strengthen Army Groups Center and North.[64]

Before the transfer orders for the Totenkopfdivision were drafted, the Russians launched the first of several massive, awesome summer offensives. On June 22, 1944, the third anniversary of the German invasion of Russia, a collection of Soviet armies larger than the entire force with which Hitler began "Barbarossa" blasted into the positions held by Army Group Center—launching the operation code-named "Bagration." In one week the Russians flattened the entire 200-mile front between Ostrov on the old Soviet-Lithuanian frontier and Kovel on the southwestern edge of the Pripet Marshes. In the three weeks that followed the Soviet assault on Army Group Center, a total of twenty-eight German divisions (about 350,000 men) disappeared permanently beneath the endless waves of Russian tanks and infantry rolling westward toward Poland and East Prussia.[65]

Summoned by OKH to help with the emergency on the central

[64] Ziemke, pp. 313-19; Seaton, pp. 434-35; Philippi and Heim, pp. 246-50; and especially Shtemenko, pp. 222-29, 231-35, for the extensive planning for "Bagration" and the ingenious deceptions the Soviets devised to keep the Germans off-balance and guessing.

[65] From the German side, the best general treatment of the offensive is still Hermann Gackenholz, "The Collapse of Army Group Centre in 1944," in Hans-Adolf Jacobsen and Jürgen Rohwer, eds., *Decisive Battles of World War II: The German View*, trans. Edward Fitzgerald (New York, 1965), pp. 355-82; which is based upon Professor Gackenholz's earlier documentary article, "Zum Zusammenbruch der Heeresgruppe Mitte im Sommer 1944," *Vierteljahrshefte für Zeitgeschichte*, 3 (July 1955), 317-33. Gackenholz was the war diarist for Army Group Center in the summer of 1944. Useful also is Werner Haupt, *Heeresgruppe Mitte, 1941-1945* (Dorheim, West Germany, 1968), esp. pp. 206-24. From the Soviet side, the memoirs of Shtemenko, pp. 238-57; and Rokossovsky, pp. 231-41; are generally thorough and reliable. Good secondary accounts may be found in Ziemke, pp. 329-45; Seaton, pp. 434-44; Carell, *Scorched Earth*, pp. 479-513; Mellenthin, pp. 282-87; Philippi and Heim, pp. 246-51; and Guderian, pp. 267-69. The five Soviet fronts that assaulted Army Group Center (First, Second, and Third Belorussian, and First and Second Baltic) together disposed of 166 infantry divisions and 40 tank brigades.

front, SSTK began its rail journey north on June 25, designated for service with the Fourth Army. The transfer of the division, however, bogged down in the confusing rail bottleneck behind the disintegrating front of Army Group Center. As a result, when the last units of SSTK detrained in eastern Poland on July 7, whence the division had been diverted to catch up with the remnants of the retreating Fourth Army, the entire central sector of the German eastern front had been erased from the map. In an effort to slow the pace of the Russian drive and establish a new front, Hitler gave the command of Army Group Center to his favorite defensive magician, Field Marshal Walter Model. Model started right in reorganizing what was left of the army group, and, to buy time to regain his balance fully, threw the best available divisions into key positions to serve as breakwaters. Accordingly, Model sent the Totenkopfdivision into the city of Grodno with orders to hold at any cost, since the loss of the city would open a hole between the right flank of the Fourth Army to the north and the left wing of what was left of the Second Army to the south. For eleven days, out numbered seven-to-one in men and ten-to-one in armor, SSTK repeatedly stood up to furious Russian attacks. Against the overwhelming superiority enjoyed by the Soviets, however, even the most stubborn resistance gained little, and the Totenkopfdivision slowed the momentum of the offensive only for a time. On July 18, with Model's permission, SSTK abandoned Grodno and withdrew to the southwest to join the mass of German divisions retreating west toward Warsaw.[66]

On July 25, with the Soviet offensive well into Poland, Model once again sent SSTK to a vital sector to stem the enemy advance. The Totenkopfdivision and the armored parachute division "Hermann Göring" were transferred to the newly reactivated Ninth Army and deployed at Siedlce, some fifty miles east of Warsaw on the main highway to the city. Here, SSTK and the Hermann Göring Division held firm for four days against the Soviet Second Tank Army and kept open the escape route to the Vistula River for the divisions of the German Second Army. On July 28, under tremendous Soviet pressure, the two divisions abandoned their defenses at Siedlce and withdrew toward

[66] Ziemke, pp. 319-30; and Klietmann, pp. 114-15.

Warsaw—turning periodically to deliver sharp counterattacks against the spearheads of the Soviet Second Tank Army. For the next eight days SSTK proved invaluable to Model, shielding as it backed slowly toward Warsaw the thousands of fleeing German soldiers who were being halted and reorganized along the Vistula by the Ninth Army.[67]

The Russian reach for Warsaw, which prompted the tragic and ill-fated uprising by the Polish Home Army of General Bor-Komorowski on August 1, marked the high point of the summer offensive.[68] In little more than one month, the Red Army had advanced nearly 450 miles, but in the process had outrun its supplies, exhausted its men, and worn out its tanks and vehicles. The Soviets suffered painfully, too, from the surprising and punishing counterattacks Model delivered east of Warsaw on August 2 and 3, and were briefly stunned to a halt. For the first time during the summer, the prospects for stopping the Russians altogether seemed favorable and Model wasted no time in setting the Waffen SS to the task.

On August 11, the recently organized Fourth SS Panzerkorps

---

[67] NA/T-312/343/7916358-6398, "Kriegstagebuch Nr. 11, AOK 9, 11. 7.- 31. 12. 44," daily entries for the period July 24 to August 10, 1944; and USDC, SS Personalakte Becker, "Vorschlag für die Verleihung des Eichenlaubes . . . Kurze Begründung und Stellungsnahme der Zwischenvorgesetzten," dated September 4, 1944, for a summary of the Totenkopfdivision's role in the defensive fighting around Siedlce. See also, Ziemke, pp. 337-45; Guderian, p. 282; and Philippi and Heim, pp. 253-54.

[68] The rising of the Home Army in Warsaw and the inability or unwillingness of the Red Army to come to Bor-Komorowski's rescue by driving the Germans from the city is still a much-disputed episode. The revolt subsequently was crushed with near indescribable ruthlessness by units of the Waffen SS and the notorious Dirlewanger and Kaminski brigades of SS irregulars. No units from the Totenkopfdivision took part in the gruesome suppression of the Home Army or were responsible for the atrocities committed against citizens of Warsaw during and after the rising. The daily entries in the war diary of the Ninth Army during August 1944, NA/T-312/343/7916354-6517, and a special report on the uprising inserted into the war diary on August 21, NA/T-312/343/7916427-6431, "Zum Warschauer Aufstand," are filled with comments expressing the army's horror and disgust with the behavior of the SS units in Warsaw. The best work on the subject of the Warsaw revolt is still Hans von Krannhals, *Der Warschauer Aufstand 1944* (Frankfurt am Main, 1964). More on SS units involved in crushing the uprising may be found in Stein, pp. 220n, 265-70; Seaton, pp. 454-56; Helmuth Auerbach, "Die Einheit Dirlewanger," *Vierteljahreshefte für Zeitgeschichte*, 10 (July 1962), 250-63; and in Heiber, ed., *Lagebesprechungen*, pp. 625n, 626-27.

(SSTK and the SS Wiking Division), commanded by SS Gruppenführer Herbert Gille, moved north and deployed along a fifteen-mile front between Tłuszcz and Stanislawow, some thirty miles northeast of Warsaw. Model personally ordered the Fourth SS Panzerkorps into this blocking position to meet what he anticipated correctly would be a major renewal of the Soviet thrust to cross the Vistula and envelop Warsaw from the north and west. When the Soviet attacks began on August 14, the SS divisions were well prepared. For seven straight days SSTK and SS Wiking repulsed a combined enemy force of fifteen rifle divisions and two armored brigades who tried to crush the SS Panzerkorps and clear the Wolomin sector.[69]

After pausing to regroup on August 21, the Russians resumed their pounding of the Fourth SS Panzerkorps on August 25—the heaviest blows falling upon SSTK. On August 26, the collective weight of eight rifle divisions, a motorized rifle brigade, and ubiquitous swarms of Russian fighter planes blasted the Totenkopfdivision from its positions east of Wolomin. For the next two weeks, the enormous Soviet force literally bulldozed the SS Panzerkorps slowly west toward Warsaw and the Vistula. On September 11, a locally successful counterattack by SSTK drove the Russian spearheads out of the northeastern Warsaw suburb of Praga—a defensive strongpoint the dazed and gaunt Totenkopf grenadiers then managed to hold until the Russian offensive temporarily spent itself on September 21.[70]

[69] NA/T-312/343/7916398-6425, war diary of the Ninth Army, entries for August 10 through 21, 1944; NA/T-312/343/7917020-6989, "AOK 9, Führungsabteilung, Kriegstagebuch Nr. 11, Anlagenband II, Tägliche Meldungen des AOK, Berichtszeit 11. 7. 44.-31. 10. 44," (microfilmed in calendar reverse), for the daily reports of the Ninth Army; and NA/T-312/343/7917249-7363, "AOK 9, Führungsabteilung, Kriegstagebuch Nr. 11, Anlagenband III, Tägliche Meldungen der Gen. Kdos., Berichtszeit 11. 7. 44.- 31. 8. 44.," for the daily reports of the Fourth SS Panzerkorps describing the Soviet attacks. USDC, SS Personalakte Becker, "Vorschlag . . . Eichenlaubes zum Ritterkreuz," dated September 4, 1944, describes the unprecedented intensity and precision of Soviet artillery fire preceding attacks by the most densely-packed infantry formations the SS had seen. See also, Ziemke, pp. 338-45; and Rokossovsky, pp. 260-66.

[70] NA/T-312/343/7916438-6507, the daily entries in the war diary of the Ninth Army for August 21 through September 21, 1944; and NA/T-312/343/7916931-6966, the daily reports Ninth Army prepared for Army Group Center for the same period.

The ensuing three-week lull around Warsaw ended abruptly on October 10, when the Soviet Fifth Guards Tank Army launched yet another offensive that compelled the Fourth SS Panzerkorps to withdraw about twenty miles northwest to the vicinity of Modlin at the confluence of the Bug and Vistula rivers. Here the front stabilized again when the Russians, who had initiated their assault too early and with insufficient strength, could not punch through the front to envelop and destroy the SS divisions. After persistent and fruitless clubbing of the well-entrenched SS Panzerkorps and the Nineteenth Panzer Division, the Fifth Guards Tank Army abandoned its attacks altogether on October 27 and another quiet period settled over the precarious front held by the Germans northwest of Warsaw. The Totenkopfdivision's exceptional combat performance, noted repeatedly in the war diary of the Ninth Army, did not escape Hitler's attention during these gloomy months. On one occasion Hitler remarked that if he had a few extra battalions to send SSTK the situation might improve, since "whenever one sent them reinforcements [they] always counterattacked successfully."[71]

While the German front in Poland remained stable during autumn 1944, the course of the war throughout the rest of Europe brought the Third Reich to the verge of collapse. The successful Allied landings in Normandy and southern France in June had been followed during July and August by a swift offensive that carried the American, British, and Canadian armies to the western frontier of Germany at the beginning of autumn. In Italy the relentless American and British advance following the capture of Rome in early June steadily pushed the Germans into the northern Apennines, while in the Balkans a renewed Soviet offensive during the summer and autumn overran the rest of Rumania and all of Bulgaria, and forced the Germans to abandon Greece and retreat north through Yugoslavia into Hungary.

The situation changed temporarily in December 1944 when Hitler launched his desperate offensive in the Ardennes, attempting

[71] NA/T-312/343/7916538-7916579, daily entries in the war diary of the Ninth Army for the period October 10 through 27, 1944, and especially those for October 12, 13, 20, and 23. Hitler's remarks about SSTK are quoted in Heiber, ed., *Lagebesprechungen*, "Mittagslage vom 6. November 1944," pp. 676-78.

to regain the initiative and achieve a decisive victory by capturing the main Allied supply port of Antwerp. Hitler's last gamble in the west, however, was a venture far beyond the capacity of the dying Wehrmacht, and only consumed Germany's last reserves of men and weapons. With his armies crumbling, his cities burning, his contempt for his people and distrust of his advisers complete, Hitler faced inevitable catastrophe with the same nihilism that was intrinsic to the Waffen SS ethos: He would destroy Germany and himself rather than yield his power or accept defeat. Thus the end of 1944 marked the incipient death spasm of Nazi Germany—a brief orgy of violence in which the Waffen SS in general and the Totenkopfdivision in particular played a central role.

Even before the end of the calamitous Ardennes campaign Hitler had become preoccupied with the prospect of one last offensive operation against the Russians that would restore his sagging prestige and the German people's faith in final victory. To the consternation of his generals, he picked Hungary as the site for the last offensive by the armed forces of the Third Reich. The German counterthrust, he directed, was to break the Soviet encirclement of Budapest—which had been completed on December 24—and reestablish contact with the German defenders trapped in the city (mainly Waffen SS troops under the command of SS Obergruppenführer Karl Pfeffer-Wildenbruch). At Hitler's personal order, the force earmarked to recapture Budapest was Herbert Gille's Fourth SS Panzerkorps (SSTK and SS Wiking). Accordingly, the two SS divisions were pulled out of the line northwest of Warsaw on December 26 and shuttled by train through Prague, Vienna, and Bratislava to Komarno in western Hungary, where they detrained and deployed for attack on December 31, 1944.[72]

The assault toward Budapest by the Totenkopfdivision and SS

---

[72] NA/T-312/343/7916662-6663, entries in the war diary of the Ninth Army for December 25-26, 1944, concerning the withdrawal of SSTK from Warsaw; Stein, pp. 233-37; Seaton, p. 500; Ziemke, pp. 383-86; Guderian, p. 313; and Heiber, ed., *Lagebesprechungen*, "Mittagslage vom 10. Januar 1945 im Adlerhorst," p. 803n. Hitler's decision to attack in Hungary with his best SS divisions was motivated partly by his desire to protect the oilfields and refineries around Lake Balaton—with the smaller Austrian fields the last source of fuel for the Wehrmacht (Weingartner, p. 133; and Seaton, p. 536).

Wiking began at dawn on New Year's Day, but carried only a few miles before it was halted by the Soviet Fourth Guards and Sixth Guards Tank Armies. For the next ten days the attack continued, grinding forward at a pace of approximately one mile per day. By January 11, the two SS divisions had suffered such losses that the relief attempt faltered altogether and was postponed.[73]

In the meantime, Hitler became even more insistent that Budapest be recaptured, and on January 8, he ordered Sepp Dietrich's Sixth SS Panzer Army transferred from the western front to Hungary. At the same time, however, he insisted that Gille's exhausted and severely weakened Fourth SS Panzerkorps resume its offensive against Budapest without waiting for Dietrich. At Hitler's direction, SSTK and SS Wiking were moved into the area between Budapest and Lake Balaton and instructed to attack to the northeast until they crossed the Danube and relieved the city.[74]

This second relief attack began on January 18 and resulted in surprising (but impermanent) progress. By the nineteenth, SSTK and SS Wiking had advanced forty miles toward Budapest and captured the town of Dunapentele on the Danube. On the following day, however, enemy resistance stiffened and the Russians held until a counteroffensive on January 27 by the Soviet Twenty-sixth and Forty-sixth Armies ended permanently the Fourth SS Panzerkorps' ill-fated attempt to recapture Budapest. The force of the Soviet blow knocked SSTK and SS Wiking momentarily off balance, but they soon managed to reestablish a cohesive defense-front north of Lake Balaton in the Bakony forest. In the cover of this dense woods, the Totenkopfdivision dug in, held against Soviet probing attacks, and awaited the Sixth SS Panzer Army, which was still in transit from the west.[75]

[73] KTB/OKW, vol. 4, pt. 2, pp. 977, 979, 987, 995, 1001, 1004, 1006; Ziemke, pp. 433-35; Seaton, p. 500; Stein, pp. 233-34; Philippi and Heim, pp. 268-70; and the thorough and detailed account in Peter Gosztony, *Der Endkampf an der Donau, 1944/45* (Vienna, 1969), pp. 116-44.

[74] Ziemke, pp. 434-37; and Philippi and Heim, pp. 268-70. Weingartner, p. 133, illuminates part of Fourth SS Panzerkorps' subsequent difficulties by pointing out that Hitler did not finally make up his mind to effect the transfer until January 20, 1945.

[75] Ziemke, pp. 434-37; Seaton, pp. 500-501; Gosztony, pp. 214-44; Philippi and Heim, pp. 268-70; and Weingartner, pp. 133-35, for the delays and tortuous progress of Dietrich's SS panzer army while in transit to Hungary. See also the

When the last of the divisions in Dietrich's SS army reached Hungary at the beginning of March 1945, plans were completed for the launching of operation "Frühlingserwachen" (Awakening of Spring), the code-name for the last attempt by the strongest formations left in the Waffen SS to drive the Russians away from the oilfields around Lake Balaton and throw them back across the Danube. The SS offensive began at midnight on March 5 from positions on the northern and southern ends of the lake and proceeded the next day in a southwesterly direction toward the Danube. For the Totenkopfdivision, "Frühlingserwachen" soon turned into a death ride. During the first three days of the operation, the SS divisions under Dietrich's command—including Fourth SS Panzerkorps and SSTK—managed to pierce the Russian lines, and by March 9 had advanced an average of twenty miles from their jumping-off points.[76]

On March 13, however, the offensive was halted by the combined effect of stiff Soviet resistance and melting snow that turned the primitive roads and surrounding countryside into an impassible mudhole. With perfect timing the Russians chose this moment to regain the initiative, and on March 16 Marshal Tolbukhin's Third Ukrainian Front went over to the offensive against the thin line held by the Sixth SS Panzer Army. That afternoon the Russian steamroller (Ninth Guards Tank Army) literally pressed the Totenkopfdivision into the mud and drove en masse into the rear of the Fourth SS Panzerkorps west of Lake Balaton. By March 17, the Russians were breaking through all along the line, and Sepp Dietrich was forced—despite contrary hysterical orders from Hitler—to authorize a general retreat toward the Austrian frontier.[77]

During the second half of March and the first week in April 1945, the remnants of the Totenkopfdivision withdrew slowly up the main highway to Bratislava and Vienna with the rump of what had been the Sixth SS Panzer Army. On April 3, SSTK halted in

---

daily summaries of the fighting in KTB/OKW, vol. 4, pt. 2, pp. 1020, 1022, 1027, 1037, 1045, 1047-48, 1050, and 1061.

[76] Stein, pp. 236-37; Weingartner, pp. 135-36; Ziemke, pp. 450-52; Gosztony, pp. 247-77; and KTB/OKW, vol. 4, pt. 2, pp. 1146, 1151, 1161, 1169.

[77] Stein, pp. 236-37; Weingartner, pp. 135-36; and KTB/OKW, vol. 4, pt. 2, pp. 1179-80, 1182, 1187, 1194-95, 1198.

the southern suburbs of Vienna as the Second and Third Ukrainian Fronts of Marshals Malinovsky and Tolbukhin converged on the city from the east and south. After more than four years of almost continuous fighting against the Russians, the elite Waffen SS divisions (including SSTK) finally had their fighting spirit broken and offered no more than a feeble gesture of resistance against Malinovsky's drive that captured Vienna. Following several days of sporadic skirmishing, the surviving units of Dietrich's SS panzer army withdrew from Vienna and retired to the west toward Linz. On April 13 the Russians captured the city, and the Sixth Guards Tank Army deployed west of Vienna in anticipation of a German counterattack. There was, however, no fight left in any of the SS divisions.[78]

When the Soviets relaxed their pressure against the Sixth SS Panzer Army on April 15 and shifted the weight of their offensive north into Czechoslovakia, the war came to an end for those left in the Totenkopfdivision. During the second two weeks of April, SS Brigadeführer Hellmuth Becker, the last commander of SSTK, led his surviving units to Linz as the final act in the drama of Nazi Germany unfolded in Berlin. On May 9, Becker attempted to surrender to the American Third Army. His offer was at first accepted upon condition that the SSTK units disarm the remaining SS guard formations in the nearby Mauthausen concentration camp. After complying with the American demands, Becker and his men surrendered to the Third Army only to be handed over forthwith to the Russians. As a consequence, Becker, most of his officers, and many of the men left in the Totenkopfdivision suffered a fate grimmer even than their long ordeal in the Russian war.[79]

[78] Weingartner, pp. 137-39; Ziemke, pp. 454-56; Philippi and Heim, pp. 282-83, 287-88; and KTB/OKW, vol. 4, pt. 2, pp. 1206-7, 1209, 1217, 1219, 1221, 1225, 1227-28, 1231.

[79] Immediately after their seizure by the Russians on May 9-10, 1945, the officers and men in the Totenkopfdivision were transported to several detention camps inside the Soviet Union. Within six months of the end of the war, many prominent SSTK officers, including Becker, disappeared, most likely the victims of secret executions. These undocumented assumptions about the fate of Becker and other missing SSTK officers were given to this writer during the Koblenz interviews of June 19-20, 1972. All three former Totenkopf soldiers in question were with the division at the end of the war. All spent varying periods in Soviet prison camps and claimed to have learned independently of the execution of Becker and other SSTK officers through the prisoner grapevine in Russia.

14. SS Bridgadeführer Hellmuth Becker (standing, foreground), last commander of the Totenkopfdivision before its attempted surrender to the American Third Army in 1945.

CHAPTER NINE

Some Observations: Ideology, Personality, and the Question of Totenkopf Criminality

T HE Totenkopfdivision's performance during the Second World War rightfully earned it a contemporary reputation as one of the most powerful formations in the German armed forces. In the French campaign of 1940 and in the assault on the Soviet Union the following spring, SSTK performed with considerable distinction in several crucial battles. From June 1941 until May 1945, with the sole exception of the three-month respite for rest and refitting in France in late 1942, the Death's Head Division fought exclusively against the Red Army. In the battle of the Demyansk pocket, on the Donetz and at Kharkov, in the battles of Kursk and Krivoi Rog, and finally in the defense of Warsaw and Budapest, the Totenkopfdivision maintained a consistent, exemplary, and remarkable combat record as a determined, fanatical, and extraordinarily effective instrument of war.[1]

As one of the original Waffen SS divisions formed during the autumn of 1939, the Totenkopfdivision also made a significant contribution to the wartime development of the armed SS. When Hitler ordered the number of SS divisions doubled after the first winter of the Russian campaign, hundreds of seasoned SS staff officers and unit commanders had to be found to make the new formations combat worthy. Many of the men chosen for these new assignments were SS officers who had distinguished themselves while serving with the Totenkopfdivision. According to the

[1] Equally impressive are the number of awards and decorations won by officers and men in SSTK. Between the summer of 1941 and the spring of 1945, forty-seven men in the Totenkopfdivision were awarded the Ritterkreuz (Knight's Cross), one of Nazi Germany's most coveted decorations for gallantry in combat. Eight of these men (all officers) also received the accompanying Oak Leaves for further heroism. Moreover, two among them (Georg Bochmann and Otto Baum) were awarded diamonds to their Oak Leaves, making them among the most highly decorated German soldiers of the war. See especially the individual biographical information on the officers and men in SSTK who received the Ritterkreuz, in Krätschmer, *Die Ritterkreuzträger der Waffen SS*.

most reliable statistics available, at least nine men who held key staff posts or were regimental or battalion commanders in SSTK during the first two years of the war subsequently became commanders of other Waffen SS divisions. Three from this same group—Max Simon, Hermann Priess, and Georg Keppler—also rose to the level of corps commanders among the fifteen Waffen SS corps that were organized before the end of the war; one of the nine, Heinz Lammerding, became chief of staff to Himmler's Army Group Vistula during the apocalyptic spring of 1945.[2]

This general record of combat achievement, however, was easily matched by the Totenkopfdivision's wartime reputation for brutality. The massacre by its units of 100 British prisoners at Le Paradis during the battle of France was the first recorded combat atrocity by a Waffen SS division. The Totenkopfdivision's own records, moreover, indicate that its officers ordered the murder of Senegalese and Moroccan soldiers later during the French campaign, and reveal that Eicke's men zealously carried out Hitler's commissar order at least through the first year of the Russian war.[3] In the summer of 1942, while still engaged in the Demyansk salient, units of SSTK also assisted in selecting and deporting captured Russian soldiers to the Reich for forced labor.[4]

In short, like the other crack formations of the Waffen SS, the wartime experience of the Totenkopfdivision was characterized by its ability to retain both its fighting spirit and combat effectiveness in defeat as well as victory, and by its utterly ruthless behavior in the execution of political and military tasks against enemy civilians and soldiers. The enduring presence of these qualities—especially in the Russian conflict—raises one of the most basic, and certainly the most difficult, questions relative to the Totenkopfdivision's role in the war: namely, what influences were decisive in producing such qualities and in molding the Death's Head

[2] USDC, SS Personalakte of Georg Keppler, Max Simon, Karl Ullrich, Matthias Kleinheisterkamp, Georg Bochmann, Otto Baum, Hermann Priess, Hellmuth Becker, and Heinz Lammerding, the Dienstlaufbahn of each.

[3] See above, chapters four and six.

[4] BAMA, III SS, 42/2, Tagesbefehle, Telegrammen, und besondere Anordnungen für die Versorgung, pp. 301-6. After he was wounded near Opochka and sent home for a lengthy convalescence, Eicke helped organize and direct the mass murder of about 18,000 Russian POWs in the Sachsenhausen camp between the middle of August and the middle of October 1941 (SS im Einsatz: Eine Dokumentation über die Verbrechen der SS [East Berlin, 1960], pp. 212-14, 220).

Division into the political and military instrument that performed and behaved as it did?

Part of the answer may lie in two interrelated phenomena: the ideological legacy of the prewar concentration camp system, and the energetic and fanatical style of leadership manifested by Eicke and the other important personalities in the SSTK officer corps. During the five years he ran the prewar concentration camp system, Eicke selected for his staff and camp guard units those SS officers who shared his extremism: he charged them with the indoctrination of the young Death's Head recruits who subsequently became the cadre of the Totenkopfdivision. The essence of the camp indoctrination was threefold. The SS recruit was drilled to obey without question every order, no matter how harsh. He learned to hate absolutely the "enemies behind the wire" as subhumans who were a lethal political and racial threat to the security of the Reich. And finally, from his superiors and from the example set by Eicke, he acquired a sense of esprit and camaraderie built around the theme that the Totenkopfverbände, with the responsibility of guarding the most dangerous enemies of the state and the racial community, constituted an elite within the SS. This particular point was most important to Eicke because of the stigma, even within the prewar SS, attached to concentration camp duty.[5]

When Eicke and the bulk of his camp personnel became the nucleus of the Totenkopfdivision in October 1939, these characteristics went with them and became the ethos of the new SS division. The gist of the concentration camp indoctrination program, with two slight variations, remained the same and became what amounted to the ideology of the Totenkopfdivision. The former "enemy behind the wire" became the mortal wartime political and racial foe beyond the frontier, and the established concept of Totenkopf elitism was expanded to incorporate the military virtues of self-sacrifice, contempt for cowardice and hardship, and the glory of death in battle.[6]

---

[5] Eicke's orders and guidelines for the ideological training of the prewar camp guards are in BAKO, NS-3/448, Befehlsblätter und Rundschreiben des Führers der SS Totenkopfverbände und Konzentrationslager.

[6] BAKO, NS-34/15, "Alfred Franke-Gricksch, Ic., SS-T.Div., Denkschrift über weltanschauliche Führung in der SS," dated February 10, 1941. This

In Russia, the Totenkopf soldier's previous SS experience and training perfectly suited the savage character of the conflict that epitomized the destructive nature of National Socialism. To Eicke's men the Soviet soldier was depicted as an Asiatic, Jewish-Bolshevik subhuman who personified the most treacherous and dangerous of enemies—the worst of those diabolical forces that would destroy the Reich and the German people unless annihilated. Exposure to the ethnic diversity and the vicious resistance of the Red Army simply reinforced this image. With their own indifference to hardship, contempt for death, and genuine hatred of the "Jewish-Bolshevik" enemy, the products of Eicke's tutelage developed a lust for killing Russians and fought with a corresponding tenacity that earned them the unqualified respect of professional soldiers like Manstein and Busch, or Wöhler and Model. Until its fighting spirit was broken at the very end of the war, the Totenkopfdivision's code of conduct corresponded almost precisely with the injunction to annihilate the enemy in combat. The natural corollaries, also hallmarks of Totenkopf wartime behavior, included the burning of villages, the murder of prisoners, and the summary execution of captured commissars and politruks.[7]

Until Eicke's death in action, these facets of the division's behavior were both strengthened and complemented by his style of division command. Even after his death the specter of Eicke's

---

memorandum sent to Himmler by the young intelligence officer (Ic) of SSTK is a most revealing piece of evidence on the ideological atmosphere in the Totenkopfdivision. The memorandum is subtly critical of the crude and harsh emphasis upon hatred of racial enemies and obedience to orders that Franke-Gricksch describes as the staple of political indoctrination in SSTK. The document concludes with an appeal that Himmler revise the ideological training in the SS to include an emphasis upon what Franke-Gricksch calls the great political, economic, and geographical issues the SS soldier needed to know to be a convinced National Socialist.

[7] See chapter six for summaries of the speeches Eicke delivered to his officers on the eve of the Russian campaign, and a description of the reaction by SSTK units to the suicidal resistance of the Red Army. Despite his exhortations to kill the enemy without pity, Eicke was careful to conceal the specifics of the ruthlessness with which SSTK fought in Russia. Before the invasion, he ordered that all matters of military and political sensitivity not be transmitted in writing, and that any written communications which might reflect badly on the division be destroyed rather than deposited in the SSTK records (BAMA, III SS, 41/7, vol. 3, p. 60, for Eicke's secrecy orders).

personality remained a dominant influence upon the Totenkopfdivision. Two of his three successors as division commander,
Max Simon and Hellmuth Becker, were his most devoted protégés and closest personal friends. Both had served with Eicke in
the concentration camps, and each had earned his complete confidence and trust. Both had been hand-picked by Eicke to command
SSTK infantry regiments in the Russian campaign, and each had
performed with the measure of ruthlessness and bravery he expected. Their long association with Eicke and SSTK and their
outstanding combat records prompted Himmler to give them
command of the Totenkopfdivision at different times during the
last two years of the war.[8]

Consequently, though neither Simon nor Becker commanded
the measure of personal devotion, fear, and respect that Eicke
had, their tenure as SSTK commanders was punctuated by a similar style of leadership and by the same kind of Totenkopf combat
performance. As an SS division commander, Max Simon earned
the special distinction of being condemned to death as a war criminal by both the Russians and the British. The unsubstantiated
Russian charges stemmed from atrocities Simon allegedly ordered
during the German withdrawal from Kharkov in the autumn of
1943. His conviction by the British resulted from the shooting of
Italian civilians he sanctioned while leading the Sixteenth SS Panzergrenadierdivision Reichsführer SS on the Arno front in August
1944. He subsequently served less than six years in prison.[9]

Hellmuth Becker's excesses in Russia before and during his
stint as commander of the Totenkopfdivision were bad enough to
embarrass even the SS. Before he became SSTK commander in
July 1944, complaints of his sexual and military misconduct by
former subordinates had provoked Himmler to launch an investigation. Though the inquiry continued on and off for the rest of the
war, Himmler was unable to punish Becker or even prevent him
from obtaining command of the Totenkopfdivision. Becker's

---

[8] USDC, SS Personalakte of Max Simon and Hellmuth Becker, especially the
Dienstlaufbahn of each, and the efficiency reports and recommendations for pro-
motions and medals for each written by Eicke before and during the war.

[9] Stein, p. 273; and the charges by the Soviet prosecutor at Nuremberg in
TMWC, vol. 22, p. 328. Accounts of Simon's conviction for the killings in northern Italy are in Stein, pp. 276, 280-81; and Reitlinger, *The SS*, pp. 245n, 450.

combat successes, the attrition of capable SS field commanders, and finally Hitler's personal admiration all combined to keep Becker in command of SSTK until the end of the war.[10]

Such individual actions and unit characteristics as those described above figured prominently in the Nuremberg Tribunal's decision to include the Waffen SS in its condemnation of the SS as a criminal organization. This controversial step established the basis for the whole postwar debate over the nature of the Waffen SS, the extent of its relationship to the general SS organization, and the degree of its involvement in the crimes attributed to the SS.

In general, two sharply contrasting views of the Waffen SS have emerged in the literature of its critics and its apologists. Among the critics,[11] a group including American and British scholars and younger historians and journalists in West Germany, the consensus is that the armed SS was responsible for its share of SS criminality, and was at least nominally a functioning part of the vast conglomerate of organizations that constituted the SS.[12] The critical view has been vociferously—and in West Germany

[10] USDC, SS Personalakte Becker, letter from Maximilien von Herff, chief of the SS Personalhauptamt, to Hans Jüttner bearing the heading "Vorkomnisse im Regt. 'Theodor Eicke,' " and dated October 30, 1943; and Jüttner's reply to Herff of November 1, 1943, indicating that Himmler already had the matter under investigation. The allegations against Becker, which included charges that he publicly raped Russian women and was insensibly drunk while in front-line command, were detailed in a lengthy letter and deposition sent to Herff on October 21, 1943 by Dr. K. H. Bockhorn, who had been a regimental surgeon in the Totenkopfdivision. In the deposition, Bockhorn listed eight other former Totenkopf officers who were willing to testify against Becker in court-martial, including Herff's deputy Alfred Franke-Gricksch. When the matter reached his desk, the puritanical Himmler was horrified by Bockhorn's charge that Becker organized and led an orgy in his regimental officers' canteen in France at Christmas 1942. While drunk, Becker allegedly splintered furniture and smashed windows, then rode a horse to death in the canteen before the fornicating revelers. Bockhorn also charged that Becker kept prostitutes in his forward command post in the Ukraine in the spring of 1943, and that to celebrate Hitler's birthday in April 1943, a drunken Becker ordered a ten-minute salvo salute to the führer from all the heavy guns in his regiment, thereby wasting precious ammunition and forcing the men in adjacent units to take cover.

[11] *TMWC*, vol. 22, pp. 512-17, for the tribunal's judgment against the SS. See also the previously cited works by Stein; Höhne; Krausnick, *Anatomie*; and Reitlinger, *The SS*.

[12] The best discussion of Waffen SS criminality remains, Stein, chapter ten, "The Tarnished Shield: Waffen SS Criminality," pp. 250-81.

quite effectively—challenged by a long publishing campaign sponsored by an organization known as the Mutual Aid Society of the Waffen SS (Hilfsorganization auf Gegenseitigkeit der Waffen SS, or HIAG). For twenty years HIAG has lobbied vigorously with the Bonn government for a full rehabilitation of the Waffen SS, and has underwritten the publication of a stream of tendentious memoirs and books by former SS generals and right-wing academics sympathetic to the Waffen SS.[13]

The thematic gist of the apologist literature has been that the Waffen SS was an organization separate, independent, and distinct from the SS; that Waffen SS officers held Himmler in contempt and frequently disobeyed his orders; and that the men of the armed SS, as front-line soldiers, were in no way associated with or responsible for the crimes committed by other SS agencies in the Reich and in occupied Europe. The effect has been the establishment of the view, widely held in nonacademic circles in West Germany today, that the Waffen SS was simply a fighting force little different from the German army, and that the men who served in the armed SS were "soldiers just like any others."[14]

The apparent dilemma posed by these widely differing views of the Waffen SS can be resolved partially through a simple examination of the Totenkopfdivision's experience in relation to the

[13] For a bibliographical summary of the apologist literature up to 1965, see especially Stein, pp. 250-58; and the same author's "The Myth of a European Army," *Wiener Library Bulletin*, 19 (April 1965), 21-22. At present, the main outlet in West Germany for the publication of pro-Waffen-SS literature is the Munin Verlag in Osnabrück.

[14] The title and theme of Paul Hausser's *Soldaten wie Andere Auch: Der Weg der Waffen SS* (Osnabrück, 1966). Among the most important works of apologist literature are the books by former Waffen SS Generals Paul Hausser, Felix Steiner, and Kurt Meyer. Hausser was also the author of *Waffen SS im Einsatz*, one of the earliest and most influential works demanding rehabilitation of the Waffen SS. The late Felix Steiner's books, *Die Freiwilligen: Idee und Opfergang* (Göttingen, 1958), and *Die Armee der Geächteten* (Göttingen, 1963), also were important in stressing the theme of a purely military Waffen SS. Kurt Meyer's popular *Grenadiere* (Munich, 1957), is perhaps the boldest and most truculent of the apologist works, arguing flatly that the Waffen SS was never involved in the commission of crimes. At present, apologist literature in general achieves its widest circulation through the HIAG-sponsored monthly magazine *Der Freiwillige*, published by the Munin Verlag in Osnabrück, which features articles about Waffen SS history, reminiscences by former SS generals, news of activities and gatherings of local SS veterans' chapters, and elaborate obituaries of prominent members.

various charges and assertions of the critics and apologists. In particular, the evidence available for tracing the movement of personnel between SSTK and the other agencies of the SS, and the materials at hand detailing the extent of the division's administrative subordination to the SS flatly and overwhelmingly contradict the apologist thesis.

To begin with, the fact that officers and men from the Totenkopfdivision ordered and committed criminal actions is indisputable. In addition to the Le Paradis episode, the murder of Black soldiers in France, and the shooting of commissars in Russia, the Totenkopfdivision was linked indirectly to crimes committed by other Waffen SS formations. In each case, the atrocity in question was ordered by a senior SS officer who had served in and been toughened by the Totenkopfdivision. The best illustrations of this point are the post-SSTK careers of Heinz Lammerding and Hermann Priess.

After joining the Totenkopfdivision in the autumn of 1939, Lammerding's rise to prominence in the Waffen SS was rapid. From his command of the engineer battalion of SSTK, Eicke picked him in December 1940 to be operations officer of SSTK. In July 1943, after four years of uninterrupted service with the division, Himmler selected Lammerding to be chief of staff to Erich von dem Bach-Zelewski's armed SS antipartisan forces. In this capacity, Lammerding planned and helped conduct a series of extensive "cleansing actions" in the Pripet Marshes during the summer and autumn of 1943 that claimed the lives of 15,000 Soviet partisans and resulted in the indiscriminate shooting of an undetermined number of Russian civilians. As a reward for Lammerding's success with Bach-Zelewski, Himmler in the early spring of 1944 gave Lammerding command of the SS division Das Reich.

In May 1944 Lammerding led Das Reich, then refitting in southern France, in the infamous "Blood and Ashes" drive against French resistance groups in the Auvergne. During the operation he had ninety-nine suspected members of the resistance publicly hanged. A month later, while enroute to the Normandy front, Lammerding sanctioned the burning of the village of

320

Oradour-sur-Glane and the massacre of its inhabitants in reprisal for the killing of an SS officer by a resistance sniper. After the war, a French court in Bordeaux tried and sentenced Lammerding to death for both the Tulle and Oradour massacres. At the time of his death in January 1971, the French were still trying without success to force Lammerding's extradition from the Federal Republic of Germany.[15]

SS Gruppenführer Hermann Priess, who commanded the Totenkopfdivision for nine months before taking over the Leibstandarte SS Adolf Hitler in the spring of 1944, was one of the main defendants in the postwar trial of a group of SS officers for the murder of American prisoners at Malmedy, Belgium, during the Battle of the Bulge.[16] It is impossible to avoid the revealing observation that five of the most widely publicized and well substantiated atrocities attributed to the Waffen SS—the massacres of Le Paradis, Tulle, Oradour-sur-Glane, Malmedy, and the reprisal killings on the Arno initiated by Max Simon—were either the work of Totenkopfdivision units or were associated with men whose personal gospel of savagery was at least a partial outgrowth of their experience in the Totenkopfdivision.

In another and more serious vein, there is a mass of evidence relative to the participation by men who served with SSTK in a wide variety of nonmilitary and criminal activities. One of the most serious charges made against the Waffen SS is the claim that men from its ranks served with the infamous Einsatzgruppen (the mobile killing units that operated behind the Russian front and shot or gassed nearly a half-million Jews and suspected parti-

[15] USDC, SS Personalakte Lammerding, Dienstlaufbahn, for Lammerding's transfers and commands subsequent to leaving the Totenkopfdivision; and Stein, p. 276; and Reitlinger, pp. 400-401 for accounts of the Oradour massacre. The version in Stein is based upon the action report on the shootings compiled by the 4th SS Panzergrenadier Regiment of SS Das Reich, a document reproduced completely in Reimund Schnabel, ed., *Macht ohne Moral: Eine Dokumentation über die SS* (Frankfurt am Main, 1957), p. 493. The inability of the French to obtain custody of Lammerding resulted from his trial and conviction as a war criminal by a German court. After serving his prison term in West Germany, Lammerding was automatically immune from extradition under the Bonn constitution's ban on the deportation of German citizens previously convicted of war crimes by German courts. See the story, "The Lammerding Affair," *Time*, 11 Jan. 1971, p. 22.

[16] USDC, SS Personalakte Priess, Dienstlaufbahn; Stein, pp. 278-80; and Weingartner, pp. 127-28.

15. Himmler with Hermann Priess (left), successor to Max Simon as Totenkopfdivision commander, and Otto Baum (right), during an inspection visit to the division in the summer of 1943.

sans).[17] In the specific case of the Totenkopfdivision this allegation is true. In August 1941 Einsatzgruppe A, whose territorial jurisdiction encompassed the Baltic States, began extensive killing operations in the rear area of Army Group North. At that time, the total strength of the Einsatzgruppe was 990 men—340 of whom were Waffen SS soldiers belonging to a unit designated "Waffen SS Battalion zur besondere Verwendung." In October 1941, when the Totenkopfdivision's losses became serious and the need for replacements acute, a whole company from the battalion serving with Einsatzgruppe A was transferred to the Totenkopfdivision and incorporated into SSTK/I. R. 3 for immediate combat duty.[18]

Far more extensive were the Totenkopfdivision's wartime associations with the concentration and extermination camp system. In the spring of 1941, a permanent home-administration to handle problems involving personnel, pay, and benefits for soldiers in the Totenkopfdivision was established in the Dachau camp and housed there for the remainder of the war.[19] The records of the Totenkopfdivision, moreover, contain numerous references to the receipt of a wide variety of supplies, especially clothing, from the workshops in the concentration camps at Dachau and Oranienburg. In addition, the reserve Death's Head formations organized

[17] See especially, Hilberg, pp. 177-256; Dawidowicz, pp. 120-21, 125-28; Stein, pp. 263-64; and Joseph Tenenbaum, "The Einsatzgruppen," *Jewish Social Studies*, 17 (1955), pp. 43-64.

[18] Identification of the Waffen SS company transferred from Einsatzgruppe A to SSTK is made in *Unsere Ehre Heisst Treue: Kriegstagebuch des Kommandostabes RFSS: Tätigkeitsberichte der 1. und 2. SS Inf. Brigade, der SS Kav. Brigade, und von Sonderkommandos der SS* (Vienna, 1965), pp. 231-33. BAKO, R-70/Sowjetunion/31, fol. 1-215, Tätigkeits- und Lageberichte der Einsatzgruppen der Sicherheitspolizei und des SD in der UdSSR vom 15. 9. 1941 bis 31. 3. 1942, especially "Gesamtstarke der Einsatzgruppe A am 1. Februar 1942," documents the continued heavy reliance of the Einsatzgruppen upon Waffen SS personnel to do the actual killing.

At the time the Waffen SS company was transferred to SSTK from the killing operations, Einsatzgruppe A had liquidated over 125,000 Jews. During the same period, a battalion commander in the Totenkopfdivision, SS Standartenführer Herbert Wachsmann, transferred as a Kampfgruppe commander to the First SS Infantry Brigade and served during that unit's big antipartisan sweeps and killing operations in northern Russia during the winter of 1941-1942 (USDC, SS Personalakte Wachsmann, Dienstlaufbahn).

[19] BAKO, NS-7/437, "Errichtung einer Heimatverwaltung für die SS-T. Div.," dated March 11, 1941.

to guard and administer the concentration camps after the creation of SSTK frequently served as a source of replacements for the Totenkopfdivision and for other SS field divisions.[20]

The movement of SS personnel of all ranks back and forth between the Totenkopfdivision and the concentration camps during the war was constant. In the period before the invasion of the Soviet Union, most of the men sent from the Totenkopfdivision to the guard units in the camps were transferred for individual reasons—usually as punishment.[21] Transfers from the concentration camps to the Totenkopfdivision during this same period were less frequent and generally involved small groups or individuals who possessed certain skills (mechanics, radio operators, doctors, etc.) required by the units of the Totenkopfdivision. Since such transfers were listed individually in the SSTK records, a large portion of which did not survive the war, the total number of men transferred from the camps to SSTK, or vice versa, cannot be determined. On the other hand, surviving documentary material does make it possible to estimate with reasonable accuracy the number of personnel exchanges between the camps and SSTK for certain periods of the war.

Between October 1939 and March 1941, for example, an in-

[20] BAMA, III SS, 42/1, pp. 73-76; 42/2, pp. 121, 465-78; and BAKO, NS-19/370, order from the SS Führungshauptamt headed "Auflösung des SS Inf. Rgts. 14," dated June 17, 1941. See also, BAKO, NS-19/374, circulars from Himmler to all SS units dated November 2 and 23, 1940, announcing the dissolution of SS Totenkopf Regiments 9 and 15, and the transfer of Totenkopf Regiment 14 from Buchenwald to the occupied Netherlands. Upon the disbanding of SSTV 9 and 15, one battalion from each was detailed for concentration camp guard duty to replace men being sent to the Totenkopfdivision. SS Totenkopf Regiment 14, which moved from Holland to Poland in the spring of 1941, murdered a number of Jews and Polish civilians in the Lublin district in June 1941 while expropriating farm animals and agricultural produce (BAKO, NS-19/370, SS IR 14[mot.], "Erfahrungsbericht über Zwangsweise Eintreibung von Getreide, Kartoffeln, usw. . . . im Distrikt Lublin," dated June 10, 1941).

[21] Eicke's practice of sending SS officers from the Totenkopfdivision back to the guard units in the concentration camps as punishment ran counter to official policy about the camp system and its wartime role. In the autumn of 1939, SS publications stressed at length the view that guard duty in the camps was no less soldierly or important than service in the front lines. The SS Totenkopf units guarding and running the camps were depicted as heroic detachments filled with exemplary SS men performing an invaluable service by protecting Germany from the internal enemies incarcerated in the concentration camps (IFZ, *Das Schwarze Korps*, 21 Dec. 1939, pp. 9-10).

complete transfer list notes a total of twenty-two SS officers sent from the Totenkopfdivision to the concentration camps.[22] In addition, individual announcements of transfers of other officers, NCOs, and SS men listed in the surviving records for the same period indicate that at least another fifty-five men were transferred from Eicke's division to the various concentration camps.[23] Since the records of SSTK for these years are incomplete, the approximate figure of seventy-seven men transferred to the camps may be taken as a conservative estimate.

After the Totenkopfdivision's first summer in the Russian campaign, when soaring casualty figures caused an urgent demand for replacements, the direction of the personnel movement between SSTK and the camps changed. Larger numbers of SS men—sometimes whole battalions—from the reserve Totenkopf regiments in the concentration camps were transferred to the Totenkopfdivision to fill depleted combat units. By August 1942, Eicke had taken so many men from the concentration camps that the guard units were being filled with older SS men dragooned from a wide variety of SS and Nazi party agencies.[24]

The SS WVHA, the parent SS agency controlling the camps, replaced the called-up guards, as the acrimonious correspondence in the SSTK files indicates, by transferring lightly wounded or convalescing soldiers from the Totenkopfdivision to guard duty in the camps. Once there, the individual camp commandants usually refused to return them to SSTK.

In August 1942, when Eicke was on leave and Max Simon was commanding SSTK, the latter wrote a long letter to Eicke describ-

[22] BAKO, NS-19/370, SS Totenkopfdivision, IIa, "Zusammenstellung über die von der SS Totenkopf-Division an andere Einheiten der Waffen SS abgegebene Führer," dated March 5, 1941.

[23] The figure of fifty-five was determined by this writer on the basis of a hand count of the transfer announcements for NCOs and SS men scattered throughout the SSTK records for the period from October 1939 to March 1941. These volumes include: BAMA, III SS, 41/5, KTB Nr. 5 und Anlagenband zum KTB Nr. 5, 7. Oktober 1940 bis 31. Mai 1941; III SS, 41/8, vol. 1; III SS, 42/1; III SS, 42/2; and III SS, 44/2, Nachschubdienst, Tagesbefehle, 25. Oktober 1939—25. August 1940.

[24] BAMA, III SS, 41/9, Lageberichte und Meldungen aus Kessel Demjansk, pp. 140-41, a letter from Heinz Lammerding to Max Simon of August 8, 1942, describing the composition of a new infantry regiment being created for the Totenkopfdivision.

ing the multitude of difficulties then facing the division. One of the most serious problems, Simon claimed, was the manpower shortage caused by the concentration camp commandants' refusal to return Totenkopf soldiers who had been transferred to the camps for temporary duty. The camp commanders, Simon fumed, ignored both the persistent demands of the Totenkopfdivision and the pleas of the men in question, most of whom preferred to return to front-line duty.[25]

In addition to the fragmentary information about the volume of personnel movement between the Totenkopfdivision and the camps, there is specific biographical data on individual officers in the Totenkopfdivision who were transferred to the concentration or extermination camps. An analysis of the assignments these men received after leaving the front reveals even more about the links between SSTK and the camp system. In particular, the careers of four men—Friedrich Hartjenstein, Anton Kaindl, Paul-Werner Hoppe, and Adam Grünewald—suggest that SS officers were exchanged between the division and the camps for a number of reasons.

Friedrich Hartjenstein joined the Totenkopfdivision in March 1940 after extensive duty in the reserve Totenkopf regiments. By October 1941 he had served successively as a company commander and staff officer in the division and had risen to the rank of SS Sturmbannführer (major). Because of the heavy losses among the officer corps of the Totenkopfdivision during the first summer of the Russian campaign, Eicke gave him command of the First Battalion of SSTK/I. R. 3. The results were disastrous. Hartjenstein proved singularly unfit to command an infantry battalion, and the severe mauling his unit suffered during the spring of 1942 was due mainly to his incompetence. In late August 1942, Eicke relieved him of command and secured Hartjenstein's transfer to camp duty.[26]

---

[25] Ibid., III SS, 41/9, long letter from Max Simon to Eicke written on August 2, 1942. The relevant portion of the letter is as follows: "As far as I know, many convalescing members of the division are now serving in the guard battalions in the concentration camps and will be held there by the commandants in question, despite the fact that they want to return to the front."

[26] USDC, SS Personalakte Hartjenstein, Dienstlaufbahn, and the efficiency report on Hartjenstein written by Oswald Pohl, the chief of the SS WVHA, and

Hartjenstein's new assignment was the command of the SS guard detachment at Auschwitz. In this capacity, he evidently redeemed himself, for on March 10, 1943, he was advanced to the position of commandant of the Birkenau extermination camp— the main killing center within the Auschwitz complex. Hartjenstein remained commandant at Birkenau until May 1944, when Himmler, as a reward for his outstanding service, transferred him to command the large slave labor camp of Natzweiler in Alsace.[27]

Anton Kaindl's SS career was a bit different. Before the war he had served on the staff of the inspectorate of concentration camps and then had moved with Eicke to the Totenkopfdivision in October 1939 as the division personnel officer. Kaindl remained a member of Eicke's staff until October 1941. At that time, Himmler had him moved back to the inspectorate of concentration camps to become chief paymaster of the camp guard units. Kaindl was transferred form the Totenkopfdivision because of his obvious administrative qualifications. At a time when the casualties of the SS field divisions were draining personnel from the camp administrative system, Himmler sorely needed SS officers with Kaindl's experience and competence. Kaindl's second term with the camp inspectorate, however, was brief.[28]

In August 1942, after a financial scandal involving the commandant at Sachsenhausen had caused a stir throughout the concentration camp system, Himmler sent the reliable and honest Kaindl to clean up the mess in the huge camp. Until the end of the war, Kaindl served as commandant of Sachsenhausen, earning in

---

dated June 8, 1943. See also, Stein, pp. 262; Hilberg, pp. 574-75; Wormser-Migot, pp. 241-42, 366, 499, 531-33, 576, 580; Hermann Langbein, ed., *Der Auschwitz Prozess: Eine Dokumentation* (Vienna, 1965), vol. 2, pp. 601, 615, 632; and Bernd Naumann, *Auschwitz*, trans. Jean Steinberg (New York, 1966), pp. 64-66, for additional details concerning Hartjenstein's tenure at Birkenau and his activities as commandant at Natzweiler.

[27] USDC, SS Personalakte Hartjenstein, Deinstlaufbahn; Hilberg, p. 707; and Langbein, ed., *Der Auschwitz Prozess*, vol. 2, 995. Hartjenstein was captured by the French in 1945 and condemned to death by a military tribunal for the mass murder of prisoners in Natzweiler. While his case was still under appeal in 1954, Hartjenstein died of a heart attack in prison in Metz (Rückerl, ed., *NS-Prozesse*, p. 127).

[28] USDC, SS Personalakte Kaindl, Dienstlaufbahn; *Dienstaltersliste der Schutzstaffel der N. S. D. A. P.: Stand vom 1. Juli 1943* (Berlin, 1943). p. 9; Reitlinger, *The SS*, pp. 259; and Hilberg, p. 559.

the process a reputation among his superiors as a scrupulously correct, thoroughly reliable camp commander.[29]

In addition, the case of Paul-Werner Hoppe demonstrates clearly how desirable officers in the Totenkopfdivision were as candidates for important jobs in the concentration camp system. Hoppe joined the SS in February 1933, and by the beginning of the war had become a key member of Eicke's staff in the inspectorate of concentration camps. In September 1939 he was among the select group of SS officers who helped Eicke plan the organization of the Totenkopfdivision, and the following month, was transferred from the inspectorate to the new SSTK as Eicke's adjutant. After eighteen months of personal service with his commander, he was rewarded in April 1941 with command of an infantry company. During the heavy fighting near Lake Ilmen in the spring of 1942, Hoppe was severely wounded in the leg. He was forced to take a convalescent leave, and after recovery found himself transferred in July 1942 to the concentration camp system as commander of an SS guard detachment in Auschwitz.[30]

The reason for Hoppe's transfer was stated clearly in a letter written subsequently by Richard Glücks, Eicke's wartime successor as inspector of concentration camps, recommending Hoppe for promotion to the rank of SS Sturmbannführer. According to Glücks, Hoppe's wound had allowed the camp system to acquire the services of a man with a unique knowledge of the entire concentration camp network. Citing Hoppe's prewar experience in the camp inspectorate, Glücks in late July 1942 suggested that Hoppe be appointed commandant of the Stutthof concentration camp near Danzig. In September 1942 Hoppe moved from Auschwitz to his new post at Danzig, where he remained until the end of the war.[31]

---

[29] USDC, SS Personalakte Kaindl, efficiency report on Kaindl written by Oswald Pohl on March 23, 1944; *Nazi Conspiracy and Aggression*, 8 vols, (Washington, D. C., 1946), vol. 7, p. 209, for a written deposition by Kaindl concerning his tenure as commandant at Sachsenhausen; *TMWC*, vol. 21, pp. 608-9, 611; and Wormser-Migot, pp. 146, 232, 319. Kaindl was tried as a war criminal by the Russians in 1947 and sentenced to life in prison. He died in a Soviet prison camp in 1951.

[30] USDC, SS Personalakte Hoppe, Dienstlaufbahn.

[31] Ibid., and a copy of Glücks's letter of recommendation for Hoppe's promotion and assignment as a concentration camp commandant, dated July 24, 1942,

Finally, the disastrous SS career of Adam Grünewald presents an interesting contrast to the noted pattern of transfers between the Totenkopfdivision and the camp system. Prior to the war, Grünewald served as commander of the detention center in Dachau and as an administrative officer in the Totenkopfverbände. With the outbreak of war, Grünewald was transferred to the new SSTK and given command of the bakery company. He performed this assignment well enough to be promoted to command of the division's procurement service, and remained with the Totenkopfdivision from November 1939 until October 1942. At that time he was reassigned to camp duty as commander of the detention center at Oranienburg—a post he held until June 1943. From Oranienburg, Grünewald moved up to the bigger assignment of commandant of the huge Vught concentration camp and deportation center in occupied Holland. His tenure at Vught became unusually notorious. After an SS investigation early in 1944 revealed that Grünewald had sanctioned especially brutal treatment of prisoners (without proper authorization) and had allowed such overcrowding in the camp's detention cells that the unsanitary conditions killed a number of women political detainees, Grünewald was removed from his command and court-martialed at Himmler's express order. As punishment, Grünewald was degraded to the rank of SS private and sentenced in April 1944 to an indefinite term of combat with the Totenkopfdivision.[32]

---

and signed by Pohl with an appended note of approval. See also, Livia Rothkirchen, "The Final Solution in Its Last Stages," *Yad Vashem Studies on the European Jewish Catastrophe and Resistance*, 8 (Jerusalem, 1970), pp. 7-29, especially pp. 25-26, for the brutalities inflicted on the Stutthof inmates by Hoppe in January 1945 to keep them from falling into the hands of the Russians alive. Hoppe's postwar fate is a classic example of Allied and West German ineptitude in prosecuting lesser-known war criminals. Hoppe was arrested by the British in Holstein in April 1946, and while in British custody awaiting extradition to Poland, escaped and went into hiding. For the next seven years, Hoppe remained free living under various aliases in Switzerland and West Germany. He was finally arrested by German authorities at Witten in the Ruhr on April 17, 1953. The disposition of his case dragged on for four years until finally, on June 4, 1957, a Bochum court for the state of North Rhine-Westphalia sentenced Hoppe to a mere nine years in prison as an *accessory* to several hundred murders while commandant of Stutthof (letter to this writer of March 27, 1975 from Oberstaatsanwalt Dr. Günter Kimmel of the Zentrale Stelle der Landesjustizverwaltungen in Ludwigsburg).

[32] USDC, SS Personalakte Grünewald, "SS- und Polizeigericht Den Haag, Feldurteil, Beglaubigte Abschrift," dated March 6, 1944, and Grünewald's

The individual careers of Hartjenstein, Kaindl, Hoppe, and Grünewald did not typify the experience of most SS officers and men in the Totenkopfdivision. On the other hand, these four cases definitely were not isolated exceptions. Among the several thousand SS officers who passed through the Totenkopfdivision during the war, there were undoubtedly many who came from or went to some type of duty in the concentration camps. The broader significance of these four examples concerns the rationale for transferring men to and from the camp system. In each case, the reason for reassignment to or from the camps was different: Hartjenstein was sent as a result of his incompetence; Kaindl because of a definite need for his talents and experience; Hoppe when a serious wound rendered him unfit for further military service; and Grünewald as punishment for his brutal performance at Vught. These four examples quite possibly document in microcosm what were the general rules governing the transfer of men between the Totenkopfdivision and the concentration camps.

There is also substantial evidence pointing to institutionalized relations between the Totenkopfdivision and SS agencies engaged in a far wider range of criminal activities. A case in point is SSTK's association with the Higher SS and Police Leaders (HSSPF) in the occupied territories.[33] During the first years of the war Himmler sent a number of men designated for service as HSSPF to the Totenkopfdivision for a period of military training. Among them were several high-ranking SS officers who spent varying periods with Eicke in 1940 and 1941 learning how to command troops in the field, and who later became conspicuously notorious for their activities as HSSPF in the German-occupied east.

The first important guest, SS Obergruppenführer Ernst Heinrich Schmauser, joined Eicke's staff in March 1940 and spent one

---

Dienstlaufbahn. See also, Helmut Heiber, ed., *Reichsführer!*, Doc. No. 301, p. 254; and Jacob Presser, *The Destruction of the Dutch Jews* (New York, 1969), pp. 464-78, for a description of life and conditions in the Vught camp at the time Grünewald was commandant. After he was sent back to SSTK as a private, Grünewald was killed in action in January 1945 while fighting with the division in Hungary (Rückerl, ed., *NS-Prozesse*, p. 126).

[33] See especially the previously cited article by Hans Buchheim, "Die Höheren SS und Polizei Führer."

month training with the Totenkopfdivision. After leaving the division, he became HSSPF for Upper Silesia and in that capacity ruled as the supreme SS authority under Himmler in the region in which Auschwitz was located. Much of Schmauser's time after 1942 was spent dealing with the logistical problems created by the immense killing operations in Auschwitz.[34]

Another SS celebrity who served briefly with SSTK in 1940, and who retained close ties long after his departure, was SS Obergruppenführer Friedrich Jeckeln. For six weeks during the spring of 1940, Jeckeln was assigned to Eicke's division as commander of the First Battalion, SSTK/I. R. 2. In the spring of 1941, Himmler appointed Jeckeln HSSPF of southern Russia, a post which included command of Einsatzgruppe C—the mobile killing unit staffed by men from the Ordnungspolizei and Waffen SS. Spurred by Jeckeln's zeal, Einsatzgruppe C murdered more than 100,000 people (mostly Jews) in southern Russia during July and August 1941. As a result of Jeckeln's gruesome success, Himmler transferred him in November 1941 to the more challenging post of HSSPF jointly of the Baltic States and northern Russia. Here he was given the task of eliminating the "Jewish-partisan menace" in the forested region behind Army Group North, and in February 1942 led an immense "cleansing action" that liquidated over 10,000 Jews, partisans, and suspected Soviet sympathizers.[35]

At his palatial headquarters in Riga Jeckeln also found enough time to amass a staggering amount of tribute from the conquered subjects in his new domain. By late December 1941 he had taken over a whole complex of warehouses in Riga and had begun to store away loot—taken mainly from Jews—that included furniture, jewelry, liquor, watches, shoes, clothing, and money. De-

[34] USDC, SS Personalakte Schmauser, Dienstlaufbahn; BAMA, III SS, 41/8, vol. 1, p. 332; Hilberg, pp. 333, 585; and Adler, *Der Verwaltete Mensch*, pp. 229-30, for Schmauser's difficulties with the firms in Upper Silesia competing for the available supply of Jews for slave labor.

[35] USDC, SS Personalakte Jeckeln, Dienstlaufbahn; and "Vorschlag für die Verleihung des Deutschen Kreuzes in Gold," dated May 23, 1944, for a description of Jeckeln's period of combat duty with the Totenkopfdivision. See also, Hilberg, pp. 193, 196, 238n, 250-51; and Adler, *Der Verwaltete Mensch*, p. 185, for accounts of Jeckeln's activities in Russia in 1941 and 1942—including his personal participation in the shooting of 4,000 German Jews who had been deported to the Riga ghetto.

spite his insatiable acquisitiveness, Jeckeln was not stingy with his booty and willingly helped supply his old friend Eicke and the hard-pressed Totenkopfdivision—then locked in ferocious winter fighting near Lake Ilmen. From December 1941 through March 1942, Jeckeln periodically sent shipments of winter clothing, fur boots, wool socks, skis, cognac, food packages, and other necessities to SSTK from the well-stocked SS warehouses in Riga. The result for the soldiers in SSTK was at least a partial mitigation of the suffering the Russian winter inflicted upon the Wehrmacht.[36]

The connection between the Totenkopfdivision and Jeckeln became more intimate—and the division's accessibility to the mountain of loot in Riga more direct—when Eicke transferred one of his staff officers to Jeckeln's command in June 1942. This officer was SS Sturmbannführer Hugo Klapsch. In Riga, Klapsch became an administrator in Jeckeln's complex of warehouses, which by then were so glutted with goods of every description that the HSSPF began using them as partial supply dumps for the SS agencies and Waffen SS field divisions operating in northern Russia. The Totenkopfdivision, however, did not long enjoy the benefits of Klapsch's patronage, as the heavy losses of the summer of 1942 led to SSTK's temporary withdrawal from Russia the following October.[37]

[36] BAMA, III SS, 42/2, pp. 444, 465, 478; III SS, 41/10, Funkspruche und Telegrammen, vol. 3, p. 469. Vital supplies such as clothing and shoes were not the only valuables collected from murdered Jews and sent to the Totenkopfdivision during the war. In May 1943 Hans Frank, the governor general of Poland, shipped 500 watches collected in Auschwitz to the Totenkopfdivision for distribution among the men as gifts. The Leibstandarte SS Adolf Hitler and SS Das Reich divisions also received allotments of 500 watches from Frank, who promised Himmler he would send each of the three Waffen SS divisions 1,000 watches from among the 94,000 that by then had already been collected in Auschwitz (*TWC/Green Series*, vol. 4, case 4, *U.S.* v *Oswald Pohl*, pp. 709-14, copies of letters exchanged between Frank and Rudolf Brandt, Himmler's adjutant, and between Brandt and Oswald Pohl). See also, Hilberg, p. 616; and Arthur Eisenbach, "Operation Reinhard: Mass Extermination of the Jewish Population in Poland," *Polish Western Affairs*, 3 (1962), pp. 80-124, especially 109.

[37] USDC, SS Personalakte Klapsch, Dienstlaufbahn; and a summary of the correspondence, efficiency reports, and other materials in Klapsch's SS service records. Klapsch succumbed quickly to the degenerate influence of Jeckeln, became an alcoholic, and subsequently was demoted to an insignificant SS administrative post in Cracow.

The friendly cooperation between Eicke and Jeckeln was atypical of the tenor of relations between Waffen SS commanders and the HSSPF. All Waffen SS units not

The unique nature of the Russian conflict also gave Himmler an opportunity to send to the Totenkopfdivision those senior SS and police commanders he had selected for "special tasks" in the east. With Eicke, these SS officers were exposed to the racial and ideological realities of the struggle in Russia, and learned quickly how the SS waged war against its subhuman foe. In one instance, a Himmler-selected trainee sent to Eicke for orientation on the east ended as a most embarrassing casualty.

On July 19, 1941 SS Gruppenführer Paul Moder joined SSTK in Russia with combat rank as an SS Sturmbannführer attached to the motorcycle battalion. From October 1939 to June 1940, Moder had been SS and police commander (SS und Polizei Führer) in Warsaw, and just prior to joining SSTK had served as a staff officer with SS Oberabschnitt Ost. Moder came to the Totenkopfdivision pending Himmler's decision on a new police assignment for him in the east. At his own request, Moder was permitted an extension of his stay, and became directly involved in the extremely bitter fighting south of Lake Ilmen in the autumn of 1941. On February 8, 1942 Moder was killed in action at the height of the Russian winter counteroffensive in the Demyansk sector.[38]

Moder's more notorious contemporary was luckier while serving with SSTK. On July 7, 1941 SS Oberführer Jürgen Stroop was posted to the Totenkopfdivision with the combat rank of SS Obersturmführer (first lieutenant), and served with the division

---

at the front theoretically were under the jurisdiction of HSSPF's, who were Himmler's immediate deputies in command of all SS and police units in a given occupied region or Wehrkreis. The HSSPF thus served to protect Himmler's authority against efforts by many vigorous Waffen SS commanders to exercise independent control over their own formations. See especially, BAKO, NS-19/neu-1665, copy of a teleprinter message from Himmler to the SS Führungshauptamt of March 5, 1942, in which the Reichsführer SS expresses concern about SS control over the Waffen SS and issues instructions for tightening the authority of the HSSPF over Waffen SS units in the occupied territories. These conclusions and the same document are in Buchheim, "Die Höheren SS und Polizei Führer," pp. 362-66, 380-82, and 383; and the same teleprinter directive is also reproduced in Heiber, ed., *Reichsführer!*, pp. 107-9.

[38] USDC, SS Personalakte Moder, Dienstlaufbahn; and a summary of the materials in Moder's SS service records, especially an undated report on his service with the Totenkopfdivision and death in action, prepared by the First Reserve Battalion of SSTK and addressed to the HQ of SS Oberabschnitt Spree in Berlin.

for two months in the Third Battalion of SSTK/I. R. 3—earning in the process the Infantry Assault Badge for participation in hand-to-hand combat. On September 15, 1941 Stroop transferred to the reserve battalion of the Leibstandarte SS Adolf Hitler for a month before moving to the Ordnungspolizei to prepare for the "special task" (Sonderauftrag) of serving as Himmler's racial expert in the Caucasus.[39]

The Totenkopfdivision thus earned the singular distinction of having in its ranks one of the vilest, most repulsive thugs in the entire SS. As SS and police commander in Warsaw in the spring of 1943, Stroop directed the final liquidation of the Warsaw ghetto. The combined SS, police, and army units he commanded were resisted furiously and heroically—though hopelessly—by the Jewish resistance fighters in the ghetto. Until the fighting ended in mid-May, Stroop personally supervised the deportation or summary executions of those Jews who surrendered, blew up the venerated Tlomacki Synagogue to celebrate the "victory," and then commemorated the whole operation by compiling a lengthy summary, complete with battle reports and photographs, in a handsome, leather-bound volume.[40]

As a reward for his Warsaw success, Himmler on September

[39] USDC, SS Personalakte Stroop, Dienstlaufbahn; and a series of letters exchanged among Jüttner (the SS Personalhauptamt) and Stroop's immediate superior, SS Gruppenführer Wilhelm Koppe (the HSSPF Warthe) between July and October 1941 concerning Stroop's transfer to SSTK and Himmler's desire to employ him in the occupied territories. Stroop's receipt of the Infantry Assault Badge is confirmed in ibid., letter from Hellmuth Becker to Stroop of January 21, 1943. The requirements for the award are described in *Handbook on German Military Forces*, p. 48.

[40] USDC, SS Personalakte Stroop, Dienstlaufbahn; Hilberg, pp. 323-26; and Ackermann, p. 164. The best account of the ghetto uprising is Reuben Ainsztein, *Jewish Resistance in Nazi-Occupied Eastern Europe* (New York, 1974), pp. 619-71. A copy of Stroop's lengthy report on the liquidation of the ghetto, entitled: "Es gibt keinen jüdischen Wohnbezirk in Warschau mehr," is in *TMWC*, vol. 26, Doc. No. PS-1061, pp. 639-93. Among the photographs Stroop had taken of himself, his SS men, and the Jewish defenders during the destruction of the ghetto, there is one picture which, when compared with an earlier photograph snapped by an unknown SS cameraman, documents visually a second individual link between SSTK and the Warsaw atrocity. In Stein, facing page 92, the SSTK soldier in the center of the picture with his gloves off (a photo taken during the battle of Kharkov in March 1943), is the same man in the photograph in Poznanski, *Struggle, Death, Memory* (page is unnumbered, approximate center of the volume), forcing a group of Jews at gunpoint out of the burning Warsaw ghetto in May 1943.

13, 1943 appointed Stroop HSSPF for Greece—a post then critically important in the wake of the surrender of Marshal Badoglio's Italian government to the Allies. After army and SS formations had occupied all of Greece, Stroop established his HQ in Athens and for the next two months busied himself with directing the deportation of Jews from the Greek mainland to Auschwitz.[41]

One of the most illuminating examples of the versatility demonstrated by Eicke's SS officers when serving in other branches of the SS is the career of SS Oberführer Erich Tschimpke. Prior to the creation of the Totenkopfdivision, Tschimpke served with Eicke as chief supply officer for the inspectorate of concentration camps. In October 1939 he transferred to the Totenkopfdivision with similar title and responsibilities. Tschimpke's organizational and administrative talents were considerable, and in the spring of 1941 they attracted the personal attention of Himmler. In April the Reichsführer SS posted Tschimpke to the Einsatzstab Reichsführers SS (Himmler's operational staff for coordinating the activities of the Einsatzgruppen and SD units in Russia), and assigned him to solve the supply and logistical problems of the SS and police units that were to operate in the rear areas once the Russian campaign began. Tschimpke performed flawlessly in keeping the Einsatzgruppen, police, and SD units well supplied, and remained with Himmler's Einsatzstab until September 1942. At that time, Himmler transferred Tschimpke to the Ordnungspolizei, with a titular promotion to police president of the city of Chemnitz.[42]

The energetic Tschimpke, however, soon grew restless behind his desk and in the winter of 1942 began to pester Himmler to

---

[41] USDC, SS Personalakte Stroop, Dienstlaufbahn; Dawidowicz, p. 394. At the end of the war, Stroop was apprehended in the American Zone, tried, and condemned to death as a war criminal. He was then turned over to the Poles, who tried and publicly executed him on July 9, 1952, on the site of the former ghetto. (Hilberg, p. 714; Ainsztein, p. 905 n. 2; and Rückerl, ed., *NS-Prozesse*, p. 58 n. 60.

[42] USDC, SS Personalakte Tschimpke, Dienstlaufbahn; and a summary of the materials in Tschimpke's SS service records. See also, BAMA, III SS, 42/2, pp. 20-21; and BAKO, NS-19/neu-1842, circular order from Himmler to Chef der Ordnungspolizei, SS Personalhauptamt, and the SS Führungshauptamt of September 19, 1942; and BAKO, NS-19/neu-1842, letter of November 28, 1942 from the SS Personalhauptamt to Himmler concerning Tschimpke's appointment.

transfer him back to the field. After some hesitation, the Reichsführer SS consented and in March 1943 secured for Tschimpke through Alfred Rosenberg's Ostministerium (Ministry for the Eastern Occupied Territories) an administrative position in the Ukraine. Tschimpke was appointed a Gebietskommissar (district commissioner) under the jurisdiction of the Reichskommissar for the Ukraine, Erich Koch. Owing to a procedural mix-up, Tschimpke had to be reassigned as a Gebietshauptmann (district captain) and SS garrison commander at Hegewald in the Ukraine, but subsequently received the Gebietskommissariat of the Korosten district in the autumn of 1943.[43]

Tschimpke remained a member of Koch's Ukrainian administration until the spring of 1944, when the Soviet advance rolled over his fiefdom and forced a general German withdrawal from the Ukraine. His job erased by the Red Army's offensive, Tschimpke requested Himmler to return him to front-line service with a Waffen SS division. Himmler, however, demurred, as he obviously considered Tschimpke a man whose ability and past experience qualified him for more significant tasks. As a result, the Reichsführer SS in April 1944 assigned Tschimpke as a special officer to the staff of the HSSPF in Italy—at that time SS Obergruppenführer Karl Wolff, the former chief of Himmler's personal staff. Tschimpke's main duties with Wolff involved liaison work with the Fascist militia of Mussolini's "Salo Republic," and the arming and training of an Italian SS legion Wolff was organizing. In this capacity, Tschimpke spent the remaining year of the war.[44]

Aside from Tschimpke, there were several other high-ranking SS officers who moved into important positions in other branches

[43] BAKO, NS-19/neu-1842, "Der Reichskommissar für die Festigung Deutschen Volkstums, Stabshauptamt, an RFSS, Persönlicher Stab," dated March 12, 1943; and ibid., copy of a teleprinter message from Tschimpke to Himmler of May 25, 1943; and copy of a letter from Tschimpke to Himmler, dated July 7, 1943.

[44] Ibid., NS-19/neu-1842, letter of July 24, 1943, from SS Obersturmbannführer Rudolf Brandt, Himmler's adjutant, to SS Obergruppenführer Hans Adolf Prützmann, the HSSPF for southern Russia; and copy of a teleprinter message from Tschimpke to Himmler of March 29, 1944. See also, USDC, SS Personalakte Tschimpke, Dienstlaufbahn; and the other materials in Tschimpke's SS service records for the period after 1941.

of the SS after serving for varying periods with the Totenkopfdivision. SS Hauptsturmführer Alfred Franke-Gricksch, an
officer in the SS Totenkopfverbände from 1935 to 1939, joined
SSTK in October 1939 and worked as an intelligence officer until
March 1941. At that point, he was transferred to the Hauptamt of
the Sicherheitsdienst, where he remained until returning to active
Waffen SS duty in August 1942 with the SS Polizeidivision. The
appearance of kidney stones forced Franke-Gricksch to return to a
desk job, and in January 1943 he was assigned to the SS Personalhauptamt (Central Personnel Office). Here he spent the rest
of the war in personnel and administrative work.[45]

The circumstances surrounding Franke-Gricksch's transfer
from the Totenkopfdivision to the SD in March 1941 are especially interesting, and illustrate graphically Himmler's intention
of giving capable SS officers experience both in combat and in
those SS agencies involved in rear-area activities. Franke-
Gricksch questioned his reassignment to the SD, for on July 23,
1941, he received a personal letter from Rudolf Brandt, Himmler's adjutant. Brandt assured Franke-Gricksch that his transfer
to the SD was neither a form of punishment nor an indication of
Himmler's displeasure, but rather was in line with the
Reichsführer SS's policy of rotating SS officers between the front

[45] USDC, SS Personalakte Franke-Gricksch, Dienstlaufbahn; and a summary of
the other materials in Franke-Gricksch's SS service records documenting his
career from 1941 to the end of the war. Franke-Gricksch became a key member of
the SS Personalhauptamt, and was regarded by his boss, SS Gruppenführer
Maximilien von Herff, as the second-best officer in the SS personnel organization.
Franke-Gricksch's obvious abilities prompted Gottlob Berger, chief of the Waffen
SS Recruiting Office, to try repeatedly to draft him back into the Waffen SS (ibid.,
letter from Maximilien von Herff to Gottlob Berger of November 13, 1943, informing Berger once and for all that Franke-Gricksch would not be released to the
Waffen SS).
In May 1943, Franke-Gricksch visited Auschwitz to inspect the killing facilities. He was so impressed by what he observed that he composed a lengthy
memorandum for von Herff entitled "Umsiedlungsaktion der Jüden." In the
memorandum, Franke-Gricksch detailed with obvious relish how the "most modern methods" at Auschwitz made it possible to dispose of 10,000 corpses every
twenty-four hours. The memorandum traces all the steps in the killing process,
from the arrival of the trains in the special siding to the burning of the corpses in
the crematoria. The original of this document evidently is lost amid the still-
unindexed collection of Nuremberg Prosecution Documents. A typed copy made
from one of the three carbons of the memorandum is in the possession of this
writer.

and the rear so each could have combat experience. This policy was reaffirmed a year later when Himmler issued a general order directing an extensive exchange of officers between the SS administrative, legal, and medical services and the Waffen SS.[46]

The career of SS Hauptsturmführer Ernst Hellerich provides another good example of how well this policy of personnel rotation worked, and shows how effectively front-line experience in the Waffen SS was applied in the SS rear-area services. Hellerich had served before the war in the SS Totenkopfverbände and was among the original contingent of SS officers transferred to SSTK in the autumn of 1939. From then until November 1942 Hellerich served as the administrative officer for the engineer battalion of SSTK. When the division was pulled out of combat for rest and refitting in October 1942, Hellerich was transferred to the staff of the HSSPF Russland Süd in Kiev with the title of SS economist (SS Wirtschafter). This important office had been created by Himmler in June 1942 for all the HSSPF in Russia and the Balkans. The SS Wirtschafter, as the deputy of the HSSPF, coordinated and controlled all economic and administrative activities (including executions and the running of concentration camps) conducted by SS agencies and units operating within the territorial jurisdiction of the individual HSSPF.[47]

Hellerich remained with the HSSPF of southern Russia, SS Obergruppenführer Hans Adolf Prützmann, until the Soviet autumn offensive of 1943 forced the general German evacuation of the Ukraine. According to Prützmann's efficiency reports, Hellerich was an outstanding Wirtschafter, and was chiefly responsible for organizing the successful evacuation of all the SS units from the Dnepropetrovsk area. His success with Prützmann led to Hellerich's transfer as SS Wirtschafter to the staff of the HSSPF

[46] USDC, SS Personalakte Franke-Gricksch, letter from Brandt to Franke-Gricksch of July 23, 1941. Himmler's directive for the exchange of personnel between the SS and the Waffen SS is in BAKO, Au-NS-19/415, "Austausch von SS Führern zwischen Front und Heimat," dated April 10, 1942. Interesting also is a reply from Oswald Pohl to Himmler, in BAKO, Au-NS-19/415, dated May 16, 1942, with a list of SS officers from the WVHA who had been transferred to active duty with the Waffen SS.

[47] USDC, SS Personalakte Hellerich, "SS WVHA, Amt A V, Beförderungen in der Waffen SS," dated December 7, 1942. See also, Buchheim, "Die Höheren SS und Polizei Führer," pp. 387-88; and Hilberg, p. 557.

Schwarzes Meer early in 1944, where he again organized a successful withdrawal of the SS units strung along the extreme southern end of the Russian front. In October 1944 Hellerich was posted to Amt B I (food supplies) of the SS WVHA, and served there for the rest of the war.[48]

Among the senior medical officers who served with the Totenkopfdivision, there were very few who at one time during the war were not attached to some other SS or police agency. The most notorious SS medical practitioner to serve with the Totenkopfdivision was SS Sturmbannführer Dr. Erwin Ding. Before the war Ding had served as a surgeon in the SS Totenkopfverbände and as camp physician in Buchenwald. In October 1939 he moved to SSTK as adjutant to the chief surgeon of the division, and remained with Totenkopf until August 1940.[49]

After leaving the Totenkopfdivision, Ding joined the staff of the Hygienic Institute of the Waffen SS, and was assigned the job of organizing and conducting the infamous typhus experiments carried out on prisoners at Buchenwald in 1942 and 1943. As a result of his experiments with injections of typhus bacilli, Ding was responsible for the deaths of nearly 600 inmates of the Buchenwald camp.[50]

SS Brigadeführer Dr. Bruno Rothardt's SS medical career was a bit different. Rothardt came to the Totenkopfdivision from the medical staff of the SS Verfügungstruppe in October 1939 and served with Eicke as physician to the Totenkopfdivision until January 1941. From then until November 1942 he worked in the

[48] USDC, SS Personalakte Hellerich, Dienstlaufbahn; and an efficiency report on Hellerich signed by Prützmann on October 20, 1943. See also, ibid., letter to Oswald Pohl from the former HSSPF Schwarzes Meer, SS Obergruppenführer Richard Hildebrandt, dated September 18, 1944; and an SS WVHA transfer notice for Hellerich dated October 10, 1944.

[49] USDC, SS Personalakte Ding, Dienstlaufbahn; and "Beförderungen in der Waffen SS," dated October 3, 1942, and signed by SS Brigadeführer Dr. Karl Genzken as chief of the Waffen SS Medical Service.

[50] *TWC/Green Series*, vol. 1, "Medical Case," pp. 50-52, and 557-73, for evidence relative to Ding's role in the typhus experiments. See also, Elie A. Cohen, *Human Behavior in the Concentration Camps*, trans. M. H. Braaksma (New York, 1953), pp. 93-97; Kater, *Das "Ahnenerbe" der SS 1935-1945*, pp. 227-28; and Hilberg, p. 579. Ding changed his name to Ding-Schuler during the war; after being arrested and charged by the American military authorities in 1945, he committed suicide before being brought to trial.

Waffen SS Medical Service, and from November 23, 1942 until August 15, 1943, was assigned to duty with the medical staff of the State Security Police (Sicherheitspolizei). Then, in the autumn of 1943, Rothardt returned to the Waffen SS for the duration of the war—serving successively as physician to the Seventh and Fourth SS Panzerkorps.[51]

The long SS medical career of Brigadeführer Dr. Oskar Hock contained a similar pattern of movement. Before joining the Totenkopfdivision in February 1941, Hock had worked on the medical staffs at Dachau and Sachsenhausen and in the medical service of the Waffen SS in Berlin. From February 15, 1941 until November 9, 1942, Hock practiced as a regimental surgeon in the Totenkopfdivision. Following his release from SS military duty, he was sent to the medical staff of the Ordnungspolizei in Berlin and kept there until the shortage of SS medical personnel forced his return to the Waffen SS in mid-1944. For the last nine months of the war Hock, like his former colleague Dr. Rothardt, served as an SS corps physician—first to the Third SS Army Corps and then with the powerful Second SS Panzerkorps.[52]

In sum, the materials drawn together here reveal several relatively clear patterns with respect to the Totenkopfdivision's relations with other SS agencies, and much about the extent of its integration within the general structure of the Schutzstaffel. To begin with, there was absolutely nothing in the history or experience of the Totenkopfdivision suggesting that the division and the men who served in it ever belonged to an organization separate and distinct from the institutional structure of the SS. From the day of its creation until the end of the war, SSTK remained bound by the general political, racial, and administrative laws of the SS. Even when it was committed to action and under the operational control of the army, the Totenkopfdivision was constantly subject to the disciplinary and administrative authority of the Reichsführer SS and consistently depended upon other SS agencies for supplies, equipment, and replacements.[53]

[51] USDC, SS Personalakte Rothardt, Dienstlaufbahn; and a summary of the other materials in Rothardt's SS service records.

[52] USDC, SS Personalakte Hock, Dienstlaufbahn; and a summary of the other materials in Hock's SS service records.

[53] Based on the experience and example of the Totenkopfdivision, the conclusions developed by this writer vary sharply from those of Robert A. Gelwick,

Moreover, among the officers, NCOs, and SS enlisted men who fought in the ranks of the Totenkopfdivision there were many who had come from or later went to SS agencies or affiliates engaged in nonmilitary tasks. Personnel exchanges between SSTK and the extermination centers, the concentration camps, the Einsatzgruppen, the SS antipartisan units, the staffs of the HSSPF, the SD, the domestic police forces of the Reich, the administrative agencies of the occupied territories, and the main medical, personnel, and operational staffs of the SS, are all a matter of documentary record. There were, in addition, almost as many different reasons why men were transferred as there were SS agencies to which they went. In the case of the Totenkopfdivision, transfers to and from the division were initiated because of certain skilled- or experienced-manpower needs, war wounds and physical infirmity, personal antipathy and jealousy, incompetence, and friendly intervention and favoritism. Personnel movement, in short, was generated by most of the rational and irrational, logical and illogical factors that govern the circulation of people among the agencies of a vast, bureaucratized institution.[54]

More importantly, the criminal involvement of a large number of men from the Totenkopfdivision—in the form of personal responsibility for combat atrocities, or by service in branches of the SS engaged in criminal endeavors—is also a matter of docu-

---

"Personnel Policies and Procedures of the Waffen SS," Diss. Nebraska 1971. Gelwick views the Waffen SS as a purely military organization formed to field a competent fighting force, and asserts that most Waffen SS commanders regarded ideological indoctrination as a necessary evil (Gelwick, pp. 15-17, 23, and 47). In the case of the Totenkopfdivision, Eicke regarded ideological indoctrination—albeit his own crude version of Nazi political and racial theory—as essential to thorough, well-rounded training. By the time he was killed, the catalytic impact the Russian war had had upon his successful effort obviated the need for further systematic ideological training.

[54] A similar conclusion is drawn in the masterly study by Michael H. Kater, *Das "Ahnenerbe" der SS 1935-1945*, pp. 338-52, where the Ahnenerbe is analyzed in terms of its place within what Professor Kater calls the institutional chaos of the SS. The one possible reservation for the use of such terminology in describing the SS involves the dangerous inferences such usage often invites. In recent years, the assumption in vogue has been that the chaos and confusion in the SS, the overlapping functions and feuding of its various agencies, and the personality clashes of its leading figures somehow prevented the execution of orders and commission of atrocities, and generally mitigated the criminality of SS policies and goals. This view, as it is hoped the experience of the Totenkopfdivision has demonstrated, needs urgent reexamination.

mented substance. Fritz Knöchlein, Max Simon, Heinz Lammerding, and Hermann Priess (not to mention Eicke) all were responsible for the unjustified killing of either civilians or prisoners of war; while Friedrich Hartjenstein, Anton Kaindl, Paul-Werner Hoppe, Adam Grünewald, and an undetermined number of men from the Totenkopfdivision (even if one counts Schmauser, Jeckeln, Moder, and Stroop) became active cogs in the greatest deliberate process of human destruction in the history of mankind.

Against the broad background of the history of the Third Reich, the individual experience of the Totenkopfdivision was only a single tile in a giant, stupefyingly complex mosaic. If the close scrutiny of so small a fragment has merit, that merit lies in what the history of the Totenkopfdivision, as a microscopic condensation of the larger forces it represented, reveals about the character of the SS and ultimately the nature of National Socialism. The political antecedents of the Totenkopfdivision, the form and objectives of its ideological and military training programs, and the character and quality of its leading personalities fashioned it into an extraordinary instrument of war. Few other divisions in the Waffen SS, and none in the entire German army, were as representative of the ethos or as well suited for the warfare that so well characterized the destructive essence of Hitler's Thousand Year Reich.

AFTERWORD

FOR the many thousands of men who served in the SS Totenkopfdivision, the events described in the preceding pages were the
most important experiences of their lives. To them, the great
drama of the war, especially the vast cataclysm of the Russian
struggle with its unprecedented hardships and suffering, compressed the anxieties and exertions of a lifetime into the short
years of youth. The surviving veterans of the Totenkopfdivision
undoubtedly look back upon what they endured with feelings that
are deep and irreducibly personal.

This book was not written to glorify what they experienced, nor
was it conceived as an effort to condemn all of them as individuals
for belonging to an institution whose creation and development
they did not control. Many of these SS soldiers, both officers and
enlisted men, served with SSTK because they were drafted into
the Waffen SS. Some were transferred to the division from other
armed SS formations, or were assigned to Totenkopf from the SS
Junkerschulen. Throughout the war, others were sent to SSTK
from Waffen SS replacement battalions. Still others volunteered
for service in the Waffen SS and fought with the Totenkopfdivision from motives that quite simply may have been patriotic. To
suggest that all these men were sadists, criminals, or fanatics who
wantonly committed atrocities would be as ludicrous as the attempts by apologists for the Waffen SS to prove that the armed SS
was not really a part of the SS. Hopefully, this book will be read
and judged for what it is: a case study that seeks to combine objective description and critical analysis.

Moreover, as a case study of a single SS division, a formation
with distinct individual features of its own, this book draws conclusions that are necessarily limited. The experiences so evident
in the history of the SS Totenkopfdivision may well have been
modified or absent in other formations of the armed SS. Broader
conclusions about the nature and extent of personnel movement
between the armed SS and the other agencies of Himmler's empire must await a larger general study of SS manpower utilization,

343

and similar analysis in other (as yet unwritten) Waffen SS unit histories. In fact, most of the crucial general questions about the relationships among the agencies and branches of the vast SS conglomerate are still unexamined and unanswered.

There is, however, one dominant general observation that emerges with the completion of this work. The history of the SS Death's Head Division clearly reveals a line of authority from Hitler through Himmler to the Waffen SS that was short, direct, and immediate: short because Hitler's interest in and thus his authority over the Waffen SS remained constant until the end of the Third Reich; direct because there were no institutional barriers to impede his intentions when through Himmler he issued direct orders to the armed SS; and immediate because the performance of the Waffen SS enhanced Hitler's ideological confidence in its reliability—sharpening the focus of his attention as the military posture of the Third Reich deteriorated.

This is, of course, not to argue that Hitler, or even the maniacally meticulous Himmler, issued every order and directive, dictated every move and action, and decided every promotion and assignment that related to the armed SS and the SS Totenkopfdivision. The men they picked to do this for them, however, shared their beliefs and their fanaticism to such a degree as to make subordinate conduct consistently reflective of superior preference. Hence, the armed SS Totenkopfverbände Eicke created in the prewar concentration camp system were shaped into an instrument ready and capable of acting in accordance with Hitler's will. When the war required the conversion of these Death's Head formations into the nucleus of the Totenkopfdivision, the relationship of control and response between Hitler and Himmler on the one hand and Eicke and his officers on the other was strengthened rather than weakened. Himmler's establishment of centralized, systematic control over the armed SS claimed Eicke as a principal victim, as the latter's unavailing feud with Jüttner and the SS Führungshauptamt to preserve Totenkopf independence clearly demonstrates. As a result, until the end of the war the SS Totenkopfdivision remained effectively, unmistakably under Himmler's authority.

344

There were, it is true, instances of insubordination that punctuated Eicke's relations with the Reichsführer SS. There were, in addition, numerous feuds and rivalries among Eicke and his SS colleagues and subordinates. Heydrich, Jüttner, Wolff, Pohl, Gärtner, Berger, Knoblauch, Kleinheisterkamp, and even Max Simon, quarreled with Eicke over an endless variety of matters. Finally, however, all the personal friction, all the jurisdictional disputes, all the schemes to undermine, undercut, and circumvent, had at most a negligible effect upon the development and performance of the prewar Totenkopfverbände and the wartime Totenkopfdivision. In short, the rivalries and conflicts endemic in the SS leadership neither compromised or weakened the institutional effectiveness of the Totenkopfdivision, nor impaired its ability to achieve the purposes for which it was created.

That such conflicts failed to damage the Totenkopfdivision or impede its performance should be a matter of no great surprise. The clashes within the Death's Head Division and the frictions between SSTK and the other agencies of the SS were differences enclosed by a consensus. Despite Eicke's irrational behavior, his disobedience, his pilfering of equipment, and his eccentric treatment of colleagues and subordinates, he and those who succeeded him as SSTK commander never refused to execute any order basic to Hitler's and Himmler's view of the ideological purposes of the SS. Eicke's clashes with Himmler involved matters of form rather than substance—issues with respect to *how* the Totenkopfdivision could best become the instrument Hitler desired. There is, moreover, no evidence to suggest or documented incident to verify that Eicke or any of the men whose SS careers he molded ever questioned or refused to act in accordance with the racial and ideological principles of the SS.

These observations pose a final question, a larger problem, that is the ultimate harvest of this work. If the Totenkopfdivision was, in fact, a condensation, an accurate reflection, of the larger forces it represented and served, then what does this one example suggest about the institutional effectiveness of the SS? For a generation, one major analytical trend in studies of the Third Reich has focused upon the internal rivalries and anarchic divisions within the National Socialist system.[1] The contributions of this view to the enlargement of our knowledge of Nazi Germany are undeniable. It may now, however, be time to reexamine this problem from a different perspective. The SS and the Waffen SS, as the example of the Totenkopfdivision so obviously suggests, functioned extremely well despite internal tensions and rivalries, and in the face of extraordinary difficulties. This, it seems, would not have been possible without a formidable degree of institutional solidity—the presence of shared assumptions and beliefs, commonly accepted norms, and the unquestioned general values that enable large numbers of people, despite individual ambitions, dislikes, and disagreements, to work together in common purpose toward definite goals.

If this is indeed the case, and the example of the Totenkopfdivision represents such an instance of institutional solidity in the Waffen SS and the SS, then it seems the moment is right to refocus the analysis of the Nazi phenomenon and begin studying what Professor Gerhard L. Weinberg has called "the National Socialist consensus"[2] with the same diligence that has been devoted to the examination of the Third Reich's structural divisions.

---

[1] An especially detailed and specific work structured on this thesis is Edward N. Peterson, *The Limits of Hitler's Power* (Princeton, N. J., 1969).

[2] Both the term and the recommendation for a reexamination of it were originally Professor Weinberg's, and were contained in a paper he read before the Georgetown University German History Forum in October 1975. This writer is indebted to Professor Weinberg for kindly making available the unpublished draft of the essay, entitled "Recent German History, Some Comments and Perspectives."

SELECTED BIBLIOGRAPHY

PRIMARY MATERIAL

Archival Manuscript Sources

Bundesarchiv, Koblenz.

Akten des Reichsführers SS und Chef der deutschen Polizei, Persönlicher Stab (NS/19).

Befehlsblätter und Rundschreiben des Inspekteurs der Konzentrationslager und Führer der SS Totenkopfverbände (NS-3/448).

Der Chef der Sicherheitspolizei und des SD, Meldungen aus den besetzten Ostgebiete, Ereignismeldungen aus der UdSSR (R58/217, fol. 1-472).

Einsatzgruppen in Polen, Einsatzgruppen der Sicherheitspolizei, Selbstschutz und andere Formationen in der Zeit vom 1. September 1939 bis Frühjahr 1940 (B-162/29, fol. 1).

Meldungen des Chefs der Sicherheitspolizei und des SD (R58/825, R70, Sowjetunion/32, fol. 1-31).

Sammlung Schumacher (NS/437).

SS Erlasssammlung.

Bundesarchiv-Militärarchiv, Freiburg im Breisgau

Bestand Generalkommando SS Panzer-Korps, ab Juni 1943 II. SS Panzer-Korps (RS 2-2/1 bis 31).

Splitterakten der 3. SS-Panzer-Division "Totenkopf," 1939-1945 (III SS).

Institut für Zeitgeschichte, Munich

Akten des Reichsführers SS und Chef der deutschen Polizei (Microfilm Serial MA).

Miscellaneous Nuremberg Documents (NG, NO).

United States Document Center, Berlin-Zehlendorf.

SS Personalakte (cited individually by name in the footnotes).

Archival Microfilm Sources

National Archives of the United States, Washington, D. C.

Microcopy T-312, Records of German Field Commands, Armies: Armeeoberkommando 8 (Reels 54, 64, 66),

BIBLIOGRAPHY

Armeeoberkommando 9 (Reels 343, 345),
Armeeoberkommando 16 (Reels 548, 549, 556, 567, 570, 580, 583).
Microcopy T-313, Records of German Field Commands, Panzer Armies:
Panzer-Armeeoberkommando 1 (Reels 62, 63, 64).
Microcopy T-314, Records of German Field Commands, Army Corps:
II Armee-Korps (Reels 131, 132, 133),
XXVIII Armee-Korps (Reel 786),
LVI Panzer-Korps (Reels 1388, 1389, 1390).

Interviews and Correspondence

Baum, Otto. Interview of July 7, 1972 in Stetten bei Hechingen, West Germany; and letter and memorandum to the author of October 15, 1973.

Kimmel, Dr. Günter. Oberstaatsanwalt in the Zentrale Stelle der Landesjustizverwaltungen in Ludwigsburg, West Germany, letter to the author of March 27, 1975.

Koblenz interviews of June 19-20, 1972, with Gottlob Fickler, Erich Nöllgen, and Walter Peters.

Pilichowski, Dr. Czeslaw. Director, Central Commission for the Study of Hiterlite Crimes in Poland, letter to the author of April 22, 1970.

Speer, Albert. Letter to the author of October 26, 1971.

Published Documents

Apenszlak, Jacob, ed. *The Black Book of Polish Jewry: An Account of the Martyrdom of Polish Jewry under Nazi Occupation*. New York: Federation for Polish Jews, 1943.

Dienstaltersliste der Schutzstaffel der N. S. D. A. P. : Stand vom 1. Juli 1935. Berlin: Reichsdruckerei, 1935.

Dienstaltersliste der Schutzstaffel der N. S. D. A. P. : Stand vom 1. Juli 1943. Berlin: Reichsdruckerei, 1943.

Documents on German Foreign Policy, 1918-1945. (Series D) 13 vols. *The War Years, 1939-1940*. Vol. 7. Washington, D. C.: U.S. Department of State, 1956.

Greiner, Helmuth, and Schramm, Percy, eds. *Kriegstagebuch des Oberkommandos der Wehrmacht, 1940-1945*. 4 vols. Frankfurt am Main: Bernard und Graefe Verlag für Wehrwesen, 1961-1965.

Handbook on German Military Forces, 1 September 1943. Washington, D. C.: Department of the Army, 1943.

BIBLIOGRAPHY

Heiber, Helmut, ed., *Hitlers Lagebesprechungen: Die Protokollfragmente seiner militärischen Konferenzen, 1942-1945*. Stuttgart:
Deutsche Verlags Anstalt, 1962.

———. *Reichsführer!* . . . *Briefe an und von Himmler*. Stuttgart:
Deutsche Verlags-Anstalt, 1968.

Hitler's Secret Conversations, 1941-1944. New York: New American
Library, 1961.

Hubatsch, Walther, ed. *Hitlers Weisungen für die Kriegführung, 1939-
1945*. Frankfurt am Main: Bernard und Graefe Verlag für Wehrwesen, 1962.

Jacobsen, Hans-Adolf, ed. *Dokumente zur Vorgeschichte des West-
feldzuges, 1939-1940*. Göttingen: Musterschmidt Verlag, 1956.

Klietmann, K. G. *Die Waffen SS: Eine Dokumentation*. Osnabrück: Verlag der Freiwillige, 1965.

Langbein, Hermann. *Der Auschwitz Prozess: Eine Dokumentation*. 2
vols. Frankfurt, Vienna, Zurich: Europa Verlag, 1965.

Liddell Hart, Sir Basil Henry, ed. *The Rommel Papers*. London: Collins,
1953.

Nazi Conspiracy and Aggression. 8 vols. Vols. 2-7. Washington, D. C.:
U.S. Government Printing Office, 1946.

Noakes, Jeremy and Pridham, Geoffrey, eds. *Documents on Nazism,
1918-1945*. New York: The Viking Press, 1974.

SS im Einsatz: Eine Dokumentation über die Verbrechen der SS. Herausgegeben vom Komitee der Antifaschistischen Widerstandskämpfer in
der DDR. East Berlin: Kongress Verlag, 1960.

Smith, Bradley F. and Peterson, Agnes, eds. *Heinrich Himmler Geheimreden, 1933 bis 1945*. Frankfurt, Berlin: Propyläen Verlag, 1974.

Trevor-Roper, H. R., ed. *Blitzkrieg to Defeat: Hitler's War Directives,
1939-1945*. New York: Holt, Rinehart and Winston, 1964.

*Trials of the Major War Criminals Before the International Military Tri-
bunal at Nuremberg, Germany*. 42 vols. Nuremberg, Germany: International Military Tribunal, 1947.

*Trials of War Criminals Before the Nuremberg Military Tribunals under
Control Council Law No. 10*. (Green Series). 15 vols. Washington,
D. C.: U.S. Government Printing Office, 1950.

*Unsere Ehre Heisst Treue: Kriegstagebuch des Kommandostabes RFSS:
Tätigkeitsberichte der 1. und 2. SS Inf. Brigade, der SS Kav. Brigade,
und von Sonderkommandos der SS*. Vienna: Europa Verlag, 1965.

Diaries and Memoirs

Guderian, Heinz. *Panzer Leader*. New York: Ballantine Books, 1957.

349

BIBLIOGRAPHY

Halder, Generaloberst Franz. *Kriegstagebuch*. 3 vols. Ed. Hans-Adolf Jacobsen. Stuttgart: W. Kohlhammer Verlag, 1962.

Hausser, Paul. *Soldaten wie Andere Auch: Der Weg der Waffen SS*. Osnabrück: Munin Verlag, 1966.

———. *Waffen SS im Einsatz*. Göttingen: Plesse Verlag, 1953.

Hoess, Rudolf. *Kommandant in Auschwitz*. Edited with commentary by Martin Broszat. Quellen und Darstellungen zur Zeitgeschichte, vol. 5. Stuttgart: Deutsche Verlags-Anstalt, 1958.

Höss, Rudolf. *Commandant of Auschwitz*. Translated by Constantine FitzGibbon. New York: Popular Library, 1961. (English edition).

Jolly, Cyril, ed. *The Vengeance of Private Pooley*. London: William Heinemann, 1956.

Manstein, Erich von. *Lost Victories*. Edited and translated by Anthony G. Powell. Chicago: Henry Regnery, 1958.

———. *Verlorene Siege*. Bonn: Athenaeum, 1956.

Meyer, Kurt. *Grenadiere*. Munich: Schild Verlag, 1957.

Rokossovsky, Konstantin K. *A Soldier's Duty*. Translated by Robert Daglish. Moscow: Progress Publishers, 1970.

Sajer, Guy. *The Forgotten Soldier*. Translated by Lily Emmet. New York: Harper and Row, 1971.

Shtemenko, Sergei M. *The Soviet General Staff at War, 1941-1945*. Translated by Robert Daglish. Moscow: Progress Publishers, 1970.

Spears, Major General Sir Edward. *Assignment to Catastrophe*. 2 vols. New York: A. A. Wyn, Inc., 1954-55.

Steiner, Felix. *Die Armee der Geächteten*. Göttingen: Plesse Verlag, 1963.

———. *Die Freiwilligen: Idee und Opfergang*. Göttingen: Plesse Verlag, 1958.

Warlimont, Walter. *Inside Hitler's Headquarters, 1939-1945*. New York: Frederick A. Praeger, 1964.

Zhukov, Georgi K. *The Memoirs of Marshal Zhukov*. Translated by the Novosti Press Agency. New York: Delacorte Press, 1971.

Newspapers and Magazines

Die Frankfurter Zeitung, 1921—.
Das Schwarze Korps, 1936-1945. (Official newspaper of the SS).
Time Magazine, 1923—.
Der Völkischer Beobachter, 1920-1945. (Berlin edition).

BIBLIOGRAPHY

SECONDARY MATERIAL

Books

Ackermann, Josef. *Heinrich Himmler als Ideologue*. Göttingen: Musterschmidt Verlag, 1970.

Addington, Larry H. *The Blitzkrieg Era and the German General Staff, 1865-1941*. New Brunswick, N. J.: Rutgers University Press, 1971.

Adler, H. G. *Der verwaltete Mensch: Studien zur Deportation der Juden aus Deutschland*. Tübingen: Paul Siebeck (J. C. B. Möhr), 1974.

Ainsztein, Reuben. *Jewish Resistance in Nazi-Occupied Eastern Europe: with a historical survey of the Jew as fighter and soldier in the Diaspora*. New York: Barnes and Noble, 1974.

Allen, William S. *The Nazi Seizure of Power: The Experience of a Single German Town, 1930-1935*. Chicago: Quadrangle Books, 1965.

Andronikow, S. G. and Mostowenko, W. D. *Die Roten Panzer: Geschichte der sowjetischen Panzertruppen, 1920-1960*. Munich: J. F. Lehmanns Verlag, 1963.

Ansel, Walter. *Hitler Confronts England*. Durham, N. C.: Duke University Press, 1960.

Aronson, Shlomo. *Reinhard Heydrich und die Frühgeschichte von Gestapo und SD*. Studien zur Zeitgeschihte, Herausgegeben vom Institut für Zeitgeschichte. Stuttgart: Deutsche Verlags-Anstalt, 1971.

Baird, Jay W. *The Mythical World of Nazi War Propaganda, 1939-1945*. Minneapolis, Minn.: University of Minnesota Press, 1974.

Bender, Roger James and Taylor, Hugh Page. *Uniforms, Organization, and History of the Waffen SS*. Mountain View, Calif.: By the Authors, 1969.

Benoist-Mechin, Jacques. *Sixty Days that Shook the West: The Fall of France in 1940*. New York: G. P. Putnam's Sons, 1963.

Bialer, Seweryn, ed. *Stalin and His Generals: Soviet Military Memoirs of World War II*. New York: Western Publishing Co., 1969.

Billig, Joseph. *Les camps de concentration dans L'Économie du Reich Hitlérien*. Paris: Presses Universitaires de France, 1973.

Blau, George E. *The German Campaign in Russia: Planning and Operations, 1940-1942*. Department of the Army Pamphlet No. 20-261A. Washington, D. C.: Department of the Army, 1965.

Bracher, Karl-Dietrich. *The German Dictatorship: The Origins, Structure and Effects of National Socialism*. New York: Frederick A. Praeger, 1970.

Bryant, Sir Arthur. *The Turn of the Tide: A History of the War Years*

Based on the Diaries of Field Marshal Lord Alanbrooke, Chief of the Imperial General Staff. New York: Collins, 1957.

Broszat, Martin. *Nationalsozialistische Polenpolitik, 1939-1945.* Schriftenreihe der Vierteljahrshefte für Zeitgeschichte, No. 2. Stuttgart: Deutsche Verlags-Anstalt, 1961.

————, ed. *Studien zur Geschichte der Konzentrationslager.* Schriftenreihe der Vierteljahrshefte für Zeitgeschichte, No. 21. Stuttgart: Deutsche Verlags-Anstalt, 1970.

Buchheim, Hans. *SS und Polizei im Nationalsozialistischen Staat.* Duisdorf bei Bonn: Selbstverlag der Studiengesellschaft für Zietprobleme, 1964.

Bullock, Alan. *Hitler: A Study in Tyranny.* 2nd ed. rev. New York: Harper and Row, 1964.

Burdick, Charles B. *Germany's Military Strategy and Spain in World War II.* Syracuse, N. Y.: Syracuse University Press, 1968.

Carell, Paul. *Hitler Moves East, 1941-1943.* Boston: Little, Brown and Co., 1965.

————. *Scorched Earth: The German-Russian War, 1943-1944.* Boston: Little, Brown and Co., 1970.

Chaney, Otto P., Jr. *Zhukov.* Norman, Okla.: University of Oklahoma Press, 1971.

Chapman, Guy. *Why France Fell: The Defeat of the French Army in 1940.* New York: Holt, Rinehart and Winston, 1968.

Clark, Alan. *Barbarossa: The Russian-German Conflict, 1941-1945.* New York: William Morrow and Co., 1965.

Cohen, Elie A. *Human Behavior in the Concentration Camp.* Translated by M. H. Braaksma. New York: W. W. Norton and Co., 1953.

Craig, Gordon A. *The Politics of the Prussian Army, 1640-1945.* New York: Oxford University Press, 1964.

Dallin, Alexander. *German Rule in Russia, 1941-1945: A Study of Occupation Policies.* New York: St. Martin's Press, 1957.

Dawidowicz, Lucy S. *The War Against the Jews, 1933-1945.* New York: Holt, Rinehart and Winston, 1975.

Deakin, F. W. *The Brutal Friendship: Mussolini, Hitler and the Fall of Italian Fascism.* 2nd ed. New York: Doubleday Anchor, 1966.

Delzell, Charles F. *Mussolini's Enemies: The Italian Anti-Fascist Resistance.* Princeton, N.J.: Princeton University Press, 1961.

Deutsch, Harold C. *The Conspiracy Against Hitler in the Twilight War.* Minneapolis, Minn.: University of Minnesota Press, 1968.

————. *Hitler and His Generals: The Hidden Crisis, January-June, 1938.* Minneapolis, Minn.: University of Minnesota Press, 1974.

Draper, Theodor. *The Six Weeks War: France, May 10-June 25, 1940*. New York: The Viking Press, 1954.

Ellis, Lionel F. *The War in France and Flanders, 1939-1940*. London: Her Majesty's Stationery Office, 1953.

Erickson, John. *The Road to Stalingrad: Stalin's War with Germany*. Vol. 1. New York: Harper and Row, 1975.

————. *The Soviet High Command: A Military-Political History, 1918-1941*. London: Macmillan and Co., 1962.

Fest, Joachim C. *Hitler*. Translated by Richard and Clara Winston. New York: Harcourt Brace Jovanovich, 1974.

————. *The Face of the Third Reich: Portraits of the Nazi Leadership*. Translated by Michael Bullock. New York: Pantheon Books, 1970.

Gelwick, Robert A. "Personnel Policies and Procedures of the Waffen SS." Dissertation, University of Nebraska, 1971.

Georg, Enno. *Die wirtschaftlichen Unternehmungen der SS*. Schriftenreihe der Vierteljahrshefte für Zeitgeschichte, No. 7. Stuttgart: Deutsche Verlags-Anstalt, 1963.

Gosztony, Peter. *Der Endkampf an der Donau, 1944/45*. Vienna, Munich, Zurich: Molden Verlag, 1969.

Goure, Leon. *The Siege of Leningrad*. Stanford, Calif.: Stanford University Press, 1962.

Greiner, Helmuth. *Die Oberste Wehrmachtführung, 1939-1943*. Wiesbaden: Limes Verlag, 1951.

Haupt, Werner. *Heeresgruppe Mitte, 1941-1945*. Dorheim, West Germany: Podzun Verlag, 1968.

Higgins, Trumbull. *Hitler and Stalin: The Third Reich in a Two-Front War, 1937-1943*. New York: The Macmillan Co., 1966.

Hilberg, Raul. *The Destruction of the European Jews*. Chicago: Quadrangle Books, 1960.

Hillgruber, Andreas. *Hitlers Strategie: Politik und Kriegführung, 1940-1941*. Frankfurt am Main: Bernard und Graefe Verlag für Wehrwesen, 1965.

Höhne, Heinz. *Der Orden unter dem Totenkopf: Die Geschichte der SS*. Gütersloh: Sigbert Mohn Verlag, 1967.

————. *The Order of the Death's Head: The Story of Hitler's SS*. New York: Ballantine Books, 1971. (English edition).

Horne, Alistair. *To Lose a Battle, France 1940*. Boston: Little, Brown and Co., 1969.

Husemann, Friedrich. *Die guten Glaubens waren: Der Weg der SS Polizei-Division, 1939-1942*. Osnabrück: Munin Verlag, 1971.

Jacobsen, Hans-Adolf. *Fall Gelb: Der Kampf um den deutschen*

Operationsplan zur Westoffensive, 1940. Wiesbaden: Franz Steiner Verlag, 1957.

Jacobsen, Hans-Adolf and Hillgruber, Andreas, eds. *Die sowjetische Geschichte des Grossen Vaterländischen Krieges, 1941-1945, von Boris Semjonowitsch Telpuchowski*. Frankfurt am Main: Bernard und Graefe Verlag für Wehrwesen, 1961.

Jacobsen, Hans-Adolf and Rohwer, Jürgen, eds. *Decisive Battles of World War II: The German View*. Translated by Edward Fitzgerald. New York: G. P. Putnam's Sons, 1965.

Kater, Michael H. *Das "Ahnenerbe" der SS, 1935-1945: Ein Beitrag zur Kulturpolitik des Dritten Reiches*. Studien zur Zeitgeschichte, Herausgegeben vom Institut für Zeitgeschichte. Stuttgart: Deutsche Verlags-Anstalt, 1974.

Klink, Ernst. *Das Gesetz des Handelns: Die Operation "Zitadelle" 1943*. Schriftenreihe des Militärgeschichtlichen Forschungsamtes, No. 7. Stuttgart: Deutsche Verlags-Anstalt, 1966.

Kogon, Eugen. *Der SS Staat: Das System der deutschen Konzentrationslager*. Frankfurt am Main: Verlag der Frankfurter Hefte, 1946.

————. *The Theory and Practice of Hell: The German Concentration Camps and the System behind Them*. Translated by Heinz Norden, New York: Berkeley Medallion Books, 1958. (English edition).

Kolb, Eberhard. *Bergen-Belsen: Geschichte des "Aufenthaltslagers," 1943-1945*. Hannover: Verlag für Literatur und Zeitgeschehen, GmBH, 1962.

Krätschmer, Ernst-Günther. *Die Ritterkreuzträger der Waffen SS*. Göttingen: Plesse Verlag, 1953.

Krannhals, Hans von. *Der Warschauer Aufstand 1944*. Frankfurt am Main: Bernard und Graefe Verlag für Wehrwesen, 1964.

Krausnick, Helmut; Buchheim, Hans; Broszat, Martin; and Jacobsen, Hans-Adolf. *Anatomie des SS Staates*. 2 vols. Olten und Freiburg im Breisgau: Walter Verlag, 1965.

————. *Anatomy of the SS State*. Translated by Richard Barry, Marian Jackson, and Dorothy Long. New York: Walker and Company, 1968. (English edition).

Leach, Barry A. *German Strategy Against Russia, 1939-1941*. Oxford: The Clarendon Press, 1973.

Liddell Hart, Sir Basil Henry. *The German Generals Talk*. New York: Apollo Editions, 1948.

————. *History of the Second World War*. 2 vols. New York: Capricorn Books, 1972.

————. *Strategy*. 2nd ed. rev., New York: New American Library, 1967.

Mellenthin, Major General F. W. von. *Panzer Battles: A Study of the Employment of Armor in the Second World War*. Norman, Okla.: University of Oklahoma Press, 1956.

Michel, Henri. *The Second World War*. Translated by Douglas Parmée. New York: Frederick A. Praeger, 1975.

Naumann, Bernd. *Auschwitz*. Translated by Jean Steinberg. New York: Frederick A. Praeger, 1966.

Neusüss-Hunkel, Ermenhild. *Die SS*. Schriftenreihe des Instituts für wissenschaftliche Politik in Marburg/Lahn. Hannover: Norddeutsche Verlags-Anstalt, 1956.

Paget, Reginald T. *Manstein: His Campaign and His Trial*. London: Collins, 1951.

Peterson, Edward N. *The Limits of Hitler's Power*. Princeton, N.J.: Princeton University Press, 1969.

Philippi, Alfred and Heim, Ferdinand. *Der Feldzug gegen Sowjetrussland: 1941 bis 1945*. Stuttgart: W. Kohlhammer Verlag, 1962.

Poznanski, Stanislaw. *Struggle, Death, Memory*. Warsaw: Council for the Preservation of the Monuments of Struggle and Martyrdom, 1963.

Presser, Jacob. *The Destruction of the Dutch Jews*. Translated by Arnold Pomerans. New York: E. P. Dutton and Co., Inc., 1969.

Reinhardt, Klaus. *Die Wende vor Moskau: Das Scheitern der Strategie Hitlers im Winter 1941/42*. Schriftenreihe des Militärgeschichtlichen Forschungsamtes. No. 13. Stuttgart: Deutsche Verlags-Anstalt, 1972.

Reitlinger, Gerald. *The Final Solution: The Attempt to Exterminate the Jews of Europe, 1939-1945*. New York: Beechhurst Press, 1953.

————. *The House Built on Sand: The Conflicts of German Policy in Russia, 1939-1945*. New York: The Viking Press, 1960.

————. *The SS: Alibi of a Nation, 1922-1945*. New York: The Viking Press, 1968.

Rich, Norman. *Hitler's War Aims*. 2 vols. New York: W. W. Norton and Co., 1973-74.

Ritter, Gerhard. *Carl Goerdeler und die deutsche Widerstandsbewegung*. Stuttgart: Deutsche Verlags-Anstalt, 1954.

Rückerl, Adalbert, ed. *NS-Prozesse: Nach 25 Jahren Strafverfolgung, Möglichkeiten- Grenzen- Ergebnisse*. Karlsruhe: C. F. Müller Verlag, 1971.

Ryan, Cornelius. *The Last Battle*. New York: Simon and Schuster, 1966.

Salisbury, Harrison E. *The 900 Days: The Siege of Leningrad*. New York: Harper and Row, 1969.

Schnabel, Reimund, ed. *Macht ohne Moral: Eine Dokumentation über die SS*. Frankfurt am Main: Röderbert Verlag, 1957.

BIBLIOGRAPHY

Seaton, Albert. *The Russo-German War, 1941-45*. New York: Frederick A. Praeger, 1970.

Shirer, William L. *The Rise and Fall of the Third Reich*. New York: Simon and Schuster, 1960.

Stein, George H. *The Waffen SS: Hitler's Elite Guard at War, 1939-1945*. Ithaca, N. Y.: Cornell University Press, 1966.

Strassner, Peter. *Europäische Freiwillige: Die Geschichte der 5. SS-Panzer Division "Wiking."* Osnabrück: Munin Verlag, 1969.

Taylor, Telford. *The March of Conquest: The German Victories in Western Europe, 1940*. New York: Simon and Schuster, 1958.

————. *Sword and Swastika: Generals and Nazis in the Third Reich*. Chicago: Quadrangle Books, 1969.

Thach, Joseph E., Jr. "The Battle of Kursk July 1943: Decisive Turning Point on the Eastern Front." Dissertation, Georgetown University, 1971.

Tieke, Wilhelm. *Im Lufttransport an Brennpunkte der Ostfront, 1942*. Osnabrück: Munin Verlag, 1971.

————. *Tragödie um die Treue: Kampf und Untergang des III. (Germ.) SS Panzer-Korps*. Osnabrück: Munin Verlag, 1970.

Toland, John. *The Last 100 Days*. New York: Alfred A. Knopf, 1965.

Turney, Alfred W. *Disaster at Moscow: Von Bock's Campaigns, 1941-1942*. Albuquerque, N. M.: University of New Mexico Press, 1970.

Waite, Robert G. L. *Vanguard of Nazism: The Free Corps Movement in Postwar Germany, 1918-1923*. Cambridge, Mass.: Harvard University Press, 1952.

Weidinger, Otto. *Division Das Reich, 1934-1941*. 2 vols. Osnabrück: Munin Verlag, 1967-69.

Weingartner, James J. *Hitler's Guard: The Story of the Leibstandarte SS Adolf Hitler, 1933-1945*. Carbondale, Ill.: Southern Illinois University Press, 1974.

Werth, Alexander. *Russia at War, 1941-1945*. New York: E. P. Dutton and Co., 1964.

Wheaton, Eliot Barculo. *The Nazi Revolution, 1933-1935: Prelude to Calamity*. New York: Doubleday Anchor Books, 1969.

Wheeler-Bennett, Sir John W. *The Nemesis of Power: The German Army in Politics, 1918-1945*. 2nd ed. New York: The Viking Press, 1967.

Wormser-Migot, Olga. *Le Système Concentrationnaire Nazi, 1933-1945*. Paris: Presses Universitaires de France, 1968.

Ziemke, Earl F. *Stalingrad to Berlin: The German Defeat in the East*. Washington, D. C.: Office of the Chief of Military History, United States Army, 1968.

BIBLIOGRAPHY

Articles

Adler, H. G. "Selbstverwaltung und Widerstand in den Konzentrationslagern der SS." *Vierteljahrshefte für Zeitgeschichte*, 8 (July 1960), 221-36.

Alexander, Leo. "War Crimes and Their Motivation; the Socio-Psychological Structure of the SS and the Criminalization of a Society." *Journal of Criminal Law and Criminology*, 39, No. 3 (1948), 298-326.

Auerbach, Helmuth. "Die Einheit Dirlewanger." *Vierteljahrshefte für Zeitgeschichte*, 10 (July 1962), 250-63.

Baumgart, Winfried. "Zur Ansprache Hitlers vor den Führern der Wehrmacht am 22. August 1939, Eine Quellenkritische Untersuchung." *Vierteljahrshefte für Zeitgeschichte*, 16 (April 1968), 120-49.

Buchheim, Hans. "Die Höheren SS und Polizei Führer." *Vierteljahrshefte für Zeitgeschichte*, 11 (October 1963), 362-91.

―――. "Die SS in der Verfassung des Dritten Reiches." *Vierteljahrshefte für Zeitgeschichte*, 3 (April 1955), 127-57.

Datner, Szymon. "Crimes Committed by the Wehrmacht During the September Campaign and the Period of Military Government (1 September 1939—25 October 1939)." *Polish Western Affairs*, 3 (September 1962), 294-338.

Eisenbach, Arthur. "Operation Reinhard: Mass Extermination of the Jewish Population in Poland." *Polish Western Affairs*, 3 (January 1962), 80-124.

Gackenholz, Hermann. "Zum Zusammenbruch der Heeresgruppe Mitte im Sommer 1944." *Vierteljahrshefte für Zeitgeschichte*, 3 (July 1955), 317-33.

Hauck, Friedrich Wilhelm. "Der Gegenangriff der Heeresgruppe Süd im Frühjahr 1943." 2 pts. *Wehrwissenschaftliche Rundschau*, 12 (August-September 1962), 452-68, and 520-39.

Heinrici, Gotthard, and Hauck, Friedrich Wilhelm. "Zitadelle." 3 pts., *Wehrwissenschaftliche Rundschau*, 15 (August-October 1965), 463-82, 529-44, and 582-604.

Hentig, Hans Wolfram von. "Beiträge zu einer Sozialgeschichte des Dritten Reiches." *Vierteljahrshefte für Zeitgeschichte*, 16 (January 1968), 48-59.

Hillgruber, Andreas. "Die 'Endlösung' und das Deutsche Ostimperium als Kernstück des Rassenideologischen Programms des Nationalsozialismus." *Vierteljahrshefte für Zietgeschichte*, 20 (April 1972), 133-53.

357

BIBLIOGRAPHY

Koehl, Robert. "The Character of the Nazi SS." *Journal of Modern History*, 34 (September 1962), 275-83.

Krausnick, Helmut. "Hitler und die Morde in Polen: Ein Beitrag zum Konflikt zwischen Heer und SS um die Verwaltung der besetzten Gebiete." *Vierteljahrshefte für Zeitgeschichte*, 11 (April 1963), 196-209.

Levine, Herbert S. "Local Authority and the SS State: The Conflict over Population Policy in Danzig-West Prussia, 1939-1945." *Central European History*, 2 (December 1969), 331-55.

Mau, Hermann. "Die Zweite Revolution, 30. Juni 1934." *Vierteljahrshefte für Zeitgeschichte*, 1 (April 1953), 119-37.

Meier-Welcker, Hans. "Der Entschluss zum Anhalten der deutschen Panzertruppen in Flandern 1940." *Vierteljahrshefte für Zeitgeschichte*, 2 (July 1954), 274-90.

Paetel, Karl O. "The Black Order: A Survey of the Literature on the SS." *Wiener Library Bulletin*, 12, Nos. 3-4 (1959), 34-35.

———. "Die SS: Ein Beitrag zur Soziologie des Nationalsozialismus." *Vierteljahrshefte für Zeitgeschichte*, 2 (January 1954), 1-33.

Rothkirchen, Livia. "The Final Solution in Its Last Stages." *Yad Vashem Studies on the European Jewish Catastrophe and Resistance*, 8 (Jerusalem, 1970), 7-29.

Stein, George H. "The Myth of a European Army." *Wiener Library Bulletin*, 19 (April 1965), 21-22.

Sydnor, Charles W., Jr. "La Division SS 'Totenkopf.'" *Revue d'histoire de la deuxième guerre mondiale*, No. 98 (April 1975), 59-76.

———. "The History of the SS Totenkopfdivision and the Postwar Mythology of the Waffen SS." *Central European History*, 6 (December 1973), 339-62.

Tenenbaum, Joseph. "Auschwitz in Retrospect: The Self-Portrait of Rudolf Höss, Commandant of Auschwitz." *Jewish Social Studies*, 15 (July-October 1953), 203-36.

———. "The Einsatzgruppen." *Jewish Social Studies*, 17 (1955), 43-64.

Vopersal, Wolfgang. "Südlich des Ilmensees, Aus dem Kampf der SS Totenkopf-Division." 7 pts. *Der Freiwillige* (May-December 1974).

Wagener, Carl. "Der Gegenangriff des XXXX Panzerkorps gegen den Durchbruch der Panzergruppe Popow im Donezbecken, Februar 1943." *Wehrwissenschaftliche Rundschau*, 7 (January 1957), 21-36.

Weingartner, James J. "Sepp Dietrich, Heinrich Himmler and the Leibstandarte SS Adolf Hitler, 1933-1938." *Central European History*, 1 (September 1968), 264-84.

Index

359

INDEX

Heissmeyer, August, 18
Hellerich, Ernst, 338-39
Henlein, Konrad, 33 n.80
Henschel firm, 261
Herff, Maximilien von, 337 n.45
Hess, Rudolf, 34, 73
Heyde, Dr. Werner, 8
Heydrich, Reinhard, 81 n.28, 133
    n.22, 274 n.27, 345; and KZ sys-
    tem, 21-22; and Russian war, 153-
    54; in SS, 15 n.33
higher SS and police leader (Höhere
    SS- und Polizei Führer), 38, 154
    n.3, 217; significance of, 82; Waffen
    SS and, 332-33
Himmler, Heinrich, and Barbarossa,
    141 n.37, 153-54 n.3; and Becker,
    318 n.10; and Eicke, 5-8, 17-18,
    57, 57 n.37, 119-20, 126-27, 129-
    32, 147 n.49, 200 n.76, 273, 276;
    and German Army, 240 n.37, 242;
    and KZ system, 17-18, 20-21,
    22 n.50; and Le Paradis massacre,
    109 n.29; mentioned, xiii, xiv, xv,
    14-15, 18, 82, 166-67, 170, 226,
    229, 234-35, 239, 246, 249-50,
    253, 314, 317, 319, 329, 331, 335-
    36, 343; on racial standards in Waf-
    fen SS recruiting, 231-32, 232 n.24;
    and Röhm purge, 16; sends HSSPF
    to SSTK, 330-35; and SSTK, 45-46,
    48, 53 n.30, 55-56, 60 n.43, 61,
    64, 66, 70-72, 78, 112-14, 129-32,
    220-21, 231-32, 235-38, 240, 251,
    257, 260, 262-63; and SSTV, 30-31,
    33-35; supports Jüttner against
    Eicke, 133-36; and Waffen SS,
    120-21, 132-36, 337-38, 344-45
Hitler, Adolf, and Ardennes offensive
    of 1944, 307; authority over Waffen
    SS, 43-44, 48, 344; and battle of
    France, 94, 98-99, 103, 114-15, 121,
    140; and Becker, 318; and Commis-
    sar Order, 153-54 n.3; and Dem-
    yansk pocket, 215 n.7, 220-221,
    223, 233, 252 n.55; and Donetz
    counteroffensive, 266-67, 280; and
    Eicke, 214 n.6, 226, 236, 240-41,
    245, 249 n.51, 261 n.9, 273, 276-
    77; and Kharkov battles, 280, 293-
    94; and Krivoi Rog defense, 298;
    and Kursk offensive, 280-81, 290-
    91; and Leeb, 213; and Luga line,
    175 n.41, 185 n.54, 186, 195, 198;

mentioned, xiii, xiv, 14-16, 72,
    172, 344-45; and Poland, 35-38,
    43 n.14; postpones western cam-
    paign, 53 n.30, 58, 64, 72; and re-
    treat to the Dnieper, 295; and Rus-
    sia, 140-42, 148, 153-54 n.3; and
    SS offensive to recapture Budapest,
    308-10; and SSTK, 64, 72, 226,
    232, 236, 238, 240-41, 250-51,
    253, 255-56, 257-60, 263, 307, 318;
    and SSTV, 24, 27, 31, 32-35, 35-
    36 n.86; and Soviet summer offen-
    sive of 1944, 302-4; and winter
    crisis of 1941, 208; and Zitadelle,
    280-81, 290-91
Hock, Dr. Oskar, 340
Hoepner, Erich, and battle of France,
    98-101, 103; decorates Eicke,
    112 n.33; and Le Paradis atrocity,
    108-11; and Russian campaign, 152,
    154, 157, 158 n.11, 161, 168-69,
    171, 178-79, 199 n.73, 210 n.1
Höss, Rudolf, characterizes Eicke,
    14 n.29; and Eicke's influence upon,
    12 n.25
Hoffmann, Otto, and SSTK replace-
    ment controversy, 130
Holland, German invasion of, 87-89
Hoppe, Paul-Werner, as Eicke's emis-
    sary to Jüttner, 135-36; at Auschwitz
    and Stutthof, 328-29, 329 n.31;
    postwar fate, 329 n.31, 330, 342
Hostens, SSTK HQ in, 118
Hoth, Hermann, and battle of France,
    91, 110; and Russian campaign,
    267-68, 269 n.21, 278-79, 281,
    283-84, 293
Hube, Hans V., and defense of Krivoi
    Rog, 296, 298-99

Ilmenau, Thuringia, 4
inspectorate of concentration camps,
    see concentration camp inspectorate
Italy, 7, 291-92

Jeckeln, Friedrich, directs Ein-
    satzgruppen, 331; relations with
    SSTK, 331-32; supplies SSTK with
    winter equipment, 219
"Jewish-Bolshevism," Eicke's lec-
    tures on, 153; identified with Rus-
    sian enemy, 316; mentioned, 192
Jews, abuse of in Dachau, 13; depicted
    by Eicke, 29 n.68; depicted in
    SSTK training manual, 144-45; de-

INDEX

Red Army Units (*cont.*)
Third Shock Army, 212; Fourth
Guards Army, 309; Fifth Guards
Army, 288; Sixth Army, 265-70,
277, 283; Seventh Guards Army,
283; Eighth Army, 158; Eleventh
Army, 212-14, 246; Twenty-sixth
Army, 309; Thirty-fourth Army,
175-78, 212, 216; Forty-sixth Army,
309; Sixty-ninth Army, 283-84,
Tank Armies, First Tank Army,
283-85; Second Tank Army, 304-5;
Third Tank Army, 277; Fifth Guards
Tank Army, 283, 288-89, 307, Sixth
Guards Tank Army, 309, 311; Ninth
Guards Tank Army, 310; Twenty-
first Armored Group, 162-63, 167
Corps, First Guards Corps, 246;
Fourth Infantry Corps, 270; Four-
teenth Infantry Corps, 270; Thirty-
second Guards Rifle Corps, 288;
Thirty-third Guards Rifle Corps,
288-89
Tank and Mechanized Corps,
Second Tank Corps, 288; Second
Guards Tank Corps, 286; Fifth
Guards Mechanized Corps, 288;
Eighteenth Tank Corps, 288;
Twenty-ninth Tank Corps, 288;
Thirty-first Guards Tank Corps,
288-89
Divisions, Seventh Guards Divi-
sion, 222, 250; Twenty-fifth Guards
Rifle Division, 279; Thirty-third
Rifle Division, 180; Forty-second
Rifle Division, 163; Fifty-second
Guards Division, 284; Seventieth In-
fantry Division, 173 n.37; 129th In-
fantry Division, 250; 130th Infantry
Division, 250; 180th Rifle Division,
167, 169; 182nd Rifle Division, 167;
192nd Rifle Division, 180; 220th
Motorized Division, 169; 237th In-
fantry Division, 173 n.37; 364th In-
fantry Division, 250; 391st Infantry
Division, 250
Brigades, Fourteenth Guards
Brigade, 222; Fifteenth Guards
Brigade, 222; Thirty-seventh Rifle
Brigade, 250; Forty-second Guards
Brigade, 222; Fifty-second Guards
Brigade, 222; 154th Naval Rifle

Brigade, 222
Regiments and Battalions, 272nd
Ski Regiment, 222; 154th Ski Battal-
ion, 222; 203rd Ski Battalion, 222;
204th Ski Battalion, 222
Reich Labor Service, provides recruits
for SSTK, 251, 258, 260
Reich Ministry of Justice, investigates
SSTK doctors, 51
Reichenau, Walter von, 47, 111 n.32
Reichsführer SS, *see* Himmler
Reichswehr, 53
Reinhardt, Max, 157, 161-62, 168
Rhineland-Palatinate, 4, 6-7
Riga, 157
Röhm, Ernst, 15-16; shot by Eicke, 17
Rokossovsky, Konstantin K.,
281 n.37
Rommel, Erwin, 92-94, 96
Rosenberg, Alfred, 144-45, 336
Rothardt, Dr. Bruno, 339-40
Rotmistrov, Nikolai, 288
Rotterdam, German assault on, 89
Royal Air Force, 140
Rudel, Hans-Ulrich, 285 n.40
Rumania, 301
Rumyantsev (Soviet plan to capture
Dnieper crossings), 293
Rundstedt, Gerd von, and battle of
France, 87, 90-91, 94-95, 97, 99;
mentioned, 156, 210 n.1, 274 n.27
Russia, 120

SA (Sturmabteilung), xiii, 5, 15; and
blood purge of 1934, 15-16; pro-
vides recruits for SSTV, 25, 34
Sachsenburg concentration camp,
18-19, 24
Sachsenhausen concentration camp, in
development of KZ system, 19, 31,
35; mentioned, 327, 340
St. Omer, 114-15
St. Sorbin, 118
Schmauser, Ernst Heinrich, 16-17;
serving with SSTK, 330-31
Schmidt, Rudolf, 93, 146
Schneider, Rudolf, 247 n.48
Schörner, Ferdinand, 297
Schopfhauser, Hubert, 102 n.19
Schutzpolizei (security police), 6 n.10,
8
Schutzstaffel, *see* SS

368

INDEX

Schweder, Alfred, 133 n.22
SD (Sicherheitsdienst), killing partisans and Jews in Russia, 202 n.78; liquidating Russian POWs, 211-12 n.2; mentioned, 15 n.33, 337
Seela, Max, and battle of Lushno, 192-95, 196; and battle of Staraya Russa, 214 n.6; and conclusion of Operation Gangway, 226 n.18
Sennelager bei Paderborn, new SSTK regiments organized in, 238, 240, 244, 251, 254
Seydlitz-Kurzbach, Walter von, and relief operation to Demyansk pocket, 223-26; mentioned, 233
Shtemenko, Sergei M., 281 n.37
Sicily, 290
Siedlce, Poland, SSTK defends, 304
Simon, Max, commands SSTK battle group in Demyansk pocket, 216-53; condemned as war criminal by Russians, 295 n.55; critical of army, 239, 240 n.37, 241, 244, 247 n.49, 252-53; describes SSTK experience at Demyansk, 252-53; efforts to get SSTK out of Russia, 242-44, 246; mentioned, 118, 146, 162-63, 314, 325, 342, 345; orders Russian stragglers shot, 160; prewar SS career, 48-49; relationship with Eicke, 249-50, 317; reports on Eicke's death, 271 n.25; and shooting of Italian civilians, 317, 321; smuggles SSTK soldiers out of Demyansk, 244, 245 n.45; succeeds Eicke in command of SSTK, 275 n.28; wounded, 166 n.24
Skoda works, 71-72
Slavyansk, 268
Smolensk, 198
Somme River, 93, 114
Sorau-Niederausitz, 4
Soviet High Command, 277, 281, 283, 286, 288
Soviet Union, see Russia
Speer, Albert, on Eicke's relations with Hitler, 276 n.30
SS (Schutzstaffel), army antipathy to; 81-82; dispute with Nazi party, 73; Hoepner's dislike of, 99; ideological training in, 316 n.6; mentioned, xiii, 5, 23, 26-28, 31-32, 48, 61,

120, 124-25, 127, 131, 340-42, 344-46; relationship of Waffen SS to, 318; and transfers of SSTK wounded, 198 n.72
SS Death's Head units, see SS Totenkopfverbände
SS Einsatzgruppen, mentioned, 341; operations in Russia, 331; personnel exchanges with SSTK, 321-23; in Polish campaign, 37-38, 40
SS Führungshauptamt (operational office), administrative jurisdiction over SSTK, 132-36; and control of war matériel in KZs, 134-36; establishes control over reserve SSTV, 187; mentioned, 129, 131 n.20, 344; strengthens Himmler's control over Waffen SS, 136
SS Hauptamt (main office), and administration of prewar SSTV, 18, 25-26
SS Junkerschulen (officer cadet academies), 32, 81, 343; at Bad Tölz, 48, 57, 105 n.22, 112, 146; at Braunschweig, 49 n.24, 57, 146
SS Leithefte (indoctrination journals), 28-29; use in SSTK, 28 n.65
SS Oberabschnitten (regional administrative districts), 56; SS Oberabschnitt Süd, 10, 15-16; SS Oberabschnitt Südwest, 50; SS Oberabschnitt West, 51
SS Rasse und Siedlungshauptamt (race and resettlement office), 52, 60, 128-30
SS Sturmbann Brandenburg (KZ guard battalion), 24
SS Sturmbann Elbe (KZ guard battalion), 24
SS Sturmbann Hansa (KZ guard battalion), 24
SS Sturmbann Oberbayern (KZ guard battalion), 24
SS Sturmbann Ostfriesland (KZ guard battalion), 24
SS Sturmbann Sachsen (KZ guard battalion), 24
SS Totenkopfstandarten (SS Death's Head Regiments),
    SS Totenkopfstandarte I "Oberbayern," in Czechoslovakia, 33 n.80; in Poland, 37, 41; incorporated into SSTK, 46, 49, 58

369

Library of Congress Cataloging in Publication Data

Sydnor, Charles W.
  Soldiers of destruction.

  Bibliography: p.
  Includes index.
  1. World War, 1939-1945—Division histories—
Germany—Waffenschutzstaffel.   3.   SS-Panzer-Division
Totenkopf.   2.   Nationalsozialistische Deutsche
Arbeiter-Partei. Waffenschutzstaffel.   3.   SS-Panzer-
Division Totenkopf.   3.   World War, 1939-1945—
Campaigns—France.   4.   World War, 1939-1945—
Campaigns—Russia.   5.   France—History—German occu-
pation, 1940-1945.   6.   Russia—History—German occupa-
tion, 1941-1944.   I.   Title.

D757.85.S95   940.54'13'43   77-72138
ISBN 0-691-05255-7